The Economics of Art and Culture

Third Edition

Spanning the economics of the fine arts, performing arts, and public policy, this update on a classic is the go-to resource for navigating today's creative industries. Building on real-world data, engaging case studies, and cutting-edge research, it prepares students for careers in the cultural, creative, and public sectors. By avoiding mathematical treatments and explaining theories with examples, this book develops theoretical concepts from scratch, making it accessible to readers with no background in economics. While most of the theory remains timeless, this new edition covers changes in the world's economic landscapes. Updates include new sections on gender representation, cultural districts and tourism, digital broadcasting and streaming, how technology impacts the arts, and a new chapter on arts management and strategy. The authors demonstrate data-driven decision-making using examples and cases from various databases. Students learn to assess academic results and apply the learned material working with the discussion questions and problem sets.

Karol J. Borowiecki is Professor of Economics at the University of Southern Denmark. He is president-elect of the Association for Cultural Economics International, editorial board member of the *Journal of Cultural Economics and Tourism Economics*, and co-founder of *Economists Talk Art*. He shapes cultural policy by influencing some of the most important institutions in Europe, writing policy briefs, and speaking to the public and media.

Charles M. Gray is Professor Emeritus of Business Economics at the Opus College of Business and Senior Fellow at the Center for the Common Good at the University of St. Thomas in Minnesota. He is a past president of the Association for Cultural Economics International and has served as a consultant to the National Endowment for the Arts.

The late James Heilbrun was Professor Emeritus of Economics at Fordham University. He was an editorial board member of the *Journal of Cultural Economics* and a consultant to the National Endowment for the Arts.

The Economics of Art and Culture

THIRD EDITION

Karol J. Borowiecki
University of Southern Denmark

Charles M. Gray
University of St. Thomas

James Heilbrun
Fordham University

CAMBRIDGE
UNIVERSITY PRESS

Shaftesbury Road, Cambridge CB2 8EA, United Kingdom

One Liberty Plaza, 20th Floor, New York, NY 10006, USA

477 Williamstown Road, Port Melbourne, VIC 3207, Australia

314–321, 3rd Floor, Plot 3, Splendor Forum, Jasola District Centre, New Delhi – 110025, India

103 Penang Road, #05–06/07, Visioncrest Commercial, Singapore 238467

Cambridge University Press is part of Cambridge University Press & Assessment, a department of the University of Cambridge.

We share the University's mission to contribute to society through the pursuit of education, learning and research at the highest international levels of excellence.

www.cambridge.org
Information on this title: www.cambridge.org/highereducation/isbn/9780521870306

DOI: 10.1017/9781139033886

First published 1993
Second edition 2001
Third edition 2024

A catalogue record for this publication is available from the British Library

A Cataloging-in-Publication data record for this book is available from the Library of Congress

ISBN 978-0-521-87030-6 Hardback
ISBN 978-0-521-69042-3 Paperback

Additional resources for this publication at www.cambridge.org/borowiecki

Contents

Preface to the Third Edition

The *Economics of Art and Culture* explains how art and culture function within the larger economy. In particular, the book applies economic methods and theories to the study of the fine arts and performing arts, as well as public policy toward the arts. Why should this be studied?

- The arts economy is an important part of what has come to be known as our cultural capital, and is therefore vital to our self-image as a society.
- The arts industry may be small in size relative to the overall economy, but it is important for many related industries to function, such as the tourism or hospitality industries.
- Arts and culture are conducive toward the well-being of a society and can generate positive effects for the education, health, and social cohesion of citizens.
- The arts economy affects quality of life, which matters for local residents and business activity, and can stimulate creativity.

Who Will Use This Book?

This volume, as a discipline-specific overview, will be useful in classrooms and boardrooms, and accessible by students, nonspecialist policy analysts, and arts administrators, among others. In particular, the textbook will interest academic readers seeking a core text on the economics of the arts and arts management or a supplementary text on the sociology of the arts, as well as those seeking a systematic analysis of the arts. Theoretical concepts are developed from scratch so that readers with no background in economics can follow the argument, and this feature may also be appreciated by lecturers struggling with their students' varying levels of economics background. The extensive use of real-world data makes the book an invaluable resource for practitioners and also develops the student's ability to analyze and critically assess data. In our world of data-driven decision-making – these abilities may be of benefit for the student's career prospects, perhaps particularly, but not only, in the cultural and creative industries or the public sector.

This textbook has widespread appeal not only among students of Cultural Economics but also students of Arts and Cultural Management and Cultural Policy since it conveys the essence of economic concepts while avoiding complicated methodological issues that would interest only students of economics. The book could be also used as a supplementary text in teaching more advanced classes in Arts Policy and Arts Management, and Arts in Sociology, especially Parts III–V, which cover a wide range of topics, including art markets and art museums, public policy and support for the arts, arts as a profession, culture and the local economy, and the role of new technologies for the cultivation of taste. The courageous educator in the field of Fine Arts may also consider covering topics on the role of demand and supply in estimating the market price of an artwork (Part II) or Chapter 14, which discloses some realities of arts as a profession, and unveils the concepts of the "starving artist" and the superstar, among others.

The Old and the New

A great deal of time has passed since the second edition of this book appeared, and the time has been eventful. We acknowledge at the outset the most regrettable occurrence, namely the passing of coauthor James (Jim) Heilbrun. Although Jim has left us, his eloquence is present throughout this revision, and we retain his name as a coauthor. It became clear that a new and younger voice was needed to propel the project forward, and Karol J. Borowiecki of the University of Southern Denmark took on the task, bringing with him a European perspective.

On a more positive note: The fields of cultural economics, cultural policy, arts management, and the emerging economic history of the arts have leapt forward, with scholars regularly advancing the knowledge frontier with theoretical derivations, empirical verifications, and case applications. We have tried mightily to retain the insights of the "classics," among others, concepts related to the demand for and supply of culture, including the notion of production and cost, firms and markets, arts management and strategy, and arts policy. We present these fundamental topics of cultural economics while blending in the more recent contributions, selecting from the firehose of new knowledge.

Timing is everything. We incorporate some implications of a global "Black Swan" event for the arts. The COVID-19 pandemic has had implications for arts markets, patrons, organizations, and policymakers all around the world. Our approach has been to illustrate selected effects with some of the tools we develop herein. For example, the application of digital technologies toward the arts and culture, such as live broadcasting of performing arts or virtual museums, has been accelerated by the pandemic. This has clearly created new opportunities, not only for the producers or consumers, but also for those engaged with the preservation of culture. However, the technological advancements also create potential threats to some of the existing cultural institutions, increase competition for production inputs, and raise inequality among institutions or creative workers. Likewise, it remains open how artificial intelligence will transform the art world.

The textbook approaches these and many other trends from a theoretical perspective, visualized with the help of various anecdotal examples and intuitive arguments, backed with systematically collected and critically assessed data, and complemented with an outlook into what the future may bring.

Being theory-based, and hence in a sense timeless, this book equips students with state-of-the-art models to analyze cultural markets and industries in a systematic way and in ever-changing conditions. However, we do not lose the proximity to the real-world context, as we showcase throughout the book how to put economic principles into practice and illustrate how to apply theory to real-world situations.

In this textbook, we have chosen not to attempt an encyclopedic approach. Instead, we have limited the scope in the name of academic rigor and to fit into a single semester course. Arts and culture compendia abound, and they serve as useful reference works.

How to Use This Book

The book consists of five parts:

- Part I: The Arts Sector in the Economy: Size, Growth, and Significance
- Part II: The Microeconomics of Demand and Supply
- Part III: The Fine Arts and Museums
- Part IV: Public Policy and Support for the Arts
- Part V: Art, Economy, and Society

The advantage of the book structure is that instructors can largely teach the parts out of order. The chapters within Parts I and II should be taught in the order as they appear since the concepts developed here build on one another. The chapters in Parts III–V can also be taught out of order, which gives flexibility in how the teaching is organized.

Each chapter begins with "Learning Objectives," which helps students to focus on key concepts and facilitates repetition. Students may also appreciate the applied nature of the book, as theoretical concepts are contextualized with recent examples and data. The chapters end with discussion questions, cases, and problem sets to enable students the opportunity to exercise and apply the learned material. Some of the open-ended discussion questions will enable educators to test the learning outcomes of students at different levels, while the real-world character of the problem sets and the involvement of the student into the learning process will hopefully be appreciated not only by the students but also by the lecturer.

Acknowledgments

We have, as always, benefited from encounters with our professional colleagues, including readers and users of the earlier editions, and engagements with artists, arts administrators and advocates, and cultural policymakers. We wish to extend our gratitude to Tanja Krischer at Deutscher Bühnenverein; Krzysztof Bogusz, Production Deputy Director at the Grand Theater in Łódź; Nicole Chamberlain-Dupree, Executive Director of the Minnesota Marine Art Museum; Carl Shroeder, Minnesota Orchestra; Pierre Korzelius, formerly of the Museé D'Orsay; Kathleen Gallagher, an arts management faculty member at Southern Methodist University; Derek Miller, Professor of English at Harvard University; Ximena Varela and Andrew Taylor, the arts administration faculty members at American University; Neil Alper, Professor Emeritus at Northeastern University and past Secretary-Treasurer of the Association for Cultural Economics International (ACEI); John O'Hagan, Professor Emeritus at Trinity College Dublin and Past President of ACEI; Stephen Boyle, Diane Aldis, Tom Borrup, Ruth Rentschler, Marjorie Moody, Mary Edna Fraser, Mara Stenback Winke, Christina Baldwin, Dawn Bentley, Sari Karttunen, Paul Finkelstein and Mina Fisher of the Bakken Trio, Gyula Berger and Márta Ladjánszki, J. P. Singh, Camila Contreras, Carolina Barrios Laborda, Trilce Navarrete, Lucie Duggan, Marc Law; members of the ACEI; attendees at annual Social Theory, Politics and the Arts conferences; members of AIMAC (International Association for Arts and Cultural Management); and our students in courses and workshops at the University of St. Thomas, the University of Southern Denmark, University of Wisconsin's Bolz Center, and Eastman School of Music. Excellent research assistance was provided by Martin Hørlyk Kristensen. Abject apologies to any whose names have escaped our recall but to whom we are nonetheless indebted.

Borowiecki acknowledges the formative influence, generous support, and remarkable kindness provided throughout the years by Victoria Ateca-Amestoy and Víctor Fernández-Blanco. Their sudden and recent passing is a big loss for the community.

Gray is especially grateful for continued administrative support and workspace provided to emeritus faculty by the University of St. Thomas Opus College of Business, and particularly to the former department chair and fellow business economist Kathy Combs.

We dedicate this third edition to our significant others and the new children in our lives: Mel's wife, Robin, and grandchildren William, Samantha, and Nelly; and Karol's partner, Lucie, and children Casimir Gabriel and Valentin Laurence.

Jim Heilbrun Obituary

Written by Charles M. Gray and reprinted with updates and with permission from
the *Journal of Cultural Economics*, 32: 225–226

Prominent cultural economist James (Jim) Heilbrun passed away on April 8 (2008) at his home in New York City, where he was born eighty-three years ago and lived most of his life. Jim is a former member of the editorial board of this journal, but most readers would probably be more familiar with him as the coauthor of *The Economics of Art and Culture*, and he had just begun working on the third edition of that book at the time of his passing.

Jim received his undergraduate and master's degrees from Harvard University and his doctoral degree in economics from Columbia University. He was a retired professor of economics at Fordham University, where his colleagues described him as a genuine gentleman and scholar. His strong interest in urban economics shaped his early research agenda and resulted in a widely-adopted textbook, *Urban Economics and Public Policy*.

His appreciation for the New York City cultural scene, especially the New York City Ballet, naturally attracted Jim to cultural economics. I met Jim at the third international conference of the Association for Cultural Economics in Akron, Ohio, in 1984. While sitting in a hotel bar, we decided that the world needed a comprehensive overview of the economics of the arts, a book that could serve as a combination text, research monograph, and cultural policy guide. Thus began a twenty-four-year collaboration through two editions of the book and a chapter in Cherbo and Wyszomirski's *The Public Life of the Arts in America*. It was at the American Assembly that culminated in that volume that Jim most vocally objected to debasing the fine and high arts by defining them broadly and indiscriminately. As he said at that time, "Legal forms are not art!"

Jim unapologetically drew a sharp distinction between the higher arts and popular culture. He strongly favored arts education as the means of promoting investment in the consumption skills required for a deeper appreciation beyond mere entertainment. His research notably examined the decline in the high arts, especially in the United States. An examination of US opera companies revealed that while opera has been a growth industry, companies have been shifting their programming toward a more popular and less demanding repertory. Similarly, he found a significant decline in the coverage of high culture by the *New York Times*, including statistical evidence that advertising affected content. Needless to say, Jim was dismayed by these findings.

Jim continued to participate in ACEI after his retirement from Fordham, attending all biannual meetings and several interim conferences up through the 2000 gathering in Minneapolis. Even after extensive travel became too burdensome for him, he continued an active research stream.

Jim was married to well-known feminist scholar and author, Carolyn Heilbrun, long-time professor of English at Columbia University, who predeceased him in 2003. Theirs was a mutually-supportive dual-career marriage long before that became the norm. Jim is survived by his daughters Emily and Margaret, his son, Robert, and two grandchildren.

Jim Heilbrun was a gifted writer, a perceptive policy critic, and a diligent, imaginative, and productive scholar. His contributions to cultural economics were seminal, and his influence will be felt for many years to come.

Part I

The Arts Sector in the Economy: Size, Growth, and Significance

1   An Overview of the Arts Sector

LEARNING OBJECTIVES

By the end of this chapter, readers should be able to:

- Define economics
- Offer a succinct statement of the methodology of economics
- Distinguish between the aims of for-profit and nonprofit organizations
- Locate relevant data on the arts industry

In the modern era, the creation of art has occupied a special position among human activities. Some might rank it as the highest of all callings; many probably think of it as being above "mere commerce"; a few have expressed their wish that economists would keep their dirty hands off it (Caust, 2003).

Yet no matter how highly we may value them, art and culture are produced by individuals and organizations working within the larger economy, and therefore cannot escape the constraints of that material world. When the Guthrie Theater in Minneapolis hires actors or electricians, it competes in well-defined labor markets and has to pay what the market, or the unions, require. When it sets ticket prices, it has to recognize that its sales will be constrained by competition from other forms of entertainment and by the tastes and incomes of its potential audience. When governmental agencies make grants to organizations such as the Guthrie, those agencies have received their funds through a budgetary process in competition with other government programs, and the government itself raises money by making claims on taxpayers that compete with their desire to spend income in the satisfaction of private wants.

In keeping with its title, *The Economics of Art and Culture*, this book explains how art and culture function within the larger economy. The definition of "economics" that pervades these pages corresponds to that proffered by Robbins (1932, 16) and is now widely accepted throughout the discipline. Simply stated, economics is the study of how societies allocate scarce resources among alternative uses. Monetary and other resources devoted to the arts can be applied elsewhere, and the arts must compete with those other applications.

In many respects, the individuals and firms that consume or produce art behave like consumers and producers of other goods and services; in some significant ways, however, they behave differently. We hope to show that in both cases, the insights afforded by the concepts and tools of economic analysis are interesting and useful.

We investigate the art and culture industry in much the same way that economists might analyze the steel, food, or healthcare industries: We look first at the historical growth of the

3

industry, then examine consumption, production, the functioning of arts markets, the financial problems of the industry, and the important role of public policy. Individual chapters also deal with arts organizations, the arts as a profession, the role of the arts in a local economy, and the relation of rapidly evolving digital technology to art and culture.

1.1   Coverage of This Book

First, however, we must explain what part of art and culture we choose to address. For the purposes of this book, art and culture comprise the live performing arts of theater, opera, classical music, and dance, plus the fine arts of painting and sculpture and the associated institutions of art museums, galleries, auction houses, and dealers. It is important to note at the outset that we are here not defining art and culture in terms of aesthetic or social scientific discourse, but simply explaining how much of their domain we have chosen to cover in a single volume.

Obviously, the above definition leaves out some important cultural and other creative activities. Among the performing arts, we exclude motion pictures (which are not live) and nonclassical music concerts (even though they are live). We also exclude writing, publishing, broadcasting, video games, and other media, except insofar as those media afford access to the arts as defined above.

These exclusions, however, are not arbitrary. First, the two included groups are internally coherent. The performing arts categories are all live and share a common production technique: A performance takes place in a venue to which the audience must come; the performance can be repeated in exactly the same way as often as might be desirable to satisfy a larger audience. Thus, if you understand, for example, the economics of theatrical production, you also understand, in principle if not in detail, the economics of opera, ballet, or symphony production. The fine arts category is coherent in a different sense: The subgroups are jointly involved in making, buying and selling, and displaying art objects.

Second, some of the excluded categories – motion pictures, broadcasting, video games, and writing and publishing – are complex industries unto themselves and very unlike the included ones. It would be difficult to generalize about the economics of such unlike activities and impractical to attempt to cover that much diversity in a single volume. Motion picture production, broadcasting, and digital media do share many traits that would facilitate treating them jointly, but that would require another book, and several very good ones already exist.

Third, the included categories – except the Broadway theater, painters and sculptors, and art dealers, auction houses, and galleries – are organized on a not-for-profit basis in most countries, while the excluded categories are largely made up of commercial, profit-seeking firms or individuals.[1] The distinction is significant not only because we would expect economic decisions to be made differently in the two sectors but also because explicit government subsidies are largely confined to the not-for-profit group, and only firms in that sector are eligible to receive tax-deductible private charitable donations. Those forms of support make up an important part of nonprofit sector budgets, again lending coherence to the group and its problems.

Table 1.1 High culture within the economy.

	Arts	Other
Nonprofit	"High culture"	Healthcare, education, social services, etc.
For-profit	Popular music, Broadway, cinema, video games	Humdrum-manufacturing, retail, finance, etc.

Finally, the included categories are older, traditional forms that are sometimes referred to as "high" art, while those that are excluded (except writing and publishing) are newer forms that are also called "popular" or "mass" culture.[2] We do not mean to imply that this distinction reflects our own value judgments, but it is well established in the literature. We shall also point out that while some categories like broadcasting or video games are excluded from this book, we discuss in places how they relate to the arts and culture sectors. For example, we explore how media and digital technologies influence art demand and supply, and analyze the most recent trends in the consumption of digital arts (see Chapter 14).

To be sure, there are ambiguities aplenty in this delineation of the field. Writing is a traditional high art but is excluded nonetheless. Motion pictures are potentially a high art, though a relatively recent rather than a traditional form. Many movies have a more serious artistic purpose than some Broadway musicals, though the latter are included here while movies are not. Table 1.1 summarizes our delineation.

1.2 Art and Culture as a Subject of Economic Inquiry

With all its compromises, our definition does correspond to the one adopted by most economists who have worked in this field as well as the categories of "core arts" as defined by the National Endowment for the Arts. The field itself remains relatively new, with almost nothing having been written about it before the mid-1960s. Its origin can be dated from 1966, the year in which William J. Baumol and William G. Bowen published *Performing Arts: The Economic Dilemma.* This path-breaking study, which long remained the definitive work in the field, attracted wide notice and quickly drew the attention of economists to an important new concern: the financial condition of the arts in the United States. (The specific questions raised by Baumol and Bowen are dealt with in detail in Chapter 8 of this volume.)

Baumol and Bowen's study was the culmination of a decade of growing interest in the condition of art and culture in the United States. That interest was reflected in the public sector by the establishment of the New York State Council on the Arts in 1961 and the National Endowment for the Arts, at the federal level, in 1965.

By comparison, cultural ministries or their equivalents had been a part of European governments for many decades or even centuries prior to this. Artistic production flourished in the Renaissance courts of the ruling families of Italy and the Burgundian Netherlands, for whom patronage of the arts was an expression of princely virtue, power, and prestige. Dynasties such as the Medici of Florence, the Gonzaga of Mantua, and the Dukes of Burgundy provided the impetus for tremendous achievements in the arts and humanities, their territories home to some of the greatest artists of all time. In France, state-sponsored institutions of artistic production began emerging from at least the sixteenth century and this public support continued into the seventeenth century with what are possibly the earliest examples of cultural policies, implemented by Louis XIV's minister of finance, Jean-Baptiste Colbert.

Since Baumol and Bowen's significant work emerged, interest in the economic problems of the arts has grown steadily. Scholars from many countries have been active in this new field. In England, Mark Blaug and Alan Peacock wrote numerous papers on the economics of the arts, beginning in the late 1960s. In the United States, an important study by Dick Netzer on the role of government subsidies in support of the arts was published in 1978. In the 1970s, William S. Hendon and others established the Association for Cultural Economics and began publishing the *Journal of Cultural Economics*, available in print and online.[3] In 1979, the Australian economists C. David Throsby and Glenn A. Withers produced an influential study entitled *The Economics of the Performing Arts*. The Swiss and German economists Bruno S. Frey and Werner W. Pommerehne wrote *Muses and Markets: Explorations in the Economics of the Arts*, published in 1989, the same year as William Grammp's *Pricing the Priceless: Art, Artists, and Economics*. More recent English-language compendia include *A Handbook of Cultural Economics*, edited by Ruth Towse and Trilce Navarrete Hernández and published in 2020, *Handbook of the Economics of Art and Culture*, edited by Victor Ginsburgh and David Throsby, and *Beyond Price: Value in Culture, Economics, and the Arts*, edited by Michael Hutter and David Throsby. By now there is a considerable body of useful research not only on the economics but also on the management, politics, and sociology of the arts or the economic history of the arts.[4]

As a final indicator of the significance of economic studies of the arts, several universities have established arts and economics programs, most notably Erasmus University in Rotterdam and Utrecht School of the Arts, both in the Netherlands, Copenhagen Business School in Denmark, University of Valladolid in Spain, and Bocconi University in Italy. According to Eduniversal, which provides a ranking of the best master's degrees worldwide, most programs in arts and cultural management are offered at European universities. Among the fifty universities listed in 2021, about two thirds are in Europe, three can be found in the United States, another three in Australia, and thirteen in other parts of the world (Eduniversal, 2021). The number of universities from non-Western countries offering high-quality programs in cultural economics has been growing in recent years and include institutions from South America (e.g., Brazil) and Asia (China, Thailand, Indonesia, and South Korea).[5]

Several other universities have specialized in educating doctoral candidates in cultural economics. These programs usually center around a key faculty member who has the requisite interest and is able to assemble the necessary resources. For example, The Department of Economics of Trinity College in Dublin has in recent years granted more than ten Ph.D.s with a specialization in cultural economics, all supervised by Professor John O'Hagan, including one of the authors of this book. More formal doctoral programs are also emerging; among others, Labex ICCA in France, an interdisciplinary network initiated by several universities in Paris, has launched doctoral education in areas related to cultural industries and artistic production.

1.3   Estimating the Size of the Arts Sector

How important is the arts sector in the economy? Although lack of data was once a frequent lament of those studying the economics of the arts, the situation has improved in recent years. In prior editions of this book, the authors pored over the National Income and Product Account (NIPA) data for the United States, industry organization data, and even *Variety* magazine to construct estimates of sectoral size. The NIPA data provide a statistical series for every year since 1929 that is uniquely suitable for making the necessary comparison. These are the accounts in which the Commerce Department's Bureau of Economic Analysis (BEA) calculates the size of the gross domestic product (GDP), a measure of the aggregate value of all final goods and services produced by the United States economy during a single year. The GDP is the sum of personal consumption expenditures, gross private domestic investment, net exports, and government purchases of goods and services. We are now able to adapt data published by the BEA in collaboration with the National Endowment for the Arts (NEA) to our purposes.

Table 1.2 presents selected data contained in the BEA–NEA Art and Cultural Production Satellite Account for the year 2019. The choice of the year 2019 is not only dictated by data availability at the time of the writing of this book but it is also the last full "normal" year before the onset of the COVID-19 pandemic, which has significantly distorted the arts and cultural industries globally, and the effects are visible throughout the early 2020s. The total in the first line goes well beyond the coverage of this book, but we include it here for reference purposes. The traditional "core arts" include performing arts companies and art museums. The excluded categories and subcategories include support services (e.g., promoters and agents) and other activities (e.g., publishing, sound recording, and jewelry making) not directly involved in arts production. In addition, many arts activities are embedded in the activities of schools and religious organizations, so they are not included anywhere in these accounts.

The total for the core arts is $93.3 billion. To put that figure in perspective, consider the fact that in 2019, the GDP of the United States – a measure of the value of the output of all goods

Table 1.2 Value added by the core "high" arts and supporting industries, 2019.

Industry and subsector	Current dollars, millions	GDP (%)
Total	902,527	4.22
Core arts and cultural production	208,113	0.97
Selected categories and subcategories		
Performing arts	85,146	0.40
Art museums	8,112	0.04
Fine arts education	3,642	0.02
Supporting arts and cultural production	694,414	3.25

Source: Bureau of Economic Analysis, U.S. Department of Commerce. "Arts and Cultural Production Satellite Accounts". Authors' calculations.

Table 1.3 Estimated size of the EU art and culture sector, 2011.

Category	Euro, millions	GDP (%)
A. Total consumer spending on admissions to the live performing arts (nonprofit provision only)	14,726	0.11
B. Estimated art museum operating income not including private donations and government support	7,717	0.06
C. Total direct governmental assistance	63,741	0.48
D. Estimated private charitable support to art and culture	13,558	0.10
Grand total	99,742	0.75

Sources: Rows A and B – European Grouping of Societies of Authors and Composers, *Creating Growth: Measuring Cultural and Creative Markets in the EU*; Row C – Eurostat, General Government Expenditure on Cultural services (COFOG); Row D – Estimated from data for 2002–2004 in *Financing the Arts and Culture in the European Union*.

and services – stood at $21,381 billion. The arts sector as measured here amounts to only a little more than four thousandth of that sum or, to be precise, 0.44%.

It is for the reader to judge whether that is a large figure or a small one: In the same year, 2019, the value added by the food, beverage, and tobacco products industry was $286.6 billion (1.3% of GDP), while the legal services industry added value of $280.2 billion (1.3% of GDP).

Table 1.3 depicts similar data for the European Union, based on data available as of 2011. These data come from disparate sources, but they offer the same message: the art and culture sector is a small component of the overall economy.

Our point here is not to be absolutely precise about what is included or not, especially given the disagreements on definitions, but to point out the order of magnitude of the arts in the economy. The arts industry is very small in relation to the overall economy, in the United States and in other countries as well. Why, then, do we study it? The arts industry may be small in size relative to the overall economy, but it is essential for the functioning of many related industries, such as the travel and tourism industries. Before the COVID-19 pandemic, a quarter of all new jobs created across the world was in the travel and tourism sector; this amounts to around a third of a billion jobs (or 10% of all jobs), and contributed approximately 10% toward global GDP, albeit with large differences across countries (World Travel & Tourism Council, 2022). And while there are many reasons to travel, places with a good supply of arts and culture tend to attract more tourists. But there is another, no less significant reason why we study the economics of arts and culture. We do so not because the arts industry is important to the economy but because it is an important part of what has come to be known as our cultural capital, and is therefore vital to our self-image as a society.

SUGGESTIONS FOR FURTHER READING

For one account of the origins of cultural economics, see Ruth Towse, "Introduction," in Towse (1997a).

See U.S. Bureau of Economic Analysis (2022) for data on the size of the cultural sector in the United States. Readers who are especially interested in employment aspects of the arts and culture sector should find Chapter 14 useful.

For discussion and development of the cultural capital concept, see Throsby (1999).

Borowiecki and Greenwald (2023) provide in the *Handbook of Cliometrics* an overview of recent scholarship on the fast-growing field of Economic History of the Arts.

Recent scholarship on any area of cultural economics is regularly explained in nontechnical terms on *Economists Talk Art*, a platform co-founded by one of the coauthors of the book, which aims at providing research-based policy analysis and commentary for cultural policy makers, managers, and the wider public.

PROBLEM SET

1.1 Should we think of art as being above "mere commerce"? Are artistic endeavors exempt from market forces? Do artists work to support themselves or to express themselves? How does the work of an artist differ from that of, say, a tailor, a plumber, or a shoemaker? In what way(s) might the artist's work be similar?

1.2 What is the role and importance of art patronage and funding in history and nowadays? Support your answer with examples familiar to you.

1.3 By conventional measures, the arts sector is typically very small in relation to the overall economy. It is argued, however, that art and culture provide many benefits for society that may not be captured by these conventional measures.

a. On your own, prepare a list of these benefits.

b. Pair-up and try to identify the three most important benefits from your lists.

c. What attribute of these benefits makes them "societal" or "social"?

NOTES

1 But as Meiksins (2018) points out, nonprofits are infiltrating Broadway.

2 The notion of high culture as distinguished from what came to be called low or popular culture emerged in the United States in the second half of the nineteenth century. See Levine (1988, chapters 2 and 3). Levine also argues that we have recently begun to move away from such rigid distinctions (p. 255). For a theoretical treatment of the distinction, see Cowen and Tabarrok (2000).

3 The Association has also sponsored biannual international conferences on cultural economics since 1979 and a range of regional workshops: The European Workshop on Applied Cultural Economics, founded in 2003 and organized in its 10th edition in 2022, or the workshop series organized in North America, South America or Asian. For further details and news in the field see the Association of Cultural Economics International (ACEI) website: www.culturaleconomics .org.

4 Economic history of the arts may be one of the fastest-growing areas in cultural economics in recent years, with coverage in the Handbook of Cliometrics (Borowiecki and Greenwald, 2023) or Handbook of Cultural Economics (Borowiecki, 2020), and with two special issues on this area

expected to be published in 2023 in the *Journal of Cultural Economics* and *European Review of Economic History*.

5 It is unlikely a coincidence that the tourism industry in each of these non-Western countries contributes a very significant fraction toward the overall economy. As we shall see in Chapter 15, the arts sectors and tourism industry are closely related.

2 Growth of the Arts Sector

LEARNING OBJECTIVES

By the end of this chapter, readers should be able to:

- Explain the difference between size and growth
- Present various approaches to the measurement of growth
- Identify factors that matter for the growth of the arts sector
- Describe the arts industry (sector, market, etc.) status and trends

Given our contention that the arts industry is crucial to our self-image, we are naturally curious not only about its size but also about changes in its status over time. If it is growing rapidly, we are likely to think better of the state of our society than if it is growing slowly or stagnating. We begin this chapter by tracing the growth of the live performing arts in the United States from 1929 to 2020, using data available over that interval, with special attention to the impact of technological innovation. We then examine more recent trends in the United States as indicated by an index based on the NIPA subaccounts introduced in Chapter 1. We give some attention to overall trends in selected other nations, including Canada, Australia, and parts of Europe. In this context, we finish by describing the development of the principal forms of the live performing arts – theater, symphony, opera, and dance. Growth of activity in the fine arts and the growth of art museums are taken up in more detail in Chapters 10 and 11.

Although we may all agree that the arts are more than "mere entertainment," they are a form of entertainment, nevertheless, and must compete with other forms in the budgets of interested consumers. The historical perspective adopted in this chapter allows us not only to measure the arts' long-run growth but also to see how they have fared in competition with other kinds of recreation, and especially with other forms of spectator entertainment. In addition, it shows us how well the live arts have stood up against the endlessly accelerating flow of technological innovations, from talking pictures through television to Internet streaming, and from vinyl recordings through the compact disc to the MP3 player and streaming on demand, which have transformed the *non*live entertainment industry over the same span of years.

2.1 Measuring Growth

Beginning in the early 1960s, observers of culture in the United States began to speak of a "cultural boom" that had started at the end of World War II. The considerable attention given to this alleged boom by the media in the 1960s probably indicated that Americans were increasingly self-conscious about the nation's cultural standing and now wanted to be taken seriously as contributors to, or at least appreciators of, high art and culture.

How can we measure the growth rate of the arts or decide when or whether the arts have enjoyed a boom? In economics (and on Wall Street), it is conventional to judge the growth rates of industries by comparing them with each other and with the growth rate of the economy as a whole. Such a comparison is useful in evaluating the position of the arts in US society. If the arts sector is growing faster than the overall economy, then that would be a sign that the arts are becoming more important to the American people as time passes. In that case, we could probably all agree that culture is, indeed, booming in the United States.

2.2   Competition among Forms of Recreation

Attendance at arts performances competes for the consumer's time and money with other recreational activities. The terms of the competition are periodically revolutionized by technological innovations – for example, the invention of the phonograph and motion pictures in the late nineteenth century, the introduction of the motion picture soundtrack in 1927, the commercial development of television immediately after World War II and then of long-playing records, audio tape systems, home videocassette recorders, compact disc recordings, videodiscs, and streaming on demand. By comparing the trend of consumers' spending on the performing arts with the trend in outlays for other spectator activities and recreation as a whole, we gain insights into both the competitive position of the performing arts and the impact on that position of some of the major technological innovations.

The first five rows of Table 2.1 shows consumer spending on the performing arts and related categories of recreational activity as a percentage of disposable personal income (DPI) from 1929 to 2020. Trends over time for the spectator categories are highlighted in Figure 2.1, in which the percentages of DPI spent on admissions to the performing arts, motion pictures, and spectator sports are plotted in the form of index numbers, with the base year 1929 = 100. For any given year, the index number is calculated as 100 times the ratio of the percentage of DPI spent on admissions in that year to the percentage for the year 1929. For example, Table 2.1 shows the percentages of DPI spent on admissions to the performing arts to be 0.08 in 1970 and 0.16 in 1929. Dividing the former by the latter produces a ratio of 0.5 for 1970, which, when multiplied by 100, yields the index of 50 for 1970 that is plotted in Figure 2.1. The straightforward meaning of that number is that in 1970 the share of DPI that consumers spent for admission to the performing arts stood at 50% (or half) of its level in 1929. In other words, consumers were spending a smaller proportion of their income on admissions to the performing arts in 1970 than they had done in 1929. The share of income spent on admission to the performing arts returned only in the early 2000s to the 1929 level, and in 2015, it was 52% above the 1929 level, before falling again in 2020 due to the COVID-19 pandemic.

One can place the performing arts sector in perspective by looking at the larger categories of which it is a part. Table 2.1 shows that consumer spending on recreation as a whole rose from

Table 2.1 Consumer spending on admissions to spectator entertainment

	1929	1939	1947	1970	1975	1980	1985	1990	1995	2000	2005	2010	2015	2020
Consumer spending as a percentage of disposable personal income														
Recreation, total	5.30	4.95	5.48	7.27	7.48	7.28	7.64	8.26	9.06	9.36	9.18	8.62	8.53	8.38
Spectator entertainment	1.12	1.18	1.19	0.49	0.41	0.37	0.34	0.38	0.41	0.45	0.50	0.57	0.53	0.17
Performing arts	0.16	0.09	0.11	0.08	0.07	0.09	0.10	0.12	0.14	0.15	0.21	0.26	0.24	0.08
Motion pictures[a]	0.88	0.95	0.94	0.25	0.21	0.15	0.12	0.13	0.11	0.13	0.11	0.12	0.11	0.02
Spectator sports	0.08	0.14	0.13	0.17	0.13	0.13	0.12	0.13	0.15	0.17	0.18	0.19	0.19	0.07
Percentage breakdown of consumer spending														
Spectator entertainment as percentage of all recreation	21.09	23.78	21.66	6.81	5.45	5.02	4.49	4.58	4.47	4.83	5.43	6.64	6.25	2.05
Percent distribution of spectator entertainment														
Performing arts	13.9	7.8	9.4	15.6	16.7	23.4	29.0	31.3	34.8	34.0	41.9	45.5	44.2	46.5
Motion pictures[a]	78.8	80.2	79.5	50.0	52.4	40.6	34.4	35.4	27.9	28.1	22.2	21.0	20.3	12.0
Spectator sports	7.2	12.0	11.1	34.4	31.0	35.9	35.5	33.3	36.8	37.9	35.9	33.6	35.3	41.5

Notes: Values for 1929, 1939, and 1947 are from the previous version of the book, while values from 1970 and onward are from the U.S. Department of Commerce NIPA accounts.

[a] In theaters only.

Source: U.S. Department of Commerce, *National Income and Product Accounts of the United States*, statistical tables, various years.

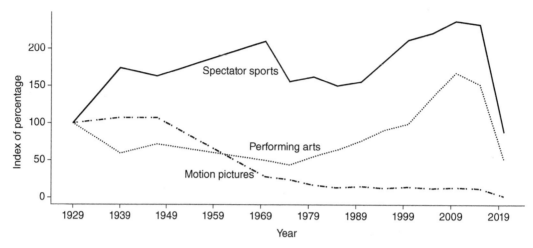

Figure 2.1 Expenditures on admissions as a percentage of disposable personal income

7.27% of DPI in 1970 to 8.38% in 2020. Real disposable income per capita rose 165% over the same period. That the proportion spent on recreation gradually increased tells us that recreation behaves like a "luxury good," something that people want relatively more of as their living standards rise.

Spending on what the Commerce Department identifies as "spectator amusements" makes up only a small part of recreation expenditure as a whole. The lower portion of Table 2.1 shows that in 1929, the earliest year for which we have data, it accounted for 21.1% of the total, and that motion pictures made up about 79% of that share. The movies were then approaching the height of their popularity. Talking pictures had been introduced in 1927 with *The Jazz Singer*, starring Al Jolson. With the advantage of the soundtrack, movies became more popular than ever during the 1930s. Through the Great Depression and the years of World War II (when travel and recreation opportunities were limited), the movies continued to claim 80% of spectator entertainment outlays.

The live performing arts did not stand up well under competition with talking pictures. The decline in real per capita income during the Great Depression may also have hurt the more expensive live performing arts in competition with the movies. Their share of spectator spending fell from 13.9% in 1929 to about 8% ten years later. Table 2.1 shows that in 1929 consumers had spent 16 cents on the live performing arts per $100 of DPI. By 1939, such outlays had fallen to just over 9 cents per $100.

2.2.1 The Impact of Television

The introduction of television broadcasting immediately after World War II had a dramatic effect on consumer behavior. In 1947, as TV broadcasting was just beginning, consumers spent 94 cents of every $100 of DPI to attend the movies. By 1975, when 97% of US homes had at least one TV set, spending for admission to the movies had fallen to 21 cents per $100, or about one-fifth of its 1947 level, and accounted for just over half of consumer outlays for spectator entertainment (U.S. Department of Commerce, 1991a, table 919). Indeed, consumers were spending as much on radio and television repairs as they were on movie admissions (U.S. Department of Commerce, 1991b, table 2.4).

While the impact of television on moviegoing was strong and clear, its effect on attendance at the live performing arts was much less dramatic. From 1947 to 1975, spending on the latter group fell from 11 cents to 7 cents per $100 of DPI. Because movie attendance was down so sharply, the share of spectator activity accounted for by the live performing arts almost doubled from 9% to 17%.

It is not difficult to see why the live performing arts should prove more resistant than the movies were to the competition of TV. Television and the movies are, in fact, technically similar, an image projected on a flat screen, while the "live" nature of the live performing arts gives them a third dimension and an aesthetic character that cannot be duplicated by the other modes. Perhaps dance provides the most obvious illustration. Television cannot reproduce the three-dimensionality of a live, on-stage performance in which dancers move through real space. Something of esthetic importance is left out. No one who has developed a taste for live ballet is likely to find ballet on television an adequate substitute for the real thing. In varying degrees, the same can be said for other live arts.

Even though some of our own research (Gray, 1995), which we revisit later in this volume, indicates that live and media arts complement, rather than substitute, each other, more recent developments may have altered the extent to which "liveness" protects the live performing arts against the competition of digital access. Today, the live arts must compete not just with broadcast versions of the performing arts, but also with broadcasts and streams of other kinds (not all of them "entertainment"), which make television, computer, and tablet viewing such an attractive leisure activity. We take a further look at the relationship between media access and attendance at the live performing arts in Chapter 3, and again in Chapters 16 and 17, which deal, among other things, with the effect of media on the cultivation of taste for the arts.

2.3   Growth of the Arts since 1970 in the United States

Figure 2.1 shows that by 1970 the ratio of consumer spending on the performing arts to DPI was half as high as it had been in 1929. The argument that the United States had been enjoying a "boom" in art and culture rests on trends that began to assert themselves in the 1960s. During the late 1950s and early 1960s, the nation had become self-consciously concerned about the situation of the arts in the United States. Comparisons, most of them unfavorable to the United States, were made with the status of the arts in other advanced industrial nations. An intense new interest in encouraging the arts developed in both the private and public spheres. Private charitable foundations (especially the Ford Foundation) greatly expanded their support for arts companies and artists. With the establishment of the National Endowment for the Arts (NEA) in 1965, the federal government, for the first time, began to subsidize artistic activity on a regular and permanent basis. State support along the same lines had begun with the establishment of the New York State Council on the Arts in 1960. (The origins of public support for the arts in the United States are treated in greater detail in Chapter 12.)

It is very likely that this combination of private and public support produced a rapid increase in arts activity during the 1970s. A variety of physical indicators reflecting such growth are displayed in Table 2.2. The top line of the table shows DPI in constant dollars, in other words, with the effects of inflation removed. It thus provides a measure of what economists refer to as "real income," the equivalent to a physical measure of income, since its year-to-year movements are not distorted by price changes. The top line is therefore a gauge of "real" aggregate growth with which to compare the growth of "real" arts activity as indicated by the other entries. Many of the indicators of real arts activity showed rates of increase during the 1970s that exceeded the growth of real income. Although figures for years before 1970 are not given in Table 2.2, some sectors, including ballet and modern dance, had also shown exceptionally rapid growth during the 1960s. Some measures of physical activity reached a high point in the late 1980s and then began to decline. Work weeks under the Actors' Equity contract with the League of Resident Theatres registered a level of 58,580 in 1990 and then slowly declined to 52,202 in 2018. Work under the Off-Broadway contract also fluctuated substantially over the same period. It should be pointed out, however, that changes in the number of work weeks shown in Table 2.2 do not necessarily indicate trends, since actors' work weeks may fluctuate widely from year to year depending on how attractive a particular season's offerings turn out to be, and 1980, an early date in the table, was a relatively strong season. That the performing arts were growing faster than the economy as a whole since the 1970s is confirmed in Table 2.1. After reaching a low of less than 7 cents per $100 of DPI in the mid-1970s, consumer spending on the performing arts rose to 12 cents per $100 in 1990 and 26 cents in 2010, which was the peak. One should not be misled by the diminutive size of these numbers, for they indicate that between 1975 and 2010 consumer expenditure on the performing arts increased more than three times as fast as DPI. That should be enough to persuade even the most skeptical observer that there was, indeed, a cultural boom since the 1970s. The rapid growth changed into a slow decline following the Great Recession that affected the economy badly, especially between 2008 and 2009. Households faced with larger cuts in personal finances were forced to decrease their overall spending, including their budgets for cultural consumption.

Competition from recordings and broadcast music, including digital streaming most recently, has likely affected attendance at symphony concerts, but the impact is not much reflected in the aggregated performing arts expenditure. Later in this chapter, we discuss changes on the supply side of the performing arts, but it is difficult to avoid the conclusion that steadily increasing competition from popular culture – exerting its effect through taste formation among the younger population cohorts – is not influencing the physical growth of arts activity (see Peterson et al., 1996). Those well-heeled consumers who are not attending the arts are doing something else instead, and there is no reason to think such competition will soon abate (see discussion in Chapter 17). Another question that remains to be answered is what will happen to expenditure on admissions to spectator entertainment in post-COVID times, a concern that we leave out for later.

Table 2.2 Growth of arts activity in the United States, 1970–2018

	1970	1980	1990	2000	2008	2014	2018	Percent change 2000–2018
Disposable personal income (billions of chained 2012 dollars)	3,637	4,906	6,817	9,480	11,610	12,844	14,556	53.6
Broadway: playing weeks	1,047	1,541	1,061	1,484	1,548	1,626	1,737	17.0
Attendance (thousands)	NA	9,380	8,039	1,1890	12,150	13,100	14,770	24.2
Road company playing weeks	1,024	1,351	1,152	772	1,125	953	1,188	53.9
Actors' Equity work weeks								
League of Resident Theaters contract	32,522	42,910	58,580	4,4423[c]	53,261	51,080	52,202	17.5
Off-Broadway contract	13,424	9,313	11,849	8,420[c]	7,083	15,351	18,175	115.9
Chicago area contract		2,093	5,344	5,851[c]	7,355	7,844	7,641	30.6
Opera, major professional companies[a]								
Performances		1,789[b]	2,283					
Attendance (millions)		2.46[b]	4.14					

Notes:

[a] Main stage, main season, includes Canada.

[b] 1983.

[c] 1997–1998 season.

Source: Broadway League Statistics, Survey of Public Participation in the Arts, NEA (1982–2019)

2.4   Influence of Changes on the Supply Side

It is an important aspect of the economics of the live performing arts that they have to be consumed at the point of production: To see *Hamlet*, one must go to the theater at a specified time. This contrasts with the case of manufactured goods, which can be produced centrally and then distributed to consumers through a network of retail outlets, and we can gain a further understanding of the growth trend in the live performing arts by examining the consequences of this difference.

As the term "consumer sovereignty" suggests, the standard assumption in the economic analysis of a free-enterprise system is that the quantity supplied responds more or less smoothly to changes in demand. For example, if the public wants more dishwashers, then the demand for dishwashers will increase (see discussion in Chapter 4), existing factories will expand output at existing locations, and a larger number of dishwashers will be distributed to consumers through existing outlets. Moreover, these outlets do not depend exclusively on dishwasher sales for their existence. Supply, therefore, responds easily and continuously to changes in demand. The situation is very different when, as in the live performing arts, the commodity has to be produced at the point of consumption. In that case, the local market has to be large enough to support a minimum-size producer before local production becomes feasible. Consequently, the adaptation of supply to demand is likely to be intermittent (or discontinuous) rather than smooth. It is well known in the study of regional economics that the local number of retail and service outlets is largely governed by such market-size or "threshold" effects (see discussion in Chapter 15). But no one would argue that the aggregate consumption and production of, for example, dishwashers, is affected by the fact that small towns do not have distributorships. We know that potential local consumers will go to larger towns to buy them. There is a good reason to think the case is otherwise for the live performing arts: Few consumers will regularly travel long distances to attend live performances, and the distance is likely to be longer for the performing arts than for a dishwasher. Aggregate consumption and production is therefore limited by the number of local places served, and discontinuous increases in the number of such places can cause abrupt surges in aggregate consumption.

With this analysis in mind, it is not unreasonable to suggest that the high growth rate of performing arts activity since the 1970s may have resulted not so much from rising consumer demand as from an increase in supply. The availability of government subsidies and additional private contributions encouraged the formation of new performing arts companies in places that previously had few or none. The same financial support also greatly increased the number and range of performance tours into previously untapped markets. In this process, a latent demand for the arts was satisfied by a sudden burst of new activity, and consumer spending on the arts increased much faster than income. If that is what happened, it is a pattern that will be difficult to duplicate in future decades, when the number of unserved markets will have diminished in relative importance.

Like the live performing arts, live spectator sporting events have to be consumed at the point of production, and trends in the spectator sports industry strongly support the argument that discontinuous changes on the supply side have important effects on spending. Figure 2.1 shows that the ratio of spectator sports admission outlays to DPI increased until 1970. This rise coincided with a period in which the number of teams increased sharply, almost doubling as the leagues expanded into new metropolitan areas in the South and West that had not previously been served. When the latent demand in these new markets was tapped, the ratio of consumer spending on admissions to their DPI soared, reaching a peak in 1970. Afterward, the number of teams continued to increase, but at a much slower rate than before, and consequently, the spending ratio declined to well below its peak level. Another period of growth began in the 1990s and ebbed in the 2010s, before collapsing due to the COVID-19 pandemic.

2.5 International Data on Arts Activity

Tables 2.3–2.11 present data on attendance at the live performing arts in seven European countries and in Canada and Australia. It is a matter of considerable interest to compare recent trends in those countries with the trend described above for the United States. If the US pattern of reduced growth or even decline of the last decade is being replicated elsewhere, then one could suggest that the dominant cause may be the same, namely, the increasing competition from popular culture and broadcasting. On the other hand, if international comparisons reveal considerable differences in trend, one might conclude that whatever may be the level of competition from popular culture, other factors produce diverse outcomes.

Tables 2.3–2.11 certainly do *not* display a picture of uniform growth across either countries or disciplines. For each country, the last column on the right shows the percentage change in attendance from the earliest date to the latest. For Germany, most of the changes were downward. For Australia, France, the Netherlands, and Norway, most or all changes were upward. Canada, the United Kingdom, Sweden, and Finland saw little change in total attendance over the period covered.

Among individual disciplines, we note that attendance at theater is down in two cases. On a priori grounds that is not surprising, since, as we have previously argued, we would expect attendance at drama to suffer from the competition of motion pictures and television. We have also argued that one would expect attendance at symphony concerts to be reduced by the competition of radio, recorded music, and more recently by digital broadcasting. The trend in the United States seems to illustrate that case, but in Europe, attendance at concerts is up strongly. The exception is the United Kingdom, where it has declined, although this observation is based on a relatively short and recent time period.

Among individual countries, Germany is an important case in which there is a well-established pattern of decline in attendance at the performing arts. (This observation would also hold if we looked only at West Germany during the period from 1979 to 1995.) From a peak of 17.75 million reached in 1998, attendance at the live performing arts fell gradually to 15.78 million in 2018, a decline of 11.1% in twenty years. As Table 2.6 shows, attendance fell across all the major sectors, except for orchestras. For an earlier period, Volker Kirchberg analyzed the German data and found partial, but not complete, confirmation of the hypothesis of a negative correlation between attendance at the high arts and at the popular arts (see Kirchberg, 1998a).

Table 2.3 Trends in attendance at the live performing arts (attendance in thousands)

Australia			Performance season				Percent change
	1995	1999	2005–2006	2009–2010	2013–2014	2017–2018	1995–2018[a]
Theater	2,336	2,465	2,723	2,847	2,956	3,223	38.0
Musicals and operas	2,722	2,430	2,614	2,849	2,742	3,088	13.4
Classical music concerts[a]	1,081	1,310	1,508	1,554	1,643		51.9
Dance	1,408	1,345	1,625	1,768	1,812	2,033	44.4
Total[a]	11,338	11,332	12,506	14,317	15,186	8,344	33.9

Note:
[a] Classical music concerts and total percentage change are calculated for 1995–2013.
Source: Australian Bureau of Statistics, Attendance at selected cultural venues and events (2007, 2010, 2014, 2018)

Table 2.4 Trends in attendance at the live performing arts (attendance in thousands)

Canada				Performance season					Percent change
	2004	2006	2008	2010	2012	2014	2016	2018	2004–2018
Theater	7,003	7,312	7,464	7,966	7,548	6,447	6,775	7,346	4.9
Opera	1,095	981	1,015	1,074	1,121	1,044	812	995	−9.1
Music	3,039	2,759	2,935	3,169	2,686	2,492	3,446	3,923	29.1
Dance	1,429	1,443	1,304	1,166	1,299	768	818	1,150	−19.5
Total	11,137	11,052	11,414	12,209	11,355	9,983	11,033	12,264	10.1

Source: Statistics Canda.

Table 2.5 shows that in the United Kingdom, attendance at some of the nonprofit live performing arts also have fallen since 2005. Data for opera, classical concerts, and musicals show that attendance declined 15.2%, 9.8%, and 8.5%, respectively. On the other hand, the trend is positive for ballet with an increase of 31.8% and also for the new category of contemporary dance that rose by 33.7%.

Table 2.8 shows data for the Netherlands for a time period from 1999 to 2019. In contrary to the United Kingdom, attendance at ballet or dance fell considerably by 39.8%, while other sectors, in particular concerts, gained substantially.

Table 2.10 shows that in Finland, too, from 1999 to 2019, attendance at orchestra concerts increased (though not as sharply as in the Netherlands). On the other hand, drama, national opera, and – over a shorter time period – dance theaters, fell by up to 22%. Consequently, total attendance at the live performing arts remained virtually unchanged from 1999 to 2019. The sudden increase in attendance at the national opera in the mid-1990s is attributable to

Table 2.5 Trends in attendance at the live performing arts (attendance in thousands)

United Kingdom	Performing season									Percent change
	2005–2006	2007–2008	2009–2010	2011–2012	2013–2014	2015–2016	2017–2018	2019–2020		2005–2019
Play/drama	8,692	8,947	9,496	9,794	10,350	10,376	10,396	9,686		11.4
Opera/operetta	1,738	1,686	1,984	1,903	1,906	1,959	1,708	1,473		−15.2
Classical concerts	3,347	3,260	3,316	3,676	3,731	3,809	3,708	3,018		−9.8
Ballet	1,527	1,571	1,540	1,997	2,083	2,051	2,326	2,012		31.8
Pantomime			5,646	5,898	5,881	6,017	6,081	5,734		2.0
Musical			9,801	10,005	9,229	9,277	9,509	8,552		−8.5
Contemporary dance	861	887	1,172	1,392	1,231	1,357	1,458	1,152		33.7
Total	16,164	16,350	17,508	18,763	19,301	19,553	19,596	17,341		7.3

Note: Total excludes pantomime and musicals that are available only since 2008–2009. For these two activities, the percentage change covers only the seasons 2009/2010–2019/2020.

Source: Department for Culture, Media and Sport, *Taking Part Survey Reports.*

Table 2.6 Trends in attendance at the live performing arts (attendance in thousands)

| | Performance season | | | | | | | | | | Percent change |
| | West Germany | | | | | Germany | | | | | |
	1979–1980	1984–1985	1989–1990	1994–1995	1995–1996	1998–1999	2003–2004	2008–2009	2013–2014	2018–2019	1998/1999–2018/2019
Plays	7,950	7,498	6,697	6,341	6,217	5,831	5,675	5,618	5,333	5,081	–12.9
Opera/ballet	6,210	5,905	5,494	5,305	5,496	6,369	5,813	5,875	5,666	5,521	–13.3
Operetta/musical	2,261	2,392	2,391	2,203	2,074	3,082	2,644	2,029	2,049	1,959	–36.4
Orchestras	1,476	1,627	1,397	1,150	1,282	1,182	1,307	1,570	1,663	1,651	39.7
Non classified	594	637	1,037	1,234	1,233	1,286	1,577	1,577	1,518	1,569	22.0
Total	10,541	10,561	10,319	9,892	10,085	17,750	17,016	16,669	16,229	15,781	–11.1

Source: Until 1995–1996 data for West Germany: Kirchberg (1999), and special tabulations provided to the author. From 1998 to 1999 data for whole Germany: Theater statistics provided by Deutscher Buhnenverein.

Table 2.7 Trends in attendance at the live performing arts (attendance in thousands)

France	Performance season						Percent change
	1973	1981	1988	1997	2008	2018	1997–2018
Theater	4,702	4,200	6,227	7,512	9,645	12,436	65.6
Classical concerts	2,743	2,940	4,003	4,225	3,554	3,553	−15.9
Dance	2,351	2,100	2,669	3,756	4,061	5,330	41.9
Total	9,796	9,241	1,2898	15,493	17,260	21,319	37.6

Source: Ministry of Culture, Les Pratiques Culturelles des Francais (2020).

Table 2.8 Trends in attendance at the live performing arts (attendance in thousands)

The Netherlands	Performance season					Percent change
	1999	2004	2009	2014	2019	1999–2019
Theater	1,987	1,988	2,503	2,268	1,721	−13.4
Opera/operetta/musical	2,390	2,979	3,810	2,432	3,638	52.2
concerts	5,372	6,637	8,623	8,092	9,364	74.3
Ballet/dance	1,164	726	663	742	701	−39.8
Cabaret	1,961	2,412	2,474	2,035	2,759	40.7
Other	1,428	861	1,509	1,789	1,235	−13.5
Total	14,302	15,603	19,582	17,358	19,418	35.8

Source: Statistics Netherlands CBS.

Table 2.9 Trends in attendance at the live performing arts (attendance in thousands)

Sweden	Performance season									Percent change
	2007	2008	2009	2010	2011	2014	2015	2017	2018	2007–2018
Theater	3,145	3,103	2,986	3,012	2,957	3,332	3,203	3,118	3,149	0.1
Classical music/ opera	1,097	1,108	1,194	1,205	1,289	1,395	1,406	1,519	1,534	39.8
Ballet/dance	805	887	821	828	682	1,085	1,016	879	807	0.4
Total	5,046	5,098	5,002	5,045	4,928	5,811	5,625	5,516	5,490	8.8

Source: Swedish Agency for Cultural Policy Analysis and Statistics, Sweden.

the opening of a new opera house in Helsinki, but even this new cultural institution has not changed the long-term downward trend of opera attendance.

For Canada (Table 2.4), we have reliable aggregate data; some of it generated specifically for this volume, covering 2004 through 2018. Attendance was up moderately for theater, and it rose strongly for music. However, opera and especially dance attendance were down, so the total performing arts visits rose only moderately.

Table 2.10 Trends in attendance at the live performing arts (attendance in thousands)

	Performance season								Percent change
Finland	1975	1985	1995	1999	2004	2009	2014	2019	1999–2019
Drama[a]	2,691	2,475	2,288	2,164	2,049	2,107	2,252	1,967	−9.1
National opera[b]	131	101	254	234	207	218	180	210	−10.4
Dance theaters[c]		41	118	180	219	198	161	140	−22.2
Orchestras[d]	677	614	951	889	874	854	1,085	1,198	34.8
Total	3,499	3,231	3,611	3,467	3,349	3,377	3,678	3,515	1.4

Notes:
[a] The Finnish National Theatre plus theaters receiving statutory state subsidy; tickets sold.
[b] Incl. national ballet; tickets sold.
[c] Dance theaters receiving statutory state subsidy; tickets sold.
[d] Members of the Association of Finnish Symphony Orchestras; total audience (in Finland). Estimate for 2019 is taken from 2018.
Sources: The Association of Finnish Symphony Orchestras, annual reports; Statistics Finland/cultural statistics (dance, drama, opera).

Table 2.11 Trends in attendance at the live performing arts and museums (attendance in thousands)

	Performance season								Percent change
Norway	1991	1994	1997	2000	2004	2008	2012	2016	1991–2016
Theater, musical	1,584	1,635	1,613	1,870	1,877	2,113	1,895	2,215	39.9
Opera, operette	180	182	220	224	192	279	337	354	96.9
Concert	1,728	1,998	2,090	2,169	2,337	2,472	2,569	2,747	59.0
Ballet, dance	288	327	293	411	460	518	590	620	115.4
Total	3,780	4,141	4,217	4,675	4,866	5,382	5,390	5,937	57.1

Source: Statistics Norway SSB.

For arts activity in Norway, we have a consistent series on attendance from 1991 to 2016. Table 2.11 shows that attendance increased steadily for all the categories covered, with a particular sharp rise for opera since 2008, related to the opening of the famous Oslo Opera House.

The pattern in Australia, based on the data from 1995 to 2017, is not unlike that in Norway. Table 2.3 shows that over a period of about twenty years since 1995, all performing arts attendance has risen, particularly that for classical music and dance. In Australia, unlike in other countries, there is no dominant form of performing arts, but instead attendance is spread fairly evenly across the forms considered here.

Australia is an interesting case also from another perspective, as the country saw a reversal of a previous downward trend in participation rates. Two national studies of participation rates in the arts show that they fell from 1991 to 1995 in seven out of eight sectors. Attendance fell in only two sectors – interestingly, these were theater and dance – but participation rates fell in four others where attendance rose less than population. The Australian Bureau of

Statistics carried out a careful review of factors – such as changes in the age or geographic distribution of the population, or changes in economic conditions – that might have explained the decline and found that they did not do so (see Australian Bureau of Statistics, 1998). One is left with adverse changes in taste and the introduction of fees at some venues as the interim explanation, to be put to the test by subsequent Australian participation studies. (See Chapter 3 for an extensive discussion of participation rate studies and Table 3.2 for detailed results in several countries.)

Data for France in Table 2.7 show mostly a decline in attendance at the performing arts from 1973 to 1981, before rebouncing to positive growth rates until at least 2008. From 1981 to 2018, participation rates rose sharply for theater and dance, whereas classical concerts have seen a modest decline over the most recent two decades.

2.6 Institutional Change in the Performing Arts

Our earlier discussion of growth in the live performing arts in the United States focused on trends in production and consumer spending. To flesh out the numbers, something must also be said about how these arts are actually produced. With specific reference to the United States, but with some degree of generalization to other regions, we address the following questions: What are the dominant institutional forms and how have they changed in recent decades? Without presuming to offer a complete history of the arts in the twentieth century and beyond, we next outline some major changes in arts institutions in the United States that have accompanied their rapid growth.

2.6.1 Theater

The world of theater in the United States changed shape almost continuously during the twentieth century. From the 1920s through the 1940s "Broadway" was virtually synonymous with "American theater." That had not always been the case, however. In the nineteenth and early twentieth centuries, theater had also thrived outside New York. There were active playhouses in all major cities and in many smaller ones. Typically, they either housed a local stock or repertory organization or were visited by touring companies, of which there were reportedly several hundred touring companies. The number of active local theaters declined precipitously, however, after the second decade of this century. Evidently, the development of motion pictures and radio broadcasting undermined the market for local theater, with the Great Depression contributing the final blow (Moore 1968, chapter 7). The Little Theater movement of the 1920s and 1930s, although it had high aspirations as an alternative to what its participants regarded as the excessive commercialism of Broadway, also failed to survive the double blow of the Great Depression followed by mobilization for war.

In the years since World War II, theater in the United States has been transformed by the development of a solidly based network of nonprofit "resident," or (as they used to be called) "regional," theaters (for a history of resident theater to the early 1970s, see Zeigler (1973)). From a mere handful of them in the late 1940s, their number has grown to more than 200 in the 1990s. The Theatre Communications Group, founded in 1961 as a service organization for the nonprofit, professional theater in the United States, had a membership of only thirty-five groups in 1966. By 1980, the number had grown to 170, and by 2022, it had grown to more than 550 (Theatre Communications Group, 2022). The growth of artistic influence has been equally as significant as the growth in the numbers of theaters. As the number of new productions per season on Broadway gradually diminished during the postwar years, resident theaters became the principal incubators for new playwrights and new productions.

While resident theater was spreading nationwide, New York was undergoing its own theatrical revolution: the development of an Off-Broadway, and later an Off-Off-Broadway theater. Off-Broadway had begun to attract attention as a phenomenon in the early 1950s. To be sure, the Little Theater Movement had been a forerunner. The Washington Square Players (later to become the Theatre Guild) began in 1914, and the Provincetown Players, famous for putting on the first productions of Eugene O'Neill, in 1916. But it was not until the early 1950s that small, artistically ambitious theaters became numerous enough to be thought of as a major alternative to Broadway (Little, 1972, chapter 2). Thomas Gale Moore tabulated a total of seventeen Off-Broadway productions for the 1953–1954 season and reported that the number of such productions grew to 134 in 1961–1962. Although the number of new productions thereafter declined, the total number of performances continued to increase. By 1963–1964, the last year of Moore's data, total Off-Broadway performances actually outnumbered those on Broadway (Moore, 1968, pp. 16–18 and table I.2). Work-week data from Actors' Equity (the trade union of the acting profession) indicate that activity in the Off-Broadway theater has fluctuated since the late 1960s, without showing any pronounced trend, except in the last two decades, which were characterized by increases (see Table 2.2).

The Off-Broadway theater is made up primarily of commercial producers but includes some ongoing not-for-profit enterprises as well. The distinction between Broadway and Off-Broadway theaters is formalized in the Equity contract under which Off-Broadway producers operate. The wage scale is lower than Broadway's, but so is house size: It may not exceed 499 seats and, except where special dispensation is given, the venue must lie outside the geographically designated "Broadway" area of midtown Manhattan.

2.6.2   Dance

The explosion of dance as a performance art in the United States is one of the major cultural events of the past fifty years. The basic facts are well known. Before World War II, there was very little professional ballet on view in the United States. Most Americans probably regarded ballet as a strictly European form, associated with a decadent, moribund aristocracy. European companies, such as the Ballet Russe de Monte Carlo, toured North America, but few US companies had yet been created. The earliest was the Atlanta Ballet, which can trace its origins back to 1929. The San Francisco Ballet began as the San Francisco Opera Ballet in 1933. Ballet Theatre, later to become the renowned American Ballet Theatre, was founded in 1940. No other permanent companies existed before World War II. The choreographer George Balanchine was brought to the United States in 1933 by Lincoln Kirstein to start a school of ballet and a permanent company. He accomplished the first goal in 1934 with the opening of the School of American Ballet in New York City but did not achieve the second until 1946, when he and Kirstein founded Ballet Society. In 1948, with official sponsorship, Ballet Society became the New York City Ballet.

The excitement generated by Balanchine's work and his company and by US tours of the great European ensembles helped to spark the dance boom of the postwar era. In 1963, the Ford Foundation announced a ten-year, $7.8-million grant "to strengthen professional ballet in the United States." By 1984, it had given $42.6 million to dance companies and related programs (Dunning, 1985, pp. 107–109). Support from the foundation was critical in helping dance organizations to achieve a modicum of financial stability during their early years of rapid growth.

While ballet was a European art form successfully transplanted, modern dance was essentially invented in the United States by pioneers, such as Isadora Duncan, Ruth St. Denis and Ted Shawn, Doris Humphrey, and Martha Graham. Yet, despite these now famous few, it cannot be said that modern dance was more than a very small enterprise with a very devoted following before World War II. After the war, however, modern dance also took part in the dance explosion.

Unlike ballet companies, symphony orchestras, opera companies, and theater groups, modern dance companies typically give most of their performances away from their home base. From the late 1960s to the 1970s, the NEA helped fuel the boom in modern dance by joining with local sponsors to finance an extensive dance touring program. This not only gave the companies more weeks of employment but also helped spread the gospel of modern dance to all parts of the country.

2.6.3 Opera

The Metropolitan Opera in New York City, founded in 1883, is the oldest US opera company. Only a few other companies now in existence date back to before World War II. However, in the late nineteenth and early twentieth centuries, the nation was also served by touring European singers who put on operas with the help of a locally recruited supporting cast. As a result, opera was somewhat better established in the United States than ballet was before the war.

Like ballet and modern dance, opera has enjoyed extraordinary growth during the years of cultural boom. When Opera America, the service organization for major professional opera companies, was formed in 1970, it had only seventeen members. By 1997, membership had grown to 110 US and 15 Canadian companies. Table 2.12 lists the ten largest US member companies together with budget size and year of founding. Of the ten, only three were started before 1950. As in the case of ballet, but on a somewhat smaller scale, the Ford Foundation contributed important financial support to US opera companies during their years of early growth: between 1957 and 1979, its grants to opera companies totaled $16.9 million (Heimenz, 1980, p. 45).

On a per performance basis, opera is by far the most expensive of the live performing arts to produce, involving, as it does, elements of all the others, combined typically with a lavish hand. Consequently, it is important economically to play to relatively full houses, so seasons tend to be short. As Table 2.12 suggests, with the exception of the very largest companies, the number of performances per season is usually well below fifty.

Table 2.12 Founding dates of the ten largest US opera companies

Opera company	Year founded	2019 Budget ($ millions)[a]	2018–2019 main season	
			No. of operas	No. of performances
Metropolitan Opera	1883	317.6	29	244
Lyric Opera of Chicago	1954	81.4	11	91
San Francisco Opera	1923	78.6	11	62
Los Angeles Opera	1986	43.8	8	39
Houston Grand Opera	1955	28.5	6	31
Santa Fe Opera	1956	25.7	5	35
Seattle Opera	1964	24.3	5	39
Dallas Opera	1957	17.8	6	26
New York City Opera	1944	5.3	6	19
Washington (D.C.) Opera[b]	1956	1.7	8	46

Notes:
[a] Budget is proxied by total functional expenses.
[b] For the fiscal year ending September 2018.
Source: Operabase, ProPublica, and financial statements from the respective opera companies

Table 2.12 reveals the immense size of the Metropolitan Opera: Its budget is almost four times the size of the next largest company in 2019. It is by far the largest performing arts company in the United States. Indeed, statistical studies of opera companies usually present their results on a with- and without-the-Met basis, in order to avoid its distorting effect on reported averages.

As we will see in Chapter 3, the popularity of opera and of ballet and modern dance is approximately equal in the United States, as measured by the proportion of the population that attends at least once a year.

2.6.4 Symphony Orchestras

Symphony orchestras are by far the oldest of the ongoing institutions in the live performing arts. The New York Philharmonic traces its origins back to 1842. The next oldest surviving orchestras are those of St. Louis (1880), Boston (1881), Chicago (1891), Cincinnati (1894), and Philadelphia (1900). Figure 2.2 presents the founding dates by decade of fifty-two major US orchestras that are members of the International Conference of Symphony and Opera Musicians. It shows that growth in the number of orchestras was greatest between 1910 and 1940, but continued at a respectable pace in the 1950s, as well. Here, too, the Ford Foundation played a major role. In 1965 Ford announced an $80.2 million grant program to strengthen sixty-one US orchestras (Hart, 1973, pp. 13–16). The foundation was concerned by the low salary level and short playing season faced by musicians in most orchestras in the early 1960s. Its aid was intended to encourage longer seasons and better pay scales and, by increasing the level of professionalism of musicians, a higher quality of performance. Three quarters of the aid was provided in the form of grants designated to build up endowment funds. It should be noted that endowment and investment income is much less important in the budgets of the other branches

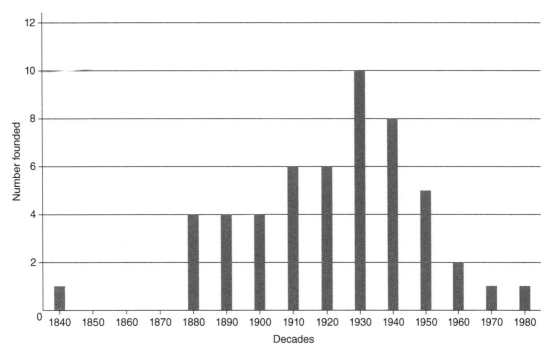

Figure 2.2 Number of symphony orchestras founded by decade

of the performing arts. In 2019–2020 it accounted for only 7.8% of opera income and for ballet and modern dance, its share is virtually nil (Opera America, 2022; Dance/NYC, 2016).

2.6.5   Relative Sizes of the Four performing Arts Sectors

Symphony orchestras are not only the longest established of the performing arts institutions we examine, but also, in the aggregate, the largest of the nonprofit group. Their gross income in 2016–17 was $2.26 billion.[1] In the same year the aggregate income of the major US opera companies was $1.14 billion and of the resident nonprofit theaters that were members of the Theatre Communications Group, $2.69 billion. Moreover, Broadway and road company gross receipts in that year totaled $2.46 billion, which tells us that in monetary terms theater as a whole is a larger industry than is the making of symphonic music or opera (Opera America, 2018, p. 54; Theatre Communications Group, 2018).[2]

In the absence of reliable ongoing data, Dick Netzer estimated the total income of the dance industry in 1983–84 as approximately $150 million (Netzer, 1986a, Table 1). Even if this figure were adjusted for growth and inflation to bring it up to 2018–19, it would remain well below the total for opera or the nonprofit theater; so it is clear that dance is the smallest of the four sectors on a monetary scale. However, opera outranks dance in monetary terms primarily because of its much greater cost of production. Attendance tells a different story. Studies of the participation rate of the US population in the various art forms, presented in Table 3.1, show ballet attendance in third place, slightly ahead of opera, but far behind theater and symphony concerts.

2.7   Summary

The trend of arts activity described in this chapter is complex and not easily summarized. First came four decades of relative decline: Consumer spending on the live performing arts as a percentage of their total disposable income fell substantially from its highest level in 1929 to a low point some forty years later, as the introduction first of "talking pictures" and later commercial television provided tough competition for the live performing arts. But a turnaround began in the 1960s when a combination of increased public and private support helped to underwrite new companies and new activities, enabling the live performing arts to tap into the demand of previously unserved audiences. Consumer spending on the live performing arts as a proportion of DPI continued to rise during the 1970s, 1980s, and 1990s, finally in the early 2000s exceeding its historic high point of 1929. This growth continued throughout the 2010s, but then it was drastically halted by the COVID-19 pandemic. We will return to a more speculative discourse on what may bring the future in Chapter 17, but disclose already now that the time when things return to "normal," that is to pre-pandemic levels, is at the time of writing often regarded as "not yet foreseeable" (e.g., Arndt et al., 2022). Moreover, the most recent global instabilities – whether the war in Ukraine, the energy crisis, record high inflation, or risk of a global recession – do not add confidence that the return to pre-pandemic trends will happen quickly. The growth or decline of the arts is visible in the expansion or shrinking of audiences as well as in the changing number of institutions. In the next chapter we look at the composition and character of audiences for the arts.

SUGGESTIONS FOR FURTHER READING

For supporting data on the long-term growth in the arts sector, see Borowiecki and Dahl (2021).

For data showing the decline in the number of new productions on Broadway, see The Broadway League (2022).

For more on how COVID-19 affected the cultural and creative sector see Naylor et al. (2021), published by UNESCO. Country specific challenges are presented for the United States by National Endowment for the Arts (2022), United Kingdom by Walmsley et al. (2022), Germany by Arndt et al. (2022), Australia by Australia Council for the Arts (2022).

PROBLEM SET

2.1 A philanthropist intends to donate a large amount of money to the live performing arts in the United Kingdom. She is mostly interested in theater and contemporary dance, and her intention is to make with the donation a significant change in the long-term. While closely studying Table 2.5 in this textbook, which presents data on attendance, she asks for your advice.

   a. Calculate the absolute change and percentage change for theater (Play/Drama) and contemporary dance over the period 2005–2019, and compare your estimates.

b. How would your answer differ for the more recent period from 2015 to 2019.

c. Discuss the strengths and limitations of using absolute change and percentage change as a measure of growth.

d. Write a brief memo outlining which of the two live performing arts should be supported to make the greatest impact.

2.2 Growth of the arts sector can be measured with the help of different variables.

a. Provide a list of variables that could potentially measure growth of the arts sector and evaluate their suitability.

b. Assess how difficult it may be for a national statistics office to collect each of the variables in a consistent and reliable way.

2.3 Choose an arts category and find suitable data that measure its growth, using two or more variables. (With some of the measures you could be creative, but try to collect at least one standard statistic.)

a. Summarize the trends in a table and/or in a figure.

b. Prepare a brief class presentation in which you present your data and the emerging trends. Outline how and where you found your data, and whether it was necessary to conduct any adjustments.

c. Evaluate critically which of the variables chosen by you is best suited to reflect the trend in the arts activity you analyze.

d. Compare your results with the overall trends presented in this book.

2.4 Evaluate and discuss what are the trends in the growth of the arts sector since the turn of the twenty-first century. Assess how the trends are affected by the wider spread of streaming technologies and digital access to culture as well as other entertainment activities.

NOTES

1 Own estimation assuming ratio of revenue to income to be the same in 2017 as it was in 2014 and using numbers from Voss et al. (2016), and League of American Orchestras (2020), reporting on FY2016–17.

2 Data on Broadway and road companies are from the official website of the Broadway Theatre Industry, broadwayleague.com.

3   Audiences for the Arts

LEARNING OBJECTIVES

By the end of this chapter, readers should be able to:

- Explain the difference between audience surveys and participation studies
- Explain what socioeconomic background means for arts participation
- Describe arts participation trends across countries and over time

In Chapter 2 we measured the growth of the arts by examining a number of indicators, including production and trends in consumer spending on admissions. In a free-enterprise economy, consumer spending is the principal source of what economists define as demand for the arts. It is the source of box office receipts for theaters, concerts, opera, and ballet; the admissions and art shop income of museums; and the royalty income of performing arts companies from the sale of audio and video recordings, and other media access. Since these forms of demand originate with the people who attend performances, visit museums, buy reproductions of art or recordings of music, or access the arts via media alternatives, surveys of arts audiences contribute importantly to an understanding of the economics of the arts. Theater managers, before establishing a range of ticket prices, want to know what kinds of people make up their audience. For example, as we explain in Chapter 4, some people are more price-sensitive than others. Museum directors want to know what sorts of visitors they are attracting. Business managers of ballet and opera companies want to find out whether they can count on attracting audiences from among those who habitually attend other kinds of performing arts. Officials at all levels of government that provide public subsidies for the arts need to know the extent to which various subgroups in the local or national population participate in arts activities. Donors of private funds want to know what kinds of audiences patronize the companies and institutions they may choose to support. Finally, economists, educators, sociologists, political scientists, and urban planners concerned with the arts are interested in information that will help them to understand the social and economic forces that determine demand for the arts.

3.1   Audience Surveys versus Participation Studies

At the outset, it is useful to draw a distinction between audience surveys and participation studies. Audience surveys are relatively inexpensive and easy to carry out. Consequently, a great many such studies have been conducted. The basic technique is to pass out a questionnaire to members of a performing arts audience as they assemble or to entrants to a museum or exhibit, and to collect the completed questionnaires before they leave. The questionnaire typically asks for information about the socioeconomic status of the respondent, including age, gender, occupation, educational background, and income level. In addition, it will usually ask about the residential location, means of transportation employed, and other circumstances of the particular visit, as well as the frequency of attendance at this company's performances or this museum, and at other kinds of events. The results of an audience survey will usually be expressed in percentage terms – for example, by showing the percentage of the audience that falls into each of several age or income classes. Table 3.3 provides an illustration of a typical format. Obviously, such surveys can produce a very detailed statistical profile of the audience that attends a particular event or patronizes a particular company or institution. And given the large number of such studies, it is relatively easy to make comparisons of audience characteristics among the categories of the live performing arts – theater, opera, ballet, and so on – and between these and museums, historic sites, and the like.

Audience surveys, however, cannot tell you anything about the behavior of the general population in relation to the arts, since they deal only with the self-selected group that actually attends. It is particularly important in deciding questions of public policy toward the arts to know what proportion of the population at large actually does attend and how the socioeconomic character of attenders compares with that of nonattenders. Information of that sort can be obtained only by a survey of the whole population. One need not, of course, ask every citizen about her or his behavior with respect to the arts: A random sample of the population will suffice, but where the behavior is as infrequent as attendance at the arts and the socioeconomic characteristics of interest cover such a wide range, the sample has to be sufficiently large. Consequently, population surveys of arts participation are expensive to carry out and are fairly infrequent.

3.2   Participation Rates in the United States

The NEA has sponsored several Surveys of Public Participation in the Arts since 1982, the most recent in 2017, which collected responses from 27,969 US adults (National Endowment for the Arts, 2019). A participant was defined as anyone who had attended an activity at least once during the twelve months preceding the survey. Participation rates are simply the number of participants divided by the adult population. Results of the NEA survey are given in the first column of Table 3.1. Among the live performing arts in 2017, musicals and operettas had the highest participation rate (16.5%), followed by theater (9.4%), performances of classical music (8.6%), jazz (8.6%), ballet (3.1%), and opera (2.2%). These figures may strike the reader as remarkably large or surprisingly small, depending on prior expectations. To put them in perspective, however, consider that, according to the same survey, 63% of the adult population watched a motion picture outside the home. Visits to art museums or galleries (23.7%) and to historic sites (28%, not reported) also outranked attendance at the performing arts.

Table 3.1 Surveys of public participation in the arts, United States

Survey year	1982	1985	1992	1997	2002	2008	2012	2017
Sample size	17,254	13,675	12,736	12,349	17,135	18,444	35,735	27,969
Attendance (% of adult population)								
Jazz	9.6	9.5	10.6	11.9	10.8	7.8	8.1	8.6
Classical music	13.0	12.7	12.5	15.6	11.6	9.3	8.8	8.6
Opera	3.0	2.6	3.3	4.7	3.2	2.1	2.1	2.2
Musicals	18.6	16.6	17.4	24.5	17.1	16.7	15.2	16.5
Theater	11.9	11.6	13.5	15.8	12.3	9.4	8.3	9.4
Ballet	4.2	4.3	4.7	5.8	3.9	2.9	2.7	3.1
Other dance	–	–	7.1	12.4	6.3	5.2	5.6	6.3
Art museums and galleries	22.1	21.9	26.7	34.9	26.5	22.7	21.0	23.7

Source: National Endowment for the Arts: Survey of Public Participation reports (1982–2017).

Audiences for the several art forms always overlap. Some people may attend only one of the performing arts or may patronize only art museums, but many others participate in several of the listed activities each year. Consequently, the "total audience" for the arts – defined as those who attended at least one arts event in the last year – will always be less than the sum of the number who participated in the individual forms. For example, in 2017, the percentages shown to attend any of the arts activities listed in Table 3.1 add up to 78.4%. But overlap among the individual audiences was such that the total number of people who attended at least one of those forms was only 54% of the population (National Endowment for the Arts, 2019).

As Paul DiMaggio and coauthors have pointed out, since a participation rate measures the percentage of a certain population that attended productions of a given institution or art form at least once during the year, it can be thought of as recording the reach of that institution or art form in the sense of measuring the breadth of its appeal. But total attendance also depends on the frequency with which participants attend, or in other words, the strength of their commitment. Thus, growth in attendance could result from increased participation, increased frequency, or both (see DiMaggio et al., 1978, p. 37).

3.3   Some International Comparisons

Table 3.2 allows us to compare participation rates in the United States, Australia, Canada, and twenty-nine European countries. In the United States, we are accustomed to conceding that Europe's long-established cultures may have a more developed taste than we do for the traditional forms of high art. It may come as something of a shock to most Americans, however, to learn that Australia and Canada, which they probably think of as even more recent converts to high culture, also appear to have higher rates of participation. Differences in the meaning of terms and in survey practices from country to country dictate that we allow a considerable margin for uncertainty when making international comparisons. That having been said, the

Table 3.2 International comparison of participation rates (rates as % of adult population)

	Classical music	Concert	Theater	Ballet/dance	Opera	Art museums	Other museums
United States (2017)	8.6		9.4	3.1[a]	2.2	23.7	
Australia (2017–2018)		38.2	16.5	10.4	15.8[b]	27.7	27.5
Canada (2016)	16	42[c]	40[d]			39	35

	Concert	Theater	Ballet/dance/opera	All museums
Austria	51.9	39.7	18.2	41.7
Belgium	36.0	32.1	21.6	39.8
Bulgaria	30.4	24.6	10.9	25.6
Croatia	35.7	21.7	11.5	28.6
Cyprus	30.5	23.0	8.5	18.4
Czech Republic	36.6	35.9	15.3	36.9
Denmark	59.7	37.7	24.9	62.5
Estonia	54.3	45.0	25.1	46.3
Finland	46.7	41.6	16.8	40.2
France	33.1	20.7	24.9	38.4
Germany	45.0	29.9	19.5	43.8
Greece	22.8	23.1	8.6	15.3
Hungary	25.8	20.2	10.7	27.6
Italy	25.7	23.8	17.0	30.8
Ireland	42.9	31.4	17.4	40.1
Latvia	55.1	42.5	24.4	49.0
Lithuania	51.2	34.0	23.2	38.8
Luxembourg	52.1	34.7	29.5	48.9
Malta	31.4	24.2	18.2	36.2
Netherlands	50.5	53.3	23.2	59.8
Norway	62.0	50.0	14.0	44.0
Portugal	19.0	13.4	7.8	17.3
Poland	21.8	15.8	10.3	24.0
Romania	25.2	15.1	10.6	20.9
Slovakia	39.7	29.5	14.8	31.2
Slovenia	50.0	32.6	15.3	35.4
Spain	30.9	21.2	14.4	28.9
Sweden	60.4	52.8	33.8	75.6
United Kingdom	37.1	39.3	21.5	52.1

Notes:
[a] Includes only ballet.
[b] Includes musicals.
[c] Includes only popular music performance.
[d] Includes comedy.
Source: United States: see Table 3.1; Australia: Australian Bureau of Statistics, *Attendance at selected cultural venues and events 2017–2018* (2019); Canada: Hill Strategies, Canadian's Arts, Culture, and Heritage Participation in 2016 (2018); European countries: Eurobarometer (2014), except Norway: Norwegian Cultural Barometer (2016).

table does seem to show that US participation rates are generally near the low end of the range for industrialized nations. The US deficiency is particularly large in the case of theater, where the participation rate is only 9.4%, as compared with figures ranging from 13.4% in Portugal to as much as 53.3% in the Netherlands or 52.8% in Sweden. In the fine arts, comparisons cannot be precise because the US figure is for "art museums and galleries," while for most other countries, it is either for "all museums." Nevertheless, the United States, with a rate of 23.7%, again appears to be near the low end of the range.

3.4   How Do Participation Rates Vary in the Population?

All studies agree that participation rates in the arts are higher for individuals who have higher incomes, higher occupational status, and greater educational attainment (as measured by the level of schooling completed). These findings appear to hold across all art forms. Equally general is the finding that educational attainment, which is also an important determinant of the other two factors, is the single most powerful determinant of arts participation. (We will substantiate this result later.)

Gender and age are also associated systematically with the rate of attendance at the arts. Women are more likely than men to participate in all categories except jazz. Except in the case of jazz, participation tends to increase with age, up to some peak in the middle years, and to fall thereafter. The age of greatest exposure, however, varies with the art form.

Because participation in the live performing arts and at art museums requires a trip to the place of production, we would expect participation rates to be higher in places where arts institutions are more numerous and accessible. Table 3.3 shows that this is, indeed, the case: They are higher in metropolitan areas than in nonmetropolitan parts of the United States in 1997. While more recent editions of the Survey of Public Participation in the Arts do not provide participation rates by the metropolitan areas, in a related exploration Borowiecki and Dahl (2021) illustrate that artistic and cultural activities are richer in bigger agglomerations. This probably reflects two mutually reinforcing effects. On the one hand, metropolitan areas offer closer proximity to arts institutions than nonmetropolitan areas. On the other hand, urban populations generally rank higher than those in rural areas in socioeconomic status.

Table 3.3 shows participation rates for various socioeconomic groups for the three high art forms in which overall participation is greatest: classical music, theater, and art museums. Data are from NEA's 1997, 2012, and 2017 surveys. The effect on participation rates of variation in income and education is shown in the two top panels of the table. Perhaps the easiest way to demonstrate the importance of these factors is to compare the highest and lowest rates within each socioeconomic classification. For example, the first column shows exposure to live classical music performances. Those with the highest income in 2012 (income data are not available for 2017) reported a participation rate of 19.4% or five times the 3.9% rate for those with the lowest income. Most striking of all, men and women with a graduate school education had a 26% participation rate in 2012, almost thirty times the rate for those with only a grade school education.

Table 3.3 Participation rates by demographic characteristic in 1997, 2012, and 2017

	1997			2012			2017		
	Classical music	Theater	Art museums	Classical music	Theater	Art museums	Classical music	Theater	Art museums
Average	15.6	15.8	34.9	8.8	8.3	21.0	8.6	9.4	23.7
Income									
Lowest	6.8	8.2	18.8	3.9	3.8	10.2			
Next lowest	12.5	13.6	31.5	5.6	5.8	14.0			
Next highest	23.4	22.1	48.6	15.1	13.5	33.8			
Highest	35.0	31.9	59.6	19.4	16.6	43.2			
Education									
Grade school	2.1	3.1	6.0	0.9	0.3	3.6	–	–	3.1
High school grad	7.0	8.5	21.5	3.1	1.8	9.9	–	2.2	10.4
College grad	21.4	21.8	48.0	15.9	14.6	37.2	14.7	16.0	39.5
Graduate school	44.5	37.2	69.8	26.0	20.0	49.3	21.9	21.6	49.0
Gender									
Male	14.2	14.6	34.3	8.0	7.3	18.7	6.8	8.2	21.1
Female	16.8	16.8	35.5	9.5	9.2	23.1	10.3	10.5	26.2
Race									
White	17.5	16.6	36.1	11.0	10.1	24.1	10.4	11.6	26.7
Black	9.6	16.4	31.1	4.0	6.2	11.9	3.9	7.7	17.1
Other	10.0	10.8	30.9	7.3	4.9	21.2	5.5	7.0	22.1
Location									
11 metro areas	18.4	19.2	42.9						
Not 11 metro	14.4	14.3	31.5						

Source: Survey of Public Participation in the Arts, 1997, 2012, and 2017

As we shall see in latter chapters, one of the principal objectives of US public policy toward the arts is to increase the rate of arts participation of the citizenry as a whole. Likewise, individual arts institutions are almost always interested in promoting participation in order to increase the size of their audience. From either point of view, it is therefore useful to know whether income or education is the more important factor in determining arts participation. For example, if income dominates, the government may wish to support a policy of heavily subsidized admissions to encourage participation by the relatively poor. On the other hand, if education is a leading factor, then admission subsidies may be less effective in widening participation than would be a range of other policies centering on education or, more broadly, on promoting familiarity with the arts.

3.4.1 Education versus Income

Separating the effects of education from those of income always poses a difficult problem for the social scientist. The difficulty arises because income and educational attainment are separately correlated with many forms of social behavior, but they are also very strongly correlated with each other. For example, from the study of criminal behavior, it is known that the well-to-do have a lower propensity for crime than the poor. But the well-to-do, on average, are also better educated than the poor. Is it their higher income or their higher educational attainment that makes them less prone to crime? Because education and income are so highly correlated with each other, it is statistically very difficult to sort out their separate effects on criminality. (In statistics this is known as the problem of "multicollinearity.") A similar problem occurs in trying to separate the effects of income from those of educational attainment in the case of exposure to the arts. However, we have already shown that exposure to the arts varies more widely by the level of education than by the level of income, which certainly suggests that education is the more important factor.

Further evidence is provided by the Ford Foundation study of exposure to the performing arts. The study sample was divided into four groups: high education with high income, high education with low income, low education with high income, and low education with low income. Rates of exposure for the four groups were compared in each category of the performing arts. The authors concluded that "the analysis confirms to a startling degree that it is indeed education rather than income that matters most. Within each educational group, the percentage attending is only somewhat higher among the high-income people than among the low-income people. But within each income group, the percentage attending is much larger among the high-education than among the low-education people" (Ford Foundation, 1974b, p. 16).

A very clear pattern emerges: The difference in the rate of exposure between those with high and low educational attainment was ten percentage points, regardless of income, while the difference between those with high and low incomes was only two points, regardless of educational attainment.

Granted that education has something to do with the development of an individual's taste for art and culture, a fundamental question remains: What exactly is the basis of the connection? Perhaps such taste is developed directly by arts appreciation courses taken in grade school, high school, or college. Or perhaps it is cultivated by a general liberal arts education without reference to special arts courses. Or more elusive still, perhaps it is developed by growing up in a home where the arts are taken seriously (which is likely to be a home where the average level of education is high). We will look into this question in Chapter 17.

3.5   Audience Characteristics

Since participation studies can tell us so much about the characteristics of the aggregate audience for particular art forms (see, e.g., Table 3.3), one might well ask why studies of individual audiences are necessary or useful. There are several reasons. The most obvious is that individual arts institutions may have unique characteristics such that they attract an audience different from the industry norm. For example, a drama company that specializes in "experimental theater" is likely to bring in a younger audience than one that emphasizes more familiar works. Second, arts institutions (other than museums that often attract a high proportion of tourists) draw most of their audience from the city or metropolitan area in which they are located. If the socioeconomic character of the population in that area differs somewhat from the national average, one would expect local audience composition to differ in the same direction.

Finally, participation studies focus on the question: Did you attend such and such arts activity at least once in the last twelve months? And, therefore, as we have already pointed out, such studies do not reflect the frequency of participation of individual respondents. The composition of the audience at a particular event, however, is affected by the frequency with which each group attends. Suppose, for example, that the participation rate in a given art form is the same for those aged 25–34 years and those aged 35–44 years and that the two population groups are equal in size. Assume, however, that participants in the latter group attend more often per year than those in the former. In that case, the latter group will, on average, make up a higher proportion of audience than the former. In short, audience studies for individual arts institutions may reveal attender characteristics somewhat different than those suggested by nationwide participation studies.

This is illustrated by the data from the Survey of Public Participation in the Arts for the years 1992–2017, which asked respondents about the frequency of attendance for the priortwelve months, and some results are depicted in Table 3.4. For example, in 2002, 2.9% of respondents reported attending classical music performances twice, while in 2017, 2.2% responded with that frequency. The overall lower frequency in 2017 mean that, while total attenders decreased from 24.3 million to 22.4 million, an approximately 3.6% decrease, total attendances, or audience size, fell from 75.4 million to 60.7 million, or a 19% decrease. A focus only on participation rates would not disclose the large decrease in audience size.

3.5.1 Audience Characteristics over Time

The question of audience age has long intrigued arts managers and economists because of its possible implication for future audience growth or decline. If an arts institution finds that its audience is either relatively old or growing older, it may well take that as a warning of future decline in audience size, because the older people, who will eventually drop out of the audience, may not be replaced one for one by younger people newly attracted to it. On the other hand, an institution that now has a relatively young audience may take that as an augur of future growth, on the theory that it can hold onto the young people as they age, while still continuing to draw new young entrants.

Whatever the age profile of their current audience, all arts institutions would now like to attract new young attenders, because they believe that they will thus be building an audience for the future. Marketing strategies may be changing to accommodate that wish. In the 1960s and 1970s, performing arts companies emphasized subscription sales because they were thought to be the most cost-effective way to sell tickets and had the added advantage, so it was hoped, of building audience loyalty (see the discussion in Chapter 7.) But a subscription purchase requires a considerable one-time payment as well as advance planning of recreational choices. These requirements are now seen as a barrier to attracting younger attenders, as well as ethnic minorities, who cannot afford a large cash outlay in advance and may also wish to avoid the rigid commitment entailed by a subscription. For this potential audience, single-ticket purchases are the preferred mode. Theater managements in the nonprofit sector have then begun

Table 3.4 Classical music annual participation frequency

Frequency range	1992 Number (in thousands)	1992 Percent	1997 Number (in thousands)	1997 Percent	2002 Number (in thousands)	2002 Percent	2008 Number (in thousands)	2008 Percent	2012 Number (in thousands)	2012 Percent	2017 Number (in thousands)	2017 Percent
0	162,608	87.5	167,406	85.6	181,604	88.2	202,275	89.9	208,586	90.1	226,294	90.6
1	10,035	5.4	11,539	5.9	9,863	4.8	9,592	4.3	10,094	4.4	10,676	4.3
2	6,133	3.3	7,627	3.9	5,951	2.9	5,605	2.5	5,649	2.4	5,523	2.2
3–8	6,318	3.4	7,627	3.9	6,980	3.4	6,046	2.7	5,579	2.4	5,637	2.3
9–20	558	0.3	1,173	0.6	1,242	0.6	1,141	0.5	1,176	0.5	1,281	0.5
Total	185,836	100	195,568	100	205,900	100.0	225,000	100.0	231,505	100	249,723	100
Attenders	23,228[a]		28,162[a]		24,296[a]		22,725[a]		22,919[a]		23,429[a]	
Attendances	56,495		73,142		75,414[b]		64,576[b]		59,636[b]		60,736[b]	

Notes:

[a] Calculated by subtracting nonattenders from total; discrepancies reflect rounding error.

[b] Calculated by estimating the average number of attendances of the sample and then multiplying with attenders.

Source: For 1992 and 1997, Gray (1999). For the years 2002–2017: data from the Survey of Public Participation in the Arts (SPPA) for the respective years.

Table 3.5 Average age of participants over time

Core art form	1982	1985	1992	1997	2002	2008	2012	Change 1982–2012
Jazz	33.1	35.2	39.6	41.0	43.0	45.7	45.8	12.7
Classical music	42.5	43.3	45.6	46.0	48.3	49.8	51.7	9.2
Opera	45.0	44.3	45.2	44.4	47.5	49.1	51.0	6.0
Musicals	41.5	42.2	43.8	44.0	45.6	46.3	48.7	7.2
Plays	41.7	41.7	43.6	43.9	45.3	47.5	49.3	7.6
Ballet	40.3	40.7	41.9	43.7	45.3	47.0	47.0	6.7
Dance	–	–	42.6	43.3	44.3	46.2	46.4	3.8
Art museums and galleries	39.7	40.9	41.3	42.7	44.7	44.4	47.2	7.5

Note: Change is shown in years and includes for dance the change between 1992 and 2012.
Source: For 1982–2012, SPPAs; authors' calculations.

"employing new marketing techniques to attract new and returning single-ticket buyers. Rush tickets for the general public, pay-what-you-can performances, flexible multi-ticket passes are just a few of the single-ticket marketing strategies newly set in place in many theatres across the country" (Janowitz, 1990, p. 36). Nowadays, it is especially the digital marketing that can help a theater attract new audiences and retain connections with existing theatergoers. The cultivation of an online presence via website and social media brings the theater closer to prospective audiences, especially to the much valued younger cohorts who predominantly use media to decide how to spend their leisure time (Finlay, 2022).

Public policymakers as well as managers of theaters and other arts institutions have a strong interest in the composition of arts audiences. As we shall see in Chapters 11 and 13, "democratizing the arts" in the sense of increasing the participation of ethnic minorities and those having lower income and occupational status and less education than the traditional arts audience has been an objective of public policy across many countries. Although one might hope that if such policies are successful, changes in audience composition would eventually show up in audience and participation studies, definitive evidence of policy impact is unlikely, given the many other social and economic factors that will have changed in the interim.

Indeed, audience composition appears to be ruled by a powerful inertia. Studies find very comparable socioeconomic profiles of audiences with regard to gender, educational attainment, occupation, and income (DiMaggio et al., 1978, p. 34, de la Vega et al., 2020). Change does seem to be occurring along one dimension, however: It is clear that audiences for some art forms have aged significantly in recent years. For example, Table 3.5, based on thirty years of data from NEA's surveys, shows that the average age of participants in the arts increased typically by about six to seven years between 1982 and 2012.

The average age of classical music audience increased by 9.2 years from 42.5 years in 1982 to 51.7 years in 2012, and it is trumped only by the age increase observed for jazz, up by 12.7 years over the time period considered here. It may be that the rapid relative growth of the arts industry over the last decades has been accompanied by other changes in audience composition that will only become evident in later audience and participation studies. Equally, the recent increase in the consumption of culture via digital means could bring changes that have yet to be explored and documented in more detail.

SUGGESTIONS FOR FURTHER READING

For an insightful discussion of the difficulties that arise in comparing national surveys of arts participation over time and to each other, see O'Hagan (2016).

For more information on patterns of participation rates in the arts see, for example, Falk and Katz-Gerro (2016) and National Endowment for the Arts (2019).

PROBLEM SET

3.1 The director of a theater wants to know what types of people make up their audience in order to decide on ticket prices. The theater director has heard about audience surveys and participation studies but has never conducted any herself.

    a. Write a brief memo to the theater director explaining whether an audience survey or participation study is more appropriate for her need by evaluating the benefits and costs of each.

    b. Suggest a viable strategy of obtaining data on what types of people make up the given audience. Be specific on whom, where, when, and how you would survey.

    c. Outline what factors should be taken into consideration in deciding about how to set a ticket price.

3.2 Price discrimination is a pricing strategy that charges customers different prices for the same product or service. Identify real-world examples of price discrimination in the arts sector and explain how this may benefit the revenues of an arts institution.

3.3 Cultural policymakers that decide about the allocation of public subsidies for the arts need to know the extent to which various subgroups in the local or national population participate in arts activities. Outline what are the main socioeconomic factors that determine cultural participation rates in a population.

3.4 Palma de Girona, a (fictive) medium-sized city in one of the EU-27 countries, is a popular location for retirement. This means that there is a relatively high share of older, wealthy, and well-educated people.

    a. What does the socioeconomic background of the population mean for participation rates at the local concert hall and art museum? (You may want to refer to Table 3.3 in the textbook.)

    b. Discuss whether the arts sector in this city should receive a subsidy.

Part II

The Microeconomics of Demand and Supply

4   Consumer Demand: An Introduction

LEARNING OBJECTIVES

By the end of this chapter, readers should be able to:

- State the law of demand
- Identify the determinants of demand and supply
- Apply the demand and supply function to selected arts goods and services
- Determine the market price

In Chapter 2, we described the growth of the audience for the arts and in Chapter 3 its size and character. It should be intuitively clear that its size, character, and rate of growth over time depend importantly on consumer behavior in the marketplace. Some consumers enjoy the arts enough to spend time and money on them. They make up the audience. Others, who differ in some way from the first group, do not enjoy them enough to become arts consumers. Are the same factors at work in both cases? What are they? We turn next to a systematic analysis of consumer choice and of what economists call consumer demand.

A number of assumptions underlie the economic analysis of consumer choice. First, because their incomes are limited, consumers cannot afford to satisfy all their material desires. They must therefore choose among the many possible goods and services. Second, these choices are made rationally. Consumers try to spend their income in such a way as to get the greatest possible total satisfaction from it. Borrowing from the eighteenth-century Utilitarian philosophers, economists use the term "utility" in place of "satisfaction," so in the jargon of economics, consumers behave as "utility maximizers." Finally, individual commodities are subject to the "law of diminishing marginal utility," to which we next turn. We will relax some of these assumptions and introduce some complexities later, but for the time being, the assumptions will make our exploration a bit easier.

4.1   Measuring the Utility of Consumption

Propositions about utility are most easily explained if we suppose that the buyer can actually measure the satisfaction obtained from each act of consumption in terms of units of utility. Let us call these units "utils." We thus assume that if you were to ask the potential purchaser of a theater ticket how much utility he or she expected to obtain from attending the performance, the answer would be, let us say, "30 utils." Since the utility obtained from consuming one more

Table 4.1 Utility of theater and orchestral concerts to a hypothetical consumer

Units purchased annually	Theater tickets		Concert tickets	
	Total utility	Marginal utility	Total utility	Marginal utility
0	0	–	0	–
1	50	50	60	60
2	95	45	110	50
3	135	40	150	40
4	170	35	180	30
5	200	30	200	20
6	225	25		
7	245	20		
8	260	15		
9	270	10		
10	275	5		

unit of any commodity is defined by economists as its "marginal utility," the consumer is telling you, in effect, that the marginal utility of a theater ticket is now 30 utils.[1]

We say "now" because the utility to be obtained from buying one more ticket depends significantly on how many tickets the consumer has already purchased. Specifically, the law of diminishing marginal utility tells us that as a person consumes more of any one commodity, holding the consumption of other goods constant, the marginal utility of that commodity diminishes.

It is important to distinguish between the total utility (TU) obtained from any one good and its marginal utility (MU). Marginal utility is the change in total utility that results from a unit increase in consumption. In economics, the Greek letter delta (Δ) denotes "change in." Accordingly, if we let Q stand for the quantity of a particular good consumed, the marginal utility of that good to a consumer is defined as $\Delta TU / \Delta Q$, where $\Delta Q = 1$. In the usual case, we assume that marginal utility remains positive as more units of a good are consumed. Hence, total utility rises. It is only marginal utility that diminishes as more units are consumed. These propositions are illustrated in Table 4.1 that shows a utility schedule for recordings purchased by a hypothetical consumer. It should be noted that because marginal utility is defined in terms of increments to total utility, the total utility of any quantity consumed necessarily equals the sum of the marginal utilities of the successive units. For example, in Table 4.1, the total utility of four tickets (170 utils) equals the sum of the marginal utilities of the first four purchased (50 + 45 + 40 + 35).

It is difficult to prove scientifically that the law of diminishing marginal utility is correct. In fact, introspection provides its strongest support. We are all consumers and will probably all acknowledge that the second bag of popcorn adds less utility than the first, the third less than the second, and so on ad infinitum for every ensuing unit consumed. There is one other persuasive argument. If diminishing marginal utility were not the general case, we would expect some individuals, who find particular pleasure in one kind of good, to spend most of their income on it and consume little else. But we do not observe such behavior, except in cases of addiction, and those we conventionally treat as "pathological." In the normal case, diminishing marginal utility apparently holds.

4.1.1 A Small Caveat

Since our example here has been theater tickets, we might easily assume that, having purchased a ticket and seen a particular show, the marginal utility of a second ticket for a subsequent performance of the same show would be zero. The buyer has already seen it. But it may also be that a first viewing whets the theater aficionado's appetite for a second, and perhaps third, opportunity. Eventually, however, diminishing marginal utility is very likely to apply.

4.2   Consumer Budget Optimization

If one accepts that consumers can measure the marginal utility of their own consumption, then it is a quite simple matter to explain how they make the choices that give them the greatest possible satisfaction from spending their income. They do so by following the rule for budget optimization, which says allocate income among commodities so that for each good purchased the ratio of marginal utility to price is the same. They thus obtain the same marginal utility for the last dollar spent on each good, which has the effect, as we shall show, of maximizing the total utility of spending.

Employing MU for marginal utility and P for price, the rule can be written algebraically as

$$\frac{MU_x}{P_x} = \frac{MU_y}{P_y} = \cdots = \frac{MU_n}{P_n}, \tag{4.1}$$

where x and y are among the n different goods consumed by an individual. In a competitive market, the single consumer cannot influence the prices at which goods are sold. How then can he or she bring about the stated equality? The answer is that the consumer can vary the quantity purchased of each good and thus bring the ratios into equality by causing the marginal utilities to change. We can demonstrate that the rule does, indeed, maximize the consumer's utility by showing that if he or she starts from a position where the ratios are *not* equal across all goods purchased, moving toward equality will produce a utility gain. Imagine an arts aficionado who has planned a "culture vulture" holiday vacation of a few days in, say, New York City or London, where various arts experiences abound. This consumer's utility schedules for her purchases over that abbreviated period are given in Table 4.1. She purchases five theater tickets at a discounted price of $10 each and attends four concerts at a cost of $20 per ticket. The table shows that the marginal utilities of the fifth theater ticket and of the fourth concert both equal 30 utils. However, their prices are not equal, so we know that the consumer's budget is not optimized. The inequality of the ratio MU / P is shown as

$$\frac{MU}{p} : \overset{\text{Theater}}{\frac{30\,\text{utils}}{\$10}} \neq \overset{\text{Concerts}}{\frac{30\,\text{utils}}{\$20}} \neq \overset{\text{Other}}{\frac{2\,\text{utils}}{\$1}}. \tag{4.2}$$

Let us assume that for all other goods purchased by this consumer, the ratio of marginal utility to price is 2 utils per dollar. This is shown by the right-hand term in Equation (4.2). To bring the ratios for theater and concerts into line with all other goods, the consumer can attend one less concert and buy two more theater tickets. Table 4.1 shows that the marginal utility of a concert thus rises to 40 utils, while that of a ticket falls to 20 utils. Prices remain the same, so the consumer saves $20 on concert tickets, which is just enough to pay for two more theater tickets. Total spending is therefore unchanged, but the consumer has gained utility: Giving up the fourth concert reduced welfare by 30 utils, but buying a sixth and seventh ticket added 45 utils, producing a net gain of 15. The consumer's final position, which satisfies the rule for budget optimization, is as follows:

$$\frac{MU}{p}: \overset{\text{Theater}}{\frac{20\,utils}{\$10}} = \overset{\text{Concerts}}{\frac{40\,utils}{\$20}} = \overset{\text{Other}}{\frac{2\,utils}{\$1}} \tag{4.3}$$

The commonsense meaning of the optimization rule should now be clear. If the ratios of marginal utility to price are not equal for all goods purchased, take dollars away from goods where marginal utility per dollar is lower and spend them on goods where marginal utility per dollar is higher. Obviously, such rearrangements will always produce a net gain.

4.3 Deriving Demand Curves

The hypothetical consumer whose optimum budget is given by Equation (4.3) obtains two utils per dollar for the marginal unit purchased in every line of actual consumption. Keeping that ratio in mind, we can use Table 4.1 to show the effect of changes in price on the quantity of theater tickets purchased. Taking Equation (4.3) as the starting point, we find that at a price of $10 per unit, the consumer obtains two utils per dollar by buying seven tickets. Suppose the price now falls to $5. Theater attendance has become a better buy. We know that the consumer will want to purchase more of them. Table 4.1 tells us how many more: In order to maintain a ratio of 2 utils per dollar at the margin, the consumer will now buy nine tickets for the holiday. Reversing direction, if the price of tickets rose to $15 the consumer (in order still to obtain 2 utils per dollar at the margin) would choose to cut purchases to five tickets.

Obviously, given our hypothetical consumer's utility schedule and the desired number of utils per dollar to be obtained at the margin, we can predict the number of tickets that she will purchase at any given price.[2] When these prices and quantities are plotted on a diagram such as Figure 4.1, they show what economists call the demand curve of one individual for theater tickets (here denoted D). Demand curves characteristically slope downward to the right, since consumers purchase more of any good as its price falls. The observation that quantity purchased varies *inversely* with price is described as the *law of demand*, and it is one of the most fundamental concepts in economics.

4.3.1 The Market Demand Curve

The demand curve of a single buyer, however, is not usually of much interest, since a single buyer is rarely important enough to influence the outcome in any market. Far more useful in economic analysis is the aggregate demand curve of all consumers of a particular product. That

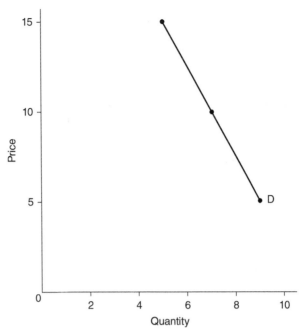

Figure 4.1 Demand curve for an individual consumer.

Demand of consumer A + demand of consumer B = market demand

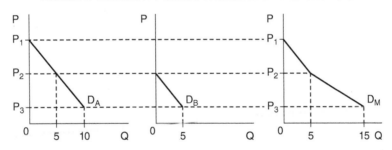

Figure 4.2 Deriving a market demand curve.

curve is often referred to as the market demand curve, in the sense that it sums up the demand brought to bear in the market by all consumers of the product in question. The market demand curve is literally the sum of the relevant individual curves. As shown in Figure 4.2, we present the demand curves for theater ticket of two individuals, A and B, and show how they (and, by extension, any number of individual curves) are added up to obtain the market curve. The latter shows the aggregate quantity of tickets consumers will buy at any given price. To obtain it we must add up the quantities that all individuals will buy at each price. As shown in Figure 4.2, we do that graphically by adding horizontally the quantities demanded by A and B at selected prices and plotting the sum as the market demand in the right-hand panel.

The foregoing example confined the consumer's choices to the few days of a "culture vulture" holiday. In general, the consumer choice principles – maximizing utility subject to a budget constraint – could easily be extended to any time period. In the remainder of this chapter and in Chapter 5, we explore more general applications, including the consequences of explicitly altering the time period under consideration.

4.4   Demand, Supply, and the Determination of Price

While developing the theory of consumer choice, we treated price as a "given." That was appropriate since the individual buyer does have to accept whatever prices are established in the marketplace. Now, however, we wish to explain *how* competitive markets establish prices. The answer will turn out to be that prices are determined by the interaction of supply and demand, and in order to explain that process, we require a supply curve as well as a demand curve.

Just as a market demand curve shows the aggregate quantity that consumers will purchase at any given price, the market supply curve indicates the aggregate quantity that producers will offer for sale at each of those prices. Demand curves slope downward to the right because consumers will buy more as the price falls. Supply curves, especially in the short run, slope upward to the right because producers will increase output and offer more for sale as the price rises. A general explanation for the upward slope is that at higher prices it becomes profitable to extend output by using productive resources in combinations that would not pay their way at lower prices. For example, a manufacturer might hire overtime labor at premium prices to increase output when prices are high enough to cover the added cost.

It must be pointed out that, in the long run, market supply curves may well be flat rather than upward-sloping. Given sufficient time to adjust, producers will be able to expand output by replicating the most efficient production methods rather than by resorting to such expensive expedients as overtime labor. Indeed, the long-run supply curve of an industry is likely to be upward-sloping only if the industry's expansion pushes up the prices of its inputs, as might occur, for example, if the supply of some inputs is constrained by natural scarcity. At this point, however, we are concerned only with the short run and can therefore plausibly assume that supply curves are upward-sloping. Because both demand and supply curves show a relationship between quantity and price, they can be plotted on a single diagram, with price on the vertical axis and quantity on the horizontal. Figure 4.3 shows hypothetical market demand and supply curves for theater tickets and provides a simple graphic solution to the problem of price determination. If the market is freely competitive, the price will tend to settle at the level where quantity supplied equals quantity demanded. Those quantities are equal at the point on the diagram where the supply and demand curves intersect. The corresponding market price is P_e and quantity sold Q_e.

P_e is also referred to as the "equilibrium price" in the sense that if the price of theater tickets is for some reason displaced from that level, market forces are automatically set in motion that tend to bring it back to P_e. The process is illustrated in Figure 4.3. If the price were at P_1 (higher than P_e), producers would offer Q_{S1} tickets for sale (corresponding to the point of intersection of P_1 with the supply curve), but buyers would purchase only Q_{D1} (as shown by the intersection of P_1 with the demand curve). Quantity supplied would exceed quantity demanded by an amount labeled "excess supply" on the diagram. To fill these unsold seats, suppliers would

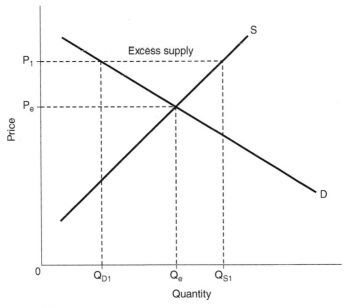

Figure 4.3 Supply, demand, and market equilibrium.

begin to lower their prices in a competitive process that would end only when equilibrium was restored at price P_e. By a perfectly analogous argument, if the price were for some reason at a level below P_e (not shown in the diagram), quantity demanded would exceed quantity supplied, giving rise to "excess demand" in the market. Suppliers would find that they could not fill all their orders for tickets at the lower price and would take advantage of the opportunity to raise prices in a process that would continue until the level rose to P_e. We show in Chapter 11 that if all markets were perfectly competitive, price–quantity solutions, such as P_e and Q_e in Figure 4.3, would be socially optimal in the sense that resources are thereby allocated, among alternative uses, in the proportions that best satisfy consumer wants. It is precisely that optimizing feature of perfect competition that makes it so attractive in the eyes of many economists.

4.4.1 Ticket Pricing in Reality

Given the rough edges of the real world, markets do not always operate with the frictionless freedom assumed in economic models. Standard theater pricing policy provides an instructive example of the inefficiencies that develop when market price is not allowed to move freely to its equilibrium level. To analyze the problem, however, it is necessary to adjust the supply and demand model to reflect the special circumstances of the performing arts. It is an obvious characteristic of any single production in the performing arts that, in the short run, the supply of tickets that can be offered exactly equals the number of seats in the house where the performance takes place (assuming that no standing room tickets are made available). Unlike the standard case in which the quantity supplied increases as price rises, so that the supply curve slopes upward to the right, the supply curve of seats for a single performing arts production is a vertical straight line, at a quantity equal to the capacity of the house.

Until fairly recently, it was a peculiar feature of theater ticket pricing that prices were established before opening night and not altered thereafter, even though the producers did not know in advance of the opening what the demand for tickets would be. The resulting difficulties can be demonstrated with supply and demand analysis. We must emphasize that the following analysis does *not* purport to show how theatrical producers choose the profit-maximizing ticket price for a new offering. That analysis is presented in Chapter 7. At this point, we look only at the short-run effects of rigid ticket-pricing decisions without explaining how the prices were arrived at.

4.4.2   The Problem of Inflexible Ticket Prices

Figure 4.4 illustrates the case in which producers have underestimated the demand for a play that turns out to be a smash hit. The play opens in a relatively small theater where the number of seats is Q_{S1}, and the supply curve is therefore S_1. In advance of opening night, the producers set the price at P_1. When the play opens, they discover that the daily demand for tickets is represented by the demand curve D_A. Consequently, at a price of P_1, there is an excess demand for seats, equal to $Q_{D1} - Q_{S1}$. Given the high level of demand, they could have charged a price of P_2 and still filled the house (see point e). By holding the price down to P_1, they sacrifice potential revenue. The lost revenue is equal to the price difference $(P_2 - P_1)$ multiplied by the number of tickets that can be sold (Q_{S1}). But the product $Q_{S1} \times (P_2 - P_1)$ is also the area of the shaded rectangle P_2efP_1; hence, that rectangle measures the lost revenue. (It is a useful property of supply–demand diagrams that revenues, i.e., sales proceeds, can be precisely measured by areas.)

One solution to the problem illustrated in Figure 4.4 – but generally limited to the unique character of Broadway productions in New York City – would be to move the play into a larger theater. For example, in a house with capacity S_2, the producers could satisfy all the excess daily demand that existed at price P_1 in the smaller house and take in the additional revenue measured by the rectangle $Q_{S1}fgQ_{D1}$, while incurring very little additional production cost.

But perhaps a theater with capacity greater than S_1 is not available. In that case, why don't the producers of this smash hit raise prices to P_2 after the play opens? Economists have often asked that question, since they like to see the price system operating efficiently and do not expect business people, who are profit maximizers, to stand in the way. The answer, apparently, is that tradition runs against altering prices (either up or down) after a play opens. The result, in the case of smash hits, however, often creates a "black market" in tickets to the underpriced show. As shown in Figure 4.4, the unsatisfied customers $(Q_{D1} - Q_{S1})$ are willing to pay prices well above P_1 to obtain seats. A customer able to buy a ticket at the box office for P_1 could resell it in a secondary market at a substantial profit. In fact, for hit shows, especially musicals, a well-organized underground ticket market had developed, the profits on which came to be known as "ice." One of the irrational results of this arrangement was that substantial revenues that might have accrued through the box office to the producers, authors, composers, and others with an ownership interest in the production, instead went to speculators and "scalpers" who had no such connection.

Next consider the case, illustrated in Figure 4.5, of a play that is *not* a smash hit. The ticket price P_1 is established before the play opens. After the run begins, the producers realize that they cannot sell all the available tickets at that price, given the demand curve D_B. There is an

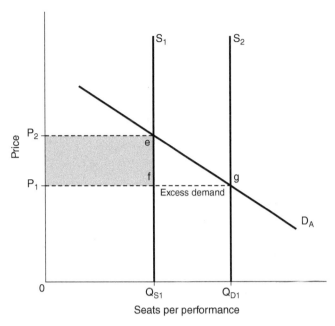

Figure 4.4 Excess demand for tickets: a Broadway hit.

excess supply equal to $Q_{S1} - Q_{D1}$. Then the question is: Why didn't they lower the price to P_2 to fill all the seats?

Again, traditional practice dictated not changing prices after the show had opened. In the case of a price reduction, there were two supporting arguments. First, those who bought tickets in advance at the higher price might be angered to find themselves sitting next to people who paid less for similar seats to the same performance. Second, lowering the price in order to sell more tickets involves both gains and losses in revenue. The additional tickets sold at price P_2 would bring in revenue equal to the area of rectangle $Q_{D1}feQ_{S1}$. However, reducing the price from P_1 to P_2 would entail a loss of revenue equal to the area of rectangle P_1gfP_2 on the seats that could have been sold at a higher price. Whether total revenue rises or falls therefore depends on which rectangle is larger, and *that* in turn depends on how responsive quantity sold is to the fall in price. If, as we assume in Figure 4.5, it is fairly responsive, a price reduction would produce a net gain in total revenue. (The responsiveness of quantity demanded to a change in price is measured by the price elasticity of demand, a highly useful gauge that is described in Chapter 5. As the attentive reader will discover, we have assumed here that the demand for theater tickets is "price elastic.")

As a first step toward pricing flexibility, Broadway theater producers agreed to a two-price system that went a long way toward solving the problem of price reductions. At noon each day, all theaters put their unsold tickets for the day's performances on sale at half price at a booth in Times Square and at two other locations in the city. From the producer's point of view, this was probably better than an across-the-board price reduction. Referring back to Figure 4.5, what they accomplished, in effect, was to maintain price P_1 for advance sales and charge something less than P_1 for the remaining unsold tickets. This is a form of "price discrimination," that is, selling the same product at different prices to different customers. But it may benefit customers as well as producers. Those who wanted assured seating, planned for in advance,

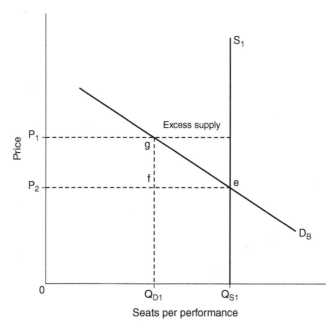

Figure 4.5 Excess supply of tickets: a Broadway flop.

could obtain it by paying the full price. Those who wanted to save money and were willing to take their chances at the last minute might be able to attend at half price.

4.5   The Rise of "Dynamic Pricing"

In recent years, with the advent of online ticket purchasing, the legalization of what had often been illegal ticket "scalping," and the rise of secondary market dealers, pricing practices have changed substantially. Ticket purchasers have become accustomed to widely varying prices for a given product, such as airline tickets, so they are far less likely to be surprised or angered to find that their seatmates paid a different price.

Broadway and other theater tickets are now customarily priced differently by day of week and time of day (e.g., matinees versus evening), and they can be adjusted over time as theater marketing staffs gain a better feel for ticket demand. Off-Broadway and regional theaters, as well as other performing arts organizations, are also implementing flexible pricing practices. The Chicago Symphony Orchestra was one of the first to implement "demand-based pricing" (Ravanas, 2008).

4.6   The Determinants of Demand

The analysis up to this point has emphasized the effect of prices on consumer choice. But there are several other factors that importantly influence demand for a particular good, including the level of consumer income, consumers' tastes, and the prices of related goods. We shall examine these in turn.

4.6.1 Income

In most cases (with exceptions to be noted later), consumers' demand for a particular commodity or service will increase as their incomes rise. We showed in Chapter 3 that the average middle-class family attends the live performing arts more frequently than does a poor family, and the average wealthy family more frequently still. Such a statement looks at the matter "cross-sectionally," that is, by comparing families with different incomes at a moment in time. But a similar relationship was found in Chapter 2 when we looked at consumption *through* time, that is, longitudinally: As the average level of family income rises in a society that is enjoying economic growth, the demand for attendance at the live performing arts increases. Since income is an obviously important determinant of consumer behavior, we shall pay a good deal of attention to its influence on the demand for art and culture.

4.6.2 Taste

Economists use the term "taste" as a shorthand way of referring to the system of preferences that so clearly affects the pattern of every consumer's demand. To take a simple example, some consumers prefer white bread to whole wheat or rye, while some prefer rolls to bread. Obviously, the aggregate of these preferences influences the demand for white bread as compared with the other types, or of bread compared with rolls. Analogously, in the realm of culture, some consumers prefer the visual to the performing arts, some enjoy the theater but have no taste for music, and some watch television in preference to attending any sort of arts activity. We all recognize that in the aggregate, these preferences must strongly affect the dimensions of our cultural life.

The tradition in economics has been to assume that consumer taste cannot be explained and that it is just as well not to try. This attitude is consistent with the philosophy of liberal capitalism, which most US economists probably endorse, namely, that it is an important function of an economy to respond efficiently to consumer preferences. If consumers want to wear hats, it is desirable that business produce hats. If tastes change and fewer hats are wanted, fewer will be produced, and that's all right, too. There is no need to agonize about the virtue of changes in taste. Whatever consumers want (provided it does them no serious harm), they should get. Thus, economists do not usually investigate taste. They simply treat it as a "given," that is, as an ultimate datum for the economy.

The case of the arts is somewhat different. A good many people, including a respectable number of economists, think it would be desirable to stimulate the consumption of art. (We examine their reasons in Chapter 12.) Art is said to be an "acquired taste," in the sense that you have to be exposed to it in order to develop the taste, and perhaps exposed under the right circumstances and for rather a long time. Therefore, to stimulate consumption, so the argument goes, we must help people to acquire the taste both by making the arts accessible and by directly stimulating exposure. The cultivation of taste is such an interesting and important question in the economics of art and culture that we devote considerable attention to it in the last two chapters of this book. As a hint to what is to come, we take note of what one prominent early cultural economist referred to as the "investment in consumption skills" that would enhance the appreciation of, say, opera (Scitovsky, 1976).

4.6.3   Prices of Related Goods

Every consumer good has substitutes. Demand for the good itself is affected not only by its own price but also by the prices of the substitutes. The quantity of tea consumers will buy depends in part on the price of coffee, the quantity of pork on the price of beef. Likewise, in the realm of art and culture, the demand for symphony tickets is affected by the price of substitutes such as compact discs or the price of admission to other entertainments. When two goods are substitutes in consumption, the relation between the price of one and demand for the other is always positive: the higher the price of admission to theatrical productions, the greater the demand for symphony tickets. Indeed, we could logically reverse that statement: We know that two goods are substitutes if empirical studies show that the price of one is positively correlated with the demand for the other.

In many instances, one consumer good is necessarily (or often) used in combination with a particular other good. In such cases, the relationship is said to be complementary. For example, the demand for automobiles depends in part on the price of the complementary good gasoline. In the field of musical recordings, the demand for compact discs is significantly affected by the price of the compact dis player that is its essential complement. In the case of the performing arts, there is an important complementary relationship between the demand for tickets and the *non*ticket costs of attending a performance, such as the costs of transportation, parking, and restaurant meals. Thomas Gale Moore, in his very early study of the Broadway theater, found that, on average, complementary expenditures accounted for about half the cost of an evening at a Broadway play or musical (Moore, 1968, table V. 9, p. 87). The demand for a given good always moves in the opposite direction to the price of its complement: If the nonticket costs of an evening at the theater rise, the demand for theater tickets falls.

4.6.4   A Hypothetical Demand Function

The connection between demand for a good or service and the factors determining it can be seen most clearly if the relationship is written out in the form of a demand equation, or, as it is often called, a "demand function." In this section, we construct a hypothetical demand equation for theater tickets.

The equation is written in the following general form:

$$Q_t = a + bP_t + cY + dP_s + eP_c. \qquad (4.4)$$

The variable on the left-hand side is the "dependent variable" – in this case, the quantity of theater tickets demanded per time period. The premise underlying the analysis is that the value of this dependent variable is explained by the factors written on the right-hand side. These are the "independent" or "explanatory" variables. The variables have the following definitions:

Q_t = quantity of theater tickets demanded per time period
P_t = the price of theater tickets
Y = average annual per capita income
P_s = weighted average price of substitutes (movies, concerts, spectator sports, etc.)
P_c = composite price of complementary goods (transportation to theater, dinner out, etc.)

a = constant term

b, c, d, e = coefficients measuring change in value of the dependent variable per unit change in the respective independent variables

Note that there is no variable to measure taste, even though we have argued that taste is a fundamental determinant of demand. That is because taste is not truly quantifiable. Instead of trying to represent taste indirectly by the use of some proxy, such as educational attainment, the analysis proceeds on the assumption that *given* the state of consumers' preferences, that is, the tastes that underlie their choices in the marketplace, the quantity of theater tickets demanded will be determined by this equation. If tastes were to change for any reason, the value of the constant term and/or of the coefficients in the equation would change, too.

To put Equation (4.4) to work, we must supply hypothetical values for all the independent variables and their coefficients and calculate the resulting value of the dependent variable, Q_t. Alternative sets of hypothetical values are shown in Table 4.2. In Case 1, we assume that the price of a theater ticket is $15, average annual per capita income is $3,000, the average price of substitute entertainments is $16, and the nonticket cost of attending the theater average $12 per person. The coefficient b has an assumed value of -5,000, indicating that for every $1 increase in ticket prices, 5,000 fewer theater tickets will be sold. Coefficient c has a hypothetical value of 40, which means that for every $1 increase in per capita income, ticket sales will rise by 40 (or for every $100 increase, by 4,000.) Note that the sign on coefficient d is positive, while that on coefficient e is negative, showing that sales of theater tickets rise when the price of substitute entertainments goes up but fall with a rise in the price of complementary goods. When Equation (4.4) is evaluated employing the hypothetical numbers assumed in Case 1, the quantity of theater tickets demanded is 106,800. (See Table 4.3 for calculations.)

We are now in a position to explain more fully the meaning of demand curves in economics. A demand curve shows the relationship between price and quantity demanded under the assumption of ceteris paribus, that is to say, when all other variables that might affect demand are held constant. In general, the important other variables are precisely those included in Equation (4.4), namely, income and the prices of substitutes and complements, plus taste, which, as already explained, is not included in the equation because it is not directly measurable.

A particular demand curve for theater tickets is implied by the relationships expressed in Equation (4.4) in combination with the values of the coefficients and independent variables assumed in Case 1. In Table 4.3, we have already calculated one point on that curve: when $P_t = 15$, $Q_t = 106,800$. To sketch out the rest of the curve, one could reevaluate Equation (4.4) at various values of P_t, while holding all other variables constant at their Case 1 levels. For example, if P_t falls to $10, Q_t rises to 131,800. However, it would be tedious to plot the entire curve one point at a time. Accordingly, we proceed as follows. An equation for the demand curve in question can be calculated from the information in Table 4.3. The values of all the terms in that table, excluding Q_t and bP_t, add up to 181,800. We can therefore write the following demand equation:

$$Q_t = 181,800 - 5,000P_t. \tag{4.5}$$

We know that this demand curve is linear (i.e., a straight line), because each time price falls by $1, Q_t rises by the constant increment of 5,000 indicated by the value of coefficient b.

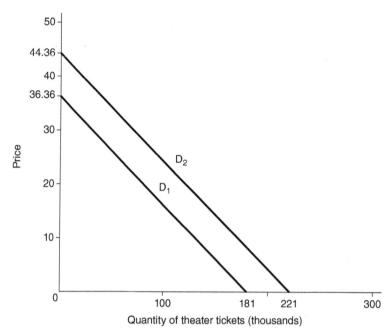

Figure 4.6 Demand curves derived from a demand function.

Furthermore, the intercepts of this curve on a price–quantity diagram (see Figure 4.6) can be obtained by analyzing Equation (4.5): If P_t falls to zero, quantity demanded rises to 181,800. That is the intercept on the horizontal axis. On the other hand, if P_t rises to \$36.36, quantity demanded falls to zero (since $181{,}800 - 5{,}000 \times 36.36 = 0$). That is the intercept on the vertical axis. Since the demand function is known to be linear, we can connect the two intercepts with a straight line, yielding the demand curve D_1 in Figure 4.6. To summarize, we have now plotted a demand curve that shows how many theater tickets can be sold at any given price, assuming that all other relevant variables remain at the levels specified in Case 1. The next step is to ask: What happens if the value of one of those variables now changes?

4.6.5 Shifting of Demand Curves

The answer is straightforward. If one of the variables previously impounded under the restraint of ceteris paribus now changes its value, the demand *function* (Eq. 4.4) necessarily yields a different demand *curve*. Economists usually refer to this as a "shift of the demand curve." The curve is said to shift to the right if demand increases, shift to the left if demand decreases. By observing the signs on the independent variables in Equation (4.4), one can see at once which way it will shift for a given change in any of the variables. The sign on income (Y) is positive, meaning that quantity demanded rises with income. Hence, if average per capita income increases, the demand curve will shift to the right. An increase in the price of substitutes (P_s) will also cause a rightward shift, while a rise in the price of complementary goods (P_c) will cause the demand curve to shift left.

In Table 4.2, the values listed for the independent variables in Case 2 are identical in all respects with those in Case 1 except that income per capita has increased from \$3,000 to \$4,000

Table 4.2 Hypothetical values of variables for Equation (4.4)

	Case 1	Case 2
Independent variables		
P	15	15
Y	3,000	4,000
P_s	16	16
P_c	12	12
Coefficients		
Constant (a)	65,000	65,000
b	−5,000	−5,000
c	40	40
d	1,000	1,000
e	−1,600	−1,600
Value of Q_t calculated from Equation (4.4) (see Table 4.3)	106,800	146,800

Table 4.3 Calculating quantity demanded from a demand function

Independent variables in Equation (4.4)	Value of terms assumed in Case #1	Contribution to value of dependent variable
a	65,000	65,000
$b \times P_t$	−5,000 × 15	−75,000
$c \times Y$	40 × 3,000	120,000
$d \times P_s$	1,000 × 16	16,000
$e \times P_c$	−1,600 × 12	−19,200
Dependent variable		
Q_t (sum of the above contributions)		106,800

per year. This $1,000 increase, when multiplied by 40 (the value of the income coefficient, c) adds 40,000 to the number of theater tickets demanded at the still unchanged values of the other variables. Q_t consequently rises from 106,800 to 146,800.

The new demand curve, D_2, is also plotted in Figure 4.6. As predicted, it lies to the right of D_1. Because, on average, their incomes have increased, consumers are now willing to buy more tickets than previously at any given price. The equation of the new curve is

$$Q_t = 221,800 - 5,000P_t. \tag{4.6}$$

4.6.6 Supply and Demand with Shifting Demand Curves

What effect will shifting demand curves have on market price and quantity sold? The answer clearly depends on the shape of the relevant supply curve. Figure 4.3 incorporated a hypothetical supply curve for compact discs drawn sloping upward to the right, to reflect the fact that in the short run increased output usually entails higher unit costs for suppliers. As shown in Figure 4.7, we again assume an upward-sloping supply curve for theater. At a given level of income as well as prices of substitutes and complements, and with a given set of consumer preferences (or taste), the demand for theater is shown by the demand curve D_1. The market is in equilibrium at price P_1 and quantity Q_1. If the average level of income should rise, consumer demand would increase, as shown by a rightward shift of the demand curve to D_2. Out of their larger incomes, consumers would be willing to pay higher prices than previously for any given quantity of recordings. Equilibrium price and quantity sold would rise to P_2 and Q_2 as producers increased output to meet the greater demand. It might seem puzzling that quantity demanded would now be greater than before ($Q_2 > Q_1$), even though price has increased ($P_2 > P_1$). This does *not*, however, contradict the earlier finding that quantity demanded *falls* when price *rises*. That conclusion was qualified by the assumption of "all other things being the same" and referred to a movement *along a given demand curve* – in fact, along the specific curve that was consistent with the assumed underlying conditions. In the present case, we specifically assume a *change* in one of the underlying conditions. Consequently, the demand curve shifts. Instead of seeing movement along a given demand curve, we observe a series of equilibrium points generated by the movement of a demand curve along a given *supply curve*. Consumers willingly pay a higher price for a larger quantity because their incomes have increased.

By analogous arguments, supply and demand analysis can also show the expected effects of demand curve shifts caused by changes in the levels of other independent variables such as prices of substitutes and complements. For example, suppose that an increase in government subsidies to musical organizations causes the number of concerts to rise and the price of concert tickets to fall. Attendance at live concerts is a substitute for buying recorded music. At the lower ticket price, some consumers will attend more concerts and buy fewer theater tickets. The demand curve for theater will shift down along the supply curve, for example, to D_3 in Figure 4.7. When the market reaches a new equilibrium, the price of theater tickets will have fallen to P_3 and the quantity demanded to Q_3.

Although consumer taste is not directly measurable, supply and demand analysis can also show, at least in terms of the direction of movement, how a change in taste will affect market price and quantity sold. For example, suppose that as a result of the cultivation of taste – investment in their music consumption skills by enrolling in a classical music course – consumers began to substitute time spent listening to music for time devoted to watching television. The demand for orchestra tickets would shift rightward, perhaps from D_1 to D_2. At any given level of ticket prices (and of other variables, including income and the prices of substitutes and complements), consumers would now buy more theater tickets than before, and their price would tend to rise.

Figure 4.7, however, depicts only the short-run outcome. In the long run, as suggested earlier, the supply curve of the concert industry might be horizontal rather than upward-sloping. In that case, as the taste for music increased and the demand curve for tickets shifted to the right, the quantity supplied would increase, while the price remained more or less constant.

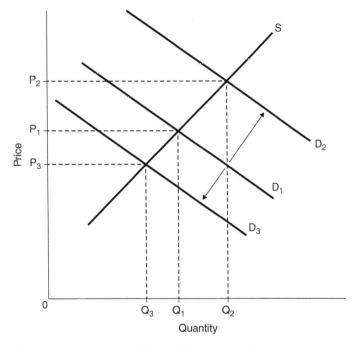

Figure 4.7 Changing equilibria with a shifting demand curve.

4.6.7   What if Many Variables Change Simultaneously?

In the dynamic real world, economic change never occurs in only one variable at a time. The discussion of actual events is usually made difficult by the fact that so many relevant forces are changing simultaneously. It is a great virtue of supply and demand analysis that it allows us to focus on one change at a time and indicates clearly the expected effects of each.

The forgoing discussion was limited to changes occurring on the demand side of the market. The demand curve was allowed to shift, while the supply curve remained fixed. To analyze other questions, it would be appropriate to hold demand conditions constant, while shifting the supply curve. One such application will be developed in Chapter 14 when we analyze the effect of a change in labor supply on the output of a theater company (see Figure 14.3 and the accompanying discussion).

4.6.8   Demand and the Black Swan Event

In an extreme case, demand could shift so far to the left as essentially to disappear. Imagine the supply curve extended all the way to the vertical axis, where at even a tiny price, attendance would be zero on the quantity axis. A black swan event such as a global pandemic cannot be added to the demand equation, but clearly it would be a serious threat to the very future of many performing arts organizations unless they can find alternative means of making their products available to maintaining their audiences and their existence until "normal" circumstances resume. We will explore some responses to black swan events in subsequent chapters, including governmental actions and entrepreneurial steps taken by arts managers.

4.7   Summary

In this chapter, we have explained the elementary theory of consumer demand, discussed the principal determinants of demand, including prices, consumer income, and taste, and shown how supply and demand interact in the market to establish prices and determine the quantity of output for all commercially traded goods. The relevance of supply and demand analysis to the arts was illustrated with some problems in theater ticket pricing. However, the full analysis of factors affecting supply in the arts is reserved for latter chapters: for the performing arts, Chapters 6 and 7; for the fine arts, Chapter 9; and for performing artists in the labor market, Chapter 14.

Because the supply and demand model is so flexible, it can be used to investigate a remarkably wide range of questions in economics. Many of these, drawn from the world of art and culture, are examined in this volume.

SUGGESTIONS FOR FURTHER READING

See the discussion in Moore (1968, pp. 84–88, 134–138) for more about ticket reselling in the secondary market.

A full analysis of the possibilities of price discrimination can be found in any textbook of microeconomic theory; we put it to further use in Chapter 9.

PROBLEM SET

4.1 The *New York Times* headline: "Broadway is Booming Despite Soaring Ticket Prices." Booming in this case refers to record attendance during the time period covered. Critically assess the headline and illustrate using dynamic supply and demand curves for Broadway tickets. Rewrite the headline to reflect your analysis.

4.2 In each of the five cases presented below, some events (causes) yield effects that can be depicted using a supply and demand framework. Show the effects of the events on the markets and indicate any changes in equilibrium price and quantity.

Market	Event	
1. A specific Saturday night concert	A popular music critic characterized the Thursday performance of the same program as "stunning."	

Market	Event	
2. Orchestra musicians	Groups of well-heeled citizens in several medium-sized cities decide simultaneously to establish major symphony orchestras.	
3. Orchestra musicians (again)	Immigration restrictions for musicians from abroad are relaxed.	
4. Drumsticks	A new, inexpensive plastic rosin dramatically reduces the cost of producing highly durable drumsticks. (This one is a little tricky.)	
5. Concerts	A fear of terrorism causes citizens to spend more leisure time at home rather than going out to concerts and other events.	

NOTES

1 A more advanced treatment of the theory of consumer choice, known as indifference curve analysis, dispenses with the unrealistic assumption that utility can be measured in quantitative units, such as utils, and assumes only that consumer can rank goods in relation to one another as more desirable, less desirable, or equally desirable (hence "indifferent").

2 The analysis has been simplified by ignoring the fact that when money income is held constant, a change in the price of any good purchased by the consumer will alter the level of the consumer's real income, thus producing effects on consumption in addition to those caused by the price change.

5   Elasticities of Arts Demand and Their Policy Implications

LEARNING OBJECTIVES

By the end of this chapter, readers should be able to:

- Measure the sensitivity of quantity demanded to price or income
- Understand the connection between changes in price and total revenue
- Apply the concept of cross-price elasticity of demand
- Interpret price and income elasticities of demand in the performing arts

The nature of demand equations and the demand curves that can be derived from them was explained in Chapter 4. We now wish to take a closer look to see what that economic apparatus can tell us about the response of consumer demand to changes in the forces on which it depends. We begin by defining a highly useful property called elasticity. Derivable from a demand equation, this measure can be employed to gauge the response of the dependent variable – quantity demanded – to changes in any of the independent variables, such as price or income, that influence it. The price elasticity of demand, for example, tells us how sensitive the consumption of a good or service is to changes in its price. Thus, the manager of a symphony orchestra who knew the size of the price elasticity of demand for its tickets could predict whether raising ticket prices would increase the orchestra's income or, to the contrary, would so discourage attendance that income would actually drop.

5.1   The Price Elasticity of Demand

The price elasticity of demand (ε_p) is defined as the percent change in quantity demanded that results from a given percent change in price, with all other things remaining the same. Using the Greek letter delta (Δ) to signify "change in," the equation can be written algebraically as

$$\varepsilon_P = \frac{\Delta Q / Q}{\Delta P / P}. \tag{5.1}$$

For some purposes, it is convenient to rearrange Equation (5.1) to read

$$\varepsilon_p = \frac{\Delta Q}{\Delta P} \times \frac{P}{Q}. \tag{5.2}$$

If price changes from P_1 to P_2 and, as a result, quantity demanded moves from Q_1 to Q_2, the equation can also be written as

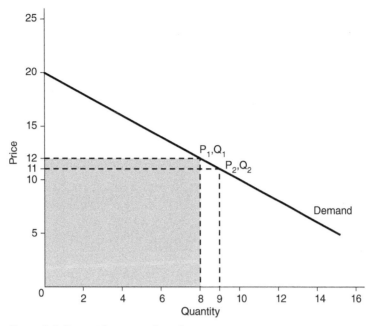

Figure 5.1 Demand curve and total revenue.

$$\varepsilon_p = \frac{(Q_2 - Q_1)/Q_1}{(P_2 - P_1)/P_1}, \tag{5.3}$$

since, in that case, $P_2 - P_1 = \Delta P$ and $Q_2 - Q_1 = \Delta Q$.

Using Equation (5.3), we can illustrate the calculation of price elasticity when the values of P and Q at two points on a demand curve are known. Consider the hypothetical case illustrated in Figure 5.1. At a price of $12, quantity sold is 8; when price falls to $11, quantity sold rises to 9. Thus, $P_1 = 12$ and $P_2 - P_1 = -1$; $Q_1 = 8$ and $Q_2 - Q_1 = 1$. Putting these numbers into Equation (5.1), we obtain

$$\varepsilon_P = \frac{1/8}{-1/12} = -1.5. \tag{5.4}$$

Price and quantity always change in opposite directions along a demand curve. As a result, ΔP and ΔQ always have opposite signs, and the value of the price elasticity of demand, using any of the previous formulas, is always negative. However, since it is confusing to compare negative numbers in terms of "more" or "less," as will have to be done in discussing elasticity, we hereafter follow the convention of dropping the negative sign.

It is a great virtue of all elasticities that as the ratio of 1% of change to another, they are "dimensionless numbers." Consequently, one can, for example, compare the price elasticity of demand for gasoline with that for electric power without worrying about the fact that gasoline is measured in gallons and electricity in kilowatt hours.

As we have already indicated, the price elasticity of demand tells you how sensitive the demand for a commodity is to changes in its price. In the hypothetical case being described, quantity demanded turns out to be quite sensitive to price changes since an 8.33% price decline induces a 12.5% increase in units purchased. The range of possible values of price elasticity is divided by economists into three classes, as follows:

$\varepsilon > 1$ is called "elastic demand"
$\varepsilon = 1$ is called "unitary elasticity"
$\varepsilon < 1$ is called "inelastic demand."

When demand is elastic $(\varepsilon > 1)$, the percent change in quantity exceeds the percent change in price, indicating that quantity purchased is quite sensitive to price.

When demand is inelastic $(\varepsilon < 1)$, quantity purchased changes by a smaller percentage than price does, indicating that demand is relatively insensitive to price.

When demand has unitary elasticity, the percent change in quantity purchased exactly equals the percent change in price but is, of course, in the opposite direction.

5.1.1 Explaining Differences in Price Elasticity

What lies behind these differences? Why is the demand for one good price elastic, for another inelastic? One significant explanation is that elasticity rises with the availability of substitutes. The more, or the closer, the available substitutes for a given good or service, the more readily consumers will switch to something else when the price of that good or service rises relative to other prices. Thus, price elasticity is always higher for a subcategory like pork, for which there are good substitutes within the larger class of meat, than it is for meat as a whole. Likewise, the price elasticity of demand is higher for meat than for food, for there are many substitutes for meat within the category of food, but none for food itself. For the same reasons we would expect the price elasticity of demand to be higher for the tickets of a single live performing arts company than for the live performing arts industry as a whole, and higher for that industry as a whole than for the entertainment sector, broadly defined to include movies and spectator sports, as well as live performance. This point will become relevant later in the chapter.

5.1.2 Price Elasticity and Total Revenue

It is important to note the connection between price elasticity and the total revenue (or gross receipts) generated by the sale of the commodity in question. Total revenue is simply price × quantity. In the hypothetical case of elastic demand shown in Figure 5.1, total revenue was $96 at a higher price of $12 $(\$12 \times 8 = \$96)$ but rose to $99 when the price was reduced to $11 $(\$11 \times 9 = \$99)$. This illustrates the rule that when demand is price elastic, total revenue rises if price falls. (Reading the illustration in the opposite direction, one can also see that total revenue falls if price rises.) There is a commonsense explanation for this result. A price fall, in and of itself, would have the effect of reducing revenue. But there is an offsetting gain because quantity rises. However, the value of ε_p is greater than 1 precisely because the percentage rise in quantity is greater than the percentage decline in price. Therefore, the gain on quantity outweighs the loss on price, and total revenue increases as price falls.

If demand is price inelastic, on the other hand, total revenue falls when price falls and rises when price rises. Again, the explanation is straightforward. The value of ε_p is less than 1 because the percent change in quantity is smaller than the percent change in price. Hence, if price declines, the loss on price exceeds the gain on quantity, and total revenue falls.

Between elastic demand and inelastic demand lies the case of unitary elasticity. This has the interesting property that total revenue is unchanged when price changes, because the percent changes in quantity and price are exactly offsetting.

It is a useful feature of a supply–demand diagram in that its dimensions are price and quantity, hence its rectangular areas in the quadrant measure dollar revenues. As shown in Figure 5.1, the dimensions of the shaded rectangle are $11 = $8 + $3,$ making the rectangle's area 96, which also equals the total revenue when price is equal to $12.

Although elastic demand curves are usually depicted as fairly flat and inelastic curves as steep, it would be a mistake to equate the slope of a demand curve with its elasticity. The former is measured by the ratio $\Delta P / \Delta Q.$ The latter contains the inverse of that ratio and the ratio P / Q (see Equation (5.2)). A straight-line demand curve, such as the hypothetical examples drawn in this and in Chapter 4, has the same slope throughout. Its elasticity, however, varies from point to point, as one can deduce from the fact that the P / Q term necessarily changes value as one moves along the curve. Indeed, below a price of $10, the demand curve drawn in Figure 5.1 becomes inelastic.

5.1.3 Price, Total Revenue, and Marginal Revenue

To analyze the behavior of producing firms (whether in the arts or elsewhere), as we do in Chapter 7, it is essential to understand the precise connection between changes in price, the elasticity of demand, and change in total revenue. The term "marginal revenue" is used to describe the change in total revenue that occurs when price is reduced sufficiently to sell one more unit of output. If we denote total revenue as TR and marginal revenue as MR, and take ΔQ to be a one-unit change in quantity sold, then in algebraic terms, $MR = \Delta TR / \Delta Q.$ In the case illustrated in Figure 5.1, reducing the price from $12 to $11 increased the quantity sold by one unit and raised total revenue from $96 to $99. Hence, the marginal revenue obtained by selling the last unit was $3.

The derivation of marginal revenue is illustrated in Table 5.1 that contains data for the hypothetical demand curve shown in Figure 5.1. Multiplying the price, in Column 1, with the quantity that can be sold at each price, in Column 2, gives total revenue for each price–quantity combination in Column 3. Marginal revenue, in Column 4, is obtained by taking the successive differences in total revenue.

Given that demand curves slope downward to the right, marginal revenue will always be less than price. This can be explained as follows. When price is reduced in order to sell one more unit, revenue is increased by the amount for which the marginal unit is sold. But there is an offset to this: We assume that sellers charge the same price to all customers. Therefore, revenue is reduced by the lower price charged for the units that could have been sold at a higher price. Hence, marginal revenue is necessarily less than price. Consider the preceding example. To sell the ninth unit, the price was reduced from $12 to $11. The ninth unit added $11 to revenue. But the eight units that could have gone for $12 each now bring in only $11. Hence, revenue from them is reduced by $1 \times 8 = $8,$ and marginal revenue turns out to be $11 - $8 = $3.$

Table 5.1 Hypothetical demand and revenue data

(1)	(2)	(3)	(4)	(5)
Demand data				
Price	Quantity	Total revenue (Col. 1 × Col. 2)	Marginal revenue ($\Delta TR / \Delta Q$)	Price elasticity of demand
20	0	0	–	
19	1	19	19	
18	2	36	17	
17	3	51	15	
16	4	64	13	
15	5	75	11	Elastic
14	6	84	9	
13	7	91	7	
12	8	96	5	
11	9	99	3	
10	10	100	1	
9	11	99	−1	
8	12	96	−3	
7	13	91	−5	
6	14	84	−7	
5	15	75	−9	Inelastic
4	16	64	−11	
3	17	51	−13	
2	18	36	−15	
1	19	19	−17	
0	20	0	−19	

The general relationship between elasticity, price changes, and changes in total revenue was explained in nonmathematical terms above in this chapter. Making use of the concept of marginal revenue, we can now state that relationship more precisely as follows:

$$MR = P\left(1 - \frac{1}{\varepsilon_P}\right). \tag{5.5}$$

For example, if the price is $20 and the elasticity of demand at that price is known to be 2.0, then we have

$$MR = 20\left(1 - \frac{1}{2}\right) = 20(0.5) = 10. \tag{5.6}$$

Since marginal revenue is positive, this confirms the earlier statement that if demand is elastic (i.e., greater than 1.0), a price reduction will raise total revenue.

On the other hand, if at a price of $20 the elasticity of demand is only 0.8, then the formula shows that marginal revenue will be negative, confirming the earlier conclusion that when demand is inelastic, total revenue is reduced if price falls:

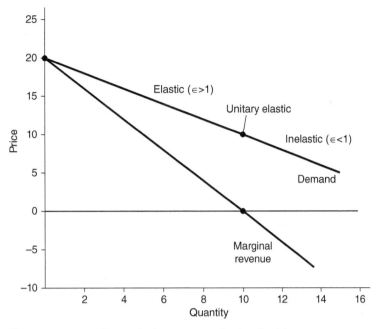

Figure 5.2 Demand, marginal revenue, and price elasticity.

$$MR = 20\left(1 - \frac{1}{0.8}\right) = 20(-0.25) = -5. \tag{5.7}$$

By testing the formula with other values of ε_p, the reader can confirm the following general results:

If ε_p = infinity, $MR = P$, then

$$\varepsilon_p > 1.0, MR > 0$$

$$\varepsilon_p = 1.0, MR = 0$$

$$\varepsilon_p < 1.0, MR < 0.$$

Figure 5.2 plots demand and marginal revenue curves from the data in Table 5.1. Marginal revenue turns negative when price falls below \$10. The price elasticity of demand drops below 1.0 at the same point.

5.1.4 Deriving Elasticity Values from a Demand Equation

In Chapter 4, a hypothetical demand equation for theater tickets (Equation (4.4)) was written in the following form:

$$Q_t = a + bP_t + cY + dP_s + eP_c. \tag{5.8}$$

The coefficients b, c, d, and e in such an equation contain information from which one can calculate elasticity values. For example, the ticket price coefficient b tells us how much the quantity of tickets demanded (Q_t) varies when the price of a ticket (P_t) changes by $1. In algebraic terms, we can therefore say $b = \Delta Q_t / \Delta P_t$. In other words, the coefficient b provides a value for the $\Delta Q / \Delta P$ term that appears in the formula for price elasticity given by Equation (5.2). Also, a consistent pair of values for P and Q are needed to calculate the price elasticity. These can be obtained by supplying a set of hypothetical values for the coefficients and variables in Equation (5.8) (which is the same as Equation (4.4)) and then solving it for the value of Q_t. For example, in Table 4.2, Case 1, we assumed a ticket price (P_t) of $15 and a value of $-5,000$ for the coefficient b. When Equation (4.4) was solved using those numbers, we obtained a value of 106,800 for Q_t.

With this information, we can calculate the price elasticity of demand for theater tickets when their price is $15 as follows:

$$\varepsilon_P = \frac{\Delta Q_t}{\Delta P_t} \times \frac{P_t}{Q_t} = \frac{-5,000}{1} \times \frac{15}{106,800} = \frac{-75,000}{106,800} = -0.70. \tag{5.9}$$

Since the demand curve D_1 in Figure 4.6 was derived from the same data used in this calculation, Equation (5.9) also gives the price elasticity of demand along that curve at the point where $P = 15$ and $Q = 106,800$.

In the real world, of course, one would not proceed on the basis of hypothetical values. To obtain a reliable figure for the price elasticity of demand, it would be necessary to employ econometric techniques to estimate the parameters of a demand price elasticity from that equation.

5.2   The Income Elasticity of Demand

Just as price elasticity measures the responsiveness of demand to changes in price while income and other variables are unchanged, so income elasticity measures its responsiveness to changes in income, when price and other variables are held constant. It is defined as the percent change in quantity demanded that results from a given percent change in income. Letting Y stand for income, it can be written algebraically as

$$\varepsilon_y = \frac{\Delta Q / Q}{\Delta Y / Y}. \tag{5.10}$$

or alternatively as

$$\varepsilon_y = \frac{\Delta Q}{\Delta Y} \times \frac{Y}{Q}. \tag{5.11}$$

or as

$$\varepsilon_y = \frac{(Q_2 - Q_1) / Q_1}{(Y_2 - Y_1) / Y_1}. \tag{5.12}$$

Although the preceding equations define income elasticity as a relationship between income and quantity purchased, it may be convenient, when suitable quantity measures are not available, to think of it as a relationship between income and consumer expenditure on a particular good. This is defensible, because in theory, the price of the good being studied is held constant over the range of observations used in calculating income elasticity, and if price is held constant, the percent change in expenditure will be the same as the percent change in the unobservable quantity. The expenditure approach is certainly convenient in studying the performing arts in the United States, where, as already explained in Chapter 2, consumer-spending data from the National Income Accounts are by far the best available historical data series.

To estimate income elasticity, the analyst obviously requires statistical observations in which the level of income displays some variations. There are two possibilities. First, one can measure variation "longitudinally," using historical time series, such as the National Income Accounts data. In that case, one might observe, for example, the year-to-year variation in consumer spending on admissions to the performing arts as compared with year-to-year variation in disposable personal income (DPI) per capita. With economic progress, DPI per capita rises through time. Thus, when income elasticity is measured longitudinally, its value suggests how consumer spending on the arts will be affected by economic growth.

Alternatively, one can measure variation in income and quantity demanded (or spending) among households at a moment in time. The data usually come from a sample survey of household income and consumption. This is described as the "cross-sectional approach," since observations are "across" households at a single date. The resulting elasticity measure answers questions such as: How do differences in income among consumers affect the consumption of art?

The range of possible values of income elasticity extends from negative through zero to positive as follows:

$$\varepsilon_y > 1 \text{ is called income elastic.}$$
$$\varepsilon_y = 1 \text{ is called unitary income elasticity.}$$
$$0 < \varepsilon_y < 1 \text{ is called income inelastic.}$$
$$\varepsilon_y > 1 \text{ is called an ``inferior good.''}$$

5.2.1 Income Elasticity, Consumer Budgets, and Industry Growth

It is important to understand the connection between these four categories and the composition of the typical consumer's budget. If a good has an income elasticity greater than 1, then consumer spending on it rises faster than their income. As a result, the proportion of income spent on the item increases as income increases. Such things are often described as luxuries, that is, goods that are consumed rarely or never when income is low, entering the typical consumer's budget only when income reaches the middle or upper range. Examples might be foreign travel, Cadillac cars, or tickets to the Metropolitan Opera.

The reader should be able to see intuitively that there is also a connection between the income elasticity of demand for a product and the rate of growth of the industry that produces it. If the income elasticity is greater than 1, aggregate consumer spending on the good (at constant relative prices) rises faster than aggregate consumer income. This implies that output by the industry in question must be growing faster than output of the economy as a whole. Table 5.2 summarizes the connections between income elasticity, the composition of the consumer's budget, and industry growth.

Table 5.2 Income elasticity of demand, composition of the consumer's budget, and industry growth

Type of elasticity	Value	Effect on consumer's budget: as consumer's income rises …	Effect on industry: as GDP rises, this industry …
Income elastic	$\epsilon > 1.0$	proportion spent on this good rises	grows faster than GDP
Unitary elasticity	$\epsilon = 1.0$	proportion spent on this good remains constant	grows at the same rate
Income inelastic	$0 < \epsilon < 1.0$	proportion spent on this good falls	grows less rapidly than GDP
Inferior good	$\epsilon < 0$	absolute amount spent on this good falls	decreases in size

If demand for a good displays unitary income elasticity, spending on it rises exactly in proportion to income, and the proportion of income spent on it remains constant as income rises. This, in turn, implies that the industry in question will grow at the same pace as the economy does.

Many consumer goods fall in the inelastic range, with income elasticities greater than 0 but less than 1. Consumer spending on them rises as income increases but less rapidly than income does. Consequently, the proportion of income spent on such goods decreases as income goes up. Food, with an income elasticity of demand around 0.5, is a good example. Such goods are important in the consumer's budget when income is low (they are sometimes classed as necessities); however, spending on them does not increase rapidly when income rises. Consequently, the industries producing such goods grow less rapidly than the economy as a whole.

Finally, there are some objects of consumption for which income elasticity is negative because quantity purchased falls as income rises. These are known technically as "inferior goods," a fitting name, since their odd behavior is accounted for by the fact that they are, for the most part, the lowest quality and therefore the cheapest members of some larger class of goods. For example, the income elasticity of demand for frankfurters is probably negative – as income rises, consumers give them up in favor of higher quality meats. Anything with an income elasticity of demand above zero is classified as a "normal good."

5.2.2   Deriving Income Elasticity from a Demand Equation

Using the hypothetical values of Case 1 in Table 4.2, we have already shown how the value of the price elasticity of demand can be derived from a known demand equation. The value of the income elasticity can be calculated in the same way. In Equation (5.8), the coefficient c shows how much the quantity of theater tickets demanded (Q_t) varies when the average per capita income (Y) of consumers changes by \$1. Thus, in algebraic notation $c = \Delta Q / \Delta Y$, which is one of the terms in the formula for income elasticity presented in Equation (5.11). The other values we require to calculate income elasticity are Y and Q. In Case 1, Y was assumed to have a value of \$3,000. When Equation (5.8) was solved using the values of Case 1, Q_t was found to be 106,800. Consistent with the values of coefficients and variables assumed in that case, the income elasticity of demand turns out to be as follows:

$$\varepsilon_y = (\Delta Q_t / \Delta Y) \times (Y / Q_t) = (40/1) \times (3{,}000/106{,}800)$$
$$= 120{,}000/106{,}800 = 1.12. \tag{5.13}$$

This result tells us that at a defined point, the demand for theater tickets is moderately income elastic. Specifically, it says that if income should rise 1% above $3,000 per capita while all other relevant variables remained constant, the quantity of theater tickets demanded would increase 1.12%.

5.3   Cross-Price Elasticity of Demand

The theory of consumer behavior tells us that the quantity demanded of a given good or service depends not only on its own price but also on the prices of substitutes and complements. Just as the price elasticity of demand measures the responsiveness of quantity purchased to changes in "own" price, so we can also define a cross-price elasticity (or "cross-elasticity," for short) that measures responsiveness to changes in the prices of substitutes or complements.

To define cross-elasticity in terms sufficiently general to cover both substitutes and complements, let us consider two hypothetical goods, j and k. The cross-elasticity of demand for j with respect to the price of k is defined as the percent change in the quantity demanded of j that results from a given percent change in the price of k. This can be written algebraically as

$$\varepsilon_{jk} = \frac{\Delta Q_j / Q_j}{\Delta P_k / P_k} \tag{5.14}$$

or, alternatively, as

$$\varepsilon_{jk} = \frac{\Delta Q_j}{\Delta P_k} \times \frac{P_k}{Q_j}. \tag{5.15}$$

Note that as in the case of price elasticity, this is a relationship between change in quantity and change in price, not a relationship between two prices. The sign of the cross-elasticity indicates whether the two goods are substitutes or complements: It will be positive for substitutes, negative for complements. Algebraically

$\varepsilon_{jk} > 0$ indicates j and k are substitutes.
$\varepsilon_{jk} < 0$ indicates j and k are complements.

The economic explanation of these statements is straightforward. If j and k are substitutes, an increase in the price of k will cause the quantity demanded of j to rise as consumers abandon the now more costly k in favor of its substitute, j. Thus, ΔP_k and ΔQ_j will both be positive, and elasticity will have a positive sign. By the same argument, if the price of k falls, the quantity demanded of j will also fall. In that case, ΔP_k and ΔQ_j will both be negative, but since one negative number divided by another yields a positive number, the elasticity will still have a positive sign.

To illustrate with an actual example, we know that organic and nonorganic fruits are substitutes in consumption. Presumably, if the price of nonorganic fruit rises while the price of organic fruit remains constant, some consumers will switch from nonorganic to organic fruit, so that the quantity demanded of the latter will increase. In fact, an empirical study of US consumption found that to be the case: The cross-elasticity of demand for organic with respect to the price of nonorganic fruit was estimated to be +0.85 (see Fourmouzi et al., 2012).

For patrons of the live performing arts, a large city obviously offers many possibilities of substitution in consumption. For example, in the Twin Cities of Minneapolis/St. Paul, the concertgoer might give up the Minnesota Orchestra in favor of the St. Paul Chamber Orchestra if the price of tickets to the former rose too high relative to the latter. Table 5.3 presents estimated cross-elasticities of demand between various sectors of the live performing arts and their substitutes. As expected, all are positive.

If the two goods are complementary in consumption, an increase in the price of one will lead to a decrease in the quantity demanded of the other. Faced by a higher price for the complementary good k, which is used in combination with j, consumers will cut back their purchases of the latter. Thus, ΔP_k and ΔQ_j will have opposite signs, one positive and the other negative, which necessarily gives the cross-elasticity a negative sign. Alternatively, if the price of k falls, the quantity demanded of j will rise. Again ΔP_k and ΔQ_j will have opposite signs, rendering the cross-elasticity negative.

An example of complementarity in consumption is provided by coffee and milk, two goods that tend to be consumed together. If the price of coffee rises, consumers will buy less coffee and will presumably need less milk to go with it. Consequently, the demand for milk will decrease.

There are complementarities in the arts field, as well. Since the customer has to travel to the point of production to enjoy the live performing arts, transportation and parking are important complementary goods. We would expect the demand for tickets to fall if the cost of these complements rose significantly.

In connection with the cross-elasticity of demand, the concepts of elasticity and inelasticity, with their precise dividing line, are not useful. However, the size of the elasticity coefficient may be of interest in indicating the strength of the indicated relationship. The closer it is to zero, the weaker the relationship. Indeed, in the polar cases of two goods that are completely unrelated in consumption, we would expect the cross-elasticity to be zero.

5.3.1   Deriving Cross-Price Elasticities from a Demand Equation

Repeating the analysis carried out for the price and income elasticities of demand, we can now calculate the values of two cross-elasticities from the hypothetical demand function data in Table 4.2. In Equation (5.8), the coefficient d measures the response of theater ticket demand to a unit change in the average price (P_s) of such substitutes as movies, concerts, and spectator sports. Using algebraic notation, $d = \Delta Q_t / \Delta P_s$, which is equivalent to the term $\Delta Q_j / \Delta P_k$ in the formula for the cross-elasticity given in Equation (5.15). To measure that elasticity, we also need values for Q_t and P_s. Taking these from Case 1 in Table 4.2, we calculate the value of the cross-elasticity of demand for theater tickets with respect to the average price of substitutes as follows:

$$\varepsilon_{ts} = \frac{\Delta Q_t}{\Delta P_s} \times \frac{P_s}{Q_t} = \frac{1,000}{1} \times \frac{16}{106,800} = \frac{16,000}{106,800} = 0.15. \tag{5.16}$$

Table 5.3 Estimates of demand elasticity, performing arts attendance

Investigator	Subsector/place	Time period	Type of study	Elasticity estimate		
				Own price	Cross price	Income
Gapinski (1986)	Theater, London	1972–1983	Pooled time series	−0.05 to −0.10	0.09 to 0.18	—
Gapinski (1986)	Opera, London	1972–1983	Pooled time series	−0.12 to −0.25	0.13 to 0.15	—
Gapinski (1986)	Symphony, London	1972–1983	Pooled time series	−0.19 to −0.35	0.44 to 0.65	—
Gapinski (1986)	Dance, London	1972–1983	Pooled time series	−0.18 to −0.81	0.21 to 2.28	—
Luksetich and Lange (1995)	Symphony Orchestras, USA	1975–1987	Pooled time series	−0.16 to −0.42	—	—
Garboua and Montmarquette (1996)	Theater, France	1987	Cross section	−1.00 to −1.47	—	—
Werck and Heyndels (2007)	Theater, Flanders	1980–2000	Time series	−0.14 to −0.16	—	1.72 to 2.35
Zieba (2009)	Theater, Germany	1965–2000	Time series	−0.26 to −0.43	0.50 to 0.60	0.60 to 1.22
Zieba (2011)	Theater, Austria and Switzerland	1969–2004	Time series	−0.12 to −0.53	—	0.34 to 0.78
Laamanen (2013)	Opera, Finland	2001–2009	Time series	−1.16	1.00	—
Zieba (2016)	Theater, opera, operetta and musicals, Austria	1972–2011	Time series	−0.41 to −0.48	—	0.81 to 2.02

Sources: Lévy-Garboua and Montmarquette (1996); Werck and Heyndels (2007); Zieba (2009, 2011, 2016, pp. 191–221, 208–216); Laamanen (2013).

Using hypothetical data from the same source, we can also calculate the cross-elasticity of demand for theater tickets with respect to the composite price of complementary goods, such as transportation to the theater and restaurant meals:

$$\varepsilon_{tc} = \frac{\Delta Q_t}{\Delta P_c} \times \frac{P_c}{Q_t} = \frac{-1,600}{1} \times \frac{12}{106,800} = \frac{-19,200}{106,800} = -0.18. \qquad (5.17)$$

Because the coefficient d, relating quantity of theater tickets demanded to the price of substitutes, carries a positive sign, the cross-elasticity with respect to the price of substitutes in Equation (5.16) is appropriately positive. On the other hand, the coefficient e, relating quantity of theater tickets to the price of complementary goods, is negative. Hence, in Equation (5.17), the cross-elasticity with respect to the price of complements is appropriately negative.

5.4   Expected Values of the Price Elasticity of Demand in the Performing Arts

Using econometric techniques, analysts have estimated the actual values of the price and income elasticities of demand for the live performing arts in several countries and over a number of different time periods. This book is not the appropriate place to explain either the complexities of such techniques or their limitations. In Table 5.3, we simply present a selection of results. However, before discussing them, it is useful to work out what elasticity values we would expect for the performing arts on the basis of prior knowledge.

It was pointed out in Chapter 4 that the price elasticity of demand for any consumer good depends primarily on the availability and quality of substitutes. If we think of the live performing arts as forms of entertainment or, even more generally, of recreation, then they have a good many substitutes, including books, newspapers and magazines, motion pictures, television and radio broadcasts, streaming of films or music, video games, eating out, spectator sports, and even recreational activities. Indeed, the list could be extended to include anything else that people might do in their leisure hours. The availability of such a large number of substitutes, of so many opportunities competing for the consumer's leisure time and spending power, suggests that we should expect a fairly high price elasticity of demand for the live performing arts.

There is an important contrary force, however. The live performing arts are almost certainly an acquired taste, meaning one that grows stronger with exposure, and the effect of that is surely to make substitutes less acceptable. Those who acquire a taste for ballet, opera, or the theater become "hooked" on the live performances.[1] Versions on film, video, or television may be pleasant, but they are no substitute for the real thing. As the passion of such devotees grows stronger, they become less concerned about the price of admission. In short, their demand becomes relatively price inelastic.

The same argument works in reverse for those who are outside the established audience. The arts are an acquired taste that they have not acquired. Few experiences can be more boring than an evening spent at a symphony concert, opera, or ballet by someone who has no understanding or appreciation of these art forms. Such people will not be easily drawn into the audience simply by lower ticket prices. Again, the acquired taste effect is to hold down the price elasticity of demand.

5.4.1 Empirical Results and Their Implications: Price Elasticity

Most studies have shown the demand for attendance at the live performing arts to be price inelastic. Table 5.3 shows the findings of eight investigations. Estimates of price elasticity are presented in Column 5. Only Garboua and Montmarquette found price elasticity to be higher than 1. The other seven estimates range from a low of 0.05 to a high of 0.53.

If these price elasticities seem surprisingly low, one reason may be that most performing arts institutions are in the not-for-profit sector of the economy. As we argue in Chapter 7, they are strongly motivated toward holding ticket prices down in order to increase attendance. But at low prices, demand is very likely to become inelastic, as illustrated in Table 5.1.

The implication that some analysts have drawn from these findings is that if performing arts institutions in the nonprofit sector are finding it difficult to balance their budgets, they may be setting ticket prices too low; for if demand is price inelastic, attendance will not fall very much if ticket prices are raised, and total revenue will increase substantially. In the hypothetical case illustrated in Table 5.1, for example, if the firm were selling tickets at a price of $5, its total revenue would be $75, but if it raised its price to $6, revenue would increase to $84.

Several cautions are in order, however. The first is suggested by the importance of private donations in helping to support nonprofit arts institutions. It has been argued that performing arts firms in the nonprofit sector are not seeking to extract maximum revenue from ticket sales alone. Instead, they look at revenues from the combination of ticket sales and private donations, and they may well believe (perhaps correctly) that the additional revenue obtainable by charging higher ticket prices across the board would be more than offset by a reduction in donations from the segment of the audience (perhaps as high as 40%) who now willingly offer donational support (see Chapter 13).

A second point to keep in mind is the distinction between the demand for the output of a single firm and that for an entire industry. The works cited here estimate the elasticity of the demand curve faced by the performing arts industry (or some major sector of it), not the demand curve faced by an individual firm. We would normally expect the firm's demand curve to be more elastic than that of the industry since elasticity rises with the availability of substitutes, and unless the single firm enjoys a local monopoly, the outputs of other local performing arts institutions are available to consumers as substitutes. Thus, the individual firm may face a price-elastic demand curve, even though the industry does not. In that case, a single firm, by raising its prices while its competitors did not do so, would diminish rather than increase its own revenue. Only if all firms in each market raised their prices simultaneously would each be able to enjoy higher revenues.

Table 5.3 also presents several estimates of the cross-elasticity of demand between the performing arts and their substitutes. As expected, these cross-elasticities are all positive, indicating that when the price of a substitute good rises, the demand for attendance at the performing arts increases. Surprisingly, the cross-elasticity turns out to be stronger than the own-price elasticity in most of these studies.

5.5   Expected Value of the Income Elasticity of Demand in the Performing Arts

On the basis of a priori reasoning alone, most economists would probably expect the demand for admission to the performing arts to be income elastic, that is, to have an income elasticity greater than 1.0. They would argue that life's essentials – food, clothing, shelter, and medical care – enter the budget first, and that goods such as tickets to the theater or opera, like trips to the Riviera or the Bahamas, cannot be considered until income reaches a fairly comfortable level. The statistical consequences of such a consumption pattern will be that as we go up the income scale from poor to rich, we find spending on the live performing arts increasing faster than income. Therefore, a study comparing consumption patterns across income classes at a given moment in time would show the income elasticity of demand for the arts to be greater than 1.0.

The same result would be expected if consumption patterns were studied through time instead of cross-sectionally. As living standards rise, more consumers pass over the threshold at which they can begin to spend on the arts. Consequently, spending on arts will increase faster than income, resulting in an income elasticity greater than 1.0.

5.5.1   Empirical Results: Income Elasticity

Two of the studies presented in Table 5.3 found the income elasticity of demand for admission to the performing arts to be in the range of around 1.0. Two further studies found it to be either below or above that level. If we take 1.0 to be the "consensus result," it is a good deal lower than many observers would have expected, given their belief that the arts behave as a luxury good in the consumer's budget.

One explanation for this outcome is suggested by the consideration of the way the need to allocate time influences consumer behavior. In Chapter 4, we assumed (implicitly) that consumption requires the expenditure only of money. In fact, it also requires time, and the amount of time available to each consumer is strictly limited by the clock. Hence, as income rises, the amount of income available per hour of consumption time increases, as does the value that consumers place on an hour of that time. Consequently, as their incomes rise, consumers are expected to substitute consumption of goods which use relatively little time for those that require more time. Attendance at the live performing arts is a fairly time-intensive activity, especially when round-trip travel is added to performance time. Hence, there is an adverse effect of time cost on attendance as income rises that tends to offset the positive "pure income effect" of greater buying power. The measured income elasticities shown in Table 5.3 are the net result of a positive pure income effect, offset in part by a negative time cost effect.

If this sounds too abstract, consider the choice between listening to a recording at home and attending a live performance in the concert hall. No doubt listening at home has gained in popularity for a number of reasons, including revolutionary improvements in audio technology and the low price and high durability of recordings, often only a mouse-click away, as compared with concert tickets. But the time factor is important, too: Mahler's Third Symphony can be heard at home in an hour and forty-three minutes. To enjoy it in the concert hall requires that plus an hour or two of time spent getting there and back.

Above in this chapter, we reviewed the connection between income elasticity and economic growth and pointed out that if the income elasticity of demand for a product is around 1.0, then, at constant relative prices, the industry producing the good could be expected to grow at about the same annual rate as the economy as a whole. If the estimates presented in Table 5.3 are accurate and generalizable, that would appear to be the long-run prospect for the performing arts industry. That's not quite an "arts boom" according to the definition offered in Chapter 2, but most arts advocate would probably settle for it as good enough.

5.6 Summary

This and Chapter 4 have dealt with the demand for the arts. We have suggested that the arts share most attributes of ordinary consumer goods, and that the standard tools of demand analysis can usefully be brought to bear on them. In this chapter we developed the concept of elasticity of demand and showed how knowledge of elasticity values can help arts administrators in the conduct of their business. Price elasticity in particular – because it affects revenue from ticket sales and therefore potentially influences budget deficits and fiscal health – is relevant not only to individual arts companies and institutions but also to those concerned with public policy toward the arts.

In the next two chapters the focus shifts to the supply side: We examine production, supply, and the behavior of producing firms in the live performing arts. On the supply side, we find some interesting divergences between the arts and the more usual sorts of goods and services, but the tools of economic analysis prove no less applicable, for all that.

SUGGESTIONS FOR FURTHER READING

Refer to Brickley et al. (2021) for an explanation of how price elasticity changes along a linear demand curve and for a practical introduction to methods of estimating actual demand functions.

The interested reader may consult any of a number of econometrics texts to gain a better understanding of how to estimate income elasticities of demand (see, e.g., Wooldridge, 2010, esp. chapter 2).

PROBLEM SET

5.1 The information in the accompanying table pertains to the annual blockbuster run for a local theater company and is the basis for the questions that follow.

    a. Plot the demand curve; calculate and plot the average total cost curve. Describe the result, especially note any oddities or problems. Provide an explanation for a variable cost figure of $0.

Fixed costs:	$160,000
Variable costs:	$0
Theater capacity:	800
Number of performances:	20

Demand data	
Ticket price	Ticket sales
$10.00	13,000
9.50	14,200
9.00	15,000
8.50	15,600
8.00	16,000
7.50	16,300

b. Calculate the total revenue and income or earnings gap for each level of output. What would you contend is the optimum ticket price? Explain. Note any contradictions.

c. Calculate the price elasticity of demand for the *first*, *middle*, and *last* pair of price–output combinations. Is this consistent with your total revenue calculations above? Explain.

5.2 Suppose the following is the demand equation for quantity (Q_d) of orchestra tickets:

$$Q_d = 1000 - 800P + 10Y + 200P_t, \qquad (5.18)$$

where P, the price of an orchestra ticket = $25
   Y, the household income = $10,000
   P_t, the price of a theater ticket = $26
   Preliminary: describe the essence of the demand equation.

a. Calculate the number of orchestra tickets sold currently.

b. Suppose the ticket manager is considering raising orchestra ticket prices to $27. Then:
   i. How many tickets will be sold if this decision is implemented?
   ii. Calculate the price elasticity of demand.
   iii. What will happen to earned revenues if ticket prices are raised?

c. Given the original information, suppose the *theater* reduces ticket prices to $23. Then:
   i. How many tickets will the orchestra sell?
   ii. Calculate the cross-price elasticity of demand.
   iii. What (if any) orchestra ticket price will restore the lost revenue?

d. Do any pricing strategies gain support from the above? Comment.

NOTE

1 Following Scitovsky (1976), we might say that committed arts patrons, having invested in their "consumption skills," more easily achieve a return to that investment.

6 Production and Cost in the Performing Arts

LEARNING OBJECTIVES

By the end of this chapter, readers should be able to:

- Understand the process of production in the performing arts
- Evaluate how to measure output
- Understand the nature and types of costs
- Explain the difference between costs in the short-run and long-run

Chapters 3–5 dealt with audiences for the arts and with the measurement and analysis of the economic demand those audiences generate in their role as arts consumers. The concept of supply was introduced in summary fashion in Chapter 4 to show how supply and demand interact in the market to yield the prices paid by consumers. We now take a closer look at the supply side. The technical process of production in the performing arts is examined in this chapter. In Chapter 7, we analyze the way in which the performing arts firm finds the optimum price–output combination by bringing together information on market demand and on its own production costs. Production and supply are organized very differently in the visual arts than in the performing arts and so are treated in Chapter 10. These chapters may be particularly appreciated by those with aspirations to manage art institutions in a most efficient way.

6.1 The Measurement of Output

In analyzing the economics of production, economists customarily begin with a concept called a "production function," a symbolic representation of how inputs link to outputs. We can write an implicit equation of the form $Q = f(K, L)$, which is a way of saying that the quantity of output depends on the capital (K) and labor (L) inputs. For example, a symphony orchestra combines musicians (L), their instruments (K), and a performance hall (more K) to produce concerts (Q).

Most examples of the production function and production have conventionally come from agriculture or manufacturing, probably because the measurement of output in those industries is relatively straightforward. A farm produces bushels of wheat or gallons of milk. A factory turns out yards of cloth, tons of steel, or cases of beer. In the service industries, including the arts, it is typically much harder to measure output. First, it may be difficult even to define satisfactory quantitative units. How do you measure the output of a bank or a police department or an art museum? Second, in the service industries a quality dimension may be important, and yet even harder to identify than quantity. For many kinds of agricultural or manufactured products, it is possible to define standard qualities. That is rarely the case in the arts. No one would argue that a symphonic performance by an amateur group is equal in quality to that of the finest professional orchestras. Yet how much different is it, and who among the general population could tell the difference? Even though we know that quality is of the very essence in the arts, we are generally at a loss to measure it directly and must fall back instead on indirect measures, or "proxies."

6.2   Output in the Performing Arts

Throsby and Withers (1979, 11ff.) discussed four possible measures of output for a performing arts firm:

1. *Number of performances.* From the point of view of cost, or supply, this is undoubtedly a good measure, since a substantial part of production cost is cost incurred per performance in the form of wages, salaries, rent, electricity, and the like.
2. *Number of separate productions.* From the artistic point of view, this may be an important measure of output. A company that puts on thirty performances each of *Hamlet*, *The Three Sisters*, and *A Streetcar Named Desire* is, in some sense, producing more artistic experience than one that concentrates on producing ninety performances of *Hamlet* alone (Throsby and Withers, 1979, p. 12). And costs, too, vary directly with the number of productions as well as the number of performances.

   While the number of performances or the number of separate productions are useful output measures with reference to cost or supply, they are deficient in two respects. First, they are not units in terms of which the demand for output can be brought into the analysis, since patrons commonly buy single seats rather than the entire house. Second, they do not measure the number of "artistic experiences" that occur in connection with a performance, which depends on the number of people who actually attend it. We therefore consider two more possibilities.
3. *Number of tickets available for sale.* This is the product of (number of performances) × (capacity of house). Since this measure is denominated in terms of seats, it does allow us to deal with demand in the same analysis as production and cost. Thus, it overcomes the first deficiency cited. However, it does not overcome the second since available tickets will not necessarily all be sold.
4. *Number of tickets sold.* This is also referred to as paid admissions and equals (number of performances) × (capacity of house) × (percent utilization of capacity). This concept measures the actual number of artistic experiences provided by a given performance, thus overcoming both of the deficiencies just cited. However, when used to measure output and cost, it introduces other difficulties that are discussed in Chapter 7. Therefore, in Chapter 7, when setting up a model of the economics of a performing arts firm, we employ the number of tickets available for sale, rather than the number of them actually sold, as the measure with which to calibrate both demand and supply.

In light of the digital distribution of cultural content by increasingly many performing arts firms, perhaps we could offer some additional thoughts to the categorization above. The number of tickets for sale or tickets sold could be calculated separately for performances broadcasted online. Here the calculation would change in the way that capacity constraints do not apply, since in the digital realm, there are no limitations in the number of seats. However, setting up a platform offering digital content is not easy and generates high fixed cost; hence, usually only large performing arts organizations can afford it (we will return to these issues in more detail in Chapter 15).

6.3   Some Basic Cost Concepts

To construct a model of the economics of the performing arts firm, we need not only a usable measure of output but also an appropriate set of cost concepts. Let us begin with the fundamental economic definition of cost. The true (or "real") cost of any endeavor, according to economists, is measured by the value of the resources that are used to carry it out. The value of those resources, in turn, is measured by the utility of the other products that were forgone when resources were used in this endeavor, rather than in the next best alternative. Since cost is thus based on the value of forgone opportunities, this has come to be known as the doctrine of "opportunity cost." Consider the following illustration. Many localities have a community orchestra staffed entirely by volunteers, and these organizations frequently offer "free" concerts to the public. Most of us would agree that the availability of these cultural events is a boon to the local citizenry, and we would particularly appreciate the fact that they are offered at no charge. But are they really free? Economists would have to say no. Although musicians, administrators, and others contribute their time "free of charge" to such enterprises, we have to recognize that time and creative energy are scarce resources. To the extent they are used in producing a community performance, they are not available for other potentially valuable pursuits. The lawyer who volunteers her time to draw up the articles of incorporation for the community orchestra is forgoing the use of her time and talents in serving other clients. Likewise, the economist playing percussion for the orchestra on rehearsal and concert evenings might have used his time carrying out research, consulting, or similar pursuits. Hence, while we may regard a community concert as "free," in fact, it is not. Many resources are used up in its production, even though there may be no explicit cost or direct money outlay for some of them. The concept of opportunity cost is particularly important when one is making judgments about the welfare effects of economic policies. We make use of it in Chapter 12 when we take up the following question: Should the government subsidize the arts?

6.4   Production Costs

The standard notions of production cost that economists have used in developing the abstract "theory of the firm" are perfectly applicable in the performing arts and are defined in this chapter. An important initial distinction must be drawn between fixed and variable costs of production. Fixed costs are those that do not vary with the level of output in the short run, including things such as the cost of plant and equipment, long-term salary contracts, debt service, insurance, and rent (if production premises are not owned). They vary with the scale of the undertaking, but once the firm sets up in business at a given scale, they are fixed and do not vary with short-run fluctuations in the level of output.

Variable costs, on the other hand, are those that do change as the level of output within the given size establishment fluctuates in the short run. A list would include costs such as wages, raw materials and supplies, and telephone and electric power charges.

Total fixed costs, TFC, and total variable costs, TVC, are measured per unit of time (say, a month or a year). Dividing by the quantity of output in the same time period (Q), we obtain the following measures of average unit cost:

$$\text{Average fixed cost } (\text{AFC}) = \text{TFC}/Q$$
$$\text{Average variable cost } (\text{AVC}) = \text{TVC}/Q$$
$$\text{Average total cost } (\text{ATC}) = \text{AFC} + \text{AVC}.$$

To ensure efficient management of the resources available to a performing arts firm, it is important to understand and monitor the cost structure. In particular, knowing the difference between fixed costs and variable costs is crucial for making the right decisions about expenses, and this in turn has a direct impact on the financial health of a firm. For example, a performing arts firm with few performances and a low attendance may be better off by accepting relatively higher variable costs and lower fixed costs. The same may be true for a firm that sees large fluctuation in demand and is unable to carry the associated risks of unforeseeable demand. In Chapter 8, we will look more closely at how the Opera de Oviedo in Spain has decreased their cost and sustained the years after the financial crisis of 2008 without loses, but we reveal already now that much of this was possible due to an optimization in their cost structure.

Moreover, knowing how high are fixed and variable costs is essential for identifying the right ticket price. We return to this in Chapter 7, when we look at when a performance "breaks even," that is, reaches a point at which enough many tickets have been sold to cover all costs. The knowledge of the cost structure can also be used to identify economies of scale. As fixed costs are spread over a larger number of tickets, the cost per ticket decreases, and this has implications for decision-making (more on this below).

Finally, the concept of marginal cost (MC) is indispensable in analyzing the behavior of producing firms. MC is the additional cost incurred in producing one more unit of output. Since fixed costs do not rise when output increases in the short run, MC necessarily equals the rise in total variable costs, when output increases by one unit. Algebraically, we can write

$$\text{MC} = \Delta \text{TVC} / \Delta Q.$$

Whenever deciding about supplying an additional unit of output, whether selling another ticket or offering another performance, the MC will be essential for making the right decision. For example, if the revenue obtained from an additional performance is higher than the MC of producing it, the performing arts institution will be financially better off organizing another show. However, if the revenue is below the MC, offering another performance may not be a wise move, as it would bring losses. For breakeven, the only viable alternative would be to increase the ticket price to recoup the losses. But even then, it is uncertain that the audiences will agree to pay it. In any case, the MC is an important metric to be considered in decisions about how much to offer, and we will continue with these concepts in Chapter 7.

6.4.1 Production Costs for a Theatrical Enterprise

In this chapter and in Chapter 7, we use a hypothetical theatrical enterprise as the prototype for production in the performing arts. We will begin by thinking about the enterprise in question as a commercial venture of the sort typical in the Broadway theater. (It is shown in Chapter 7 that the same production model is applicable as well to the noncommercial theater and such other nonprofit enterprises as opera and ballet companies.) The distinction between fixed and variable costs is very clear in a theatrical enterprise. Fixed costs are the expenses of mounting a production, what Throsby and Withers refer to as the "setting up costs." (Throsby and Withers, 1979, p. 13). These are incurred before a play opens and are in no way affected by the length of its subsequent run. Included among those fixed costs are items such as the cost of scenery, costumes and props, rehearsal wages to the cast, the director's basic fee, stagehands' wages, preopening night advertising and publicity, theater rental, and office, legal and audit expenses. Table 6.1 shows this using data for 1,953 US professional not-for-profit theaters in 2019. The production and development costs, including both payroll and nonpayroll costs, averaged $2.3 million and account for close to 30% of total expenses. Most of these costs are paid in advance of opening night by the producer, investing his or her own capital as well as funds obtained from other "backers" who become partners in the venture.

Table 6.1 Average expenses for US professional non-for-profit theatres in 2019 (in thousand US dollars)

Type of expense	2019
Artistic payroll	1,527
Administrative payroll	1,895
Production/tech payroll	1,302
Total payroll	4,725
General artistic nonpayroll	301
Royalties	179
Production/tech nonpayroll	714
Development/fundraising nonpayroll	302
Marketing/front-of-house/education	844
Occupancy/building/equipment maintenance	690
Depreciation	337
General management/operations	322
Total expenses	8,414
Total number of shows	28,332

Source: Theatre Communications Group's, *Theatre Facts*, 2019.

In a theatrical enterprise, variable costs are the operating expenses of the show, which begin on an opening night and continue at more or less the same rate for each performance. The most important of these costs are salaries of actors and stage and company managers, wages of stagehands and technical crew, and expenses for advertising and publicity. The hope of theatrical investors is that box office receipts will be more than sufficient to cover the operating costs as the play runs, including the shares going to the author and the theater, providing a surplus sufficient not only to pay back their investment but also to yield a profit.

6.4.2 How Unit Cost Varies with Output

To analyze the output and pricing decisions of performing arts firms (as we do in Chapter 7), it is necessary to show how their unit costs vary with the level of output. Following the conventional approach of microeconomic theory, we do this by plotting "cost curves" on a diagram that shows unit costs on the vertical axis and quantity of output on the horizontal, as shown in Figure 6.1. To measure the quantity of output, we choose number of performances (equivalent to "length of run"), since, as already argued, that is the unit of quantity to which the important category of variable costs is most directly related. It is important to note that, in this analysis input, prices are assumed constant. The variation of unit cost with output arises from forces inherent to the production process rather than from changes in wage rates or materials prices.

Curves showing AFC, AVC, and ATC are displayed in Figure 6.1. The AFC curve, TFC/Q, falls sharply over an initial range of outputs but appears almost to level off as the number of performances (i.e., length of run) reaches a high level. The character of this curve is mathematically determined by the fact that $AFC = TFC/Q$, and the numerator TFC is a constant. Therefore, when Q first increases beyond zero, the value of the quotient TFC/Q declines very rapidly. For example, suppose $TFC = 60$. Then as Q increases from 1 to 2 to 3, AFC falls from 60 to 30 to 20. But when Q is already large, further increases reduce the value of the quotient only a little. For example, as Q goes from 40 to 41 to 42, AFC declines only from 1.50 to 1.46 to 1.43. In fact, the AFC curve necessarily takes the form of a rectangular hyperbola, a geometric figure for which the product of the values on the two axes equals a constant. In this instance, since by definition $AFC = TFC/Q$, it is also the case that $AFC \times Q = TFC$. What are the economic implications of all this? Forsaking mathematics in favor of plain common sense, the declining AFC curve simply shows the process that business people refer to as "spreading your overhead."

The AVC curve in Figure 6.1 is drawn as a horizontal straight line. Its height above the quantity axis represents AVC of putting on a single performance of the given production. AVC is constant as output (i.e., the number of performances) increases because the inputs of labor and materials required are identical for every performance no matter how long the show runs.

MC, it should be recalled, equals the additional variable cost required to produce one more unit of output. But if AVC is constant as output rises, then the additional variable cost entailed by one more unit is always equal to the average that has been required up to that point. Thus, when AVC is constant, MC necessarily equals AVC and is also constant. Therefore, in Figure 6.1, the AVC curve also represents MC and is so labeled.

Average total cost equals the sum of AVC and average fixed cost. In Figure 6.1, the ATC curve is therefore drawn as the sum, in the vertical direction, of AVC plus AFC. Since AVC

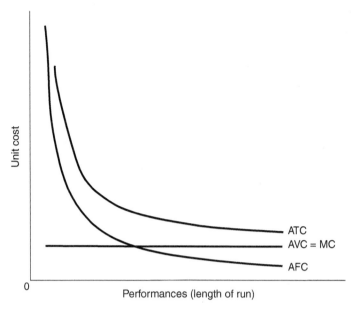

Figure 6.1 Performing arts costs and output.

is parallel to the quantity axis, the ATC curve lies at a constant distance above AFC. Like the latter, it falls sharply at first but appears almost to level off as quantity increases.

6.4.3 The Arts as a Special Case

It is a singular feature of production in the performing arts that AVC and MC are constant for all outputs. Readers familiar with the elementary principles of economics may recall that in the usual cases of manufacturing or farm production analyzed in microeconomics, the short-run AVC and MC curves are always U-shaped, and the outcome of every application turns out to be determined by their upward-sloping right-hand branches. Why are the conditions of production so fundamentally different in the live performing arts? In the usual cases, production is carried on under conditions such that the law of diminishing returns applies when the firm increases output in the short run. The law of diminishing returns says that when variable inputs (such as labor and materials) are applied in uniformly increasing doses to a fixed input (such as a factory or a farm), the increments of output obtained per added dose of inputs will eventually begin to diminish. But if the increments to output per added unit of input diminish, then the unit cost of additional output, which we have defined as MC, must be rising, and if MC is increasing then AVC must also increase. Hence, the MC and AVC curves eventually turn upward because of diminishing returns in production. In the performing arts, however, production is organized in such a way that the law of diminishing returns does not come into play. Each performance is a repetition of the same "production process" as the previous one. Output of the firm increases because we measure output by performances, but inputs are used over and over again in the same proportion as before. Thus, the conditions under which diminishing returns would occur are simply not present. This has implications for the performing arts manager in the sense that offering more performances will decrease the cost per performance and hence may lead to better financial outcomes. However, what has to be considered is the demand, and the question whether additional performances will retain a high enough audience so that the additional cost of a given performance is covered.

6.5 Summary

This chapter has extended the economic analysis of production and cost to the performing arts. Despite measurement difficulties, the arts seem to lend themselves well to this adaptation. In Chapter 7, we examine the economic behavior of firms in the live performing arts. A distinction is drawn between profit-maximizing firms, such as producers for the Broadway theater in New York City or West End in London, and firms organized on a not-for-profit basis, such as the typical resident theater company outside of New York City or London. We show that for both types of arts producers, the cost concepts and cost curves developed in this chapter play a crucial role in the explanation of behavior. Next, we will turn our attention on how to use this knowledge in order to set ticket prices.

PROBLEM SET

6.1 A theater director hires you as an analyst and assigns you the task to monitor and evaluate the institution's performance. The theater is located in a wealthy neighborhood, and it is usually sold out, as it has a low seating capacity.

  a. Provide an exhaustive list of possible measures of output.

  b. Assess critically which of the listed measures should be preferred for the institution in question.

  c. Explain how the performance of the theater could be measured beyond output? Be creative.

6.2 A smaller orchestra employs musicians. Suppose labor is the only variable input and generates variable cost (VC). All musicians are paid 20 euro per hour.

  a. Complete the table below calculating labor (L), average variable cost (AVC), and marginal cost (MC) for the first eight units of output (Q) in the short run.

  b. Draw a graph showing AVC and MC.

  c. Explain why AVC will be increasing for output where MC is higher than the AVC.

Q	VC	L	AVC	MC
1	20			
2	40			
3	60			
4	80			
5	120			
6	160			
7	240			
8	320			

6.3 By early 1800s, the German firm Breitkopf & Härtel was publishing music by Beethoven, Haydn, Mendelssohn, Schumann, and many others. One of the owners of the firm, Gottfried Christoph Härtel, was carefully measuring the production cost and using the information to make decisions. Härtel calculated that printing of a musical sheet was associated with the fixed cost of 900 pfennings (the cost of typesetting) and marginal cost (MC) of 5 pfennings per copy (Scherer, 2001).

   a. Write down the formulas for total cost, average total cost, average variable cost (AVC), and MC.

   b. Draw a graph showing the average total cost, AVC, and MC functions.

   c. Explain what are the economies of scale in this context.

   d. Advise Härtel deciding how much should he pay a composer for a one-page music sheet if the publisher expects to sell 300 copies of the composition at 15 pfennings per copy.

7   Firms and Markets in the Performing Arts

LEARNING OBJECTIVES

By the end of this chapter, readers should be able to:

- Understand how performing arts firms will set ticket prices
- Determine the supply of firms at different price levels
- Explain the difference between nonprofit and commercial sector
- Describe the implications of economies of scale

In this chapter, we investigate the economic choices – especially the price-output choices – made by performing arts firms. These choices are largely determined by the following factors:

1. The level and character of consumer demand for the firm's output
2. The method and cost of producing that output
3. The type of market in which the firm operates
4. The firm's artistic and financial objectives
5. The availability of government subsidies or of private donational support

Consumer demand was analyzed in Chapters 4 and 5 and production and cost in Chapter 6. We begin this chapter with a discussion of market types and how they influence the behavior of performing arts firms.

7.1   Types of Markets

Conventional economic analysis recognizes four types of market structure, distinguished from one another by the size and number of suppliers and by whether the goods sold are homogeneous or differentiated. Homogeneous goods are products, such as wheat, steel, or potatoes, which are graded and standardized so effectively that buyers do not care which supplier they deal with for any given grade. Products are said to be differentiated if the unique features of style, quality, design, or brand name are sufficient to convince buyers that sellers are not offering virtually identical goods. Examples of differentiated products are automobiles, magazines, toothpastes, and theatrical productions.

7.1.1 Perfect Competition

Perfect competition exists when there is a large number of sellers of a homogeneous product, and no one seller is large enough in relation to the size of the market to influence the market price. When these conditions exist, suppliers treat market prices as given and concentrate on deciding how much to produce at those prices. Agriculture, which has both homogeneous products and large numbers of sellers, would come closer to being perfectly competitive than any other industry were it not for the pervasive influence of government farm policy in setting prices and regulating output.

The analysis of perfectly competitive markets occupies an important place in economics because even though few, if any, such markets exist, the price–quantity outcome under perfect competition is theoretically clear. It is also optimal in the sense that, as a result of competitive pressures, goods will be produced to satisfy consumer preferences at the least possible economic cost. Hence, perfect competition provides a very useful theoretical benchmark with which to compare outcomes in other types of markets. (See further discussion in Chapter 11.) No market in the performing arts, however, comes close to being perfectly competitive, and there are at least two reasons for this. First, the number of sellers is never large enough. Second, the goods sold are differentiated, rather than homogeneous, even when the same work of art is being produced. Lovers of classical music will not agree that one performance of a Beethoven symphony is just like another, much less that a Beethoven symphony is interchangeable with one by Shostakovich.

7.1.2 Pure Monopoly

At the opposite pole from perfect competition is pure monopoly, where there is only one seller of the good in question. If public regulation does not interfere (as it sometimes does), the firm is free to choose the price–quantity combination along the demand curve for its product that best satisfies its objectives. It should be noted, however, that a monopolist cannot force anyone to buy at high prices. Whatever price the firm chooses, the demand curve dictates the quantity that can be sold. Performing arts firms are sometimes monopolists within a predominantly local market. The price–output choices they make, however, will depend on whether they are in the commercial sector, in which case, they will be seeking to maximize profit, or in the not-for-profit sector, in which case, their motivation will be more complex. We examine both cases in this chapter.

7.1.3 Monopolistic Competition

Just as its name suggests, monopolistic competition is a type of market structure that blends elements of monopoly with elements of competition. Typically, the industry contains a moderate to large number of sellers, whose products are differentiated rather than homogeneous. Book publishing, shoe and apparel manufacturing, and automotive repair are examples of such industry. In each of these industries, there is competition because a large number of firms are selling goods or services that are close substitutes for one another. But there is an element of monopoly, as well, insofar as each firm has a monopoly over its own brand, type, quality, or design. However, it is a crucial characteristic of monopolistic competition that there are enough sellers so that each assumes its pricing decisions will not provoke a reaction from the others. Firms are, in others words, "price independent."

Among individual sectors of the performing arts industry, the Broadway theater can be accurately described as monopolistically competitive. Thirty or more plays and musicals open during a single season and certainly compete with each other for an audience. Yet each company clearly has a monopoly over its own show and sets prices on the assumption that its own policies will not provoke a response from competitors. If we adopt a broader definition, under which all the live performing arts make up a single industry, then the industry itself, in most large cities, is monopolistically competitive. The opera company, the symphony orchestra, the dance groups, and the resident theater companies compete with each other by offering products that are unique, and yet closely substitutable as forms of artistic entertainment.

7.1.4 Oligopoly

The final major type of market structure is oligopoly. Its basic characteristic is that a few very large firms, anywhere from, say, two to fifteen, dominate the market. A larger number of very small firms may be present, as well. The product of an oligopolistic industry may be either homogeneous – as, for example, with steel, cement, and petroleum products – or heterogeneous – as in the case of automobiles, airplanes, and household appliances. It is an essential feature of oligopoly that the number of major firms is small enough so that each assumes that the others will respond in some way to its own pricing decisions and, therefore, makes its decisions taking the probable responses to them into account. For example, if a major automobile manufacturer decides to reduce prices in order to boost sales, it certainly anticipates that its rivals will somehow respond, and its decision allows for that response. In other words, these firms, unlike monopolistic competitors, are "price interdependent."

The performing arts market in some cities may appear to have the characteristics of oligopoly since a few large institutions, say, a symphony orchestra, an opera company, and one or two resident theaters, may dominate the scene. In the Twin Cities of Minneapolis and St. Paul, the Minnesota Orchestra and the St. Paul Chamber Orchestra might be thought of as a "duopoly," a subcategory of oligopoly, and each is certainly cognizant of the marketing strategies of the other. Nevertheless, even in this last case, the oligopoly analysis does not apply especially well because performing arts firms other than the Broadway theater are usually operated as nonprofit enterprises and therefore are less likely to become involved in the competitive pricing strategies typical of oligopolies operating in large national markets.

7.2   Artistic and Financial Objectives

The objectives or goals of performing arts firms depend on whether they are in the commercial or the not-for-profit sector of the economy. If the former, it can be assumed that like other commercial enterprises, their objective is to maximize profits. The price and production policies that this implies are described below in this chapter.

The motivation of firms in the not-for-profit sector, as Throsby and Withers (1979, p. 14) suggest, is best understood by separating the dimensions of quality and quantity. Each performing arts institution chooses for itself some portion of the universe of art and some mixture of tradition and innovation. Within that realm, it tries to offer performances that satisfy its own standards of excellence. Thus, its quality objectives can be thought of as embodied in its choice of repertoire and standard of performance.

We argued in Chapter 6 that because of the way production is organized in the live performing arts, the firm does not run into diminishing returns in production. It does seem likely, however, that a form of diminishing returns is encountered when the firm seeks to attain the desired standard of quality in its productions. For example, choosing inputs so as to produce a desired level of quality as economically as possible is analogous to the problem the conventional manufacturing firm faces in trying to produce a given level of output at the lowest possible cost. The solution for the manufacturer is to use inputs in such proportions that, at the margin, each contributes the same quantity of output per dollar of expenditure on it. Employing MP for marginal product and P for the price that the firm pays for an input, the rule can be written algebraically as follows:

$$\frac{MP_x}{p_x} = \frac{MP_y}{P_y} = \cdots = \frac{MP_n}{P_n},$$

(7.1)

where x and y are among the n different production inputs used by a firm. In the case of a performing arts firm establishing a level of quality, the solution is to choose inputs in such proportions that each contributes at the margin the same boost to quality per dollar of expenditure. For example, a theatrical firm would try to arrange its budget so that an additional thousand dollars spent on scenery would yield the same increment to quality as an additional thousand spent on costumes or on hiring better actors. Diminishing returns plays a part in this process because using more of any one input (scenery, costumes, and actors) while holding the others constant does seem likely to yield diminishing increments to quality.

Of course, quality is usually a subjective matter, and we are not suggesting that it can be measured in quantitative units. What we are suggesting is that rational decision-making about quality requires that the firm's directors, using their best judgment, behave as if they could so measure it.

As for the quantitative goal, Throsby and Withers (1979, 14ff.) point out that performing arts firms in the nonprofit sector try "to make their product available to as large an audience as possible. Practitioners … tend to have a crusading spirit about their profession, and the larger the audience that can be attracted the happier they are." This attitude is easy to explain. The performer would obviously rather play to full houses than to empty ones. In addition, the members of the organization typically share a belief that art "is intrinsically good and socially necessary" and should therefore be displayed before the widest possible audience.

Even the most crusading entrepreneurs for the arts, however, cannot ignore economic realities. Their qualitative and quantitative goals are therefore pursued subject to the constraint that if the enterprise is to survive, its revenues must, in the long run, cover its costs. Combining the quantitative and qualitative objectives and the constraint of a balanced budget, Throsby and Withers (1979, p. 15) conclude that the motivation of a performing arts enterprise in the nonprofit sector can be described as follows: Over an appropriate period of time, the firm tries to maximize attendance, while presenting a repertoire that meets its own quality standards, subject to the constraint that revenues from the box office plus other sources must be sufficient to cover costs. The possible other sources of revenue are primarily government subsidies and (especially in the United States) private charitable donations. As will become clear in what follows, this formulation leads to clear predictions about pricing policies of arts enterprises – both with and without outside support.

7.3   A Model of the Firm in the Live Performance Arts

Figure 7.1 depicts the demand and cost situation facing a firm in the live performing arts. The diagram reproduces the average total cost and marginal cost curves already explained in Chapter 6. Average fixed cost is not shown separately. Because AFC = ATC – AVC, it can be read from the diagram as the vertical distance between those two curves. In Figure 6.1, the cost curves were drawn with the number of performances as the measure of quantity on the horizontal axis. In Figure 7.1, the number of performances is multiplied by the capacity of the house. Thus, the horizontal axis now measures quantity as the number of seats available for sale, increasing in the rightward direction as the number of performances increases. For example, if the house contains 1,000 seats, one performance = 1,000 seats, five performances = 5,000 seats, and so on. Costs, therefore, are now measured per available seat rather than per performance. This does not affect the shapes of the curves, only their height, as measured in dollars, on the vertical axis. The advantage of calibrating quantity this way is that since consumer demand is expressed in price per seat, it allows us to plot the demand and marginal revenue curves on the same diagram as the cost curves. These are shown as D and MR in Figure 7.1. (The concept of marginal revenue is explained earlier in Chapter 6.)

A demand curve for tickets, it should be noted, shows the number of seats sold at any given price. To argue that the number of seats sold equals seats available for sale and can be converted into the number of performances at a fixed ratio, we require the additional assumption that the house is sold out for every performance (at any rate, up to the last one). That assumption may seem unrealistic, but without it, the length of the run would be indeterminate in the model depicted in Figure 7.1. With it, the quantity scale can be thought of as measuring number of performances, length of run, or total attendance.

Throsby and Withers (1979) adopted a different strategy. They elected to use as a quantity measure the actual number of seats sold over the life of a given production. That has the advantage of dispensing with the assumption of a constantly sold-out house. In fact, Throsby and Withers assume, not implausibly, that attendance per performance will fall off toward the end of the run, so that if cost per performance is constant, the cost per seat sold will rise. That gives them a marginal cost curve that rises toward its right end as marginal cost curves do in the cases of manufacturing or agricultural firms, instead of remaining horizontal, as shown in Figures 6.1 and 7.1. But that upward slope, it should be noted, results not from diminishing returns in production, as in the conventional case, but from production conditions modified by factors arising on the demand side. Thus, their model makes the unit cost depend on the conditions of demand as well as supply, which violates the usual practice in the microeconomic analysis of

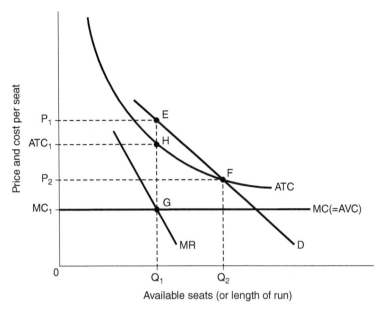

Figure 7.1 Price and output determination for a theatrical enterprise.

formulating independent explanations for supply and demand. We have chosen available seats, rather than seats sold, as the unit of output to avoid the melding of supply and demand factors and to maintain simplicity and clarity in the analysis.

7.3.1 Price, Output, and Profit in the Commercial Theater

Let us assume to begin with that the firm in question is producing a play for the Broadway theater. The firm's objective is to maximize profits by finding the best price-output combination for this production, where "output" equals the number of seats sold but also the length of run. The possible combinations are those that lie along the demand curve for the firm's play. Which will be the most profitable? The answer is that the firm should choose the price at which the last unit sold just adds as much to revenue as it costs to produce. In technical terms, this means that output should be carried to the point where the marginal revenue obtained from selling one more seat just equals the marginal cost of providing a performance for one more attendee. In Figure 7.1, MR intersects MC at point G when Q_1 seats are sold. We can see that this is the profit-maximizing output by reasoning as follows: To the left of G, MR lies above MC, indicating that additional sales would add more to revenue than to cost, thus boosting profits; to the right of G, MC lies above MR, so that additional sales would add more to cost than to revenue, thereby reducing profits. Profits are therefore greatest at point G. Moving vertically up to the demand curve from G, we see that Q_1 seats can be sold at a price of P_1, as indicated by point E. The profit-maximizing price and quantity for this production are therefore P_1 and Q_1.

At output Q_1, the average total cost per seat is ATC_1, as indicated at point H. Profit per seat is therefore $P_1 - ATC_1$, and the aggregate profit is $P_1 - ATC_1$, or the area of the rectangle P_1EHATC_1. We can describe the play depicted in Figure 7.1 as "a hit." The public's desire for tickets is strong enough that the demand curve lies considerably above the ATC curve for a range of possible outputs, and the play is able to earn back its costs plus a profit. If interest in the play had been so weak that the demand curve lay below the ATC curve at all price–output combinations, we would have to call the play "a flop," for there would be no price at which the producer could sell enough seats to break even, let alone earn a profit.

The performing arts are an example of what economists call a decreasing cost industry. Cost per seat falls continuously as output is extended through time because the fixed costs of mounting a production are spread over a larger and larger number of performances. Consequently, in the commercial sector, the longer the run, the greater the financial success. (As we see in Section 7.3.2, an analogous version of success applies in the not-for-profit sector.)

Our analysis of a Broadway production using Figure 7.1 has implied that the play would close after the number of performances is equivalent to Q_1 available seats. That conclusion, however, is based on the assumption that a single price (or, more realistically, a single range of prices) must be charged throughout the play's run. In fact, it may be profitable for the producer to extend the run beyond Q_1 by lowering prices. By the time Q_1 is reached with ticket prices at P_1, the production has recovered its fixed costs plus a profit. The additional cost of further output is only MC_1. If the producer can sell additional seats by reducing the price below P_1, while keeping it still above MC_1, it will pay to do so. The run can be profitably extended by the sale of "twofers" or by other off-price arrangements. This is a form of price discrimination through time. Like other forms of price discrimination (e.g., charging different fares for first-class and economy-class seats on airlines), it is a way of increasing the firm's profits by charging different prices to customers whose demands differ.

7.3.2 Price and Output in the Nonprofit Sector

Figure 7.1 can also be used to analyze the price–output decisions in the nonprofit sector. Assume initially that the production previously described as a commercial enterprise is now mounted instead by a not-for-profit theater company. The company's objective, as already argued, is to maximize attendance, at productions of suitable quality, subject to the constraint of balancing its budget. If no subsidies or private donations are available, it will try to produce the quantity of output at which price just covers the average total cost. The demand and the average total cost curves intersect at point F, indicating that the optimum price and quantity are P_2 and Q_2, respectively. Comparing this outcome with the result when the same play is produced commercially, we see that the ticket price is lower and total attendance (or the length of run) is greater under a not-for-profit organization.

It is unrealistic, however, when analyzing the nonprofit sector, to frame the analysis in terms of single productions. Most nonprofit performing arts companies put together a repertory of events each season. A resident theater group may mount four plays, an opera company two or three operas, a classical dance company half a dozen short- to medium-length ballets, combined into several evening-length performances. The model depicted in Figure 7.1 can handle this complication quite realistically. The quantity scale, total seats sold, now measures the "length of season" rather than the length of run, since the productions do not have individual "runs." Instead of applying to individual productions, the cost curves now refer to aggregates for the chosen repertory. Thus, total fixed costs are the aggregate production costs (i.e., setting-up costs) for the season. AFC declines because TFC/Q decreases as the season (Q) grows longer. AVC and MC now refer to the operating cost per production averaged over the season's repertory and are constant, as before.

Subscription sales now account for an important fraction of all admissions to nonprofit performing arts programs. Thus, it also makes good sense to draw a single demand curve (as we have done in Figure 7.1) that applies to the aggregate repertory rather than to think in terms of separate demands for individual productions.

Increased popularity for the offerings of a company over successive seasons would show up as a shift of the demand curve to the right. Assuming that the cost curves do not shift, the intersection of D and ATC would also occur further to the right. The increased quantity of tickets sold would indicate a longer season for the company.

For performing arts groups trying to establish themselves as permanent institutions, longer seasons are taken as an important sign of success. Imagine how difficult a professional career is for a musician or ballet dancer whose company guarantees only fifteen or twenty weeks' work over a whole year. Longer seasons strengthen a company immeasurably, both by augmenting performers' incomes and by giving them a greater opportunity to develop their skills. Undoubtedly, longer seasons also make it easier to retain top-notch performers and to design high-quality productions.

7.4   Production Costs in the Long Run

In analyzing production costs, economists draw a useful distinction between the long run and the short run. Up to this point, our analysis of production and cost has dealt only with the latter, which is defined as a period short enough so that one or more factors of production are effectively fixed in quantity. In the case of manufacturing – the conventional example dealt with in microeconomics – the fixed factor is plant and equipment. The short run is the period in which the manufacturer has to decide how much output to produce, and at what prices, from the firm's existing plant. The long run is defined as a period long enough so that *all* factors of production become variable. In the manufacturing case, that means a period long enough so that the firm could plan to build one or more new plants, discard old ones, or even go into a new line of business.

What are the analogous definitions in the live performing arts? In the case of plays offered in the commercial theater, the short run is the life of a single production. Over that period the play's production costs, comprising all expenses that were committed before opening night, are a fixed cost. The producer's decisions are limited to deciding how long the play should run and at what ticket prices. The long run in the commercial theater is a period over which the producer can contemplate mounting additional plays or musicals, different in type, larger or smaller in scale, in the same or other venues.

We argued that it is unrealistic to think in terms of single productions in the not-for-profit sector, since most companies put on a season or repertory of productions each year. This logic applies equally well to theater, opera, ballet and modern dance, and symphony concerts.

Accordingly, the short run for the nonprofit performing arts organization is best defined not as the run of a single production but as the length of one season. The season is the planning unit. The individual productions are conceived not singly but as a package, complementary to one another. While it may sometimes be possible to change course in midseason, that is rarely done. Thus, the production costs for a given season are essentially fixed once the season begins, which gives "the season" its economic character of being "the short run." The long run is then a period longer than a single season. In the long run, management can contemplate putting on more or less elaborate productions, a longer or shorter season, a season comprising a larger or smaller number of individual productions, or it can move to a different venue or even go out of business.

One of the most interesting questions that can be asked about any production process is: How do costs per unit of output behave when the scale of production increases? By scale, economists mean the size of the producing enterprise, with size measured by physical output when plant and equipment are operated at designed capacity. If we plot scale on the horizontal axis and average unit cost on the vertical, we generate the firm's long-run average cost curve. So another way of putting the preceding question would be: What is the shape of the firm's long-run average cost curve?

The question is interesting in part because there is no a priori answer; each industry has to be investigated empirically. Three possible long-run cost patterns are denoted as follows: economies of scale, if unit cost falls as the scale of output increases; constant returns to scale, if unit cost is unchanged; and diseconomies of scale, if unit cost rises. In most cases, the outcome will be some combination of these tendencies. In manufacturing, for example, firms in most industries enjoy economies of scale up to some minimum efficient size, after which there is a broad range of output marked by constant returns to scale. At very large scales, diseconomies may set in. Evidence on this last point, however, is hard to come by. Indeed, in a competitive world, we would not expect to find many firms that had expanded into a range where unit costs were increasing, since such behavior would be self-destructive.

7.4.1 Economies of Scale in the Live Performing Arts

Since the season is the planning unit for most nonprofit performing arts enterprises, length of season, as measured by the number of performances – or, for symphony orchestras, the number of concerts – is the appropriate indicator of scale for studying the behavior of costs in the long run. (This is analogous to the use of plant size as the measure of scale in the manufacturing case.)

The existence of economies of scale in the live performing arts has been confirmed empirically a number of times. Baumol and Bowen (1966, pp. 201–207, 479–481), probably the earliest to do an empirical study, found that for most of the eleven symphony orchestras in their sample, cost per concert fell significantly as the number of concerts per year increased. In the typical case, unit cost did not decline over the entire range of outputs. Rather, it reached a minimum at a point that varied across orchestras at somewhere from 90 to 150 concerts per year and then leveled off.

The authors speculated that the observed economies of scale probably arose from two sources. Most important would be the fact that up to some point an orchestra can play more concerts without investing in more rehearsal time. For example, if it sells subscriptions in three series (say, Thursday evenings, Friday evenings, and Sunday afternoons), it can perform the same music three times a week. If demand picks up to the point where a fourth series is justified, it can play the same music a fourth time without additional rehearsal expense. A second source of economies of scale (probably less important) is the fact that the administrative expense of running the orchestra need not increase with each increase in the number of concerts performed. Thus, "overhead" can be spread over more output, reducing the level of average fixed cost per concert as the season lengthens.

Savings analogous to both economies of scale should be available to producers of theatrical repertory, opera, ballet, or other kinds of dance. Hence, we would expect to find economies of scale operating in all kinds of live performance arts. An early study by Globerman and Book (1974) used a sample of Canadian symphony orchestras and theater companies to confirm the existence of economies of scale in orchestra performance up to a level of about 115 performances per year. For theater companies, they found that economies of scale extended much farther: "minimum cost per performance ... was obtained at approximately 210 performances." They surmised that the greater economies of scale available to theater groups reflected higher fixed costs per production in theatrical activity, as compared with symphony concerts.

Lange et al. (1985) also confirmed the existence of economies of scale for symphony orchestras. They found that average cost per concert declined as output rose from 1 to 65 concerts per year, was constant over the wide range between 67 and 177 concerts, and rose sharply at higher outputs. The authors speculated that greater commitments to touring or special events, or other differences in the type or quality of output, might explain the higher unit costs encountered by orchestras giving the most concerts per year, but they were unable to confirm that statistically.

Finally, Last and Wetzel (2010) studied the productivity of German public theaters from 1991 to 2005 and observed that these institutions did not operate on an optimal level. The authors' conclusion was that some theaters failed to exploit economies of scale.

7.5   The Effects of Donations and Grants

Firms in the commercial sector of the live performing arts do not receive government grants and are not eligible to accept tax-deductible charitable donations. Consequently, they rise or fall on their ability to sell tickets at the box office or (very rarely) to sell movie or other ancillary rights to their artistic properties. Nonprofit firms, on the other hand, do sometimes receive public funds and are also eligible to accept tax-deductible private donations. In fact, the principal reason they are organized on a not-for-profit basis is to become eligible for such tax-deductible private support. The Americans for the Arts organization estimates that charitable contributions by individuals, business firms, and foundations accounted for approximately 40% of total operating income of nonprofit performing arts institutions (Americans for the Arts, 2021). Indeed, such support is so important in the United States that we devote much of Chapter 13 to it.

Grants-in-aid from the federal government, through the National Endowment for the Arts, and from state and local governments, through their arts councils, are also significant

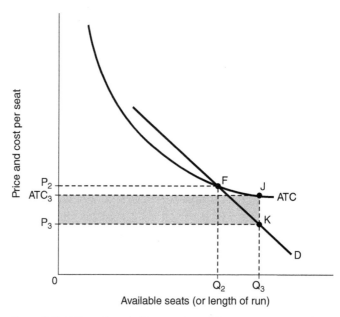

Figure 7.2 Effect of a subsidy on price and output: a nonprofit performing arts firm.

in the budgets of nonprofit firms. The arguments for and against public subsidies are carefully weighed in Chapter 13. This is the appropriate point, however, at which to examine the probable effects of both private donations and government grants on the price–output decisions of nonprofit performing arts producers.

Donations and grants may be given either with conditions attached that specify how they must be spent or as unrestricted contributions that can be used in whatever way the recipient chooses. Since aid to nonprofit performing arts institutions usually takes the unrestricted form, we assume it in the following analysis (see Throsby, 2008b).

Once the objective of nonprofit firms in the performing arts is understood, the probable effect of grants and donations on their price–output choices becomes clear. We have argued that their objective is to maximize attendance, while presenting a repertoire that meets self-imposed quality standards and is subject to the requirement of a balanced budget. Assume initially that the quality of the chosen repertoire is not affected by the availability of donations or grants. In that case, the effect of such contributions will be to allow the firm to reduce ticket prices and thus expand attendance. This result is illustrated in Figure 7.2, in which the demand and average total cost curves are carried over from Figure 7.1. (The marginal revenue and marginal cost curves have been omitted, since they are irrelevant when profit maximization is not the objective.) In the absence of donations or subsidies, the firm operates at point F. Q_2 tickets are sold at a price of P_2, which just covers the average total cost. When contributed income becomes available, prices can be set below the level of cost, by an amount that reflects the available subsidy. In this instance, they are reduced to P_3 (at point K) and attendance rises to Q_3. The average total cost per seat at output Q_3 is $\left(\text{ATC}_3\right)$, as indicated by point J. There is now a deficit per seat of $\text{ATC}_3 - P_3$. The aggregate deficit of $Q_3 \times \left(\text{ATC} - P_3\right)$ is indicated by the shaded rectangle and, if the firm's financial forecasts are accurate, just equals the amount of contributed income that is available. The diagram has been drawn so that the contributed income covers 40% of total expense, approximately the proportion that obtained in the performing arts during the 2010s (see, e.g., Voss et al., 2016).

It may be too restrictive, however, to assume that the quality of output established by a nonprofit performing arts firm is unaffected by the availability of contributed income. Although dollars can be wasted in the arts as elsewhere, it is nevertheless true that higher quality performances and productions generally cost more to put on. Consequently, it is likely that some firms will try to improve the quality of their productions or will choose a higher quality repertoire when financial aid is available to help cover the higher cost (Throsby and Withers, 1979, pp. 23–24). Indeed, donations and grants are sometimes given expressly for the purpose of improving performance or production quality. If the beneficiary responds to that stimulus by raising quality, the average total cost curve shown in Figure 7.2 would shift upward when donations or grants become available. Assuming demand to be unaffected by the change in quality, the decline in ticket prices and the rise in attendance would then be less than depicted in Figure 7.2. If, however, the demand curve were to shift upward in response to higher quality, there would be an additional impetus both to greater attendance and to higher prices. In either case, at the end of the process in which quality was adjusted, we would expect prices to be lower and quality and attendance higher than they would have been in the absence of contributed income.

It has already been pointed out that donations are nowadays an important source of income to nonprofit performing arts groups. Hansmann (1986) notes that a large fraction of the donations received from individuals appears to come "from people who actually attend the groups' performances." The willingness of these donors to contribute is likely to be inversely related to ticket prices. Consequently, he argues for (and develops) a theory of behavior in which the nonprofit firm explicitly takes into account the effect of its ticket prices on donations. He considers various possible objectives for the firm, among which the goal of maximizing aggregate revenue from ticket sales and donations is only one. Needless to say, his theory is far more complex than the one that has been presented in this chapter.

7.6 Institutional Size, Market Structure, and Innovation

Although donations and grants are sometimes given for the purpose of underwriting new productions or raising the general level of quality attained by performing arts companies, they may indirectly exert an opposite influence as well. Contributed income, especially when it is given in the form of "challenge grants," is usually associated with institutional growth. The receiving organization is encouraged not only to seek "matching" funds but also to add administrative staff assigned to development, marketing, and financial administration. Sometimes contributions are earmarked for the acquisition of a larger hall in which to perform. The inevitable result of such growth is a large increase in overhead costs, and that may, in subtle ways, affect artistic policy.

It has often been noticed that as institutions grow, they become more conservative. The very phrase "the establishment" connotes conventionality, inflexibility, and unwillingness to take risks. In a study of the repertories of English nonprofit theaters, O'Hagan and Neligan (2005) tested the hypothesis that institutional size is positively related to conventionality or, to put it the other way, negatively associated with innovation and risk taking. They obtained data on forty English theaters covering seasons of the late 1990s. O'Hagan and Neligan (2005) measured conventionality by means of an index equal to the average number of times that each play in a given theater's repertory was produced by all theaters covered by the study. High values of the conventionality index imply that there is conformity in the repertoire, while low values suggest innovativeness. O'Hagan and Neligan's (2005) results show that conventionality of repertory increases with institutional size, as measured by the size of the company's house. In other words, holding other variables constant, the more seats it has to fill by appeal to the market, the less innovative a company is likely to be. It is hard to avoid the conclusion that theatrical groups (and probably other performing arts institutions, as well) grow less creative as they become more successful, at least as success is measured in the marketplace.

7.6.1   Competition Encourages Artistic Innovation

But there is a second part to this story, leading to a more optimistic conclusion. An increase in subsidies as a proportion of total income was found to lower the conventionality index. As the authors put it: "Without subsidy, performing arts organizations may be forced to present mass-appeal shows, as submission to box office demand ensures greater financial security and very often survival." Hence, companies that, to a larger degree, depend on box office sales will tend to offer more conventional repertoires. On the other hand, performing arts companies that rely on state subsidies can afford to offer "riskier," more innovative repertoires.

Second, O'Hagan and Neligan (2005) find that the average index of conventionality was lower in London than elsewhere. The authors hypothesize that the much higher level of innovation found on the London stage is attributable in part to the intense competition with higher density and wider variety of theatres. Even though larger companies may be more conformist, larger markets apparently lead, by way of greater competition, to increased innovation.

These findings are encouraging because they suggest that as the audience for the arts grows larger in any locality and the number of local companies increases, competition will bring greater diversity, more risk taking, and increased creativity. Thus, in the longer run "more" may also mean "better."

7.7   Summary

In this chapter, we have presented a model of the performing arts firm – applicable alike in the fields of theater, ballet, opera, and symphony – that predicts how firms will set ticket prices and determine the length of run or, in the case of repertory production, length of season. It was shown that ticket prices will tend to be lower and, therefore, the length of run longer in the nonprofit than in the commercial sector. The model also suggests that economies of scale exist in the live performing arts: As the length of run or season increases, cost per seat declines.

The chapter opened with a description of the four kinds of market structure – perfect competition, oligopoly, pure monopoly, and monopolistic competition – that, according to standard economic analysis, differentially affect firms' price and output decisions. It was pointed out, however, that only the last two are relevant for the analysis of the arts. The chapter closed with a summary of O'Hagan and Neligan's research on the repertory of nonprofit theater companies (O'Hagan and Neligan, 2005), which showed that market structure also has a strong effect on qualitative aspects of performing arts output: Where the market is larger and therefore more competitive, as in London, theater companies are more innovative or, in artistic terms, more creative than are otherwise similar companies in smaller markets. The interesting implication of this finding is that as local audiences grow larger, local performing arts producers will probably become less risk averse and hence more creative.

SUGGESTIONS FOR FURTHER READING

Microeconomics textbooks, such as Perloff (2018), provide a more detailed and technical introduction to production functions.

See Neligan (2006) for information on how competition among theater companies and institutional size affects repertoire conventionality.

PROBLEM SET

7.1 You are asked to provide economic advice to a commercial theater. Suppose the theater has a marginal cost (MC) of producing output q given by $MC = 4 + 2q$. Assume that the market price for a theater performance is €10.

  a. What level of output will the theater produce?

  b. Suppose the theater's average variable cost is given by $AVC = 4 + q$ and fixed costs are known to be €4. What is the profit earned in the short run?

  c. How would your answer change if fixed cost was equal to €12, and should the theater continue its production in the short run?

7.2 A firm in the performing arts finds that, at its current level of production, marginal revenue is smaller than marginal cost $(MR < MC)$. Explain what it should do if it wants to maximize profits. Provide the intuition and support your answer with a graph.

7.3 In the chapter, we have approached the concept of production costs in the long run by focusing on the performing arts.

  a. Evaluate whether art museums can benefit from economies of scale. In particular, discuss what are the differences between the sources of economies of scale between art museums and the performing arts. Provide examples.

  b. Can you think about a situation when diseconomies of scale come into existence (that is when cost per unit of output increases with higher production)? What would be the implications for optimum output?

7.4 **(Advanced)** Suppose that to produce one concert, a string trio requires exactly three instruments: one violin (X), one viola (Y), and one cello (Z). Which of these three types of production functions – perfect substitutes, Cobb–Douglas, or perfect complements – seems most appropriate given the substitutability of these inputs? Hint: Ponder some specific examples, such as $Q = (1/3)(X + Y + Z)$, $Q = XYZ$, and $Q = \min\{X, Y, Z\}$. Students with no background in economics may also need to consult a microeconomics textbook, such as Perloff (2018).

8 Productivity Lag and the Financial Problem of the Arts

LEARNING OBJECTIVES

By the end of this chapter, readers should be able to:

- Explain the concepts of productivity lag and earnings gap
- Outline when an "artistic deficit" may arise
- Describe factors that may mitigate productivity lag

Economists and laypersons alike understand "economic growth" to mean growth in output per capita, in other words, the happy situation in which a society's total production grows faster than its population, so that more goods and services become available per person. Only when a nation's economy consistently produces such growth its citizens can enjoy a steadily rising standard of living. But what can bring this about? The answer is a rise in productivity. Assuming for simplicity that the length of the work week and the proportion of the population that is working remain constant as the economy grows, a given rise in productivity, which is the name economists give to output per work hour, will bring about an equivalent increase in output per capita and therefore in living standards.

From 1947 to 2020, nonfarm business productivity in the US economy has increased by an average of 2.2% per year (US Bureau of Labor Statistics, 2022). However, the growth rate since 2007 – corresponding to the "Great Recession" – has fallen to 1% annually. In addition, the pattern has not been uniform across industries. In particular, output per worker has risen much faster in manufacturing than in certain kinds of service industries, such as education, nursing home care, barbershops, automotive repair, gourmet food preparation, and – relevant for the purposes of this chapter – the live performing arts. Such industries are said to suffer from "productivity lag." Diverse as their outputs may sound, these industries have in common a single characteristic that inhibits increases in output per work-hour. In each of them, it is difficult, perhaps impossible, to substitute machinery for labor, and more machinery per worker is an important source of increased productivity.

As we show in this chapter, interindustry differences in the trend of productivity have one very important consequence: They cause related but opposite differences in the trend of unit costs. The cost of services in which output per work-hour increases slowly rises relative to the cost of goods for which gains in output per work-hour are more rapid, and the cost of services such as education or the live performing arts, in which output per work-hour is almost unchangeable, rises most of all. The connection between lagging productivity and rising cost in the live performing arts was first explored by Baumol and Bowen (1966), whose seminal work has been cited earlier, and they explicitly introduced the dilemma of how to finance the live performing arts in the face of ineluctably rising unit costs. Because this dilemma is pervasive in the performing arts, we give it a great deal of attention in this chapter.

8.1   The Productivity Lag Argument

The argument we make here, on the basis of Baumol and Bowen's analysis, can be summarized as follows. Costs in the live performing arts will rise relative to costs in the economy as a whole because wage increases in the arts have to keep up with those in the general economy, even though productivity improvements in the arts lag behind. It is not suggested that artists must be paid the same hourly wage as workers in other jobs, since working conditions and the nonmonetary satisfaction obtained from employment differ across occupations. Rather, the argument is that all industries, including the arts, compete to hire workers in a nationally integrated labor market and that artists' wages must therefore rise over time by the same proportion as wages in the general economy to enable the arts industry to hire the workers it needs to carry on.

In any economy, there are several possible sources of growth in physical output per work-hour. These include:

1. *Increased capital per worker.* If workers are provided with more machinery, output per work-hour rises: Ten workers with two front-loaders and two trucks can move more earth in an hour than ten workers with one front-loader and one truck.
2. *Improved technology.* Technology can be defined as the state of knowledge about methods of production. The introduction of bulldozers and front-loaders to replace pickaxes and shovels, for example, was an improvement in technology that vastly increased output per work-hour in the earth-moving trades.
3. *Increased labor skill.* Obviously, if workers are more skillful, they can produce more output per hour. Skills may be improved by either education or on-the-job training.
4. *Better management.* If managers develop more efficient ways of organizing the production process, output per work-hour will rise.
5. *Economies of scale.* In some production processes (there is no rule about this), output per unit of input rises when the scale of production increases. Automobile manufacturing is a prominent example. Such industries are said to enjoy economies of scale and, among other things, display increased output per work-hour as the scale of output rises. (Economies and diseconomies of scale were discussed earlier in Chapter 7.)
6. *Economies of scope.* These economies arise when a single firm can produce multiple products at a lower unit cost than multiple firms. The single firm can spread supply chain and centralized function costs over those products (Panzar and Willig, 1977, 1981).

As one might guess from this list of causes, productivity increases are achieved most readily in industries that make use of a lot of productive equipment. Output per worker can then be increased either by using more machinery or by investing in new equipment that embodies improved technology. As a result, in the typical manufacturing industry, the amount of labor time needed to produce a physical unit of output declines dramatically decade after decade.

The live performing arts are at the other end of the spectrum. Machinery, equipment, and technology play only a small role and, in any case, change very little over time.

That is not to say that technological improvements are entirely absent. For example, stage lighting has been revolutionized by the development of electronic controls and audience comfort has greatly been enhanced by air-conditioning, which also facilitate longer seasons and more flexible scheduling. But these improvements are not central to the business at hand. As Baumol and Bowen (1966, p. 164) point out, the conditions of production themselves preclude any substantial change in productivity because "the work of the performer is an end in itself, not a means for the production of some good." Since the performer's labor is the output – the singer singing, the dancer dancing, the pianist playing – there is really no way to increase output per hour. It takes four musicians as much playing time to perform a Beethoven string quartet today as it did when it was first published in 1800.

Of the six sources of increased productivity cited, only economies of scale and of scope offer much hope to the performing arts, and even those might be quickly exhausted within a given organization. Economies of scale might take the form of longer seasons, and economies of scope may be realized when, for example, a dance company offers dance classes in addition to a performance series, spreading its studio expenses over both teaching and rehearsal functions. With only those limited factors to rely on, the live performing arts, as Baumol and Bowen (1966, p. 165) emphasize, "cannot hope to match the remarkable record of productivity growth achieved by the economy as a whole." As a result, cost per unit of output in the live performing arts is fated to rise continuously relative to costs in the economy as a whole. That, in brief, is the unavoidable consequence of productivity lag.

On the other hand, industries in the "progressive" sector, in which productivity rises at a substantial rate, find themselves in a very favorable position. They can raise wages each year at the same rate at which productivity improves without increasing their unit labor costs at all. Hence, their prices need not rise, even though their wages do.

8.2   Algebraic Explanation of the Effects of Productivity Lag

These propositions can be supported by formal analysis. Let us define the following terms:

w = wage per hour
opw = physical output per work-hour (productivity)
ulc = unit labor cost = w/opw
k = annual rate of increase in output per work-hour in the general economy

Subscripts 0 and 1 will be used to indicate values in successive years, beginning with year 0. We make the following assumptions:

1. There is no *general* inflation. When we speak of cost increases in the live performing arts, we mean increases relative to a stable general price level.
2. Productivity, measured by physical output per work-hour, rises by k percent per year in the general economy.

3. Productivity does not rise at all in the live performing arts. Therefore, productivity lag in the arts sector is k percent per year.
4. Wages in the general economy rise at the same rate as opw does, namely, k percent per year.
5. Wages in the arts also rise by k percent per year so that the arts can remain competitive with other industries in the labor market.

Given these assumptions, we can show:

a. Unit labor costs remain constant in the general economy, allowing prices to remain constant, even though wages are rising.
b. Unit labor costs rise in the arts sector at a rate equal to the rate of productivity lag.
c. It follows from statements a and b that costs rise in the arts relative to those in the general economy at the same rate at which arts sector productivity lags.

The algebraic argument is as follows:
In the general economy in year 0, we have

$$ulc_0 = \frac{w_0}{opw_0}.$$

In year 1,

$$ulc_1 = \frac{w_1}{opw_1} = \frac{(1+k)w_0}{(1+k)opw_0}.$$

But since the $(1+k)$ terms cancel out,

$$ulc_1 = \frac{w_0}{opw_0} = ulc_0.$$

Thus, wages in the general economy can rise at the same rate as productivity without causing unit labor costs to increase.

In the live performing arts in year 0,

$$ulc_0 = \frac{w_0}{opw_0}.$$

In year 1, recalling that wages increase while productivity does not, we have

$$ulc_1 = \frac{w_1}{opw_1} = \frac{(1+k)w_0}{opw_0}.$$

Substituting ulc_0 for $\frac{w_0}{opw_0}$, we find that

$$ulc_1 = (1+k)ulc_0.$$

Thus, unit labor costs in the arts sector rise by k percent per year, which is the annual rate by which the growth of arts productivity "lags." Since unit labor costs are constant in the general economy, it also follows that costs in the arts rise k percent per year relative to those in the general economy.

8.2.1 A Numerical Example

If this derivation seems overly abstract, it can easily be illustrated numerically. In Table 8.1, the upper panel shows the situation in a hypothetical manufacturing industry where productivity is increasing. Assume that widgets are the product. Output per work-hour is therefore measured by widgets produced per worker per hour. The first row shows that *opw* rises from thirty widgets in 2015 to thirty-six in 2020, an increase of 20%. Wages, shown in the second row, rise at the same rate as productivity, increasing from $15 per hour in 2015 to $18 an hour in 2020. Unit labor cost, equal to wages per work-hour divided by output per work-hour, is shown in the third row. In 2015, it was *ulc* = $15 / 30 widgets, or 50 cents per widget. In 2020, unit labor cost remains unchanged. Wages have risen 20%, so has output per work-hour, leaving *ulc* still at 50 cents per widget. Thus, wages in a progressive industry can rise as fast as productivity without causing any increase in costs.

The lower panel of the table shows the situation in a hypothetical symphony orchestra, a live performing arts institution in which productivity is stagnant. We assume the following production conditions. The orchestra consists of 100 musicians. It plays five concerts per week in a hall that seats 1,600. Potential admission (the "output" of the orchestra in productivity terms) is therefore 8,000 per week. The musicians work forty-hour a week. Output per work-hour of the orchestra is therefore 8,000/40, or 200 admissions. Since there are 100 musicians, output per work-hour per musician is two admissions. This is shown as *opw* in the first row of the lower panel and is unchanged from 2015 to 2020.

The second row of the lower panel shows that wages per hour for players in the orchestra rose from $40 in 2015 to $48 in 2020, an increase of 20% that matches the upward movement of wages in the general economy. Unit labor costs for the orchestra are shown in the third row. In 2015, hourly wages were $40 and output per work-hour was two admissions, yielding *ulc* = $20 per admission. By 2020, wages had increased to $48 an hour, while *opw* remained at 2, so that

Table 8.1 Hypothetical illustration of productivity lag

	2015	2020	Percent change, 2015–2020
Widget industry			
Output in widgets per workhour (*opw*)	30	36	20
Wage per hour (*w*)	$15	$18	20
Unit labor cost (*ulc*) per widget = *w/opw*	$0.50	$0.50	0
Symphony orchestra			
Output measured by admissions per workhour (*opw*)[a]	2	2	0
Wage per hour (*w*)	$40	$48	20
Unit labor cost (*ulc*) per widget = *w/opw*	$20	$24	20

[a] Size of the concert hall = 1,600; concerts per week = 5; potential admissions per week = 8,000; number of musicians = 100; musician work hours per week = 40; orchestra hours per week = 4,000; output per work hour: admissions per week ÷ orchestra hours per week = 8,000 ÷ 4,000 = 2.

unit labor cost increased to $24 per admission. These hypothetical numbers show that in the live performing arts, unit labor costs rise over time by the same rate at which productivity gains in the arts lag behind those in the general economy.

8.3   Historical Evidence on Costs

The historical record strongly supports the hypothesis that because of productivity lag, unit costs in the live performing arts increase substantially faster than the general price level does. A great deal of such evidence was unearthed by Baumol and Bowen (see Baumol and Bowen, 1966, p. 165). Their earliest cost data are for productions at the Drury Lane Theatre in London in the eighteenth century. They compared average cost per performance at the Drury Lane in the seasons 1771–1772 through 1775–1776 with costs per performance of the Royal Shakespeare Theatre in 1963–1964. In that period of almost two centuries, cost per performance multiplied 13.6 times. Over the same period, a historical index of overall British prices shows them to have increased only 6.2 times. These increases can also be expressed as compound annual rates of growth, that is, as the annual growth rate that, if applied to the starting figure and compounded over the period in question, would result in the indicated final magnitude. On that measure, theatrical costs increased 1.4% per year, while the annual rate of increase for the general price level was only 0.9%.

In the United States, Baumol and Bowen put together a nearly continuous cost history for the New York Philharmonic Orchestra beginning in 1843 (Baumol and Bowen, 1966). Between that date and 1964, cost per concert rose at a compound annual rate of 2.5%, while the US index of wholesale prices rose at an average of 1.0% per year. As Baumol and Bowen point out, the apparently small difference between these numbers leads to a startling divergence in costs when compounded decade after decade: The orchestra's cost per concert multiplied twenty times over in 121 years, while the general price level only quadrupled.

For the years after World War II, Baumol and Bowen (1966) analyzed data on twenty-three major US orchestras; three opera companies; one dance company; and a sample of Broadway, regional, and summer theaters. In every group, the same results showed up: Cost per performance increased far more rapidly than the general price level. Moreover, they found a pattern in the postwar experience of Britain's Royal Shakespeare Theatre and London's Covent Garden (venue for the Royal Opera and Royal Ballet) so strikingly similar to US experience that they were encouraged to speculate that the structural problem of production in the live performing arts is one "that knows no national boundaries." The results have been echoed more recently and in other countries as well. For example, Last and Wetzel (2010) study the productivity of German public theaters for the period from 1991 to 2005 and conclude that also these boundaries have been crossed by Baumol's cost-disease.

8.4   The Consequences of Productivity Lag, or, Why Worry about It?

The facts of productivity lag are not in doubt. Everyone agrees that it causes costs, and presumably prices, in the live performing arts to rise relative to costs in the general economy, and that in the long run, an extraordinary divergence in prices can occur. But one may well ask, so what? Why should we worry about it? After all, many service activities besides the arts are afflicted with productivity lag. It takes a barber just as long to cut hair, or a professional basketball player just as long to play a full game, now as it did fifty years ago. Consequently, the prices of those activities (and many others in which technological improvements are absent or unimportant) have risen far more rapidly than the general price level. Yet we hear no outcry about a haircutting crisis or an impending financial collapse of the basketball industry. Why should we worry about productivity lag in the live performing arts? Why not let the arts suffer whatever consequences the uneven progress of technological change metes out for them?

The answer must be that the arts are a matter of special social concern and that we are therefore unwilling to leave their fate to the dictates of the market as we do haircuts and gourmet meals. This, however, is not the place to discuss how or why the arts may be different; those questions are taken up in detail in Chapter 12. At this stage, we simply explain the two principal points made by those who are concerned about the effects of productivity lag.

First, as we have already seen, productivity lag leads to steadily rising ticket prices for the live performing arts. This, in turn, makes it increasingly difficult to attract people of low or moderate income to the audience. The availability at relatively low prices of nonlive entertainment via the mass media – television, motion pictures, recordings, and on-demand streaming (precisely the modes in which technological progress has been important) – makes it even more difficult to attract the relatively poor. We have documented in Chapter 3 the fact that in US arts audiences, those with low or even moderate incomes are grossly underrepresented. Anyone who believes that this virtually automatic exclusion of the poor is socially undesirable is likely to be alarmed at the inexorable rise in ticket prices dictated by productivity lag.

The second unfortunate effect of productivity lag is that it puts the nonprofit institutions responsible for most of our live performing arts under unremitting financial pressure. Because relative costs are continuously increasing, they are under great pressure to raise ticket prices faster than the general rate of inflation, a strategy that is not easy to carry out and that they probably find philosophically repugnant. While it is difficult to demonstrate rigorously, it seems reasonable to believe that a nonprofit firm would find it easier to balance its budget in a technologically progressive industry, where unit costs are stable or falling year by year, than in a lagging one, where real costs are constantly moving upward, and prices charged to customers must do likewise.

The financial problems facing performing arts groups as a result of productivity lag were emphasized by Baumol and Bowen (1966, chapter 6, p. 12). For them and for later writers, a company's "earnings gap," defined as the difference between its expenditures and its earned income, has appeared to be the most useful (though far from unambiguous) measure of the financial strain it faces. In general, the gap is covered by some combination of private donations and government subsidy. Later in this chapter, we discuss the size of the gap in some typical arts organizations, whether it has been growing relative to expenditures, and how it has been financed. First, however, we must look at some possible countervailing forces to the effects of productivity lag.

8.5   Offsets to the Effects of Productivity Lag

By countervailing forces to productivity lag, we mean not policy responses initiated by the arts institutions themselves but rather economic effects that can be expected to operate on their own to ease indirectly the pressures generated by productivity lag. The first of these is rising living standards.

8.5.1   The Effect of Rising Living Standards

The problem of productivity lag exists only because there is persistent technological progress in the general economy, which causes a rise in output per work-hour, and in real wages, in other words, a rise in per capita income. Income per capita, as we have seen, is one of the determinants of demand for the arts. Regardless of what the exact value of the income elasticity of demand for art turns out to be, we can be certain that it is well above zero. Therefore, as income rises, other things remaining the same, the demand for art will increase. In the case of the live performing arts, the demand curve for tickets will shift to the right: At any given price level, the public will be willing to buy more tickets than it did previously. Thus, while productivity lag causes ticket prices to rise, which would lead to a decline in quantity demanded, rising income to some extent offsets that effect by stimulating ticket purchases. This does not mean that productivity lag causes no problems but only that rising living standards will work to mitigate them.

Perhaps an analogy is in order. Because of productivity lag in the business of high-quality food preparation, the price of a meal in a gourmet restaurant has risen sharply in recent years. That may cause some anguish for both customers and owners, but it has not prevented the gourmet restaurant business from growing. A similar effect is likely in the live performing arts. Baumol and Bowen were criticized for failing to emphasize this possibility. But Baumol has corrected that failure in more recent work (Baumol and Bowen, 1966, pp. 182–183).

8.5.2   The Effect of Economies of Scale

It was shown in Chapter 7 that the live performing arts display systematic economies of scale in production. When the length of run or season is taken as the measure of scale, the unit cost of output falls as output rises because the fixed costs of any one production or any given repertory can be spread over more performances as their number increases. This effect works in tandem with rising living standards. As per capita income increases, demand curves for admission shift to the right, more tickets are sold, and performance seasons grow longer. The resulting decline in unit costs can help to offset the cost-increasing effect of productivity lag.

8.5.3   The Effect of Economies of Scope

As suggested earlier in this chapter, a dance company that also operates a dance school will likely be able to spread some overhead costs – space utilization and back-office functions, for example – over these multiple products. Likewise, a theater company may rent out a dark stage for corporate presentations, and an orchestral association may sponsor popular concerts on otherwise idle nights. But these cost savings and revenue enhancements are ultimately limited, and they have the potentially negative effect of requiring additional staffing with specialized skills that do not serve the organization's core mission.

8.5.4 Income from the Mass Media

Although technological progress has had little direct effect on the live performing arts, its indirect impact via the mass media is potentially large. In the past hundred years, technological change has given us (in rapid sequence) the phonograph record, motion pictures, radio broadcasting, television, long-playing records, tape recording, satellite and cable systems, videocassette recorders, compact discs and videodiscs, and, most recently, online streaming and live broadcasting. Each of these innovations provided a market for live or nonlive performance arts that could yield significant income to groups producing the actual performance. Such income could help to offset the adverse budgetary impact of productivity lag. Symphony orchestras, to pick the most obvious example, might earn royalties from the sale of prerecorded music or fees from live-streamed online concerts. Theater, ballet, and opera companies, in addition to earning royalties from the sale of prerecorded music or videos, could be paid for performances on streaming platforms or cable TV. Indeed, in the analogous case of professional sports, earnings from television far outweigh income from ticket sales.

Unhappily, this potential revenue has not materialized. Royalties from recordings are trivial for most US symphony orchestras, and the trend has been down. Income from television performances has been equally disappointing. A retail grocer, standing in front of his shop, was asked how business had been that day. He replied: "It was kind of quiet in the morning. Then in the afternoon it slowed down." That is also the story of culture on commercial television. In the early days of commercial television, the networks made a modest effort to present high culture on the tube. Even then, however, the number of performances contracted for was so low, when measured against the size of the arts industry nationwide, that the income earned from broadcasting could be described only as negligible.

Is there thus no hope for performing arts institutions to benefit from technological advancements? Some believe that a solution to the recurring financial problems of performing arts institutions is offered by the digital broadcasting technology. Broadcasting of performances, either as live streaming or encores, may enable not only the widening of the overall audiences but also generate additional revenue flows. One of the first cultural institutions to broadcast their performances was the Metropolitan Opera in New York when it launched its broadcasting series in 2006. The transmission was initially directed at national cinemas and selected theaters abroad but by 2019 expanded to cover more than 2,300 venues in 72 countries. In that year, Met's Live in HD series generated $28m revenue, accounting for a significant 9.1% of the institution's operating revenue (The Metropolitan Opera, 2021). Similar ventures were also launched by some of the major institutions in Europe: The Berlin Philharmonic launched its online streaming service in 2008, while a year later followed the Royal National Theatre in London.

High-definition transmissions quite obviously influence the cinema industry, where digital projections became additional and often nonnegligible income revenues. As noted earlier, the cinema sector is beyond the focus of this book; however, we may be able to assess the potential of performance art broadcasting by looking at revenues generated through transmissions to cinemas.

Some estimates on the importance of broadcasting to digital cinemas can be obtained from box office revenues, as provided in a report by Hancock (2015). In 2014, cinema broadcasting generated revenue of $277.2 million that consisted in almost half from broadcasting of traditional performing arts, that is, opera (25%), theater (15%), and ballet (7%). Considering, in addition, transmissions of concerts (17%), either classical or popular music, and art exhibitions (3%), we come to the total share of cultural content broadcasting to be just above two-thirds of all transmissions to cinemas. The observed and forecasted revenues are certainly very promising, but we have to remember that the broadcasting technology is still in its early stage and hence a novelty. Whether the high demand will persist will become clearer over the next years as we observe how consumers respond to broadcasted options.

The COVID-19 pandemic has also forced organizations worldwide to consider alternative distribution channels. O'Hagan and Borowiecki (2021) explore challenges that orchestras have faced since the turn of the last century and in what way COVID-19 posed new problems that impacted orchestral music. In doing this, they highlight the possibilities regarding revenues from digital streaming of classical music. They show that streaming revenue in 2016 accounted for around 16% of global classical recorded music revenues, rising within two years to 37%. The highest percentage in 2018 was in the United States, at 60% of total revenue, with the figure for Europe at 22%. The US figure may be then seen as the potential for earning revenue from paid for streamed orchestral concerts.

Another concern is the distribution of the profits obtained in the digital projections market. With transmissions of performance arts across international borders, the markets become globally much more interrelated and cultural institutions are exposed to increasing competition. The first-movers seem to have substantial market power as indicated, for example, by the Met, whose broadcasting revenues account for about 46% of global revenues in 2014 obtained from opera transmissions to cinemas. Such a significant market share might encourage the Met to be lavish with their production budgets. Take, for instance, their 2014 production of "Prince Igor," which allocated $169,000 of its $4.3 million budget to a poppy field set, assembled from silk flowers (Maloney, 2014).

One could thus raise two big concerns. First, does live broadcasting decrease live attendance at the broadcasting venue, that is, are there any signs of "cannibalization" of box office revenues? And second, how is attendance at local, lower tier performing arts institutions affected by a sudden exposure to competition in the form of live HD broadcasts of some of the world's best (and most expensive) performances. We shall return to both issues in Chapter 16.

8.6   Competition with the Mass Media for Inputs

Despite some success stories of some of the leading performing arts institutions, the mass media failed to yield significant income for the live performing arts more in general. Moreover, they have actually made matters worse in that sector by bidding up prices of the professional inputs that both the mass media and the live performing arts employ. Of course, the performers whose incomes have increased as a result of this labor market competition will not regard it as a bad thing. But the institutions that employ them to produce live performances will find their personnel costs rising at a very uncomfortable rate.

Since the wage effect referred to here is transmitted from one sector (the mass media) to another (the live performing arts) through competition to hire in the labor market, it bears a strong formal resemblance to the productivity lag effect. The point is that performers of "star" quality, such as Meryl Streep, Tom Hanks, or Andrea Bocelli, can command enormous salaries when they work in motion pictures or on television. They earn such salaries because the mass media now have a vast audience in an international market, and the presence of a star performer can make a big difference at the movie box office or (for TV and streaming) in the ratings war (Frank and Cook, 1995; Rosen, 1981). Inevitably, wage inflation at the upper end exerts an upward pull on the wages paid to actors and singers who play "supporting" roles, and so eventually, the whole spectrum of performance wages is drawn upward, not only in the mass media but also in the live arts, which must compete with the mass media for talent. A similar effect probably operates for other artistic personnel, such as stage, music, and dance directors, whose services are required by both the mass media and the live performing arts. In Chapter 14, we reexamine this matter from a labor market perspective.

The process just described might be called "the mass media wage effect." Whatever we call it, however, it is not a new story. In his study of the economic history of US theater, Thomas Gale Moore (1968, pp. 14–15) found that during the 1930s, a decade of nationwide deflation brought on by the Great Depression, operating costs on Broadway actually rose. He attributed this increase to the arrival of sound in Hollywood. The first "talking picture" was *The Jazz Singer*, which opened in 1927. Thereafter, Hollywood developed a ravenous appetite for singers, dancers, and composers, for writers who could compose dialogue, actors who could project it, and directors who could put it all together. The longtime home of these talents was the Broadway stage. Hollywood began to hire them away in the 1930s and in the process drove up wages and costs on Broadway, despite the fact that in the nation as a whole, prices and costs had gone down (Moore, 1968, pp. 14–15).

In assessing the problem of costs in the live performing arts, the mass media wage effect must be thought of as additive with the effect of productivity lag: It is evil tidings piled on top of bad news.

8.7 Productivity Lag and the Growth of Music Festivals

Bruno Frey has pointed out that the growth of music festivals, especially notable in Europe, can be regarded as both a response and an offset to productivity lag (Frey, 1994a). He argues that music produced at festivals, such as Salzburg in Austria, Glyndebourne in England, or Wexford in Ireland, has enjoyed cost advantages over music produced in the conventional home venues of opera companies or symphony orchestras for several reasons. First, festival labor costs usually do not include labor overhead items such as retirement benefits, health insurance, and vacation time that are paid by the artists' permanent employers. Second, they are not hampered by the union and/or government restrictions that often burden production in the home venue. The first of these advantages would make for a lower level of costs at festivals, the second for a slower rate of cost increase.

Demand factors have also contributed to the rapid growth of festivals. Perhaps most important, festivals are complementary to vacation time, and vacation time has been increasing rapidly as incomes rise. Demand also benefits from the relative decline in transportation costs (measured in both money and time) that makes festivals increasingly accessible. However, Frey concludes that the very success of festivals is likely to undermine their cost advantages in the long run, so that they will not remain a permanent offset to the ill effects of productivity lag on conventional performing arts production.

8.8   Costs and Revenues in the Performing Arts

Table 8.2 provides an account of costs, revenues, and the earnings gap of three nonprofit organizations in the performing arts in 2019, all located in New York City and well known: the New York City Ballet, the American Ballet Theater, and the Alvin Ailey American Dance Theatre. The table is useful for several reasons. First, by listing the major components of cost and revenue, it tells us a good deal about how performing arts firms actually carry out their functions. Second, it allows us to look systematically at the relative magnitudes of the principal financial categories. Finally, it gives us a precise definition of the earnings gap.

The table reveals that personnel costs, which include salaries and wages, and related expenses like employee benefits and payroll taxes, make up between 47% and 71% of total expenditure in these dance companies. Artistic personnel, the workers among whom productivity lag is bound to be a problem, account typically for nearly three-quarters of that (New York City Ballet, Inc., 2020). Note I – Schedule of functional expenses). Nonsalary costs, however, are clearly nonnegligible, amounting up to about 50% of the total. The three largest nonsalary categories are occupancy (4–9% of all outlays), transportation and per diem costs incurred while on tour (up to 6%), and nonsalary advertising and promotion costs (4–5%).

The earnings gap is generally defined as the difference between operating expenditures and earned income. Earned income in the case of the selected performing arts companies, as illustrated in Table 8.2, comprises both earned and contributed income. The former can be further divided into two distinct types (not shown separately in the table). Ticketed income is revenue from the sale of tickets to performances for which the company itself is the financially responsible producer. Such performances are usually limited to those at the company's home base. When the company is on tour, that is, performing away from home, it usually does so in return for tour fees. These are paid under contracts between the company and a "presenting organization" at each stop on the tour.

8.8.1   The Role of Presenting Organizations

If a ballet company based in New York City tours through Indiana, its performance in South Bend might be sponsored by a local presenting organization calling itself, say, "South Bend

Table 8.2 Typical expenditures and income for select dance companies, 2019

	New York City Ballet			American Ballet Theatre			Alvin Ailey Dance Foundation		
	Dollar amount	Percent of total	Percent of subtotal	Dollar amount	Percent of total	Percent of subtotal	Dollar amount	Percent of total	Percent of subtotal
Total expenditure	$91,775,751	90		$49,002,829	75		$45,352,857	77	
Salaries and wages	$45,422,721		49	$19,280,890		39	$17,113,353		38
Compensation of officers	$1,437,326		2	$1,369,193		3	$2,106,409		5
Employee benefits, payroll taxes, and pensions	$19,308,881		21	$6,616,610		14	$4,298,518		9
Advertising and promotion	$3,238,583		4	$2,513,522		5	$1,664,429		4
Occupancy and related costs	$6,008,597		7	$1,829,989		4	$3,892,132		9
Travel, conferences, meetings	$964,262		1	$2,287,824		5	$2,638,310		6
Depreciation and financial costs	$5,915,049		6	$2,771,150		6	$3,223,397		7
Total other expenses	$9,480,332	10		$12,333,651	25		$10,416,309	23	
Income	$91,173,379	100		$47,153,046	100		$48,602,296	100	
Earned	$66,111,906	73	100	$24,874,870	53	100	$37,257,104	77	100
Program services Revenue	$51,172,079		77	$23,738,059		95	$24,900,379		67
Investment income	$1,352,359		2	$789,455		3	$2,998,945		8
Sales, royalties, and miscellaneous	$13,587,468		21	$347,356		1	$9,357,780		25
Contributed	$25,061,473	27	100	$22,278,176	47	100	$11,345,192	23	100
Fundraising	$5,362,376		21	$3,195,804		14	$4,278,125		38
Government grants	$2,850,883		11	$206,010		1	$539,730		5
Other contributions	$16,848,214		67	$18,876,362		85	$6,527,337		58
Earnings gap (expenditures – earned income)	$25,663,845	28		$24,127,959	49		$8,095,753	18	

Source: IRS 990 forms from Guidestar.org and ProPublica.org.

Arts." That organization would guarantee a fixed payment to the ballet company, would advertise and sell tickets to the performance, rent a hall, and take financial responsibility for the whole enterprise. In the unlikely event that ticket sales more than cover expenses, the local presenter is entitled to keep the net proceeds. Likewise, it is responsible for covering any deficit.

Because local presenting organizations play a crucial role in the distribution of performance art in a nation as large as the United States, it is appropriate to add a few words about the often-complex economics of their operations. During the course of a season, they will typically present a variety of touring attractions, for example, a symphony orchestra, a ballet company, a modern dance group, and a chamber music ensemble. They may also sponsor a number of vocal or instrumental soloists. Subscriptions can then be solicited for one or more groups of these offerings. Single ticket sales will, of course, also be promoted.

Since very few arts performances break even, presenting organizations, too, are likely to require unearned income to cover a financial gap. For that purpose, they can tap the same sources available to the performing institutions themselves: individual and business contributors, who can make tax-deductible donations, and government organizations that can provide subsidies. In the case of local presenters, subsidies are more likely to come from a state or local council on the arts than from the National Endowment for the Arts. (The economics of private donations is discussed in Chapter 12 and public support in Chapter 13.)

Fee-based income will be most important for companies that do a great deal of touring. A typical ballet company earns less than a quarter of its performance income from fees. The proportion would be somewhat higher for the average symphony orchestra and would be close to 100% for the typical modern dance company, which tours widely and rarely performs except on the basis of a contracted fee.

Nonperformance-earned income in the performing arts may sound like a contradiction in terms. It is not. Companies that own their own hall can earn income by renting it to others during the offseason or any other time it might go unused. More generally, many companies have discovered that they can earn worthwhile income by selling souvenir programs, books, posters, and T-shirts at their own performances.

8.9   Earned versus Unearned Income

The share of total revenue accounted for by earned as compared with unearned income – or, as the latter is often called, "contributed income" – varies widely among firms and across art forms. Symphony orchestras have the lowest earned income ratio among the five major categories. They are in general the oldest institutions in the nonprofit performing arts industry, with many of them having been established in the nineteenth century. Consequently, they have long-standing ties with well-to-do patrons, especially with what is sometimes referred to as "old money." Private contributions accounted for almost 43% of their total revenue in 2017, and income from endowments (funds that are the result of generous past benefactions) made up an additional 10%. As a result, earned income amounted to only 44% of total revenue for the average symphony orchestra (League of American Orchestras, 2020). Another example of a long-standing institution is the Metropolitan Opera, whose contributions account for about half of income, twice the size of box office, and increased from $133.5 million in 2010 to $166 million in 2019 (The Metropolitan Opera, 2020). In fact, the ties with patrons are so elaborate that the longest part of the Met's Annual Report 2019 consists of the acknowledgment of contributors (thirty out of fifty pages). At the other end of the scale, modern dance companies rely on earned income typically for more than two-thirds of their revenue. As already pointed out, these companies generally do not have a home base at which to sell tickets. Most of their earned income therefore consists of fees received for performances on tour. Since modern dance companies tend to be relatively small and relatively new, they do not attract private contributions as readily as larger and older institutions do, and tend to rely more heavily on government grants (Smith, 2003, appendix table 3).

8.9.1 The Earnings Gap

Since total income approximately equals expenditures and the earnings gap equals the difference between expenditures and earned income, it follows that the earnings gap also approximately equals unearned income. The relative size of the gap is usually measured by taking the gap as a percentage of expenditures. Changes in the gap can be measured as changes in either its absolute or relative size over time.

The New York City Ballet depicted in Table 8.2 has a total expenditure budget of $91.8 million in 2019. Earned income amounts to only $66.1 million, leaving an earnings gap of $25.7 million. In relative terms, the gap equals 28% of expenditures. More than three quarters of that is covered by private contributions: 27% from individuals, 16% from corporations, and 15% from foundations (not shown separately in the table) ("Note H – Public support" in the report by New York City Ballet, Inc., 2020). These proportions have changed substantially in recent years. Twenty years ago, foundations would have been the leading source of private donations to dance companies, with individuals a close second and corporations a very distant third. The sharp rise in the relative share of corporate contributions testifies to the fact that ballet (and modern dance), once regarded suspiciously in the United States, is now considered "mainstream."

8.9.2 Is the Earnings Gap Growing?

If expenditures and earned income grow at the same rate, the earnings gap will grow in absolute size, but its relative size will be unchanged. On the other hand, if expenditures grow faster than earned income, not only the absolute but also the relative size of the gap will increase. Writing in the mid-1960s, Baumol and Bowen found that for a number of institutions, the relative size of the gap had increased during the postwar period (Baumol and Bowen, 1966). On the basis of that experience, they estimated that in the next ten years, expenditures would grow at between 5% and 7% per year, while earned income would rise only 3.5–5.5% yearly, resulting in continued relative growth of the gap (Baumol and Bowen, 1966, pp. 388–393).

Fortunately, that did not happen. Expenditures continued to increase rapidly, but in some disciplines, earned income rose faster, so that the gap in some areas declined in relative size. Data from the Ford Foundation show that from 1965–1966 to 1970–1971 the gap as a

Table 8.3 The earnings gap (contributed income as a percentage of total revenue)

	2005	2010	2015	2019	Percent change (2005–2019)
New York City Ballet	39	40	19	28	−11
American Ballet Theatre	51	49	44	49	−2
Alvin Ailey Dance Foundation	22	9	26	18	−4

Source: IRS 990 forms from Guidestar.org and ProPublica.org.

percentage of total expenditures rose for symphony orchestras and nonprofit theaters, but it fell for opera, ballet, and modern dance companies. Schwarz and Peters's study indicates that in the 1970s the relative size of the gap fell substantially in ballet, modern dance, and nonprofit theater, declined slightly for symphony orchestras, and was approximately stable in the field of opera (Schwarz and Peters, 1983).

More recent data are summarized in Table 8.3. As previously, the earnings gap is expressed here in proportion of total expenditures. The table indicates that the gap continued to decline until 2019, but it also shows the volatility of this measure.

On the whole, then, dire predictions that productivity lag would lead to a relentlessly increasing earnings gap proved to be incorrect. What happened? As we indicated earlier in this chapter, a number of factors can work to offset the effects of productivity lag. In this instance, expenses of performing arts companies did increase more or less as predicted, but earned income rose at an equal or slightly higher rate, so the relative size of the gap began to decline. But what explains the rise in earned income? Evidently, ticket prices rose much faster than the general price level without causing a drop in attendance (see discussion in Chapter 2). Hence, box office revenues, adjusted for inflation, rose substantially. Thus, productivity lag persists in the arts, but so do some of its potential offsets.

8.9.3 Interpreting the Earnings Gap

Something more must be said by way of interpretations. Since performing arts firms in the non-profit sector cannot normally operate with a cash deficit, an earnings gap cannot exist unless unearned income is available to cover it. As we have seen, such income flows from both private donations and public grants. Emphasis on the earnings gap as the starting point in a financial analysis leads one to think of unearned income as a passive factor that responds after the fact to the financial needs of the company. But we could just as well look at it the other way round and argue that the existence of unearned income makes it possible for a performing arts firm to finance expenditures in excess of earned income. A very large earnings gap for a given firm might indicate not that the firm is in serious financial trouble but rather that it has succeeded in finding generous outside support, probably in response to its very high quality of operation.

Still, there is a sense in which firms operating with a large earnings gap may seem to have given hostages to fortune: Suppose that government grants are cut back because of a fiscal squeeze or that private donations decline because of a change in tax law or a serious economic recession. Is it not safer to depend on ticket income a little more and public or private charity a little less?

8.10   Is There an "Artistic Deficit"?

Faced with the continual upward pressure on costs generated by productivity lag, firms in the live performing arts might be expected to seek ways of economizing by gradually altering their choice of repertory or their production process. For example, theatrical producers might look for plays with smaller casts or plays that could be mounted with a single rather than multiple stage sets. Or they might try to compensate for higher costs by shunning artistically innovative plays that do not draw well at the box office and so have to be "carried" by revenues from more conventional offerings. Consistent with Chapter 7 analysis of the effect of market structure on innovation versus conformity in the theater, we would expect this to occur most often in smaller cities where a single company might have a virtual monopoly on professional production. Orchestras and opera companies, too, might be driven away from innovative or "difficult" material by box office considerations. Or operating on the cost side, they might select programs with an eye to reducing rehearsal time or hire fewer outside soloists or other high-priced guest artists. Ballet companies could cut down on the use of specially commissioned music or choreography and could eschew new productions that require elaborate sets or costumes. (This topic is revisited in Chapter 14.)

Although economics clearly teaches us that firms will respond to rising input costs by economizing in their use of the offending inputs, economists interested in the arts are likely to be disturbed when they find firms in the performing arts doing just that. They are offended at the notion that *Hamlet* is no longer viable because its cast is too large, or that piano concertos will be less frequently heard because soloists (or at any rate the well-known ones) have become too expensive. Hilda and William Baumol express their dismay at the notion that rising costs should narrow "the economically feasible range of artistic options" (Baumol and Baumol, 1985, p. 17). When that occurs, it has been said that performing arts firms are reducing their fiscal deficit by incurring an "artistic deficit."

However, the decision to economize in the use of inputs often constitutes a last resort for the management of performing arts institutions. Such resistance to cost minimizing efforts is exemplified in the case of Holland's world-renowned orchestra – Royal Concertgebouw – which reported a significant deficit in their financial summary in 2013. The managing body interpreted the negative figures as a sign that the institution would be forced to cease its operations. Despite the gravity of this unprecedented financial crisis, reducing the size of the staff and employing musicians on a part time basis was not deemed a viable strategy; a decrease in the institution's artistic scope was the last thing the management would consider (Van Lent, 2014). This example highlights not only the management's unwillingness to compromise on the artistic quality of a top international orchestra, but also the difficulty in navigating its financial and creative success, which often require contradictory concessions. It is worth noting that this problem is peculiar to the performing arts. In the fine arts – for example, in architecture – we fully expect practitioners to adapt their "products" to changes over time in the relative prices of alternative inputs. We are not surprised to find that modern buildings are devoid of the elaborate hand-carved stonework that decorated important buildings in earlier times. Indeed, the esthetic rationale of the modern movement in architecture was precisely to design buildings that could use machine-finished materials in place of the increasingly costly hand-finished ones.

Table 8.4 Percentage of Broadway plays with cast size greater than thirty

	Percent
1950s	69
1960s	67
1970s	31
1980s	24
1990s	38
2000s	27

Source: Davenport (2011).

In this instance, it is not too strong to say that the necessity of adapting was the challenge that gave rise to a whole new school of design.

What makes the performing arts different is the fact that the past provides much of the substance that we wish to see performed. We do not want *Hamlet* with half the characters omitted because of the high cost of labor, nor do we wish to give up symphony concerts in favor of chamber music recitals simply because symphonies employ too many musicians. We want the "range of artistic options" to include the option of hearing or seeing performances of great works that were invented under very different economic circumstances than our own. There would indeed be an artistic deficit if today's companies became financially unable to present for us the great works of the past.

Have our performing arts institutions, responding to financial pressure, already begun cutting back along some dimensions of quality? Are we even now the victims of an artistic deficit? Baumol and Baumol (1985) showed that average cast size for all nonmusicals produced on Broadway fell from 15.8 in 1946–1947 to 8.1 in 1977–1978. Table 8.4 provides an updated insight into this matter by showing the share of Broadway plays with cast size greater than thirty from 1950s to 2000s. While more than two-thirds of Broadway plays had a cast greater than thirty in the 1950s and 1960s, only between a quarter and one-third of plays have a larger cast more recently. Figure 8.1 tracks data compiled by Derek Miller (2016) that extends the Baumol and Baumol's (1985) findings and covers all Broadway productions. Cast size recovered a bit from its nadir, and has stabilized, varying around what we might presume to be the artistic minimum. A study of opera repertory in the United States (Heilbrun, 2001) has shown that from 1983 to 1998 companies have increasingly produced popular operas at the expense of new or less well-known works. This could be interpreted as evidence of a growing artistic deficit in that field.

8.11 Innovation in the Performing Arts?

There are also voices of dissent against Baumol's cost-disease hypothesis. One such example is Tyler Cowen (1997), who outlines two reasons why the performing arts are not stagnant in

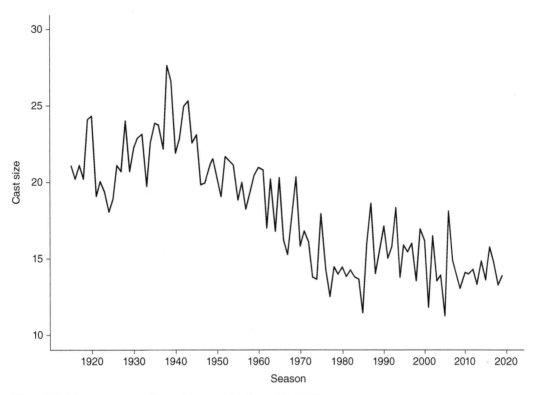

Figure 8.1 Mean cast size of Broadway productions, 1915–2020.

terms of productivity, compared with other economic sectors; they spark both innovation in process and innovation in product.

Innovation in process is visible primarily via the significant improvements in the technology of electronic music reproduction. Not only has the quality of recordings improved significantly over the past few decades, but the ease of access has also increased, with most repertoires available online to millions nowadays. Furthermore, a rising number of performing arts institutions expand audience reach (and generate new sources of financial revenue) by broadcasting their shows to cinemas and arts centers around the world, as we have discussed in Section 8.5.4. In terms of consumption units, electronic or digital reproduction has made the performing arts vastly more productive.

There has also been a considerable improvement in product innovation, which is not quite apparent if we rely solely on a comparison of the time needed to perform Beethoven's string quartet in the past and nowadays, as this approach assumes both inputs and outputs as constant.

The Beethoven example makes the performing arts and artistic production appear as a stagnant, unchanging activity. In reality though, a quartet in today's terms is significantly more productive than it was in the 1820s, because it can perform a range of other works by more recent composers – the repertoire is undeniably greater. In addition, creative musicians and composers push the boundaries of product innovation also by availing of new, innovative settings for their performance. An extreme example is that of the best-known pieces of the late twentieth-century German composer Karlheinz Stockhausen – the *Helicopter String Quartet*. The experimental work is performed in the air and involves a string quartet, four helicopters with pilots, as well as audio and video equipment and technicians (Stockhausen, 1996).

The increasing variety of musical compositions and performance settings clearly constitute a productivity increase, but the rising cost of labor can also be offset by some innovative cost-saving procedures. The use of light can sometimes be employed as a substitute for an elaborate (and expensive) stage set, while modular stage elements can be reused for different performances. Cost-minimizing efforts may result in the development of a contemporary – often minimalistic – scenography. It was due to such cost-saving measures that the Opera de Oviedo, despite being located in the periphery of Spain, remained one of the two opera houses in Spain that sustained the Spanish financial crisis of 2008–2014 without making loses (the other being the renowned Gran Teatre del Liceu opera house in Barcelona) (PUCK, 2012). Oviedo Opera begun further not only to rely on borrowed costumes and stage sets but also to lend out their own costumes and sets. On their webpage, in fact, the institution offers more than twenty productions to rent (including costumes and stage sets) for all types of theaters and production companies.

Examples of labor cost saving can also be found in dance performance. Taneli Törmä, a Finnish contemporary dancer and choreographer, finds the cast for his performance "Behind My Skin" among local volunteers. In the call for volunteers, published via social media, the artist offers a three-day workshop and states that the required thirty volunteers "can be 15–100 year's old and don't need to have any dance or performance background," – this allows him to draw relatively easily and almost for free on a pool of performers (Törmä, n.d.).

It remains debatable whether and how some of these decisions and strategies enlarge the previously discussed artistic deficit or are detrimental to the lives and earnings of artists (see Chapter 14 for more on artists' earnings). However, the examples demonstrate how performing arts can survive and perhaps even thrive economically despite the increasing financial problem in the form of high labor cost.

8.12   "Coproduction" in the Arts

In this section, we resurrect the production function from Chapter 6, written there as $Q = f(K, L)$, where output (Q) depends on the amount of capital (K) and labor (L) applied to production. Our examples of output in the arts were all observable and measurable, including the number of admissions, number of concerts, or number of tickets sold.

But in many areas of enterprise, especially the services, the "output" depends on the effort not just of the supplier but also of the customer or service recipient. For example, if we discuss educational output, the number of graduates will indicate the volume of production, but it does not adequately portray the actual amount of learning taking place. Teachers (L) and school buildings (K) will not be successful if students fail to put forth effort. Students must learn how to learn. Similarly, in health care, patients must take their medicines and otherwise heed medical advice in order to achieve the best outcomes. In these cases, active engagement by the customer or service recipient is known as "coproduction," where output is "coproduced" by those on both the demand and supply sides of the market.

In these examples, enhancing student and patient skills will improve the outcomes, even if the usual quantitative output measures fail to reflect these improvements. The same may be said of the arts. We might modify the production function to include the role of the audience: $Q = f(K, L, A)$, where Q is no longer an observable measure of output, but more broadly it indicates something like "audience satisfaction." A concert hall is still a component of productive capital (K), and musicians comprise an important part of labor (L), but audience engagement (A) enhances the overall experience. We read in Chapter 3 about the importance of familiarity with the arts in promoting attendance, and here we state that finding more formally. This means that arts organizations can enhance their impact by investing in larger and better performance spaces, employing superior musicians or actors, and by investing in their audiences.

Thus, we find that orchestras offer young people's concerts, theaters offer classes and workshops for all ages, and, to take a specific example, the Minnesota Opera provides audience "skill-building" programs, including a course in "Opera 101" on their website. All of this means that while cost pressures cannot be easily resolved, the arts organizations can still be more impactful by enhancing customer consumption skills.

8.13   Summary

This chapter introduced the problems associated with productivity lag in the performing arts. Rising costs and higher ticket prices threaten to reduce the audience for the arts, but these difficulties may be at least partially offset in a growing economy by rising consumer incomes, increasing taste for the arts, and falling unit costs attributable to economies of scale and scope. Furthermore, arts organizations can be more impactful in the face of cost pressures by investing in their audiences. One can thus remain guardedly optimistic about the continued financial viability of the performing arts. However, there is considerable evidence that growth of the earnings gap has been forestalled in part by assorted innovations but also by an increasing artistic deficit.

SUGGESTIONS FOR FURTHER READING

On new and alternative forms of finance and funding in the cultural and creative industries, see the special issue in the *Journal of Cultural Economics* (Loots et al., 2022).

PROBLEM SET

8.1 What is meant by the concept of "productivity lag" as applied to the performing arts? Illustrate your answer with an example. How might productivity lag exacerbate the problem of an earnings gap? How, if at all, might an "artistic deficit" arise in this context? What factors, if any, might mitigate the difficulties resulting from productivity lag?

8.2 The results of a productivity lag are sometimes known as a "cost disease" or "Baumol's disease." In what sense is it a disease? And why Baumol?

8.3 A typical concert played by a given symphony orchestra lasts 2 hours, requires 75 musicians, and is performed in a concert hall with a capacity of 1,500. Calculate the productivity of a musician, measured as the output by admissions per work-hour.

8.4 Suppose the average hourly wage of a musician playing at the symphony orchestra has increased from 30 euro in 2013 to 45 euro in 2023.

a. What is the unit labor cost in 2013 and 2023, assuming that productivity has not changed.

b. What are the percent changes in wage per hour and unit labor cost over the period studied?

c. Discuss the implications of your results for the future financing of this symphony orchestra.

9 Economics of Arts Management and Strategy

LEARNING OBJECTIVES

By the end of this chapter, readers should be able to:

- Explain why arts organizations exist
- Evaluate structures of arts organization
- Outline when principal-agent problems may occur
- Offer a succinct statement of strategy in the arts

Chapters 7 and 8 offered some insights into performing arts markets and the operations of organizations, with specific implications for pricing, output, and costs. Some readers may have regarded those implications as resulting from the intersections of assorted lines and curves rather than the deliberate consequences of human decisions – and to some extent those impressions are correct. Those earlier chapters implicitly assumed that costs are easily measurable, information is easily available, and all market participants are rational utility maximizers. While these assumptions may be useful for suggesting general tendencies or creating a standard by which to benchmark current practice, they may be less useful as guides to actual decision-making by the manager of a not-for-profit organization.[1]

In this chapter, we extend economic tools beyond these "ideal" analyses to offer some insights into how economics can inform our understanding of the actual management of arts organizations, including governance structures, assignment of decision rights, and the nitty-gritty of pricing and strategic positioning. To these ends, we draw upon the seminal work of two Nobel-prize-winning economists, Ronald Coase and Oliver Williamson, neither of whom ever exhibited a professional interest in cultural economics, but both of whom nonetheless help us to understand more about arts organizations. Their work constitutes elements of what is known as the "new institutional economics," which acknowledges that institutional realities can get in the way of theoretical niceties. More recent work by Richard Caves (2000; 2002), a relative latecomer to cultural economics, has brought some of the concepts to bear on our understanding of arts markets and organizations.

In Section 9.1, we summarize the essential relevant insights and tools, and in the remainder of the chapter, we will explore selected implications. Principal-agent theory will inform a discussion of decision rights and incentive compensation within organizations, contract theory will aid our understanding of what are known as organizational boundaries, and transactions-cost economics will provide insights into both the existence of organizations and their strategic positioning.

9.1   Markets versus Hierarchies: Why Arts Organizations Exist

It is easy to take the existence of a symphony orchestra or an opera company for granted. They just are! Yet most readers of this book are likely aware of independent performing professionals who perform as soloists or coalesce temporarily as a string quartet or a group of dancers.

Imagine a dance performance developed and offered in the absence of an existing organization. A group of dancers, desiring to generate income from the use of their skills, decides to create and present a dance performance. Each of them contracts with each other to combine their efforts; each contracts separately with a choreographer, who will create a dance for the group and perhaps also direct the performance, and with a business manager, who will see to rehearsal and performance space rental and take care of other details such as advertising. Then perhaps each independently solicits payment from potential audience members.

The number of separate transactions or contracts required to make this event happen approaches the mind-boggling. And failure to perform by just one participant could result in multiple contract breaches. Far better for a dance company to offer the event and sell tickets to patrons is to employ a choreographer, a business manager, and dancers, and perhaps to vertically integrate to own both rehearsal and performing space, to offer the event and sell tickets to patrons. The number of independent transactions is reduced substantially.

This was the insight proffered by Ronald Coase and fine-tuned by Oliver Williamson, both of whom were awarded the Nobel Memorial Prize in economics for their efforts (Coase, 1937; Williamson, 1983, 2010). Coase (1937) points out simply that organizations and their decision-making hierarchies come into existence when the consequent reduction in transactions costs justifies the costs of creating and operating an organization. That opens the door, as it were, for taking economics concepts and tools inside the organization to explore nonmarket resource allocation decisions.

Williamson (1983, 2010) developed a framework illustrating how the interplay of human and environmental factors can lead to market failure, a situation defined by an inefficient distribution of goods and services in the free market, and then proposed vertical integration to remediate market failure.

9.2   The Structure of Arts Organizations

Like any hierarchical organization, not-for-profit arts firms constitute a series of sequential principal–agent relationships. With reference to Figure 9.1, a governing board – which may or may not be truly representative of assorted stakeholder groups – typically has responsibility for establishing an overall strategic direction and goals, and then empowering a chief executive officer (CEO, usually an executive director or president) to develop and implement the means to achieve the goals. The relationships among hierarchical levels are effectively described by principal–agent theory (sometimes also known as agency theory), whereby resources are allocated not by impersonal market forces but by interpersonal professional interactions characterized by asymmetric information. Within an organization, a supervisor (the principal) assigns

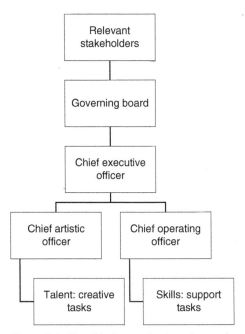

Figure 9.1 Simplified organization chart, of an arts organization.

responsibility over a set of tasks to a subordinate (the agent), who then carries out the tasks as stipulated. Problems arise when the principal and agent have divergent interests, and the principal must expend resources to ascertain whether and how well the agent has carried out the assigned tasks.

In the not-for-profit arts organization, the board is the principal and the CEO is the agent. The CEO in turn becomes a principal by employing and empowering agents further down in the hierarchical structure, what we may call the chief artistic officer (CAO), typically referred to as the music director, artistic director, or some similar label, and a chief operating officer (COO), perhaps with a formal title of vice president for operations.

The CAO has the responsibility for overall artistic quality, including artistic vision, selection and hiring of talent, and overseeing exhibits or performances. The COO has responsibility for all support functions, ranging from finance to marketing, which keep the organization's house in order. The CAO and COO are agents of the CEO, who must ensure that all internal resource allocation decisions are consistent with the organization's goals.

Neither the board nor the CEO, acting as the principal, is likely to have the time or means for constant monitoring of their agents, giving rise to what is known as "asymmetric information" – the agent knows more about his/her performance than does the principal. To some extent, the alignment of interests is achieved via commitment to the organization's mission and goals (Byrnes, 2008). However, incentive conflicts, including unethical and illegal behavior on the part of CEOs, have been known to arise in the not-for-profit sector generally and in the arts specifically.

CEOs may seek to enrich themselves with excessive perks, such as lavish travel expenses charged to the organization, at the sacrifice of achieving organization goals. The CAO may ignore budget realities in pursuit of artistic excellence, only to sink the organization into dire fiscal straits. A ticket manager may secretly divert a portion of the admission proceeds into a personal bank account.

A key to avoiding any of these self-serving behaviors is a careful assignment of decision rights combined with more overt alignment of individual interests with the organization's goals (Fama and Jensen, 1983). The board of directors may specify limits on the CEO's expenditure choices and also defer some CEO compensation pending achievement of organization goals.

9.3   Solving the Principal–Agent Problem in Art Commissions

This chapter has a focus on arts organization, but it is useful to consider the self-serving behaviors of art market participants more widely. Principal–agent problems may occur also in the case of any commissions or hiring more in general. The problem is that the objective of the principal – the employer, for example, an arts organization – and that of the agent – the employee, for example, a musician or dancer – are not necessarily aligned. Some agents may be just driven by the earnings and the status, but do not want to provide larger efforts than necessary.

Solving the problem is not always easy, but an interesting application is shown in research on art commissions in history. Consider when patrons (principals) commission from artists (agents) large oil paintings of figurative subject or public art that require months or years of work. The emerging conflict of interest is that quality of the painting requires the artist's time and effort, which is neither negotiable before the artwork is commissioned nor measurable after the painting is delivered. An economics textbook solution to contractual problems between patrons and artists in the case of unverifiable quality and when interests of the agent and the principal are not aligned would be to condition payments on measurable variables related to quality.

Intrigued by the principal–agent problem between patrons and painters, Etro and Pagani (2012) show what solution was in force in seventeenth-century Italy: Prices and payments were based on the number of human figures depicted. The number of human figures is measurable and, especially for the case of historical paintings, it is correlated with the quality of a painting, as human figures are particularly difficult to paint and hence require time and effort of the painter. By studying contracts between patrons and painters in seventeenth-century Italy, Etro and Pagani show that prices were indeed higher with a rising number of human figures (holding many other characteristics of the painting constant, such as the size). Designing the price based on the number of human figures can be thus viewed as a way for patrons to enhance quality by paying indirectly for it.

Applying some of these insights to the management of arts organizations nowadays is not straightforward, but the aspiring principal should always keep in mind whether her objectives and those of her agents are aligned. If they are not, the manager may consider introducing certain arrangements to incentivize the behavior of the subordinates so that their acting becomes realigned with the organization's goals.

9.4   Boundaries of the Organization: Independence, Collaboration, and Merger

Two world-class orchestras compete in the same metropolitan market and have made very different choices pertaining to performance venues. After many decades of performing in a sound-challenged university auditorium, the Minnesota Orchestra constructed its own performance space, the acoustically acclaimed Orchestra Hall, in downtown Minneapolis.

Across the Mississippi River, the Saint Paul Chamber Orchestra (SPCO) has a long-term contractual relationship with the Ordway Center for the Performing Arts in downtown St. Paul, where it presents about half of its annual concerts. Otherwise, it is essentially an itinerant musical ensemble, performing at a variety of venues – usually churches or synagogues – throughout the metropolitan region.

Many other performing companies make similarly divergent choices regarding performance venue. How can we explain such differences? Figure 9.2 portrays a simplified value chain for the performing arts whereby the services of a group of talented musicians are made available to an audience under the auspices of an organization and a performance venue.[2] Each of these stages adds value to the process. Without the musicians, there would be no music; without the organization, the task of assembling the performing resources would be too daunting; and without the venue, audiences would have no access to the performance. The lingering question is: Whether it makes more sense for the venue to be "vertically integrated" into the musical organization or to remain separate?

The relevant rule is that an organization will vertically integrate – in this case, build or acquire and maintain its own performing space – if the associated incremental costs justify the associated incremental benefits. The more-or-less 100 members of the Minnesota Orchestra will simply not fit in a typical house of worship, nor would capacity be sufficient to cover the costs entailed with a larger organization. By contrast, the thirty-six musicians in the SPCO are easier to transport, and they more easily fit onto smaller stages.

Another aspect to consider, of course, is that ownership and maintenance of a performing space requires staff with skills unrelated to the core activity of the organization. The desired return to such a large physical investment requires booking as many revenue-generating uses into the facility as possible in order to cover the costs. Accordingly, the Minnesota Orchestra

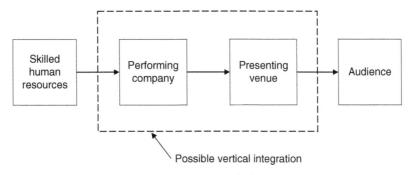

Figure 9.2 Simplified performing arts value chain.

has a dedicated eleven-person facilities staff that does not include allocated services from the finance, marketing, and development functions. The SPCO has no corresponding function, and hence no such staffing and expenditure needs.

The Ordway Center for the Performing Arts has a twelve-person operations staff and an eleven-person production staff, plus allocated sales and other support functions. The costs of these positions are spread over three core tenants – the SPCO, the Minnesota Opera, and the Schubert Club – as well as the Ordway's own season of road shows, dance performances, and other presentations. This affords the Ordway some scale economies that may not be available to the Minnesota Orchestra in its operation of Orchestra Hall.

9.5   Strategy in the Not-for-Profit Arts: Value Creation and Sharing

Almost all arts organizations are local in nature, which means that their geographic scope – including relevant market and rivalries – are inherently limited. Adapting the language from Chapter 7, some may see themselves as monopolists. Only the largest metropolitan markets host more than one major art museum, symphony orchestra, or opera company, and those organizations can easily come to regard themselves as occupying a monopoly position that requires no active strategic positioning.

That would be a mistake, however. Audiences have many alternative uses of their time and budgets, and they will seek out the combination of uses that maximizes their utilities, given costs of information, ticket outlays, and other constraints.

A strategy can be defined as that set of policy plans and actions that maximize value creation for essential stakeholders, such as audiences and other community members.

Strategic positioning can go even further and may include the definition of a target audience, based among other factors, on the visitor status: domestic or foreign tourists, or locals. In Italy, for example, museum attendance is primarily driven by foreign tourism, which is attributable to the high interest in Italian cultural heritage by international visitors. Not surprising, many museums across Italy have very similar exhibitions. One example are the life and works of Leonardo da Vinci, which are exhibited, among other places, in the Museo Leonardiano in Vinci, Museo Leonardo da Vinci in Florence, National Museum of Science and Technology in Milan, or Museo il Genio di Leonardo da Vinci in Venice. In contrast, Copenhagen appears to be a city that puts a particularly high emphasis on the well-being of locals and quite clearly above that of tourists. For example, the planned development of a state-of-the-art Natural History Museum of Denmark, which is expected to become a major tourist attraction, is critically regarded by many locals. The project encountered quite some protest since locals do not necessarily wish that their quarters become too touristic, and hence possibly overcrowded and expensive. Therefore, a requirement imposed on the planners and developers of the museum is that it becomes an attractive place to the locals as well. It is perhaps not surprising that while Denmark is not – in relative terms – a prime location for cultural tourism, it is a country characterized by some of the world's highest self-reported well-being.

A clearly defined plan of action designed to achieve a long-term goal is conducive toward its achievement. The choice of that specific goal will not always be straightforward though and may include the navigation of policies that balance quality against quantity, flat versus hierarchical organizational structures, or weight tourist activity against preferences of the locals. Furthermore, efficient arts management and strategy may not only benefit the arts institution but could have wider implications for innovativeness within a society. Borowiecki and Navarrete (2017) show the importance of policy and strategies of cultural heritage institutions in Europe, which can be conducive to innovation. In short, the economic tools and concepts presented here are surely worthy of consideration by aspiring management of arts organizations and cultural policymakers.

SUGGESTIONS FOR FURTHER READING

Addleson (2001, 169–170) forcefully makes the point that simplifying assumptions are less useful as guides to actual decision-making by the not-for-profit manager.

For a more detailed treatment of the value chain in the arts context, see Preece (2005).

See Castañer and Campos (2002) for propositions that relate organizational factors to artistic innovation, and Borowiecki and Navarrete (2017) on how policy and strategies can be conducive toward innovation at cultural heritage organizations in Europe.

PROBLEM SET

9.1 A famous actress and a film producer sign a contract. Which is the agent and which is the principal? Does it matter for analysis purposes?

9.2 The fiancé of your colleague is an emerging artist and offers to paint your portrait. You would like to have a portrait, but you do not have the time to supervise the artist. Should you offer to pay by the hour, pay a fixed fee, or pay based on the quality of the painting, and why? What will the artist most likely prefer to?

9.3 Arts organizations are built on multiple tensions between artistic and managerial values. Discuss the accuracy and significance of this statement and outline what are the emerging implications for efficient arts management.

9.4 Choose a not-for-profit cultural institution that you are familiar with or interested in and develop its strategic plan. (If such plan already exists, you can instead assess its critically.) Identify the essential stakeholders and provide a couple of specific approaches of value creation and sharing. Deliver a presentation of your results in class.

NOTES

1 Not-for-profit and nonprofit organizations are not necessary the same. Nonprofits are formed explicitly to benefit the public good, while not-for-profits exist to fulfill a mission (an organizational objectives). In the arts sector, there are many not-for-profit organizations that can (and need to) make profits, but all money earned through pursuing business activities or through donations goes right back into running the organization, and the main goal is the mission.

2 The value chain concept originates in the work of Porter (1985).

Part III

The Fine Arts and Museums

10 The Market in Works of Art

LEARNING OBJECTIVES

By the end of this chapter, readers should be able to:

- Understand the difference between a primary and secondary art market
- Explain how demand and supply affect the market in works of art
- Describe the concepts of expected return and risk, and how they interrelate
- Evaluate whether art is a good investment

It is said that Van Gogh sold but a single painting during his lifetime. Yet in 1987 one of his paintings, *Irises*, sold at auction for nearly $54 million and garnered headlines around the world. In 1990, one of his portraits brought $82.5 million, and at that time more than a few knowledgeable dealers in art works expected prices of selected works to exceed $100 million in the near future. That has come to pass many times over, but first came the great crash.

The recent record of that price movement of paintings is depicted in Figure 10.1. The chart is based on the Art Sales Index calculated by Renneboog and Spaenjers (2013), which covers over a million artworks sold globally between 1957 and 2007, and has been extended by us until 2021.[1] From 1957 through the early 1980s, art prices increased steadily, with a temporary sharper rise and then fall in the early 1970s. Beginning in 1985, the prices of impressionist paintings (not shown separately here) began to grow more rapidly, and soon thereafter, the other price rises accelerated. This period coincided with what we identified in Chapter 2 as the "boom" in the arts, but the boom ended with the "crash" of 1990 and the years immediately following. By 1994, a gradual recovery was under way, with a much sharper increase over the early 2000s so that the 1990 peak was reached in 2007. However, in the same year came the Global Financial Crisis that brought the prices into a long-lasting downward trend lasting until the end of the 2010s.

What causes an art boom or crash? Why are some works of art so expensive, while others so cheap? Why do some paintings increase in value, while others decline? What are the implications for creators and purchasers of art? Are some museums being priced out of the market, and will the broader public then experience diminished access to great art?

In this chapter, we examine the process by which artists make their creations available to purchasers, including the role of dealers, auction houses, and other modes of sale. We also inquire into why and how individuals, firms, and others decide to acquire art. These decisions create the supply of and demand for art, and the interaction of supply and demand helps explain both the levels of art prices and changes in those levels.

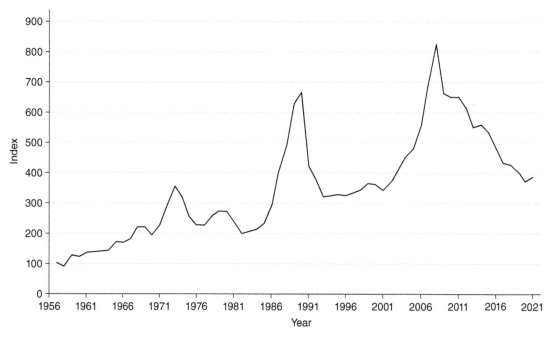

Figure 10.1 Art Sales Index, 1975–2021.
Source: Art Sales Index from 1957 to 2007, calculated by Renneboog and Spaenjers (2013), and Art Price Index from 2008 to 2021.

10.1 Some Preliminary Considerations

The concepts of supply and demand, as developed earlier, must be refined so that they more nearly fit the face-to-face nature of markets in art. Following some preliminary definitions, an overview of market structures and processes in the arts sets the stage. Then our focus will be the supply side of the market, particularly the behavior of the artist. The demand for the arts is approached through a description of the theory of asset demand and an application of that theory to arts markets. As the reader is now well aware, full understanding of the market – the price of art and the amount sold – requires the exploration of both supply and demand.

In Chapter 1, we tackled the very practical matter of defining art for the purpose of inclusion in this volume. Now, we briefly address the matter again, with a specific focus on the visual arts. Edward Banfield, a noted political scientist and art collector, issued a caveat before defining art for his purposes: "Highly civilized people can define art in profoundly various ways. Here art will be defined as that which has the capacity to engender in a receptive viewer an aesthetic experience" (Banfield, 1984, p. 21).

While we cannot disagree with this definition, it only substitutes one question for another: What is an aesthetic experience? Leslie Singer (1978) evaded such metaphysical entrapments by noting that works of art have two attributes: decorativeness (size, weight, medium, physical condition, subject matter, etc.) and intellectual appeal (art historical significance, quality of work, artist reputation, etc.) (Singer, 1978, pp. 21–39). These attributes apply to paintings, drawings, sculptures, and related collectibles. We consistently use paintings as a convenient example in illustrating the nature of the markets in question. Principles that apply to the market in paintings can easily be extended to markets in other media.

We must also reintroduce two concepts – transaction costs and information costs – that help us to understand the functioning of the markets and the roles played by some of the participants. Transaction costs refer to the costs, over and above the payment for goods sold, incurred by all parties in bringing about a transaction. Examples from the buyer's perspective would include time spent looking for and examining merchandise, waiting in lines, and discussing alternatives. For example, it is to reduce the sum of transaction costs that shoppers seeking only a few grocery items are willing to pay a price premium at a convenience store rather than spend time searching through a supermarket and standing in a checkout line.

Imperfect information in a particular market means that participants in a transaction may not be well informed about things, such as product quality, resale value, and the price and availability of substitutes. However, obtaining accurate information may be costly in terms of time, effort, and even money. The higher is the cost of being wrong, the more likely is a potential buyer to expend resources in obtaining better information. Otherwise, the buyer lacks the assurance of obtaining what he or she really wants or needs.

10.2 Arts Markets

Readers of popular business periodicals such as *Business Week*, *Forbes*, and the *Wall Street Journal* surely noticed the increasingly frequent coverage of transactions in art objects. The art boom has been eminently newsworthy since about the 1980s. According to a writer in *Forbes*:

Almost unnoticed, art has turned from an obscure, chaotic, and esoteric market to an organized and highly sophisticated market. Works of art have become quasifinancial instruments, because the art market itself has become more of a financial market (Lee, 1988, pp. 65–66).

Like "genuine" financial markets, the market in paintings really consists of at least two components: a primary market and a secondary market. We explore the nature of each of these markets in turn.

10.2.1 The Primary Market

The primary market is one in which original works are sold for the first time. As is the case in any other market, the resulting price reflects the operation of the forces of supply and demand. This market includes artists' studios, art fairs and festivals, galleries, and similar outlets.[2] As might be expected, participants in the primary market are hampered by imperfect information and encounter considerable transaction costs. The works of new artists – the "unknowns" – and the new works of more established painters are traded in this market. Purchases of art via primary market participation may entail a fair amount of risk, largely because the intellectual appeal is uncertain for many people (I may not know art, but …), even though the decorativeness attributes may be more widely recognized and understood (… I know what I like). Neophyte buyers may not know what works are being offered for sale, whether they are of high quality, or where the works are available without considerable expenditure of time and effort.

The process by which the primary market in paintings operates is much like that of other markets. The prospective buyer goes to the point of sale, perhaps a studio or gallery where works are displayed, often – but not always – with prices attached. Prices may, in fact, be in a price list posted or available at the front desk. In a typical scenario, an artist may have established an exclusive relationship with a dealer who arranges an exhibition of the artist's work. Under such an arrangement, the artist provides the creative work, and the dealer contributes market knowledge and experience. The prices that they attach to the works reflect the "reserve price" of the artist plus a best guess of what the work can command over the reserve price. The reserve price is the minimum the artist is willing to accept in bringing a work to the market. Setting the price is tricky; it should exceed the reserve price without being too high for buyers.

To the extent that the artist and her representative may be uncertain of the price that a given work can command, they may rely on a "feel for the market" or use such rule-of-thumb practices as "markup pricing." The feel for the market is based on experience in selling the artist's work in the past, the prices of similar works at the present, and knowledge of trends in buyer preferences. For new artists who have yet to establish themselves, a dealer may keep prices low in the first show. A sellout encourages slightly higher prices for a subsequent show. Markup pricing in most markets is a standard percentage of increase – say, 50% – above the costs of production. Usage in this market is necessarily less precise, since a very large component of the production costs consists of the opportunity cost of the artist's time, and this value itself may be unclear.

Figure 10.2 depicts a hypothetical market for a given work of art. As developed in Chapter 4, the market demand curve is the horizontal sum of the individual demand curves in the market. The supply curve is vertical at a quantity of one, there being, after all, only one of a unique work. Conceptually, the "market clearing" or equilibrium price is P_1. Actual sale at this price depends on attracting the individual who is willing to pay this price. Since the new artist cannot rely on this fortuitous circumstance, she will likely choose instead to set a price, P_2, above her reserve price, P_r, but below P. Any of a number of potential buyers who deem the acquisition worthwhile at this price may make the purchase on a first-come, first-served basis. The buyer is very likely to preserve a substantial amount of "consumer surplus," which is the difference between what she actually paid and what she would have been willing to pay.

New works of well-known artists may also be sold through dealers who have represented them historically. However, auction houses, which are described more fully in Section 10.2.2, are increasingly active in the sale of these works. Some of the reasons for this evolution are presented below.

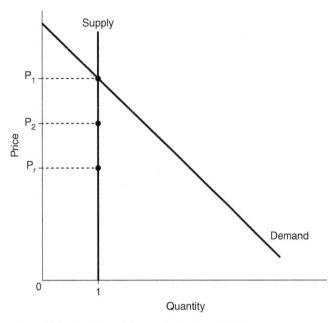

Figure 10.2 Supply and demand: single work of art.

10.2.2 The Secondary Market

The exchange of existing works of art constitutes the secondary market, and in contrast with the primary market, participants are likely to have very good information about artists and their "seasoned" works. The acquisition of recognized work in this market is not so risky as the purchase of unknowns. News about the art world can be obtained at the corner newsstand. Furthermore, traditional art journalism is complemented by the numerous electronic magazines, podcasts, and art blogs that provide content, ranging from art critiques and commentary, through art news and interviews with artists, to insider art world gossip.

Information costs in secondary art markets have fallen in recent years. Not too long ago, dealer markups were routinely two to four times the wholesale price. Auction house commissions, by contrast, may total no more than 25% of the sale price. Another innovation is that galleries more frequently post prices of exhibited works. Newcomers to these markets may be surprised to learn that prices have not always been posted. By keeping prices private, dealers could size up potential buyers and quote a price in keeping with a subjective estimate of willingness to pay. Posted prices are felt by some to protect potential buyers from possible "gouging." The fact remains, however, that so long as purchase is voluntary, the buyer may be regarded as willing to pay the price if the transaction occurs.

"An auction is a sale in which a good or service is sold to the highest bidder." (Perloff, 2018, p. 514) Auctions are used when markets have neither breadth (numerous buyers and sellers) nor depth (a number of closely related products that can be considered substitutes, even if imperfectly). Under such circumstances, market interaction does not produce a

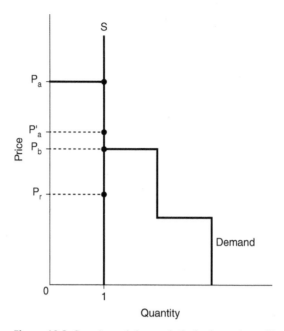

Figure 10.3 Supply and demand: limited number of buyers.

standard valuation reflected in a market price. As we show below, sale at auction may gain the maximum price for the seller.

Works of art are typically sold via what is known as an "English auction," where the price is raised until a single bidder remains. One feature of such a process is that all bidders know the current high bid for a work. The most famous auction houses are the British firms of Christie's and Sotheby's, each of which has offices and auction rooms in many countries, including the United States. Figure 10.2 can also be used to illustrate the operation of such a process. If the top price that anyone is likely to offer is P_1, a large number of potential buyers – represented by the smooth demand curve – can be expected to drive the price up to P_1, providing maximum revenue for the seller and eliminating any consumer surplus.

The more likely case might be represented by Figure 10.3, where the demand curve is discontinuous and a stair step line indicates a limited number of potential buyers with varying preferences. The most eager purchaser, Bidder A, who might be willing to pay as much as P_a, need only offer P_a' to top the bid of Bidder B, at P_b. The price received by the seller still exceeds the reserve price, P_r, by a substantial amount, while the successful bidder preserves some consumer surplus. For example, if Bidder A would have been willing to pay as much as $100,000 for a painting but needs to offer only $91,000 to top Bidder B's top offer of $90,000, then A receives $9,000 in enjoyment from the painting above what she actually paid.

In the event that the highest bid fails to exceed the reserve price, as illustrated by Figure 10.4, the painting will be "hammered down" at the reserve price and "bought in." This means that the seller rejects the bid of P_1 and, in effect, buys it from herself, but the appearance of an actual sale is maintained. If she were not willing to accept less than $1 million,

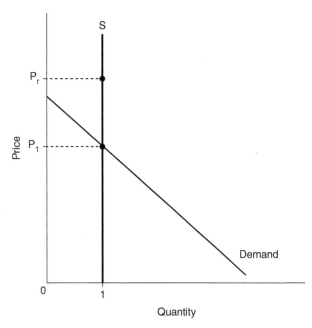

Figure 10.4 Art auction bid below reserve price.

but bidding ceased at, say, $800,000, then her representative might offer a bid of $1 million. Although the casual observer may think that a sale has occurred, in fact, the current owner simply keeps the work.

10.3 The Supply of Art

Not too long ago, James Rosenquist wrote that "art isn't really done for any reason other than a means of the artist's self-expression" (Rosenquist, 1982, p. 25). While this may be consistent with many artists' professed self-images, it certainly is not consistent with sustained material well-being. Some of the motivations of artists are developed more fully in Chapter 14, where we seek to understand how and why artists choose their professions. Suffice to say at this point that most economists (and most artists as well) recognize the commercial motivation for producing art.

Artistic products can be regarded as either commissioned or speculative. Commissioned works are those that are specifically requested by a client who is familiar with the artist's technique, such familiarity having been gained from previous exposure. Portraits typically are commissioned, and established artists are more likely to secure commissions. William Grampp recounts numerous examples even of old masters acquiescing to specific expressions of consumer preference. More often than the lay public may realize, paintings have in the past been made to order, altered, and updated, adding a new child to a family portrait or more luxuriant growth to a landscape (Grammp, 1989, pp. 46–51).

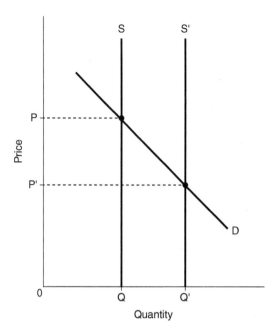

Figure 10.5 Price impact of supply increase by artist.

Speculative works are those produced by the artist with no guarantee of sale. The artist invests time, talent, and materials in producing art that may – or may not – subsequently be purchased for an acceptable price. As already described, these works are offered in the primary market. Schneider and Pommerehne view that the supply of works of art in the primary market is dependent on two factors: the costs of production and the expected selling price (Schneider and Pommerehne, 1983, p. 42). This is consistent with our theoretical considerations on the economics of art supply from Chapter 4, and it essentially means that the higher the production cost, the less willing is the artist to produce a work, while the higher the expected selling price, the more likely is the artist to bring a work to market. In the case of unique works, this boils down to an "either/or" decision. Either the market conditions support a supply decision, or they do not.

A painter may offer his or her works to the market sparingly, seeking to avoid an oversupply that may depress the price. This is illustrated in Figure 10.5, which depicts the market in the works of a particular artist. An increase in supply, with a shift in the supply curve from *S* to *S'*, causes a decline in the market price from *P* to *P'*. Works produced at a rapid pace may also be retained in the artist's own inventory as a hedge against unexpected price increases. This is one means by which an artist can take advantage of being "discovered." Another means is through a resale right, or *droit de suite*, which is a legal entitlement in the European Union (EU), in the state of California, and in Australia. This right entitles an artist to a fixed percentage of the sale price of a work whenever it changes hands. The California and Australia law provides for payment to the artist or heirs of 5% of the sale price, and the EU rate is 3%. It is probably safe to say that most economists would agree with a concise evaluation proffered by a prominent news magazine: "The law ... is daft" (*The Economist*, 1997, pp. 18–19). Like any interference in the market mechanism, it results in unexpected and perhaps unwanted consequences, as we demonstrate in Section 10.5.

10.4 The Demand for Art

The demand side of the market includes a number of participants, including collectors, dealers, museums, corporations, and anyone else with a desire to possess a work of art. Museums are the subject of Chapter 11, and we postpone further discussion of their participation until then. Although the other market participants may differ in size, awareness, and taste, they share enough characteristics for us to lump them together and simplify the discussion a bit. We refer to buyers of paintings as "households," but our analysis can easily be extended to all of the other purchasers.

Households must make a number of decisions regarding the disposition of their income. The first decision is how much to spend and how much to save. The amount spent must then be allocated among a very large number of consumer goods and services. The amount saved will be divided among a number of assets, both real and financial. Although the US Department of Commerce classifies acquisitions of works of art as consumption expenditure, they might more properly be regarded as additions to a household's asset portfolio. In that regard, they are akin to savings.

When households are considering the acquisition of assets, they weigh, at least implicitly, a number of attributes of those assets. According to the theory of asset demand, the decision to acquire art depends on the following: wealth, or the total resources available to the household; expected return on the asset relative to the return on all potential substitutes; expected risk, or the degree of uncertainty associated with the return on the asset relative to that of other assets; liquidity, or how quickly and easily the asset can be converted to cash; and tastes and preferences. Although usually taken as given, here we mention them explicitly because of their importance in arts markets (see the discussion in Chapter 4).

A change in any of these elements can cause the demand curve for paintings to shift, and a favorable shift will result in a price increase and an increase in earnings for those currently offering the paintings for sale (as well as a potential increase in earnings for other current owners). Each of the demand factors is discussed more fully in upcoming sections.

10.4.1 Wealth

Households that are wealthy can buy more assets, including art, than those that are not wealthy. Accordingly, we would expect purchases of most types of art to increase as household wealth increases. Among the exceptions to this general rule are the so-called inferior goods, purchases of which may actually decline as wealth rises. Examples from the art world might include reproductions or art posters, which in many households are relegated to the basement or storage closets in response to growing affluence. The degree to which asset demand responds to wealth changes is known as the wealth elasticity of demand, similar in concept to the price and income elasticities of demand. It is written as

$$\varepsilon_W = \frac{\Delta Q / Q}{\Delta W / W},$$

(10.1)

where Q is quantity demanded and W is wealth. If ε_W is greater than 1, this means that the quantity demanded is very responsive to wealth changes, and such assets are regarded as luxuries. If ε_W is less than 1, the asset is more likely to be a necessity. If ε_W is less than 0, the asset may be one of those reproductions. In an approximation of these measures, Michael Bryan found the value of the "real economic growth elasticity" for paintings to be about 1.35 (Bryan, 1985, p. 4). This supports the contention that paintings, in general, can be considered luxury goods. This may help to explain the recent and substantial Japanese entry into the art market. As Japanese wealth has grown, one would expect increased purchases of luxury goods and acquisition of assets.

10.4.2 Expected Return

The return on an asset measures how much we expect to gain from holding that asset. Ignoring transaction costs, the return can be written as

$$r = \frac{C + P_{t+1} - P_t + S}{P_t}, \tag{10.2}$$

where r is return, expressed as a percent, C is a dividend or coupon payment received, expressed in monetary units, P_{t+1} is the expected price in the next time period, P_t is the actual purchase price, and S is the nonpecuniary benefit derived from ownership. For a work of art, we would expect that C would equal zero, but it might, in fact, be negative, when such things as insurance premiums, maintenance, and other outlays are taken into account. Normally, S would have some positive value. For a typical financial asset, such as a corporate bond, S would likely be zero and C would have some positive value.

An example may help illustrate the role of expected return. Suppose a dealer quotes the price of a painting at $5,000 and the collector has reason to believe that this particular artist will soon gain popularity, leading to a substantial increase in the prices of his paintings. If the collector feels that she will be able to sell the painting in a year for $6,000 and that while it is in her possession, she will derive esthetic pleasure worth another $1,000, then the return from holding the painting for a year would be calculated as

$$r = \frac{6,000 - 5,000 + 1,000}{5,000} = 0.40 \tag{10.3}$$

or 40%. If this exceeds the return on other assets and seems not to entail a great deal of risk, the collector will acquire the painting.

The pure speculator, someone who is not likely to derive esthetic benefits, will require a higher expected monetary return to be persuaded to purchase the work. For this person, $S = 0$, and the expected return reduces to

$$r = \frac{6,000 - 5,000}{5,000} = 0.20 \tag{10.4}$$

or 20%. If everything else is the same, the speculator is less likely to acquire the painting than is the collector since the expected return has fallen by half.

Equation (10.2) can be rewritten to identify the highest price that a collector and a speculator are likely to offer for a painting. We can solve P_t as follows:

$$P_t = \frac{C + P_{t+1} + S}{1+r}.$$ (10.5)

Suppose both the collector and the speculator expect that a painting will sell next year for $6,000, and that the best return either could expect on an alternative financial asset is 15%. The only difference is that the collector still derives $1,000 worth of esthetic pleasure from holding the painting for a year, hanging it on a wall, impressing her friends. The speculator will be willing to pay a price of

$$P_t = \frac{6,000 + 1,000}{1+0.15} = 5,217.$$ (10.6)

The collector, on the other hand, would be willing to offer

$$P_t = \frac{6,000 + 1,000}{1+0.15} = 6,087.$$ (10.7)

If the collector and the speculator are bidding at auction for the painting, the collector will outbid the speculator. The role played by esthetic pleasure in setting art prices causes some analysts to regard speculators as unlikely to remain in the art market for long. Uninformed speculators may also regard the market as too risky, and below we turn our attention to that attribute of art. But first, we revisit the issue of the *droit de suite*.

Imposition of a tax on resale of an asset, such as a painting or other work of art, changes the value that an initial buyer is willing to pay. A 4% *droit de suite*, such as that imposed by the EU for artworks of the value as in our example, alters the collector's offer as follows[3]:

$$P_t = \frac{6,000 - (0.04)6,000 + 1,000}{1+0.15} = 5,878.$$ (10.8)

While this amount still outbids the speculator, it is less than the offer without the *droit de suite*. Thus, the real burden of paying the tax, designed to aid the artist, falls at the outset right back on the artist.

10.4.3 Risk

The amount of risk associated with an asset affects the quantity demanded. In our presentation and use of Equation (10.2), we presumed that various parties could predict the selling price of a painting in a year. Both the collector and the speculator acted as if the painting would sell for $6,000 a year. In fact, they may be very uncertain of what the selling price will be. A simple example may help to illustrate the role of risk.

Suppose two paintings, one by an established artist and one by a new discovery, happen to be priced at $5,000 each. The painting by the established artist is expected to sell in a year for $6,000, while the work of the unknown may sell for as much as $10,000 – or as little as $2,000. If each of these outcomes is equally likely, we would say that the expected value of the price in a year is the average of the two possible outcomes, or also $6,000. However, buying the latter painting entails the possibility of a substantial loss. The buyer who prefers a sure $6,000 (a gain of $1,000) to a range of $2,000–$10,000 (with a possible loss of as much as $3,000) would buy the established work. Such a person would be described as "risk-averse," and most of us seem to be risk-averse most of the time.

To summarize, if we are confident that a work of art – say, a Picasso – will increase in value, we are more likely to acquire it. If we are far less certain about the future course of the asset's price, we are less likely to be interested in purchasing it. Most contemporary paintings rather actually depreciate in value, like automobiles. According to one knowledgeable gallery owner, "The percentage of contemporary paintings that are resold at a profit is minuscule" (Robin Graham, owner of Graham Gallery, quoted in Lee, 1988, p. 67). Consistent with this anecdote, a comprehensive study of 19,000 art galleries across more than a hundred countries in 2015 revealed that selling contemporary art is least profitable. In comparison, art galleries specializing in Old Masters have a profit margin about three times as high as galleries selling contemporary art, while those with a focus on the nineteenth-century art perform about twice as well (Resch, 2016, Figure 11).

10.4.4 Liquidity

An asset that can be readily converted to cash – sold in a secondary market – is likely to be more attractive, and hence command a higher price, than one that is not so liquid. The work of a master can be resold; however, that of a novice may or may not be resold. The former is more liquid than the latter.

In general, the development of arts markets has made many works more liquid. Not too many years ago, Robert Anderson was able to say: "The vast majority of collectors and most domestic museums give little or no thought to resale possibilities when buying art works. Even in private collections holding periods typically span generations; paintings are usually sold only to settle estates" (Anderson, 1974, p. 15).

Works of art may, in the past, have been owned for forty years and more; nowadays, over such a period, paintings are often resold multiple times and typically reappear on the market more frequently (Mei and Moses, 2005). A collector can quickly sell a painting through the major auction houses.

10.4.5 Tastes and Preferences

In considering most markets, economists take tastes and preferences as given. We choose to vary from that practice because of the unique nature of arts markets. Most consumers are able to recognize the quality of, say, tomatoes, and we can be fairly certain of the quality and usefulness of items that are widely advertised. We have a lot of information and/or experience in consumption.

To the extent that the arts are a luxury good, however, many possible buyers by definition do not enter the market until they are sufficiently wealthy. Hence, they are less likely to have experience in purchasing and face the prospect of investing a great deal of their time and energy in learning about the market. But the fact that they have become wealthier may also indicate that the value of their time has increased. This creates a potential conflict that may be resolved in different ways. Some collectors may rely on "experts," the art critics, gallery owners, and others who may be in a position to divine (shape?) current public taste. Others can economize on information costs by purchasing, and then reselling, only recognized works, thereby reinforcing the superstar phenomenon in the art world, where works of the most recognized creators, whether living or dead, often command extraordinary sums, while new talent encounters ever higher hurdles.

10.5 Art as Investment

Now that we have developed the underpinnings of both supply and demand in the art market, we may inquire whether art is a good investment. Several studies have sought to ascertain precisely that, and we review some of the findings. Table 10.1 lists both the average return and the risk for a variety of "household investments" for the period of 1957–2007. In this case, return is the capital gain plus any additional monetary payment (e.g., the coupon or interest payment received on bonds) on a variety of assets, and risk is measured by the standard deviation of annual rates of return.[4] Among assets other than art, corporate stock as measured by the S&P 500 offered the highest returns (an annual average of 6.6%), but it was also somewhat risky, with a standard deviation of 16.5. This means that investors who prefer high returns and are not particularly worried about risk (we would call them risk-neutral or, in the extreme, risk-seeking individuals) would exhibit a preference for corporate stock compared with, say, corporate bonds or Treasury notes. At the other extreme, those who have a strong distaste for uncertainty might opt for the least risky asset that offers at least a reasonable return. In this case, the global government bonds not only offered a reasonable average return of about 3.1% over the period covered, but they also entailed relatively low risk.

Of special note is the riskiness of paintings, with a standard deviation nearly as high as that of gold over the period covered. Paintings would appear to be superior to gold by both risk and return measures, as they offered a higher return and less risk. But a quick review of Figure 10.1 reminds us that the volatility of paintings as an investment is nonnegligible. The high rates of return on art investments in the 1980s or during the early 2000s were exceptional, but they should not be taken to indicate that it is easy to make money in art. On the contrary, investing in most art, in most periods, might well lead to losses rather than profits, for it is only after the fact that we find out what the profitable choices would have been in any given era. "The history of art connoisseurship tells us that the main lesson imparted by the test of time is the fickleness of taste whose meanderings defy prediction" (Baumol, 1987, p. 1). Ownership of artworks may well represent a very rational choice for those who derive a high rate of return in the form of esthetic pleasure. They should not, however, let themselves be lured into the purchase of art by the illusion that they can beat the game financially and select with any degree of reliability the combination of purchase dates and art works that will produce a rate of return exceeding the opportunity cost of their investment.

Table 10.1 Returns and standard deviations of alternative household investments, 1957–2007 (in percent)

	Rate of return	Standard deviation
S&P 500 stocks	6.6	16.5
GFD global stocks	6.3	16.2
Art	4.0	19.1
Dow Jones corporate bonds	4.0	9.7
Global government bonds	3.1	8.2
Commodities	3.0	11.4
US government bonds	2.7	10.6
Gold	2.4	24.2
T-bills	1.4	2.1
US real estate	1.1	4.1

Source: Renneboog and Spaenjers (2013).

The fickle nature of the market is further illustrated by an account in the *New York Times*: "The price of paintings by Sandro Chia rose from $10,000 to $60,000 after the influential collector Charles Saatchi bought seven. But when Mr. Saatchi sold them all without explanation, the Chia star fell as fast as it had risen" (Passell, 1990).

It should not be particularly surprising then that studies of different time periods and varying data sources reach conflicting conclusions on the investment value of art. One conclusion that all observers would agree on, however, is that investing in art for financial gain is an unusually risky business that is best left to well-informed professionals.

It is now normal to consider art a bankable asset – for the very wealthy at least – but the art market is too volatile and risky for most investors (*The Art Newspaper*, 2022)

Another highly volatile art market that has evolved, mostly between 2018 and 2021, is the market for non-fungible tokens or NFTs. An NFT is a unique digital identifier that is used to certify authenticity and ownership of artworks, and this allows artists to overcome galleries or auction houses and to sell directly to buyers. Given the ease of transaction and saving in intermediary fees, the NFTs are transforming the traditional art market and attract buyers from outside the art world. The downside is that these markets are particularly volatile, and while spectacular price increases, hyped by the media, attract many new market participants, equally remarkable price drops, in the range of 70% within a matter of a few months, are possible as well (Nansen, 2022).

Periods of extraordinary rise in art prices undoubtedly helped some artists and pleased some investors. It has had seriously adverse consequences, however, for art museums and their audiences, since museums have been virtually priced out of the market for great works of art. They simply cannot afford to pay tens of millions of dollars for a single work. (A rare exception is the well-financed Getty Museum in California, which in 1990 acquired at auction the Van Gogh work mentioned at the very beginning of this chapter and in 2014 paid $65.1 million for a painting by the Édouard Manet, another nineteenth-century pivotal figure (Reif, 1989)). It is the world's wealthy private collectors who have bid art prices up to their highs. Unhappily, the works they purchase will not be available for viewing by the art-loving public, unless they lend, donate, or bequeath them to museums. It is to the economics of art museums that we turn in Chapter 11.

SUGGESTIONS FOR FURTHER READING

For discussions and analyses of the *droit de suite*, see McAndrew and Dallas-Conte (n.d.) and Banternghansa and Graddy (2011).

The topic of imperfect information and such related matters as informational asymmetry are treated in greater detail in Perloff (2018, chapter 19).

For a critical review of studies of the art market, see Frey and Eichenberger (1995). This special issue of the *review* also contained several other treatments of art as an investment.

Digital resources on art markets are manifold. Examples include the podcast series "*The Week in Art*," provided by *The Art Newspaper*, digital magazines (e.g., ARTnews), online reports (e.g., McAndrew, 2022), or analyses provided by corporate art market participants, including the two auction houses Sotheby's and Christie's.

For a curious example of the long-run return of art collected by the economist John Maynard Keynes, see Chambers et al. (2015).

PROBLEM SET

10.1 According to a major New York art dealer, "Art has been transformed into a financial instrument." Use this statement to explain the following:

    a. Why did the Art Sales Index decline in the early 1990s?

    b. Devise an explanation for why a number of major corporations have established art collections. How might a period of rising market interest rates affect such acquisitions? Explain.

10.2 The painting "*Salvator Mundi*" was allegedly purchased for £45 at Sotheby's in 1958. It was later attributed to Leonardo da Vinci and sold for £70 million in 2005 and then again for about £350 million in 2017.

    a. Calculate what has been the average annual return over each period of ownership.

    b. The painting has undergone years of restoration since 1958 and research ensued to uncover the true identity of the artist. By referring to the concepts of demand and supply, explain how the knowledge about the artist's identity has increased the price so markedly.

10.3 A recent article in the *Guardian* stated that: "Auction houses are recording a boom in sales after a return to pre-pandemic levels of supplies of works."

    a. Assess critically whether art is a good investment. In your answer discuss what are the risks and liquidity issues associated with art investment.

    b. Would your answer above differ if the time horizon of the investment was forty years?

    c. Explain whether a collector or a speculator is willing to pay a higher price for an artwork, and why?

NOTES

1 The creators of all of these indexes customarily caution the potential investor that a combination of objective measures and the subjective analyses and opinions of art experts go into their construction. Furthermore, the indexes are aggregated over a multitude of transactions, so they cannot be regarded as a reliable indicator for any single work of art or artist.

2 Singer further divides the art market into a tertiary component. This seems to us unnecessarily complicated, as the first two will describe the market quite nicely. But any such classification scheme abstracts from the usual blurring between categories. For example, dealers participate in the secondary as well as the primary market, while auction houses extend their reach into the primary market.

3 See Directive 2001/84/EC of the European Parliament and of the Council of 27 September 2001 on the resale right for the benefit of the author of an original work of art.

4 Standard deviation measures how much the observed values of a work of art vary from their average values. The standard deviation is calculated as $\sigma = \sqrt{\dfrac{(X - \mu)^2}{N}}$, where X is the value of a work of art at some time, μ is its average value over the period covered, and N is the number of different values observed over the time period covered.

11 The Economics of Art Museums

LEARNING OBJECTIVES

By the end of this chapter, readers should be able to:

- Explain the different roles of a museum
- Describe the trends in museum attendance and the profile of museum visitors
- Evaluate a museum's cost and revenue sources
- Discuss the problem of distribution of art among museums

Museums are essentially collections of objects, or sometimes experiences, that reflect and convey a cultural heritage over time. Art museums preserve and present the artistic elements of that cultural heritage. All museums face persistent questions of how to allocate resources among their multiple functions, how to manage their investment portfolios (including works of art), and how to pay for it all. In this latter regard, museum managers wrestle constantly with what prices to charge for gallery admission, given that their missions may be incompatible with excluding *anyone* by imposing an admission fee. This chapter addresses these and related issues. Although the emphasis is on museums and museum policy in the United States, the fundamental principles and conclusions may be generalized to other nations as well.[1]

11.1 What Do Museums Do?

The Museum Data Files, developed and maintained on behalf of the Institute of Museum and Library Services (IMLS), include entries for 2,620 art museums in the United States (Institute of Museum and Library Services, 2018). Of these, over 200 – including some Canadian and Mexican museums – are regularly surveyed by the Association of Art Museum Directors (AAMD, 2018), and the results of those surveys inform much of the discussion to follow.

Alma S. Wittlin (1970, p. 2) pointed out that museums are characteristically flexible because "they allow a wide gamut of differences in the use people make of them," and that "many, if not most, visitors to a museum hardly distinguish between learning and recreation." The variety of functions performed by art museums reflects the breadth of the demands the public makes on them. Their principal business may be to collect and display art, but they perform several other functions as well, notably, conservation, research, and education (Murray, 2020). Table 11.1, drawn from the 2014 and 2017 AAMD surveys, presents a breakdown of the

Table 11.1 Museum operating expenses, percent allocation by category, 2014–2017

	2014	2017
Arts-focused activities	33	31
Temporary exhibitions, curatorial, collections care and management, education, library		
Revenue-generating activities	24	23
Store, development, membership, benefit events, facilities and catering, restaurant, marketing and PR		
Administration	16	15
Administration, IT		
Infrastructure	21	20
Building maintenance, utilities, security		
Other	6	10

Source: Association of Art Museum Directors, "Art Museums by the Numbers," 2015 and 2018.

expenditures of nonprofit art museums among categories, which reflects the broad range of functions. Arts-related outlays constitute almost one-third of total expenditures in 2017, the largest overall category, as might be expected. It may surprise the casual museum patron to learn that "revenue generating activities" comprise almost a quarter of total outlays. Elements of this category illustrate the range of complementary activities at many museums, including stores and restaurants.

Conservation (collections care and management) is an important component of the arts-related category. We note that conducting conservation "in house" requires hiring a trained conservator and maintaining an up-to-date laboratory. According to one commentator (Storch, 1990, pp. 92–94), the setup costs for such a facility, plus annual cost of materials and supplies and a conservator's salary, can be a considerable sum. Consequently, only the largest art museums do it themselves. Those museums that do not neglect the problem (and some do) contract, for the service, with outside specialists in conservation or with other museums that have the requisite facilities.

Educational programs are another significant category of the arts-focused activities. Such programs comprise activities such as public lectures, art appreciation courses, programs in cooperation with local public schools and colleges, teacher training programs, and courses for academic credit. (Of course, if we were to adopt a broader definition of learning consistent with Wittlin's previously quoted statement, much of the expense of collection and display could also be labeled educational.) Clearly, museum directors and their boards of trustees believe that providing an education program is one of their civic responsibilities. Moreover, it is an important one to carry out if they wish to retain or expand subsidy support from their local government. But an education program also serves a museum's self-interest by building an appreciative audience among which the institution's future financial supporters may be found. Casual empiricism in support of this point includes the inevitable lineups of yellow school buses outside major US art museums on nearly any weekday during the school year. (We pursue this topic later in this chapter as well as in Chapter 12.)

Research in an art museum consists in trying to determine as precisely as possible the origin, authorship, and character of each object in the collection. Since that is the responsibility of the curator, we can assume that some fraction of expenditure listed in Table 11.1 as curatorial is allocable to research. Also assignable to research would be the cost of maintaining a library, which is listed explicitly in the table. In addition, a part of the outlay for exhibitions might be classified as research, since important research is often carried out when new exhibitions are mounted.

Finally, Table 11.1 shows that revenue-generating activities, including development and membership, accounted for a sizeable portion of operating outlays. These are the costs of obtaining ongoing or episodic financial support for a not-for-profit organization. Membership programs seek to enroll ordinary citizens who are willing to pay, say, $50, $80, or $100 a year to become a "friend" of the museum. "Development" is the polite word for large-scale fundraising. If membership is fundraising at the retail level, development is fundraising at the wholesale level. The development staff try to obtain large charitable donations from wealthy and/or generous persons or foundations, as well as grants from state or federal agencies. They, as well as the senior curatorial staff and the members of the board of trustees, also work at persuading wealthy private collectors to donate or bequeath works of art directly to the museum. Rooms or even entire wings of museums may be named in honor of patrons who donate a large collection or pay for the construction of an addition to the galleries.

11.2 Attendance at Art Museums

Attendance at art museums may be taken as a reasonable indicator of the public's interest in the fine arts. Table 11.2, which incorporates data from several Surveys of Public Participation in the Arts up until 2017, shows some variability but no clear trend in adult visits to art museums.

As an early point of reference, the 1982 survey found that 22.1% of all adults reported having visited an art museum or gallery in the previous twelve months. After some intervening ups and downs, this figure was 23.7% by 2017. Because of changes in survey methodology and in arts experience delivery methods (especially the Internet) between the earliest and most recent time periods, we must interpret this apparently minor change with care.

The surveys also allow us to compare the public's rate of attendance at museums of art with its propensity to engage in other recreational activities. The 2017 participation rate at art museums is higher than that for any of the individual live performing arts, among which the highest rate is 16.5% for musical plays and operettas. On the other hand, it has historically been below the participation rate for such other entertainments as movies away from home and sports events, which typically fall in the 35–60% range.

It was pointed out in Chapter 3 that participation rates in the arts rise dramatically with increases in individual income, occupational status, and educational attainment. Table 3.2 showed that these generalizations hold for art museums as well as for the performing arts. We have also discussed in Chapter 3 that for the performing arts, education is a more important determinant of participation than income.

Table 11.2 US adults attending an art museum, performing arts or other leisure activities, selected years (values in percent)

	1982	2002	2008	2012	2017
Visual arts					
Art museum or gallery	22.1	26.5	22.7	21	23.7
Performing arts					
Musical plays	18.6	17.1	16.7	15.2	16.5
Jazz	9.6	10.8	7.8	8.1	8.6
Classical music	13.0	11.6	9.3	8.8	8.6
Opera	3.0	3.2	2.1	2.1	2.2
Ballet	4.2	3.9	2.9	2.7	3.1
Leisure activities					
Cinema	63.0	60.0	53.3	59.4	-
Sports events	48.0	35.0	36.2	30.4	-

Source: National Endowment for the Arts, Survey of Public Participation in the Arts.

Table 11.3 Comparison of art museum visitors and selected performing arts attenders, 2012 (values in percent)

	Art museum or gallery	Classical music	Opera	Ballet	Theater
Gender					
Male	42.9	43.9	41.3	36.0	42.1
Female	57.1	56.1	58.7	64.0	57.9
Race and ethnicity					
White	76.0	83.2	78.0	79.4	80.7
Hispanic	10.1	5.5	7.8	9.2	6.4
African American	6.5	5.1	6.2	6.9	8.5
Asian	5.6	4.9	7.4	3.4	3.0
Other	1.8	1.3	0.6	1.1	1.4
Income					
$20,000 or less	8.4	7.8	7.4	8.5	7.9
Over $150,000	17.0	18.2	22.3	17.6	16.5
Education level					
Not high school graduate	2.4	1.9	1.5	2.0	2.0
Graduate school	23.5	29.6	37.0	28.6	24.2

Source: Survey of Public Participation in the Arts, 2012.

11.3 A Profile of Museum Visitors

Because the rate of museum attendance rises strongly with education, income, and occupational status, it follows that art museum audiences will rank higher on those socioeconomic measures than will the US population as a whole. Table 11.3, drawn from the 2012 Survey of

Public Participation in the Arts (SPPA), allows us to compare the socioeconomic character of art museum visitors and audiences for selected live performing arts. What it shows us is that museum visitors as a whole do not rank as high on socioeconomic measures as do performing arts attenders. A greater proportion of art museum visitors have education of less than the high-school graduate level or incomes of less than $20,000 than at the performing arts. There are also fewer of those who earn over $150,000 among museum visitors, especially in relation to opera. In other words, on socioeconomic measures, museumgoers are somewhat closer to the US average than are performing arts attenders, especially those who attend classical music or opera.

11.4 Museums as a Decreasing Cost Industry

We look now at the cost conditions under which museums operate. This will provide the background needed for the discussion of the contentious question of museum entrance fees. The analysis focuses especially on the display function, since that is by far the costliest, and, of course, it is to see the museum's displays that the public would be asked to pay an admission fee.

The question we wish to answer is: How does the cost of making the museum's displays available to the public vary with the level of public admissions? In this formulation, admissions serve as the measure of output for the display function. The analysis deals only with short-run variation; hence, the museum's galleries (its "plant") are assumed to be fixed in size. What we are really asking, therefore, is: How does cost vary with output in the short run, or in other words, what is the shape of the short-run cost curves for the display function? The answer, we argue, is that the display function operates under conditions of short-run decreasing unit cost.

Figure 11.1 shows the relationship between daily display function cost per visitor and the number of visitors per day. The shapes of the curves displayed in Figure 11.1 are deduced from what we know about the way museums operate, and they are generally supported by available empirical work. It is useful to divide the cost of operating the display function into two parts. (1) Basic operating cost for the galleries includes heating, lighting, maintenance, insurance, office staff, and basic security service. These can be thought of as the minimum costs that must be incurred if the galleries are to open each morning. They are a fixed sum that does not vary with the number of visitors per day. The cost per visitor of this component therefore falls as the number of visitors increases. (2) The museum also incurs a marginal cost (*MC*) for each person/visit to cover the cost of additional security, information, and cleaning personnel imposed by attendees.

In Figure 11.1 we assume, for the sake of simplicity, that marginal cost per visitor is constant. It is therefore shown as a horizontal line in the diagram. (In fact, once basic operating costs have been incurred to open the museum for the day, the marginal cost of a visitor might well be zero over some relatively low range of visits.) Basic operating cost per attendee is not shown separately, but we know how it behaves: Since it consists of a fixed component divided by an increasing quantity, it would have the shape of a rectangular hyperbola, sloping downward exactly like average fixed cost in Figure 6.1. By adding this component vertically onto

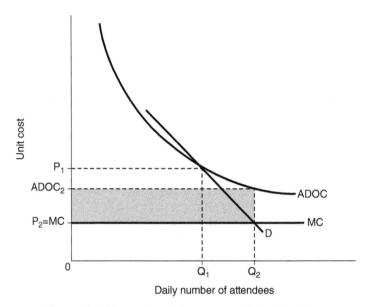

Figure 11.1 Economies of the museum display function.

marginal cost, we generate the downward-sloping average daily operating cost curve ($ADOC$) in the diagram. (Basic operating cost per visitor can be read as the vertical distance between MC and $ADOC$.) Thus, the museum display function operates under conditions of decreasing unit cost because, as more visitors enter, the basic cost of opening the galleries to the public can be spread over more visits.

11.4.1 Full Cost versus Marginal Cost Pricing

To analyze the effect of charging for admission, we need information about the public's willingness to pay for visits. In Figure 11.1, curve D shows the demand for visits as a function of the price charged. If the museum wished to set a price just high enough to cover the full cost of the display function, it would charge the price indicated by the intersection of the demand curve and the average daily operating cost curve: At a price of P^1, Q^1 visitors would enter per day and the average daily operating cost would exactly equal the price charged. The display function would break even. Some analysts who oppose government subsidies for museums have argued strenuously in favor of that (Haag, 1979).

However, at output Q_1, marginal cost is well below price. Charging price P_1 therefore violates the welfare rule, which says that price should be set equal to marginal cost. There is a measurable welfare loss to society in charging price P_1, indicated by the fact that potential visitors between Q_1 and Q_2, who are willing to pay more than the full marginal cost of their visit, but not a price as high as P_1, are nevertheless denied attendance. (This welfare argument is developed more fully at the beginning of Chapter 12.) On the other hand, if the museum followed the welfare rule, it would set price at the level indicated by the intersection of D and MC: At price P_2

there would be Q_2 visits per day. The welfare rule would be satisfied, but because price would be below cost, the display function would incur a daily operating deficit of $Q_2\left(ADOC_2 - P_2\right)$, equal to the area of the shaded rectangle in Figure 11.1.

Because the size of the potential deficit is large, the issue raised here is not a trivial one. We will use the financial report of the Minneapolis Institute of Art (Mia, as it presents itself) to illustrate our point. Operating expenditures of Mia totaled in excess of $39 million in 2016. Program expenses (the display function, education, and other direct and indirect services to visitors) accounted for more than $35 million of that. Dividing by the 2016 attendance of 760,000 yields an average cost per visit (or $ADOC$) in excess of $46.00. That is far above the probable marginal cost per visitor, which may in fact be close to zero. It also greatly exceeds the zero entrance fee that Mia charges. The certainty that charging a price equal to marginal cost would result in operating deficits for museums is a powerful argument for providing them with government subsidies. The question of subsidies and/or alternative ways of covering museum deficits is discussed further in Chapters 12 and 13, as well as in the section of this chapter dealing with museum finances.

The analysis to this point has overlooked the phenomenon of congestion that may occur at very popular special exhibitions, or, as they have come to be known, "blockbusters." (See the discussion of this topic below in this chapter.) Crowding at an exhibition reduces the pleasure obtained by viewers. This reduction in pleasure can be thought of as a cost that visitors who enter a congested exhibition impose on other simultaneous visitors and can be treated as an increase in marginal and average cost, starting at the point when visitors begin to get in each other's way. If the museum were setting fees equal to marginal cost, such an increase in marginal cost would justify higher charges for blockbusters than for ordinary exhibitions. The higher fees, if set correctly, would reduce congestion to the optimal level and make some contribution toward covering the deficit incurred during uncongested periods.

11.4.2 Entrance Fees and Equity Considerations

To this point the discussion of admission charges to museums has dealt only with what economists call the "efficiency" issue: It was argued that charging a price in excess of the presumably very low marginal cost would be inefficient in the sense of violating the $P = MC$ welfare rule. But charging for admission also raises issues of "equity" or "redistribution." Historically, most art museums in the United States have charged visitors little or nothing not because they understood the economist's arcane welfare rule, but rather because they believed it was their mission to make great art available to the masses, and they feared that substantial entrance fees would prevent the relatively poor from partaking. It is therefore worthwhile to ask whether entrance fees, even those as low as the marginal cost of an admission, would in fact tend to filter out low-income visitors.

There is not much empirical evidence on this question. However, Kirchberg (1998b) studied a representative survey of Germans in order to evaluate whether entrance fees are a significant barrier to visiting museums, and how individual socioeconomic characteristics matter. He finds that entrance fees affect visits by people with lowest incomes about five times as much as people in the highest income bracket. However, it is not only income that matters, but also education and occupation. The conclusion by Kirchenberg is that entrance fees will potentially not only affect museum's revenues and the number of visitors, but it will also change the socioeconomic composition of the attendance and may "contribute to an elitist composition of museum attendances" (Kirchberg, 1998b).

While these conclusions have unlikely changed in more recent years, the accessibility to museums has been enhanced by digital technologies as increasingly many museums become virtual and freely accessible to anybody, independent of their status or background. We will address these topics in more depth in Chapter 16.

11.5 Entrance Fees and Overall Fiscal Health

In addition to income from admission fees, museums obtain revenue from sales in museum stores and cafeterias. Museum managers should be concerned with whether and to what extent these may be regarded as "complementary" goods. A hypothetical example should illustrate the potential importance of cross-price elasticity, developed in Chapter 4, in the museum sector. Suppose for simplicity's sake that we can describe the three outputs of a museum as gallery visits, museum shop sales, and museum restaurant sales. Most museums provide gallery access to visitors of lesser means in a variety of ways, including specific days set aside for free entry. A museum's management, considering whether to add a second free-entry day, should consider the impact on other revenues. Table 11.4 offers some hypothetical figures.

The addition of a second free day increases the average number of total visits on that day by 500 persons. Of those, 100 formerly paid an admission fee of $5, but now are able to take advantage of free admission, resulting in $500 of forgone revenues. The 400 new visitors make purchases in the shop and restaurant that yield an average net of $2 and $1, respectively. The 100 persons, who formerly paid for admission, having saved $5, spend more than previously in the shop and restaurant, as indicated. Finally, the museum saves on selected staffing outlays on the free day. The result, as illustrated, is a net revenue increment of $1,200 per free day. There may also be some indirect or secondary effects, such as goodwill, increased individual and organizational giving, and so on. Steiner's (1997) study of a

Table 11.4 Calculation of net effect, hypothetical change in museum admissions policy, in US dollars

Component of change	Amount
Loss due to 100 displaced visitors at $5	−$500
Net museum shop earnings, spending by 400 new visitors at $2	800
New restaurant earnings spending by 400 new visitors at $1	400
Net museum shop earnings, increased spending by 100 previous visitors at $2	200
Net restaurant earnings increased spending by 100 previous visitors at $1	100
Personnel savings, reduced ticket sellers, and entry monitors	200
Total amount	$1,200

single museum failed to turn up evidence of such cross-price responses, although her theoretical model certainly pointed to the strong possibility, and museums may be well advised not to reject such pricing alternatives.

11.6 Acquisition Policies of Art Museums

Art museums reported spending $2.81 billion acquiring works for their collections in 2018. In addition, they reported donations of artworks valued at $2.49 billion (Association of Art Museum Directors, 2018). The latter figure may err on the low side because some museums were unable to estimate the value of the works they received as gifts.

Donations of works of art that appreciated in value after the donor purchased them are strongly affected by provisions of the federal tax code. This important question is examined in detail in Chapter 13.

Acquisition policies have always been a sensitive topic in the museum world. Directors and boards of trustees are reluctant to tip their hands for fear of adversely affecting the art market. In their annual reports, they do show aggregate cash expenditures for acquisitions, and they are happy to list the works acquired, but they do not have to report the prices they paid or the estimated value of donated works. They are eager to avoid controversy, and as we see in the next section, in the museum world, nothing more easily leads to controversy than decisions affecting a museum's holdings.

11.7 Managing a Museum's Collection

When economists look at an art museum, they see an institution that has a large stock of capital held in the form of works of art and of buildings in which the art is either displayed or stored. But why "stored"? If display is their principal function, then why not show the entire collection? The answer is that few museums have the gallery space to display all their holdings simultaneously. As a result, some pieces are consigned to the basement. These are likely to be either works in a style that is no longer considered interesting or less important pieces in a category of which they have better examples on display. Works in storage are known as "the reserve." In some cases, they exceed by many times the number of pieces actually on display.

To an economist, the problem of managing a museum's collection, which is its capital, appears to raise some of the same questions that occur in managing the assets of a business firm. Unlike a commercial enterprise, the museum is not trying to maximize profits. But it is presumably trying to attain some set of definable objectives, for which it ought to deploy its assets efficiently. With this in mind, an economist might ask whether the right balance has been struck between the quantity of art owned and the amount of building space available to display it. For example, a museum with a large number of high-quality pieces in its reserve might be better advised to build more gallery space rather than to spend funds purchasing more works of art that it lacks space to display. In economic terms, it is a matter of comparing at the margin the benefits to be obtained by investing an additional dollar in building gallery space as compared with the benefit of investing that dollar in additional works of art and then spending the money where the benefit per dollar is greatest.

11.7.1 The Problem of "Deaccessioning"

The trade-off between investing in art or in structures is a relatively simple matter to discuss. Much stickier is the question of how to manage the museum's art holdings themselves. It might seem reasonable for a museum that owns a relatively large number of paintings by postimpressionists Vincent Van Gogh and Henri Rousseau, but none by Annibale Carracci, an important sixteenth-century Bolognese mannerist, to sell a Van Gogh and a Rousseau and use the proceeds to buy a Carracci. An economist might say, "They're just trying to deploy their assets rationally." But when the Baltimore Museum of Art tried to do just that in 2020, it ran into a storm of protest and decided to pull out just two hours before the auction (Sheets, 2020). "Deaccessioning" of major works – the term refers to selling an object out of the museum's permanent collection – almost always leads to controversy.

The justification usually given for deaccessioning is that it allows the museum to better meet its chosen objectives. The criticism often comes from those who disagree with the objectives. A museum as large as the Metropolitan may wish to cover the field of art very broadly and has the resources to do so successfully. In that case, selling a Van Gogh and a Rousseau to buy a painting that will help fill a gap in the collection would seem to make sense.

Small- or medium-sized museums, on the other hand, may decide to specialize in the art of one period or country and will therefore deaccession objects that fall outside of their chosen field and use the proceeds to buy additional works within that specialty. A case in point, reported by Evan Roth (1990), is the Walker Art Center in Minneapolis that some years ago decided to concentrate on contemporary, especially twentieth-century, US art. In May 1989, at Sotheby's in New York, it auctioned twenty-two very fine nineteenth-century US paintings and announced that the proceeds, amounting to $10.5 million, would be used to buy works that "better reflect the artistic mission of the museum." But Roth reports that "the sale was not universally well received" and quotes Jonathan Yardley of the *Washington Post* as complaining that "thanks to selling off giants of the 19th century, the museum has the money to buy up more pygmies of the 20th." Evidently, Yardley disagrees with Walker's objectives. Sarah Montgomery (1992) has suggested that fear of being proved wrong may be one reason museum professionals resist deaccessioning: Because critical judgment about art does change with time, what they sell off today may be viewed tomorrow as having "special aesthetic value." Far safer, they think, to keep currently uninteresting works in storage.

Deaccessioning does raise difficult questions. Some argue that it will shake the confidence of potential donors, who do not like to think that the works of art they reluctantly part with may later be sold by the museum on the open market, perhaps passing back into private hands. There are also those who would argue that museums violate public trust if they dispose of any object that has been given into their safekeeping.

Perhaps one of the feasible solutions is a concept that became known as the "Ellis Rule," which permits deaccessioning, provided that the deaccessioning museum ensures the institution or individual to whom it sells commits in some binding form to equal or higher conservational standards and equal or higher public access (Dickieson 2018). It is thus a procedure that maintains the *status quo*, and yet the ownership of an artwork changes and potentially also the place of exhibition. In any case, the topic of deaccessioning remains current as it is also visible with a recent introduction of laws allowing museums in the United Kingdom to dispose of objects where there is a compelling moral obligation to do so (Department for Digital, Culture, Media and Sport, 2022).

11.8 Some Questions of Distribution

The preceding section, which dealt with the problem of rationally managing a single museum's collection, leads us to the important question of the distribution of art among museums. It is a puzzling fact that our larger museums have extensive reserves holding many objects, which, though rarely displayed, may be of a higher quality than works currently on display in smaller museums. Would not the less well-endowed places be delighted to have a few of the rejects in the basement of the Metropolitan? Montias (1973, p. 214) points out that this sort of misallocation of social resources is made worse by the fact that museum directors have virtually no incentive to refuse a bequest. The result, he thinks, is that works of art "often end up in places that have no need for them."

When a misallocation of resources exists, a correction can yield social gains (theoretically measurable in monetary units). If an appropriate way can be found to divide those gains between the affected parties, it is possible that all of them can be made better off in the process of overcoming the misallocation. In the case of museum holdings discussed here, economic intuition suggests that there must be a conceivable arrangement by which less well-endowed institutions could rent – perhaps indefinitely – underutilized objects from museums that are, in effect, overstocked. Economists point out that when voluntary trades are made in the marketplace, both parties benefit; otherwise, they would not have agreed to the trade. Hence, if the arrangements suggested here were carried out voluntarily, we could assume that both the lender and the borrower gained from the transaction. Perhaps the problem is that museum directors and boards of trustees would prefer to spend their available funds (however meager) buying art to add to the museum's collection rather than renting it. "Renting" sounds decidedly second rate when compared with the accomplishment implied by "new acquisition." But with art prices in the marketplace rising to the levels that are referred to on all sides as astronomical, the time may be near when novel arrangements for sharing existing museum resources will become acceptable.

Stephen E. Weil, a long-time museum administrator now retired from the Smithsonian Institution, reaches a similar conclusion, but without using explicitly economic arguments. He sees no reason why large and small museums need to pursue identical policies. Instead, he calls for a division of labor "with each size of institution specializing in what it did best." He suggests that large museums could serve as the principal repositories and caretakers of our material heritage and the primary source of loans. Small museums would concentrate on presenting special exhibitions and other programs that drew on the collection resources of the larger museums and addressed the esthetic, historic, political, and scientific issues relevant to their communities (Weil, 1990). Small museums could thus give up trying to do what they cannot do very well, that is, collect art, while concentrating on what they are uniquely well suited to do, that is, mount exhibits relevant to their own communities. In this way, Weil argues, the museum field as a whole could best serve the public interest. He admits, however, that the scheme leaves medium-sized museums out of account. They would probably have to go on pretty much as they have done, both collecting and exhibiting.

Weil has also pointed out that joint acquisition by several museums is another constructive response to the nearly prohibitive current cost of adding to a museum's collection. He cites several cases in which US museums have jointly purchased works of art under an agreement that provides for the regular circulation of the objects among the partners. For example, in 1975, a group of museums in the state of Washington formed the Washington Art Consortium for the purpose of purchasing a collection of US drawings and other works on paper. Each participant, Weil (1983, p. 151) writes, "is guaranteed the right to show the entire collection for at least four months during any two-calendar-year period." The National Endowment for the Arts (NEA) supported this cooperative effort with a $100,000 grant in 1975. And more recently, as Blumenthal (1995) puts it, "… tough economic times in the arts are making for interesting new institutional bedfellows." His *New York Times* article describes many such sharing arrangements, some funded by private foundations.

11.8.1 Collection Sharing and Franchising on a Large Scale

Several major museums now see collection sharing on an international scale as a way to serve wider audiences while simultaneously augmenting their own income. To take one early example, in October 1991, the Museum of Fine Arts in Boston announced an agreement with a Japanese group to supply art from the Boston museum's extensive collections to a new museum planned for the city of Nagoya. According to the announcement (MNEWS, 1991), the Boston museum would "develop both long-term and temporary exhibitions" from its own holdings for the Nagoya museum. It would "also make its expertise available in all areas of the new museum's operations, and would be appropriately compensated for its services."

An even more elaborate scheme for collection sharing has been implemented at the Solomon R. Guggenheim Museum in New York City (Kimmelman, 1990, 1992). The Guggenheim specializes in twentieth-century European painting, of which it has one of the world's greatest collections, reportedly numbering around 6,000 pieces. Its building, a deservedly famous structure designed by Frank Lloyd Wright, can display only a few hundred objects at a time. A small annex has been added, but further expansion at the existing site is impossible. The solution, in addition to a branch in the SoHo district of lower Manhattan (now closed), is a "franchising" system, under which additional "Guggenheims" are being established at selected locations globally. The cost of constructing them is borne by foreign governments or localities eager for the prestige and tourism such a facility would undoubtedly confer. Artworks to fill these branches are on loan from the Guggenheim in New York, which also provides curatorial services and receives appropriate fees in return. The additional income would enable the Guggenheim to round out its collection by purchasing late-twentieth-century works. Table 11.5 lists the various Guggenheim museums and their sites.

Table 11.5 Guggenheim museums

Museum and location	Established	Closed
Solomon R. Guggenheim Museum, New York City	1959	–
Peggy Guggenheim Collection, Venice, Italy	1980	–
Guggenheim Museum, SoHo, New York City	1992	2001
Guggenheim Museum Bilbao, Spain	1997	–
Deutsche Guggenheim, Berlin, Germany	1997	2013
Guggenheim Hermitage Museum, Las Vegas	2001	2008
Guggenheim Museum, Las Vegas	2001	2003
Guggenheim Guadalajara, Mexico	2007	2009
Guggenheim Abu Dhabi, United Arab Emirates	2025[a]	–

[a] Expected opening date.

Theoretically, the franchise plan does help overcome the misallocation of resources, which, as we indicated earlier, is implied by large, undisplayed reserves of art. Nevertheless, many observers worry about its risks. First, that the Guggenheim may become financially overextended in playing the game of international expansion and thus risk losing control of the collection it exists to protect; second, that by emphasizing autonomy, the scheme tends to undermine the alternative of cooperation between museums; third, that the art itself will be at risk when shipped back and forth across the globe to rotate the stock at the new Guggenheim satellites. We take up the risks of transporting art to international exhibitions at the end of the next section.

11.8.2 Special Exhibitions, Tours, Blockbusters!

Special exhibitions and tours have a major impact on the geographic distribution of art display. In effect, these events substitute the transportation of art for the transportation of people. In the last thirty years, they have grown enormously in frequency and importance (Dobrzynski, 1996). Many formats are possible. A museum of almost any size may decide to put on a special exhibition of the work of some artist, school, or period in which they own a nucleus of at least a few objects. The bulk of the exhibition will consist of works borrowed from other museums or from private collectors. Since the expense of organizing such a "loan exhibit" (including curatorial staff time, packing and transportation charges, and insurance) is considerable, the organizers will usually try to spread the costs by sharing the exhibition with other museums, in effect, putting the show on tour. The Department for Digital, Culture, Media and Sport (2021) estimated that national museums in the United Kingdom undertook about 2,300 loans of more than 71,000 objects in 2019. Since the typical exhibit travels to several museums and is usually a "featured attraction" wherever it goes, the total impact of these endeavors is surely impressive.

These events increase the availability of art to the viewing public along two dimensions. First, there is a "concentration effect": They bring together far more works with a unifying theme than the viewer could otherwise hope to see in any one place. The impact is powerful, and the museumgoer is far more likely to come away with lasting esthetic impressions than would be the case if only a few works of any given type were on view during a single visit. Second, there is a

Table 11.6 Selected blockbuster exhibits, 2019

Exhibit and site	Attendance
"Diane Arbus: Box of Ten Photographs," Smithsonian, Washington D.C.	1,677,000
"Tutankhamun: Treasures of Golden Pharaoh," La Villette, Paris	1,423,170
"Trevor Paglen: Sites Unseen," Smithsonian, Washington D.C.	1,132,800
"Tiffany Chung: Vietnam, Past Is Prologue," Smithsonian, Washington D.C.	968,200
"Between Worlds: Art of Bill Traylor," Smithsonian, Washington D.C.	960,500
"Camp: Notes on Fashion," Metropolitan Museum of Art, New York	687,449
"Jean-Michel Basquiat/Egon Schiele," Foundation Louis Vuitton, Paris	676,503
"Munch: A Retrospective," Tokyo Metropolitan Art Musem, Tokyo	669,846
"DreamWorks," Centro Cultural Banco do Brasil, Rio de Janeiro	663,265
"DreamWorks," Centro Cultural Banco do Brasil, Belo Horizonte	605,674

Source: "Art's most popular 2020," *The Art Newspaper* (2020, p. 3).

"distribution effect": Special exhibitions and tours carry this concentration of works, with its powerful esthetic impact, to places that may be remote from major collections. (Incidentally, it should be pointed out that traveling exhibitions are shown not only at museums but also at local "arts centers" that have exhibition space, but no collection of their own.)

Special exhibitions of sufficiently grand size, or blockbusters, are usually loan exhibitions dealing with the work of a major (and very popular) painter, such as Van Gogh, Degas, or Matisse, or that bring to the public works not readily accessible, such as the King Tut exhibit of Egyptian art or the exhibition of masterpieces from the Buckingham Palace. Museums may sometimes charge a special admission fee for a blockbuster, and so may come out ahead financially on a particularly well-attended exhibit. In addition, when an exhibition goes on tour, the institution that organized it is entitled to collect participation fees from the museums it visits. According to the NEA, most special exhibitions do not make money. However, they do attract visitors, and "for most museums, attendance translates ultimately into income." Table 11.6 depicts a list of the world's best attended exhibits in 2019; it is worth noting that four of the top ten blockbuster exhibits have been hosted by the Smithsonian in Washington, D.C., but also two shows were organized in Paris.

To be sure, the vogue for special exhibitions has its detractors. Blockbusters usually attract major support from corporate sponsors. Some observers object that in their eagerness for corporate support, museums are permitting themselves to be commercialized and losing sight of their artistic objectives. Others argue that emphasis on special exhibitions has undermined the public's willingness to attend just for the sake of studying the regular collection. There are staffing problems, as well. The larger museums, having attractive collections, must process an enormous number of loan requests, which puts a heavy and, from their point of view, unproductive burden on their professional staff. Finally, some art lovers worry about the potential for catastrophic loss should an airplane crash while carrying irreplaceable masterpieces to an internationally organized blockbuster. This fear was realized when some art was lost in the well-publicized crash of Swissair flight 111 in September 1998. One critic who raised that objection (as well as some others) did, however, admit that some appalling acts of vandalism and burglary have occurred in major museums during the ordinary course of business (Haskell, 1990, p. 9).

11.9   A Note on "Superstar" Museums

Bruno Frey has introduced the concept of "superstar" museums to describe the status and behaviors of such destination institutions as New York's Metropolitan Museum of Art, Chicago's Art Institute, the Prado in Madrid, the Louvre in Paris, the Hermitage in St. Petersburg, the Uffizi in Florence, the Rijksmuseum in Amsterdam, and other "must-sees" for visitors to their host cities. Superstar museums feature world-famous artists and paintings (Frey, 1998, pp. 113–125).

The superstar museums are widely regarded as having a favorable economic impact on their communities, and many are actively engaged in "cultural tourism," a concept covered in greater depth in Chapter 15. They are under substantial pressure to continue to satisfy customers, what Frey calls a "visitor orientation," whereby preservation, conservation, and art historic research become relatively less important. Formerly, the curatorial staff selected or designed exhibits that they felt the visitor *should* see.

11.10 Museum Revenues

The analysis of performing arts company finances in Chapter 8 focused on the problem of the "earnings gap" that was defined as the difference between total expenditures and earned income. The revenue shortfall was covered by unearned income, consisting of government grants and income contributed by private supporters. Following Baumol and Bowen's lead (Baumol and Bowen, 1966), it was pointed out that productivity lag in the performing arts intensified their financial problem. The term "earnings gap" implies its opposite, the notion that performing arts companies could conceivably balance their budgets out of the earned income. After all, the commercial theater does it. So do promoters of rock concerts and other profit-making live popular entertainments, and it is taken for granted that not-for-profit performing arts companies will also charge a price for admission. In that context, one of the tasks of economic analysis is to explain why ticket revenue might fall short of expenses, leaving an earnings gap.

We adopt a different perspective in dealing with art museums. Many of them were founded with the intention that they be open to the public free of charge. There were and are commercially operated museums, but not in the field of art. Since the earned income of art museums was traditionally close to 0 and, in any event, was never expected to cover expenses, the term "earnings gap" seems inappropriate. Let us look at their finances without emphasizing that term.

Table 11.7 shows the sources of art museum operating income, according to the two most recent surveys. Earned income accounted for only 27% of the total in 2014 and remained unchanged in 2017. Admission fees rank highly, but the highest revenue is obtained from museum shops. We have already seen that there are strong economic arguments against using high admission fees to increase museum income, as their relatively modest role in generating revenues is not necessarily to be regretted. On the other hand, policymakers have encouraged museums to raise as much net income as they can by operating a restaurant, bookstore, or gift shop for visitors in order to reduce their dependence on outside financial assistance. New

Table 11.7 Museum income, fiscal 2014 and 2017

	FY 2014	FY 2017
Total income	Percent by type or source	
Government	18	15.5
Federal (NEA, NEH, IMLS, other)	6	6
State	4	2
County	2	3
City	4	4
Other	2	0.5
College and university	3	3
Memberships	8	7
Household	7	6
Corporate	1	1
Gifts and grants	25	26
Household contributions	10	10
Corporate contributions	4	4
Foundations and trusts	7	8
Benefit events	4	4
Total earned	27	27
Admissions	7	7
Educational events	1	1
Exhibition fees	2	1
Restaurants and catering	2	3
Facility rentals	1	1
Museum store	8	8
Other	6	6
Total endowment income	21	22
Total[a]	102	100.5

[a] Total does not sum 100 due to overlapping categories.
Source: Association of Art Museum Directors,
"Art Museums by the Numbers," 2015 and 2018.

York's Metropolitan Museum of Art, which does everything on a large scale, has gone as far as to open "satellite" shops in Connecticut and New Jersey. But the nationwide growth of museum shops has led to a counterattack by commercial interests, who point out that various tax exemptions give stores operated by not-for-profit institutions an unfair advantage. Accordingly, they have brought pressure on Congress to amend the tax law.

Clearly, museums are heavily dependent on unearned income to balance their budgets. It should be noted, however, that as a result of generous past support from wealthy donors, many museums have large endowment funds. Table 11.7 shows that investment and endowment income made up 21% of total income in 2014, which slightly increased to 22% by 2017. Even so, in 2017, the yield covered 30% of the difference between earned and total income. To that extent, museums do not have to scratch and scramble to meet their expenses. Nevertheless, museums are heavily dependent on contributed funds. As revealed in Table 11.7, government grants and donations by individuals, corporations, and foundations accounted for 54% of total income in 2014 but somewhat fell to 51.5% in 2017, reflecting the rising importance of the earned income.

11.10.1 Contributed Private Support

Private support contributed by individuals, foundations, and corporations amounted to 25% of total museum revenue in 2014, which slightly increased to 26% by 2017.

Some evidence indicates that the substantial effort that art museums put into fundraising pays off quite handsomely (SMUDataArts, 2019). This is a provocative result, for as long as the return from a dollar spent is more than a dollar gained, logic suggests that museums should spend even more than they do to raise money. The economics of private contributions to arts organizations, including museums, is discussed in detail in Chapter 13. There we pay special attention to the controversial role of corporate support.

11.10.2 Federal Assistance to Museums

The largest single federal expenditure on behalf of museums is the annual appropriation for the Smithsonian Institution. Created by Congress in 1846, the Smithsonian is now by far the largest museum in the United States, if not in the world. The Smithsonian operates nineteen museums, including several devoted to the arts. Collectively in 2013, they absorbed $916.9 million of federal funds, out of $1,218.8 million allocated to museum programs and research institutes. In 2021, Congress appropriated $773.9 million toward its total budget of $1,383.1 million (Smithsonian Institution, 2021).

In the arts, the federal government also assumes responsibility for the operating costs of the National Gallery of Art in Washington, D.C. Congress appropriated $141 million for that purpose in 2013 toward operating expenses of $168 million. Art museums not directly owned or operated by the national government may receive federal support through a number of channels, including the Institute of Museum and Library Services, the NEA, and the National Endowment for the Humanities (NEH) (National Gallery of Art, 2021).

11.10.3 The Institute for Museum and Library Services

Created by Congress in 1996, the IMLS is the main source of federal support for libraries and museums. The vision of the agency is to support access to museums so that individuals and communities "learn from and be inspired by the trusted information, ideas, and stories they contain about our diverse natural and cultural heritage" (Institute of Museum and Library Services, 2022). This was to be accomplished by providing museums with direct operating support to help cover their general expenses, as well as specific program support. At the federal level, grants for general operating support were a new idea and a radical departure from the already established practice of the NEA and NEH. The two endowments give grants only for well-defined purposes – usually a "project" or "program" of some sort, for which the applicant submits a detailed proposal – and specifically avoid general operating support. (It is different at the state level: State arts councils frequently give general operating support to well-regarded institutions within their own states.)

If a federal agency is going to offer general operating support to museums, the logic of the situation might suggest that every qualified museum should receive its pro rata share as a virtual entitlement. The National Museum Services Board, which provides museum policy advice for the IMLS, thought otherwise. It was decided from the beginning that museums should compete for the available funds through an application procedure. To ensure that the large museums would not soak up most of the available funds, a maximum allowable amount per grant was established; this maximum was $112,500 in 2000. This means, in effect, that museums with larger operating budgets receive proportionately less aid than do very small institutions. Within the universe of museums, IMLS programs are therefore highly redistributive. That may be perfectly consistent with the general tendency of US arts policy to favor programs that will carry art to underserved areas or constituencies. Undoubtedly, it also serves the political purpose of garnering votes for the agency by spreading benefits to as many congressional districts as possible.

It must be pointed out that the IMLS assists all types of museums, not just museums of art. They define the term "museum" broadly enough to include aquariums and botanical and zoological parks, as well as museums of history, natural history, science, ethnography, and specialized interests, such as medical history, horticulture, and even antique steam engines. In the face of that competition, art museums receive slightly less than one quarter of IMLS grant funds.

11.10.4 The National Endowment for the Arts

In 2017, the NEA awarded $3.8 million in program funds to museums. That made museums the NEA's eighth largest program category, exceeded by design ($7.6 million), theater ($7.3 million), music ($6.4 million), arts education ($5.7 million), media arts ($5.4 million), multidisciplinary work ($4.7 million), and dance ($4.1 million).[2] Beginning in 1997, the NEA restructured its granting categories in accordance with its strategic plan, focusing on function rather than on the type of recipient, and grants to museums appeared under several program areas, including Creation and Presentation, Education and Access, and Heritage and Preservation. A detailed examination of recipients is now required to ascertain funding to museums.

11.10.5 The National Endowment for the Humanities

The NEH also provides a degree of support to art museums. Since the study of art falls within the "humanities," the fields covered by the two endowments naturally overlap. Support for museums is offered by both. Museums are eligible for NEH aid from its Division of Preservation and Access (National Endowment for the Humanities, 1998). However, since these funds go to museums of every type as well as to historical societies, archival collections, and other recipients, art museums receive only a fraction of the total. In the field of art, the NEA is obviously the more important source of funding. In the typical case, an NEH grant would be given in support of a special exhibition (often a traveling exhibition) and an accompanying catalog and public education program. Emphasis on the last two elements is, of course, consistent with the endowment's mission to support education and scholarship in the humanities.

11.10.6 State and Local Government Support

Direct state and local government support for art museums is even more important than federal support. Table 11.7 shows that while the federal share in art museum budgets is equal to 6% in both years, the state and local share is equal to 10% in 2014, and, after a small fall, to 9% in 2017. Not counted here is the considerable value of the indirect subsidy museums receive from local government because their land and buildings, like those of other nonprofit institutions, are exempted from the local property tax.

In some cases, a museum's connection with local government goes back to the legal arrangements under which the museum was founded. New York City, for example, gives extensive operating and capital construction support to museums that have been built on public land, even though the museums themselves are private philanthropic corporations, rather than entities of the local government.

11.11 Summary

Art museums do seem to occupy a special place in the local public consciousness. We can only speculate as to the reasons. Perhaps the high visibility of the grandiose or otherwise architecturally significant buildings they inhabit makes them particularly potent symbols of civic pride. Or it may be that their role in conveying culture to the people is especially attractive to taxpayers in a society that has always insisted on its devotion to popular education. (The question of government subsidies for art and culture is further analyzed in Chapters 12 and 13.)

SUGGESTIONS FOR FURTHER READING

See Dickieson (2018) for a discussion about the future of art museums with a focus on deaccession.

Several art museums provide attractive digital resources; see, for example, the British Museum Podcast and Blog, the *Smithsonian Magazine* (available online), the Louisiana Museum of Modern Art Youtube Channel, or explore what your local museum offers online.

PROBLEM SET

11.1 Museums are said to be "decreasing cost firms" with respect to the number of daily visitors. Use this description in responding to the following:
   a. Sketch and label the average and marginal daily operating cost curves for a museum. Superimpose upon these curves and clearly label both representative demand and marginal revenue curves.
   b. Identify the price and admission level associated with the "profit-maximizing" admission charge; an "efficient" admission charge; and a "break-even" admission charge. Discuss the implications of each of these in light of reasonable assumptions regarding the museum's mission.

11.2 At a recent meeting of the Board of Trustees of the Hochkunst Art Museum, the staff reported on some capital spending options. The museum currently owns approximately 4,000 works of art but has room to exhibit only 800 of these at any one time. An important painting – a significant work of a Late Nineteenth Century Minnesota Pointillist – has been offered to the museum by the current owner for $15 million, which is less than the estimated market value of $25 million, but far in excess of the current capital budget of $2 million. The staff estimates that the 1,000 least important items in inventory could be sold *en masse* for a total of some $5 million; the next least important 1,000 items would bring in an additional $10 million.

Alternatively, the museum could double its exhibition space and gain extra facilities for related functions by constructing an addition to the existing building. The total cost of $15 million would preserve the architectural integrity of the museum building.

The museum must choose which of the projects to pursue: acquisition, expansion, or operate as usual. The board, comprised largely of well meaning but inexpert civic and business leaders, is in a muddle. Your task is to help them identify the factors affecting their decisions, including the judgments they must make, the beneficiaries of either course of action, the value of the outcome of each alternative, and whatever else you deem relevant (including alternatives not represented here).

Prepare an executive presentation outlining and motivating your recommendation.

NOTES

1 Museums can be found in as good as every country of the world, including in Afghanistan, Burundi, Cuba, and North Korea. UNESCO estimates that there were around 104,000 museums worldwide in 2021, but the distribution is not even, with Europe and North America accounting for about two-thirds of that number (UNESCO, 2021).

2 The United States has the largest number of museums (33,082) out of which about 2,600 are art museums (Institute of Museum and Library Services, 2018). Europe recorded about 19,000 museums, including at least 5,600 art museums (EGMUS, 2022). The country with the fastest growing number of museums is China, which more than doubled the number of museums from below 2,500 in 2010 to about 5,500 in 2020 (Zhang, 2022); this corresponds to the opening of more than five museums each week on average.

Part IV

Public Policy and Support for the Arts

12 Theory and Practice of Government Support for the Arts

LEARNING OBJECTIVES

By the end of this chapter, readers should be able to:

- Discuss whether the arts should be subsidized
- Explain the collective benefits of the arts
- Describe equity considerations as a justification for subsidy

Although history tells us that the arts have been subsidized by Medici princes, Austrian emperors, Russian czars, English parliaments, and French republics, the question, "Should the government subsidize the arts?" still strikes policymakers as eminently worthy of debate. Economics brings some useful tools to that debate. In this chapter, we build on material in earlier chapters to explore the economic theory of government intervention as applied to the arts, along with descriptions of how that theory has been applied in selected nations. In Chapter 13, we review practices of private support for the arts and how that private support interacts with government support, again with selected illustrations.

12.1 Elements of the Economic Theory of Arts Support

The dominant tradition among economists holds that given the existing distribution of income, competitive markets in most circumstances can be relied on to satisfy consumer preferences optimally. According to this view, there are two principal grounds for justifying government subsidies or other forms of intervention.

The first would be that markets are not competitive and display other imperfections. These are the efficiency arguments, so called because some form of "market failure" has led to an inefficient allocation of resources, which it is the task of intervention to correct. Moreover, economists are in substantial agreement about which imperfections justify what sorts of government intervention. Debate therefore focuses not on the theoretical arguments for intervention but on whether the art and culture industries, in fact, operate under the justifying conditions of identifiable market failure.

The second justification for intervention would be a belief that the existing distribution of income is unsatisfactory. We say "belief" to emphasize the fact that judgments about the distribution of income cannot be scientific but are necessarily based on ethical conviction. This is the so-called equity argument: Subsidies are called for not because markets are working inefficiently, but because it is alleged that some participants lack the income to buy a minimum fair share.

12.1.1 Optimization in Perfectly Competitive Markets

In Chapters 4 through 7, we built the argument that supply and demand interact in competitive markets to produce an optimum allocation of resources. In Chapter 4, we showed that demand for a given good or service reflects the utility consumers expect to obtain by using it and that prices along any given demand curve show the amount that consumers would willingly pay for the corresponding quantities.

Thus, in Figure 12.1, the prices recorded along the supply curve S show the marginal cost of supplying the successive quantities of shoes measured along the horizontal axis. At a price of P_1, Q_1 pairs are supplied, indicating that the marginal cost of the last pair sold is equal to P_1. Furthermore, since factor markets are also assumed to be perfectly competitive, shoe manufacturers, in order to hire inputs, must pay them an amount equal to what they could earn in their next best employment. Therefore, the marginal cost of the last unit measures the opportunity cost to society of the resources employed in its production, that is to say, it measures the value of the other products that were forgone when resources were used up to make this pair of shoes.

By analogous reasoning, we can see that social welfare would also fall if shoe output were reduced below Q_1. At quantities below that level, the demand curve, which measures marginal utility, rises above the supply curve, which measures the marginal cost. Thus, if we failed to produce units to the left of Q_1, the loss in utility to consumers would exceed the reduction in cost to society. Again, aggregate social welfare would be reduced.

Thus, Q_1, the equilibrium level of shoe production under perfect competition, is clearly the optimum, since social welfare would be reduced if output were either greater or less than that amount. By the extension of this argument, one can see that if all markets were perfectly competitive, so that price everywhere equaled the marginal cost, the allocation of resources would be optimal throughout the economy.

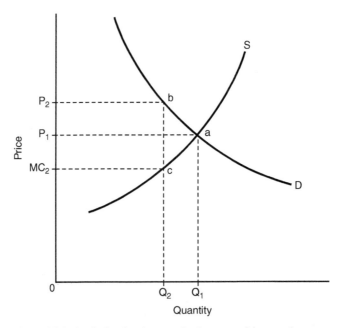

Figure 12.1 Optimization in a perfectly competitive market.

12.1.2 The Problem of Market Failure

When markets work sufficiently well, we rightly let them operate on their own. We do not ordinarily find it necessary for the government to intervene in the markets for running shoes, cellular phones, or tennis rackets. We do not have a national shoe policy or a national tennis racket policy or policies to influence the output of countless other consumer goods. Instead, we accept the market outcome. Why should the arts be an exception? Why not leave arts output to be settled in the marketplace alongside the output of running shoes, cellular phones, and tennis rackets? A possible answer, which we now look into, is that markets do not always operate efficiently, and market failure, as it has come to be called, provides an argument for public intervention. The principal causes of market failure are monopoly, externalities, public goods, declining cost industries, and costly information. We examine them in that order and ask in each case whether they seem to operate in the fields of art and culture. If they do, that argues strongly in favor of corrective public policy.

12.1.2.1 Monopoly

Monopoly is a cause of market failure because the monopolist is in a position to restrict output and earn extra profits by raising prices above the marginal cost level that would prevail under competition. Because output stops short of the level at which marginal cost equals price, some consumers are denied goods for which they would pay more than the incremental cost of production. Such an outcome is economically inefficient. It would occur, for example, if output were restricted to Q_2 in Figure 12.1, instead of expanding to the competitive level of Q_1, since over the range from Q_2 to Q_1, the price consumers are willing to pay always exceeds the marginal cost.

As explained in Chapter 7, arts institutions frequently operate as monopolists within their local market. Rarely is there more than one art museum, professional symphony orchestra, opera, or ballet company in a US city. This is not usually treated as a source of market failure, however, because most arts institutions are organized on a not-for-profit basis. If they charge prices above the marginal cost, it is not because they are trying to maximize profits, but because they operate under conditions of decreasing cost, so that the marginal cost is always below the average total cost of production. The problem of decreasing cost industries is discussed in Section 12.3.1.

12.1.2.2 Externalities or Collective Benefits

Externalities exist when the activities of one firm or individual affect other firms or individuals in ways for which no compensation is paid. For example, if a power plant produces air pollution, it imposes damage costs on nearby firms and residents for which they are paid no compensation. Pollution is the classic case of an external cost. But externalities can also be beneficial. When a suburban homeowner maintains a highly visible flower garden, neighbors and passersby obtain an external benefit for which they cannot be charged. Because externalities, whether positive or negative, are not mediated through markets, the resources used in their production are not subject to the rationalizing influence of the price system. They are an important cause of market failure.

Since the arts are often alleged to be a source of external benefits, but rarely of external costs, only the benefit case is examined here. To avoid prejudging its applicability to the arts, however, we illustrate it by reference to education. Education produces both a private benefit to the person receiving it and an external benefit to society at large. The private benefit consists of higher earning power and greater ability to take part in and enjoy the nation's material and immaterial culture. The external benefit is the advantage conferred on the rest of society by the education of each individual member. In a democratic community, each citizen is affected by the way others vote and carry out their civic responsibilities. Each of us gains if our fellow citizens are literate and well informed rather than ignorant. Consequently, your education confers a benefit on the rest of us, over and above what you personally gain from it. Since this kind of external benefit is conferred broadly on the members of society, who consume it collectively, it can also be called a "collective benefit."

Figure 12.2 shows both the private and the external (collective) benefits attributable to the education of a hypothetical individual. Years of schooling are measured along the horizontal axis and cost and benefit per year along the vertical. The curve D_P measures the marginal private benefit that the individual obtains from successive years of schooling. We assume that the marginal benefit declines as years of schooling increase. D_P is also the individual's demand curve for education, since it measures what he or she would be willing to pay for each additional year of schooling. The marginal cost of schooling, indicated by the curve MC, is here assumed constant per incremental year at level C_1. If the individual were required to pay the market price for schooling, he or she would purchase it up to Q_1, the level at which price just equals marginal private benefit.

While this outcome is optimal for the individual, it is suboptimal from the viewpoint of society as a whole, because it fails to take account of collective benefits. Each year of schooling acquired by the individual student confers a collective benefit on the rest of society, the value of which is measured by curve D_E. (How this value could be determined is discussed below.) Accordingly, society as a whole would be willing to pay up to the amounts measured along D_E to encourage the individual to buy successive years of schooling. In short, D_E is society's demand curve for the collective benefits of a single individual's education.

Adding together the private and collective benefits of each year's schooling, we obtain curve D_S which measures the marginal social benefit of education. Graphically, D_S is the vertical sum of D_E and D_P and represents the social demand for education. From society's point of view, the optimal amount of schooling for the individual is Q_2 years, the level at which the marginal social benefit of an additional year just equals its cost. We can now see that Q_1, the free-market solution, is not optimal. The market, left on its own, will ignore external benefits and therefore produce too little output. Externalities thus cause market failure.[1]

How can society prevent market failure in the face of externalities? The answer is it can encourage production by paying a subsidy equal to the marginal value of the externality. In the hypothetical case illustrated, if a subsidy lowered the cost from C_1 to C_2 per year, the individual would freely choose to pay for Q_2 years. The amount $C_1 - C_2$ equals the value of the marginal external benefit of year Q_2. Thus, public policy can, in theory, solve the efficiency problem posed by the existence of collective benefits.

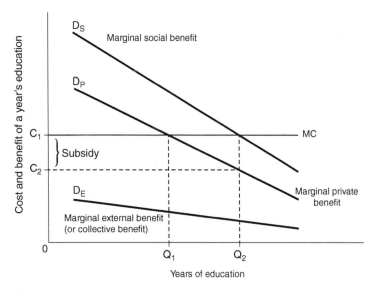

Figure 12.2 Private, external, and social benefits of education.

12.1.2.3 Do the Arts Produce Collective Benefits?

Does the analysis developed to describe the benefits of education apply equally well to art and culture? It is clear that the arts, like education, confer private benefits on those who consume them. These benefits consist of the joy, stimulation, and enlightenment that individuals gain when they attend the live performing arts, visit museums and galleries, or are otherwise engaged with works of art. But after such individual pleasures are accounted for, however rich and exciting they may be, is there anything additional that should be classified as an external or collective benefit? The question is controversial; no aspect of the economics of art has been debated at greater length, which in itself suggests that the answer is not unambiguous. Perhaps that is inevitable, for it is in the nature of the case that the external benefits of art and culture are likely to be diffuse and unobservable. Each of the alleged external benefits in the list that follows has been endorsed by at least one economist studying the arts. We have added doubts and qualifications where that seemed appropriate.

1. *Legacy to future generations.* A number of eminent economists have suggested that preserving art and culture as a legacy to future generations qualifies as a collective benefit (see Baumol and Bowen, 1966, pp. 384–385; Netzer, 1978a, p. 23; Peacock, 1969, pp. 330–331). The argument is that both those who enjoy the arts and those who do not would be willing to pay something today to ensure that art and culture are preserved for the benefit of future generations who are not here to register their preferences.

Here we introduce the concept of "cultural capital," as defined by Throsby (1999, 6): "[C]ultural capital is the stock of cultural value embodied in an asset. This stock may in turn give rise to a flow of goods and services over time." According to Throsby's definition, cultural capital would include tangible elements, such as architecturally significant buildings and works of art, and intangible elements, such as shared values and beliefs – those embodied in literature and music. The contention is that most of us would wish to endow our descendants with a stock of cultural capital as rich as the stock we inherited from the past.

The legacy argument is a powerful one but does require qualification: Suppose that the private sector on its own takes such a strong interest in art and culture that preservation is amply ensured without government subsidy? In other words, one may agree that handing on the cultural tradition is a genuine external benefit and yet believe that the marginal value of still more "legacy" is so low that it does not warrant subsidy.

2. *National identity and prestige.* Some people take pride in the stock of cultural capital possessed by their society – whether city, region, nation, or other identifiable group. At one time, the United States seemed poorly stocked with cultural capital; the country had produced few painters, singers, dancers, choreographers, conductors, or musicians of "international stature." That deficit no longer exists. There is a degree of collective benefit that at least some Americans feel at the great reputations and legacies of artists, such as Jackson Pollock, Jean-Michel Basquiat, and Georgia O'Keeffe; musicians and composers, such as Yo-Yo Ma, Leonard Bernstein, Jessye Norman, Suzanne Farrell, and John Williams; and dancers and choreographers, such as Twyla Tharp, Martha Graham, and Alvin Ailey.

Although these feelings of national pride are real enough, some observers may believe them unworthy of support. Perhaps national and subnational pride are among the sins of this age that ought not to be subsidized (see, e.g., Throsby and Withers, 1979, p. 179). Or if, say, regional prestige is worthy of support, how are we to know whether it is more effectively promoted by subsidizing a local art museum or by building a sports stadium at public expense? Cultural economist Alan Peacock was an early advocate for verifying not only that arts subsidies are a possible way of reaching a valid objective but also that they are the most cost-effective way.

3. *Benefits to the local economy.* Arts activity may provide spillover benefits to other producers in the local economy. This can occur in either of two ways. First, the arts may attract out-of-town consumers who, in addition to buying tickets to a local performance or visiting a museum, also spend money in local shops, restaurants, and hotels. This spending stimulates the local economy exactly as merchandise exports would. Second, the presence of cultural amenities may help a city to induce new firms to locate there instead of somewhere else.

While strictly local economic benefits may appeal to local citizen voters, they would not seem to justify payments by a national government, for there is no reason why a national government should wish to subsidize arts activity in order to attract tourists or firms to one city rather than another. From the point of view of the nation as a whole, the arts can provide an economic stimulus only to the extent that they attract tourists or firms from abroad. Even from a locality's point of view, we must bear in mind the caveat that there may be more effective ways of stimulating the local economy than by subsidizing the arts (see Netzer, 1978a, pp. 24–25; Seaman, 1987). (These matters are taken up in greater detail in Chapter 15.)

4. *Contribution to a liberal education.* As Baumol and Bowen put it, if it is generally conceded that "a liberal education confers indirect benefits upon the community, the same must be true of the arts" because they are an indispensable part of a liberal education (Baumol and Bowen, 1966, p. 385). Or, expressed in the terms introduced above, education enhances the stock of cultural capital, generating collective benefits. While this would appear to be a powerful argument, it is not often mentioned, perhaps because it seems to imply that only art education, rather than its production and distribution outside any specific educational setting, deserves subsidy. In fact, such a narrow reading of policy implications is unwarranted. Consumers can

learn about art in any institutional setting they find congenial. We return to the important question of art education in the final chapter of the book.

5. *Social improvement of arts participants.* It has sometimes been alleged that participation in the arts makes us better human beings by exercising our sensibilities or by exposing us to the highest and best achievements of our fellows, constituting thereby an investment in the cultural capital introduced above. Thomas Gale Moore, citing A. C. Pigou's belief in the "elevating influence" of arts consumption, agrees that "a good play or good opera may, in fact, improve the quality of citizens" (Gale Moore, 1968, p. 117). Throsby and Withers, only partly in jest, respond by asking, "What happens to citizens who see bad plays and bad opera?" They add that there is no scientific evidence to support the alleged beneficial effect of art on individual personality or behavior (Throsby and Withers, 1979, pp. 176–177). Perhaps listening to Beethoven's string quartets or studying the paintings of El Greco, however delightful the experience may be, does not, in fact, have much "elevating influence." Moreover, the claim that art improves the citizen or elevates the soul smacks so much of snobbism that it is likely to be counterproductive in building public support for the arts, and it risks seeming to diminish art's principal function for the individual, which is to provide esthetic pleasure.

Now, these strictures may seem to contradict the view that the arts provide a collective benefit by contributing to a liberal education. Perhaps the contradiction is avoided if we explain that, yes, we would like our fellow citizens to have a liberal education so that they understand the collective traditions of our art and culture, but that there is no scientific evidence that understanding art and culture makes them better individuals in the sense of being less prone to violence, envy, greed, or other unpleasant psychological disorders.[2]

6. *Encouraging artistic innovation.* It is commonly recognized that invention – or, more broadly, scientific, technological, and managerial innovation – is a major source of economic progress. It is also understood that innovation would be inhibited if its initiators were unable to claim adequate rewards for their risks and efforts. That is why we allow technical inventions to be protected by patents. In the field of the arts, however, innovation cannot be patented. Specific works of art, such as a painting, musical composition, or piece of choreography, are protected by copyright. But copyright does not afford any protection to the innovative principle – for example, a new technique in painting, or a new dance style – that is embodied in the specific work, and failure to provide such protection may be socially inefficient. Artistic experiment is costly and subject to failure. When it fails, the artist or not-for-profit organization who made the attempt must bear the full cost (and without the tax offsets available in business situations). But when it succeeds, the innovators cannot prevent others from using the new technique free of charge. Consequently, the scales are loaded against artistic innovators, and they probably undertake less experiment than would be socially desirable. Both Moore and Netzer regard this as a form of market failure that justifies subsidies to the arts (Gale Moore, 1968, pp. 121–122; Netzer, 1978a, p. 24). Netzer points out that the same problem occurs in the physical and social sciences and that "the federal government has a long tradition of subsidizing experimentation on just these grounds" (Netzer, 1978a, p. 24, n. 12).

A word of caution is in order, however: As a practical matter, one cannot assume that much of the available public subsidy would be used to encourage innovation and experiment. Grant-giving bodies have a strong inclination to play it safe by shunning experimentation, perhaps for sound political reasons. They know that opponents of public support like to reinforce their case by citing what seem to them to be objectionable experimental arts projects that received public support.

12.2 External Benefits as Public Goods

We must now take up the important question of how the actual value of external benefits from the arts might be determined. These external or collective benefits, if they exist, have the character of what economists call a "public good," which is a good that displays one or both of the following characteristics. First, it is subject to joint consumption, meaning that one person can consume it without diminishing the amount that remains for others to enjoy. Examples include diverse programs, such as national defense, air pollution control, and public health. Joint consumption is certainly not a characteristic of ordinary "private" goods: Two people cannot wear the same pair of shoes at the same time. Second, a public good is generally not subject to exclusion, meaning that once the good exists, there is no way of preventing someone's benefiting from it, even if that person refuses to pay for the privilege. And since no one can be compelled to make a specific payment for the privilege of consuming it, a public good cannot be financed, as ordinary goods are, by prices charged in the marketplace by a private producer. Instead, they must be paid for (though not necessarily produced) by the public sector, hence the term "public goods."

On reflection, it should be clear that the external benefits allegedly produced by the arts have the characteristics of a pure public good: They are subject to joint consumption, but not to exclusion. The benefit that one person's daughter will enjoy thirty years because the arts have been preserved for posterity will not diminish the benefit that someone else's son can obtain from the same source, nor can parents be compelled to pay for that prospective benefit by threatening to exclude their offspring from consuming it, for such exclusion is impossible.

In the case of ordinary goods, we know that competitive markets will generally guide production in accordance with consumer preferences. If public goods cannot be sold in the marketplace, however, how can society assure that they, too, are produced in the right quantities to satisfy consumers? The correct answer, in theory, is that the government should poll its citizens to find out how much they are willing to pay for alternative levels of the public good and then provide it up to the quantity at which the public's willingness to pay (WTP) for one more unit just covers its marginal cost.

Police service, for example, is a locally provided public good. If town authorities were trying to decide how large a police force to provide, they might ask each citizen how much he or she would be willing to provide for a first police officer, a second, a third, and so on. The aggregate amount indicated for each quantity would be a point on the public's demand curve for the collective good called police service. The optimum quantity to provide would be found as the point of intersection between this demand curve and the labor market supply curve for police officers.

In the case of the externalities of art and culture, there are no physical units (such as the number of police officers) in which to calculate the optimum quantity to produce. What we can try to find out, however, is whether the public (who, after all, should be the final judges in this

Table 12.1 External benefits of art and culture: An Australian survey

	Agree or strongly agree (%)	Neither (%)	Disagree or strongly disagree (%)
Artists should have freedom of expression	76	21	3
The arts should be an important part of education	73	22	5
Artists make an important contribution to Australian society	73	22	5
The arts in Australia reflect the diversity of cultures present in Australia	71	23	5
The arts help you understand perspectives that are different to your own	71	24	5
The arts make for a richer and more meaningful life	68	26	6
The arts should receive public funding	63	29	8
The arts allow me to connect with others	53	36	11
There are plenty of opportunities for me to get involved in the arts	47	40	13
The arts are not really for people like me	29	30	42

Source: Australia Council for the Arts, "Creating Our Future: Results of the National Arts Participation Survey," August 2020, p. 48.

matter) believe that there are any external benefits from art and culture, and, if so, how much they would be willing to pay for them. Aggregate WTP can then be compared with the current level of government subsidies to see whether actual subsidies fall short of, equal, or exceed the value the public puts on arts externalities.

The Australia Council for the Arts carried out a sample survey of Australians in order to study consumer attitudes toward the externalities of art and culture (Australian Council for the Arts, 2020). The first step was to ask questions designed to reveal whether respondents believed the arts to have properties that could be identified as external benefits. For example, one question, intended to test the idea that national prestige is an external benefit of the arts, asked whether respondents agreed with the statement that "Artists make an important contribution to Australian society." Seventy-three percent either agreed or strongly agreed with the statement. Table 12.1 shows the responses to all of the questions (some of which have been abridged to save space). The results imply that there is an overall acceptance of public benefit stemming from the arts.

12.2.1 Eliciting WTP for External Benefits

In a survey of residents of Sydney, Australia, Throsby and Withers (1983) attempted to estimate the public's WTP for the external benefits of the arts. Respondents were asked: What is the maximum you would want paid out of your taxes each year to support the arts at their current level? "Current level" was specified so that the answers could be interpreted as measuring the demand for the collective benefits of the arts that accrue at a specific level of arts output, rather than as indicating a desire for more arts activity.

Table 12.2 Willingness to pay for the arts out of taxes (Australian dollars per year)

	Mean	Median
With full tax liability	96.7	18.2
With no tax liability	154.8	20.2

Source: Throsby and Withers (1983).

Economists have long recognized that in a voter survey, it would be difficult to elicit answers indicating true WTP for public goods. Two kinds of strategic bias could occur. On the one hand, if voters understood that they would be required to contribute whatever amount they said they were willing to pay, they would have an incentive to understate their true willingness in the belief that other people's contributions would pay for a sufficient supply. This is the well-known "free-rider" problem. On the other hand, if voters were told that they would not have to make any payment to back up their stated willingness, they would have an incentive to overstate their preference for the public good in the hope of encouraging a greater supply at no personal cost.

Throsby and Withers handled the strategic bias problem by posing the question both ways to each respondent. One answer (full payment required) could then be regarded as indicating the lower boundary of WTP, while the other (no payment required) would indicate the upper boundary. Presumably, the true value would fall somewhere between those limits.

Results of the WTP questions are summarized in Table 12.2. When no tax liability was suggested, mean WTP turned out to be $155 (Australian) per person. With full tax liability, the mean was reduced to $97. Both results far exceeded the actual level of expenditure of tax receipts on the arts in Australia, which at the time amounted to only about $6 per capita. It must be recognized, however, that mean values can be pulled upward by a small number of extremely high responses. Median values are not subject to that effect. The medians in this case were $20 and $18, still greatly in excess of actual tax outlays at the time. Thus, whether or not economists believe that the arts produce significant external benefits, Throsby and Withers's (1983) study demonstrates the Australian public's conviction that they do and furthermore that those benefits justify subsidies considerably in excess of current levels, even when it is understood that taxpayer liability would rise accordingly.

In the years since the Throsby and Withers (1983) study, economists and other policy analysts have conducted WTP studies of arts support in multiple locations and jurisdictions, and essentially without exception they confirm a public WTP that exceeds actual support (e.g., see the reviews in Noonan (2003) and Throsby (2003)).

12.2.2 Declining Cost Industries

A declining cost industry is one in which the average unit cost of production falls continuously over the range of output demanded in the market. In Chapter 11, it was shown that museums commonly operate under those conditions. Figure 11.1 illustrated the resulting dilemma. As long as average cost is declining, marginal cost must lie below it. To achieve breakeven, the museum has to charge a price equal to average cost, but that price will necessarily be higher than the marginal cost. The result is a form of market failure in the sense that the norm of setting price equal to the marginal cost is violated. In the case illustrated in Figure 11.1, if the museum charges a price P_1, then the potential visitors between Q_1 and Q_2, who are willing to pay more than the full marginal cost of their visit, but not a price as high as P_1, are denied attendance.

Public subsidies are one way of trying to correct this problem: The museum charges marginal cost prices for admission (e.g., P_2 in Figure 11.1) and therefore runs a deficit, but the deficit is covered by a yearly public subsidy. However, there is a drawback to this arrangement from the social welfare point of view: Taxes levied to cover the deficit may have harmful effects – for example, by driving a wedge between marginal cost and price elsewhere in the economy – that offset the welfare gain from using marginal cost pricing at the museum.

Private charitable donations and membership fees offer a solution that avoids the harmful effects of tax finance. The museum could employ marginal cost pricing for admission to its exhibits and then cover the difference between total costs and total admission revenues by soliciting charitable donations and selling annual memberships to interested members of the public. This approach is a version of the "two-part tariff" scheme that many economists regard as the best available solution for declining cost industries. A two-part tariff describes any scheme under which units of output are sold at the marginal cost, thus satisfying the marginal cost-equal-to-price rule, while the producing organization's deficit is covered by a periodic, lump-sum fee required of all potential users. It is an advantage of this arrangement when employed by a museum that those who are directly interested in the institution and presumably benefit from it also cover its deficit, instead of imposing the burden in the form of taxes on distant third parties. However, a distinction can be made between local and national tax finance. Since museums provide a largely local service, using general local tax revenues to cover their deficits is consistent with the intent of the two-part tariff: Those paying the taxes are at least potential users of the subsidized service.

As these comments suggest, the museum case is particularly complicated. Museums typically perform several functions, and subsidies may therefore be justified on several grounds. The declining cost problem as discussed is entirely independent of the question of external benefits. Thus, even if it is decided that deficits resulting from marginal cost pricing should be covered by donations and membership fees rather than out of tax funds, we may still wish to subsidize museums because they preserve art for future generations, perform an educational function, or are the source of other external benefits.

12.2.3 Lack of Information

Markets cannot operate with complete efficiency unless all participants have full information about the goods and services being sold. Consumers, for example, have to be aware of all the available options if they are to make optimal choices. Ignorance on the part of consumers is therefore a source of market failure. The arts are rightly said to be an "acquired" taste, meaning that the consumer has to be familiar with them to enjoy them and that once consumers do become knowledgeable, their demand is likely to increase markedly. But consumers are not in a position to acquire the taste if they lack information about the arts. ("Information" is here understood broadly as including not only "facts" but also the opportunity to experience the thing itself.)

In the field of art and culture, two ill effects might result from the lack of information. First, a number of consumers will be deprived of potential utility because they are ignorant of the arts and therefore do not partake. Because art is an acquired taste, we are entitled to believe that the loss is potentially substantial. Second, because demand falls short of its potential, many arts enterprises will be prevented not just from growing, but also from achieving the economies of scale of which we know they are capable, resulting in a higher unit cost of production.

Many ordinary commercial activities face the same problem and are able to deal with it by advertising and promotion. Netzer pointed out, however, that this solution is less feasible for arts enterprises because "the markets for most art forms are segmented, specialized, and too modest in size to make mass advertising campaigns profitable." He concludes that government subsidies to encourage widespread production of the arts are justified as a way of overcoming ignorance by giving consumers "firsthand experience of them" (Netzer, 1978a, p. 26).

12.2.4 Productivity Lag and Subsidies for the Arts

The hypothesis that productivity lag is bound to cause a long-run increase in the real cost of the performing arts, first proposed by Baumol and Bowen (1966), has often been cited by arts advocates as a justification for government subsidies. Without subsidies, it was asserted, either ticket prices would have to rise continuously, which would end all hope of reaching new audiences, or else performing arts companies would face increasingly large deficits that would ultimately force many of them out of business. The productivity lag hypothesis was analyzed in Chapter 8, and it was shown that there are some alternatives to these gloomy predictions. Leaving those qualifications to one side, it must now be emphasized that productivity lag per se does *not* provide justification for government subsidy.

Productivity lag is a market process that would cause unit cost to rise in any technologically unprogressive industry. But there is no reason to subsidize an industry simply because it is technologically unprogressive. Given that its real costs are rising relative to those in more progressive industries, it is best to let its prices increase to reflect the rise in real costs. As long as markets are operating efficiently, those higher costs will be absorbed optimally by the economy. We would all be better off if there were no technologically unprogressive industries, but since there are, matters are made worse, not better, if we use subsidies to prevent market prices from reflecting their true costs. Lag or no lag, subsidies can be justified only by some form of market failure or else by the distributional or merit good considerations to which we turn next.

12.3 Equity of Arts Production and Access

Up to this point, we have been concerned with "efficiency" arguments, whereby public support of the arts may overcome market failures and improve the efficiency with which the economy fulfills consumers' wants.

We turn now to arguments for public support that involve considerations other than efficiency in the allocation of resources. The principal justifications to be taken up are those concerned with equity in the distribution of income, wealth, and access to the arts, which may belong to a special class of "merit goods" for the production of which consumer preferences are a deficient guide.

12.3.1 Merit Goods and the Distribution of Income and Wealth

Concerns with the distribution of income and wealth can enter the discussion of public support for the arts in two ways. First, how do the existing distributions affect access to the arts? Does inequality of income and wealth make art and culture so inaccessible to the poor or other identifiable groups as to constitute a justification for public subsidy? A second question is almost the reverse of the first: Not how does the distribution of income and wealth affect access to the arts, but how do subsidies to the arts affect the existing distribution of income? Are subsidies likely to help the poor at the expense of the rich or vice versa? In either case, are the distributional consequences a problem?

Before going further, we take a moment to clarify our language, not taking for granted terms that have been used earlier in this volume. We refer to "income" as the periodic flow of purchasing power into the household, whether in the form of wages and salaries, interest or rent payments, or from other sources. These payments permit us to maintain our standard of living. "Wealth" refers to the accumulation of income net of current expenditures and manifests in the form of real estate, financial investments, and other liquid and illiquid assets.

It is well known that both income and wealth vary enormously by identifiable population subgroups in the United States – to the extent that the distribution affects arts access. We take up first the question of how the existing inequality of income affects participation in the arts.

12.3.2 Egalitarian Arguments

It was shown in Chapter 3 that audiences at the performing arts and visitors to museums include very few people with low incomes. According to the SPPA (see Table 11.3), those with incomes below $20,000 made up at most 8.5% of arts audiences in 2012, although they accounted for 17.4% of the US population. In contrast, 8.3% of the US population with incomes above $150,000 account for more than 17% of arts audiences (National Endowment for the Arts, 2015). Clearly, the poor were greatly underrepresented in the audiences for art and culture. Subsequent surveys show very little change in these patterns.

Although education is a more important determinant of arts participation than income, it is nonetheless true that at market prices, the relatively poor (including a large number of youths and students) simply cannot afford much live art and culture as we define those goods. Thus, the desire to ensure as nearly as possible universal access to our civilization's cultural tradition provides one of the most powerful arguments for subsidizing the arts. As Netzer puts it: "There is something intrinsically abhorrent about a policy of making the cultural and artistic heritage of our civilization available to only, say, the richest 20% or 30% of our population, the group to which enjoyment of the arts would be limited in the absence of all support outside the marketplace" (Netzer, 1978a, p. 19).

This is essentially a moral argument. It reflects the fundamental belief of Western societies that every individual should have equal opportunity for self-development. Moreover, the problem is not only that access is limited by high prices and low income, but there is also a regional dimension. As Baumol and Bowen pointed out (Baumol and Bowen, 1966, p. 379), many communities simply lack the facilities and institutions to present the performing arts or the fine arts with any regularity at a professional level. Subsidies are therefore needed to help distribute art and culture geographically as well as to increase its accessibility to the relatively poor.

12.3.3 Arts Subsidies and the Distribution of Income

If the unequal distribution of income provides a strong argument for subsidizing the arts, it may seem paradoxical to suggest that current arts subsidy programs might actually increase the existing inequality. Whether arts subsidies help the poor at the expense of the rich or the other way around depends on how the distribution of subsidy benefits compares with the distribution of tax costs across income classes. Because the well-to-do participate in arts activity so much more frequently than do those with lower incomes, it should not be surprising if they also reap a large share of any subsidy benefits.

We must recognize that art subsidies can have distributionally perverse results in any country unless either the tax system is fairly progressive or assistance to the arts includes a large number of programs clearly directed to the benefit of the low-income population. That is the "bad news" about the distributional effects of arts subsidies. The "good news" is that unfavorable effects on the distribution of income would not weaken the general case for subsidies. As Musgrave has argued, the allocation and distribution functions should be handled separately in the public sector. If a public spending policy can be justified on efficiency grounds, it should be undertaken for that reason. If necessary, its distributional effects should be corrected by other policies that aim at achieving whatever the community believes to be the "correct" distribution of incomes (Musgrave, 1959, chapter 1). Moreover, subsidy programs that effectively concentrate their benefits on the low-income population would not, in any case, have perverse effects on income distribution.

12.3.4 Merit Goods

Economic theory tells us that if society wishes to redistribute income from rich to poor, it is better to make the transfers in cash rather than by providing specific goods or services to the poor at subsidized prices. Redistribution in kind – for example, subsidized low-income housing – can at best be as good as cash but can never be better and may well be worse. The reason is that it may provide beneficiaries with goods or services that would not be their first choice if they were given cash to spend as they pleased. Nevertheless, we find that governments frequently do assist the poor by offering them specific goods at subsidized or even zero prices. Low-income public housing and medical care are important examples in the United States. A possible explanation for subsidies in such cases is that the objects in question are what economists call "merit goods." This term was introduced by Musgrave to describe those goods that society has decided it would be desirable to provide in quantities greater than consumers would wish to purchase at market prices (Musgrave, 1959, pp. 13–14). Instead of accepting consumer preferences as binding, the public or its legislative representatives decide to impose their own: A subsidy is paid to reduce the price of the merit good, thereby increasing the quantity consumed.

Throsby and Withers believe it can be inferred from the public pronouncements of politicians in the countries they studied that "merit good considerations have probably been the most significant single explanation of government involvement in the arts" (Throsby and Withers, 1979, p. 192).[3] Art is regarded as a good thing or, more precisely, as an *especially* good thing. Politicians are therefore willing "to support the arts even though they acknowledge that the resulting activity exceeds that which consumers would demand if left to their own devices" (Throsby and Withers, 1979, p. 193).

What exactly are merit goods? The concept has been much debated by economists. Some would say that merit goods are simply those things that a majority of the public or its representatives have agreed are so worthy of consumption that they deserve to be subsidized. According to this explanation, good housing, health care, and the arts are merit goods because there is a political consensus favoring public support. This is not very satisfactory, however, because it does not tell us *why* a majority believe these objects of expenditure deserve special treatment.

If we ask *why* merit goods are special, a possible explanation is that they are a class of goods and services with the unique quality of being better for people than they realize. For example, consumers may be ignorant of the importance of adequate health care. Left to their own devices, they would consume too little of it for their own good. By subsidizing it, we lower its price and encourage them to consume more. With respect to the arts we would probably want to word that a little differently. The point would not be that the arts are "better" for people than they realize in some therapeutic sense, but rather that the ignorance of the arts is keeping many people from experiences that they would greatly enjoy, if only they knew about them. This, however, is a justification for subsidies that we have already offered under the category of market failure due to the lack of information. (Merit goods arguments have an annoying tendency to overlap with arguments made for public subsidy on other grounds.)

Another possible explanation of the term "merit goods" would be that it describes a class of goods and services that have some sort of "inherent worth" or "intrinsic merit" that distinguishes them from ordinary consumer goods. Netzer appears to take that position when he writes of the NEA's policy of subsidizing a wider distribution of modern dance throughout the United States: "Underlying that decision is the general merit-goods assumption that more exposure to modern dance is a good thing." In the same vein, he argues that a decision to subsidize the Metropolitan Opera "must be based on a straightforward 'merit-goods' argument: the Met is a good thing that can be perpetuated only with fairly large amounts of public subsidy" (Netzer, 1978a, pp. 27, 123). This is not so much an explanation in economic terms as it is a value judgment (the Met is a good thing) that lies outside the realm of economic discourse.

12.4 Direct Public Support of the Arts in Practice

In this section, we offer a survey of the means by which units of government in the United States and elsewhere support the arts, viewed through the theoretical lens developed above. Prior to 1965, government support of art and culture in the United States was uncoordinated and haphazard. States and communities often underwrote performance venues, such as municipal or university auditoriums, and supported high-profile institutions such as art museums, but there existed no coherent national policy.

President John F. Kennedy took an interest in the federal government's relationship to the arts. In 1962, he appointed the philanthropist August Heckscher to the position of special consultant on the arts. Among other things, Heckscher recommended the establishment of a national arts foundation with the power to offer grants to arts institutions and to state arts councils. Shortly afterward, President Kennedy was assassinated, and it fell to President Johnson (in this case as in so many others) to carry the Kennedy proposal to fruition.

At first, there was a good deal of congressional opposition to the idea of federal financial support for art and culture. Netzer (1992a) reported that southern Democrats and conservative Republicans (there were also liberal Republicans in those days) expressed the usual fear that government subsidies would lead to government control. Opponents also argued that government funding would reduce the incentive for the private support that was a justly cherished US tradition. Nevertheless, in 1965 Johnson obtained from Congress and signed legislation establishing not one foundation but two: the National Endowment for the Arts (NEA) and the National Endowment for the Humanities (NEH). The legislation authorized initial funding of $10 million to each of the endowments, but actual appropriations were well below that level in the first few years. By 1979, however, appropriations for the NEA had climbed to $149.6 million. When adjustment is made for inflation, that was to be the endowment's largest annual appropriation.

Since its founding, NEA has been a political football and a pawn in the US "culture wars," generally supported by more liberal administrations, and threatened, even to the point of elimination, by more conservative interests. In order to survive, NEA has adjusted its policies and programs over time in pursuit of that ever-shifting fine line between strengthening the nation's artistic capital and stepping on the wrong toes. One might argue that there still is no coherent national policy, but rather a series of shifting policies in accordance with the tenor of the times. NEA policies and practices at any given time can be found on the NEA website, cited above.

12.5 Summary

We have presented a wide range of arguments favoring the use of government subsidies for art and culture. The strongest ones can be summarized as follows.

Over and above direct benefits to participants, the arts produce external benefits for society as a whole. The most important of these, we believe, are the cultural legacy preserved for future generations, the contribution made to a liberal education, and the collective benefits produced by artistic innovation. These are all part of a society's cultural capital. WTP studies conducted in countries around the globe indicate that the general public does believe the arts produce external benefits and is willing to make substantial tax payments to support them.

The decreasing cost nature of museum output is an additional justification for subsidy, as is the fact that the enjoyment of the arts is an acquired taste about which many consumers lack the information and experience to make informed choices.

Equity considerations provide further justification for subsidy. The egalitarian ethic suggests that all citizens should have at least some access to the nation's heritage of art and culture. To that end, subsidies are required to overcome the barriers of high prices and low incomes and the somewhat different problem of geographic inaccessibility.

12.5.1 The Case against Public Subsidies

Sydney Smith and a friend were walking in Edinburgh one day when they overheard a heated argument between two people who leaned from upper windows on opposite sides of a narrow street. Smith remarked that they would never agree because they were arguing from different premises.[4] So it is in this debate. Those who are suspicious of any extension of government power will not easily be persuaded that a case exists for subsidizing the arts. On the other hand, those who believe the government can play a constructive role even in what is fundamentally a "free-enterprise economy," will have relatively little difficulty justifying arts subsidies as a way of advancing "the general welfare."

SUGGESTIONS FOR FURTHER READING

An overview of alternative perspectives on whether the government should subsidize the arts is presented by Tyler Cowen (2006).

For a full analysis of the survey method for evaluating WTP for public goods, see Mitchell (1989). Selected additional arts-and-culture-related WTP studies include Morrison and West (1986), Santagata and Signorello (2000), Thompson et al. (2000), Riujgrok (2006), Plaza (2010), and Chang and Mahadevan (2014). For an overall assessment of the technique and additional references, see Throsby (2003) or Ginsburgh (2017).

The point that redistribution in kind can never be more valuable than cash is demonstrated rigorously in almost every intermediate microeconomics text. See, for example, Perloff (2018), pp. 166–167.

PROBLEM SET

12.1 Suppose we agree that government should subsidize the arts. The nonprofit music industry can serve as a frame of reference for your response.

Use supply and demand curves to identify the differential effects of the following:

a. Subsidy of the performing artist

      b. Subsidy of the arts (music) organization

      c. Subsidy of the arts (music) audience

12.2 The marginal cost to offer a theater performance to an additional theatergoer is equal to €5. Demand for theater is given by the demand function $P = 20 - Q$, where P is the price of the performance and Q is the quantity of performances offered. The marginal external benefit (the collective benefit) of attending a performance is equal to €2 per attendance. In response to outcries by cultural economists, the government introduces a subsidy of €1 per attendance. Is overall welfare improved or reduced by the subsidy? Support your answer with a graph.

12.3 What is the likely effect of a government subsidy for public theater on the mix of public and private theater institutions? Explain.

12.4 During the COVID-19 pandemic, the culture sector has been heavily subsidized by many governments around the world. For example, the French government provided a rescue package worth €2 billion ($2.4 billion) to art museums, and the greatest expected beneficiaries have been the Louvre, Musée d'Orsay, and the Centre Pompidou.

      a. Discuss whether the arts deserve the right to receive subsidies. In particular, assess critically whether the arts produce predominantly individual benefits or also collective benefits.

      b. Discuss how financial public support can serve as an instrument to increase equity of arts production and access.

NOTES

1 In his classic article R. H. Coase (1960) showed that if the number of affected parties is small enough so that transactions costs are low, we would expect them to arrive at a bargaining solution in which the effects of externalities are fully and optimally taken into account. In the case of education, however, the number of parties is clearly too large for such a solution.

2 This is not to say that arts participation does not matter positively for life satisfaction, which it likely does (Steiner, 2016). Furthermore, the well-being of a person is related to her artistic endeavors (Borowiecki, 2017; Borowiecki and Kavetsos, 2015).

3 They quote supporting statements of politicians in Australia, New Zealand, Canada, Great Britain, and the United States.

4 Smith's remark is reported in Auden (1956), p. xiv.

13 Private Support for the Arts

LEARNING OBJECTIVES

By the end of this chapter, the reader should be able to:

- Describe different forms of art support
- Explain the economics of "indirect" government support
- Evaluate the costs and benefits of private versus public support

Artistic institutions earn income by selling tickets to performances or, in the case of museums, by charging for admission. But in every economically advanced country, they also receive substantial additional support (the unearned income referred to in Chapter 8) either from the government in the form of grants or from private individuals and businesses in the form of charitable donations. In Chapter 12, we developed the theory of public support for the arts, illustrated with applications in the leading Western economies. In this chapter, we examine and analyze private support for the arts, mostly in the form of household, corporate, foundation, and other donations. We also explore the economics of "indirect" government support in the form of tax forgiveness for private donors, as well as the interactions between public and private support known as "crowding out" or "crowding in."

13.1 An International Comparison of Arts Support

Comprehensive international comparison of the level of direct public support for the arts was collected by Eurostat in 2019. The European statistical office provides data on the amount of support per capita in member states of the European Union and some neighboring countries, which we complement with data for the United States, Canada, and Australia. The results, summarized in the first column of Table 13.1, reveal a wide range in the level of direct support per capita. Iceland tops the list, spending €662 (ca. $743 in 2019), followed by Norway (€450), and Denmark and Switzerland (€302 each), while the United States ranks last, spending only €3.7 ($4.2) per person. The exclusion of indirect aid makes governmental support in the United States look much less generous than in fact it is. Direct support consists of cash grants or payments. Indirect support occurs when a government forgoes potential tax revenue through some provision favorable to arts institutions. Examples in the United States are the exemption of arts institutions from the local property tax and, even more important, provisions in the federal and state tax codes that create an incentive for taxpayers to make charitable contributions to non-profit arts organizations. In both cases, the foregone revenue is equivalent to an expenditure

Table 13.1 Level and source of government support for the arts

Country	Direct spending in Euros per capita, 2019	National (%)	State/regional (%)	Local (%)
Iceland	662.2	45	0	55
Norway	450.4	50	0	50
Switzerland	302.4	0	50	50
Denmark	302.3	33	0	67
France	254.1	29	0	71
Netherlands	227.1	40	0	60
Australia[a]	170.3	39	35	26
Germany	162.1	–	–	–
Ireland	156.7	50	0	50
Spain	123.0	20	20	60
Poland	102.4	29	0	71
Italy	78.9	33	0	67
Portugal	55.9	33	0	67
Canada[b]	4.3	36	44	20
United States	3.7	11	27	62

Notes:

[a] For the 2017–2018 season.

[b] Is for nonprofit, performing arts companies in 2018.

Source: Europe: Eurostat, General government expenditure by function (COFOG), United States: Grantmakers in the Arts, *Public Funding for Arts and Culture, 2019*, Australia: A New Approach (ANA), *The Big Picture: Public Expenditure on Artistic, Cultural and Creative Activity in Australia*, Canada: Statistics Canada, Performing arts, sources of public sector grants & Performing arts, not for profit.

by government. Indeed, in the United States the sums lost through such provisions have been called "tax expenditures." There are though also examples of indirect support in Europe, most notably in the form of reduced value added tax (VAT) on cultural goods and services.[1] Too often in casual intercountry comparisons of subsidies to the arts, the writer mentions only direct expenditures, and then only those of the central government, resulting in a very distorted picture. Unfortunately, the level of indirect aid to the arts in any country can only be estimated. An older, but careful study by Mark Schuster of the NEA put it at $10 per capita in the United States in 1984 (Schuster, 1985, table 4). Since that date, marginal income tax rates in the United States have fallen, which would reduce the value of indirect support, but charitable giving has greatly increased, which would raise its value. In the absence of later data, if we were to add $10 to the figure shown in Table 13.1, it would leave the United States still at the bottom of the list, along with Canada.

Considering the division of direct public support between levels of government, it has to be noted that, historically, there was a wide range of variation reflecting differences in political traditions and in the historical development of government.[2] However, in 2019, the overwhelming picture is that of a dominant local government support for the arts, which accounts for not less than 50% of direct spending in all countries covered (except Canada and Australia). This is in line with the notion that local authorities are believed to be better at assessing which project deserves the most public support. (We will return to the role of the arts in a local economy in Chapter 15.)

Countries in which the local government provides more than two-thirds of direct aid include France and Poland (each 71%), and Italy, Portugal, and Denmark (each 67%).

We turn next to the mathematics of indirect aid.

13.2 The Mathematics of Indirect Aid, or Tax Expenditures

Private donations to nonprofit institutions are encouraged in the United States by provisions in both the federal income tax code and the state codes in states that levy an income tax. Under the federal code, taxpayers who "itemize" their deductions are allowed to include as a deduction from their taxable income the amount of their cash contributions to such institutions, up to a limit that varies from 20% to 50% of adjusted gross income, depending on the circumstances. Although these provisions were originally adopted as a matter of tax equity (if a taxpayer donates part of her income to charity, then that part is no longer available to be spent or saved at the individual's discretion, and it might be regarded as unfair to count it as "income"), they have been retained as a matter of deliberate policy to foster private support of charitable undertakings. Contributions are tax deductible by the donor only if made to not-for-profit organizations that qualify under guidelines set by the Internal Revenue Service. Among these are the requirement that there be no distribution of net income or "profit" to any party and the rule that the organization may not engage in political activity or attempt to influence legislation. Obviously, nonprofit organizations in the fields of art and culture take care to abide by the rules so that they can continue to receive contributions that are tax deductible by the donor. Individual artists, of course, are not eligible to receive such contributions, since for tax purposes they are treated as profit-making sole proprietors. But for that reason, they are permitted to testify or lobby in legislative matters, just like other citizens, and in fact, they often provide important support for legislation favoring the arts. Although the terminology of this subject may be complex, it is important to bear in mind that donations are deductible not from tax liability but from taxable income. Arithmetically, what happens under US tax law is that the donor's tax liability is reduced by an amount equal to the donation multiplied by the tax rate in that person's marginal tax bracket. The higher the individual's marginal tax rate, the greater the tax reduction per dollar given away; hence, the less the cost of the gift to the donor, the stronger the tax-based incentive to make donations. The amount of tax saved by the individual is also the amount of revenue lost by the government on account of the charitable deduction. It is this lost revenue that constitutes the indirect support given by government to the nonprofit sector.

These relationships are clarified in Table 13.2. Algebraic definitions of terms are given at the left. The two columns at the right show the outcome for (A), a donor in the 50% bracket, which was the highest just before the Tax Reform Act of 1986, and for (B), a donor in the 37% bracket, the highest current rate. Under the 1986 Act, the highest rate had been 33%, but modifications introduced by the Revenue Reconciliation Act of 1990 lowered the top rate on ordinary income to 31%. In 1993, under President Clinton, it was raised to 39.6%, and then in 2018, under President Trump, it decreased to 37%.

Table 13.2 Mathematics of charitable donations

	(A) Pre-1986	(B) Current
TI = taxable income	$100,000	$100,000
t = marginal (or bracket) tax rate	0.50	0.37
G = deductible gift	$1,000	$1,000
tG = tax saved by donor = revenue loss to government	$500	$370
$(1-t)G$ = cost of gift to donor	$500	$630

The table allows us to examine the economics of charitable deductions from two different perspectives. Looked at chronologically, it shows that when marginal tax rates were reduced after 1986, the cost to donors of making gifts rose. In other words, the tax incentive to give money away was weakened: A gift of $1,000, which would have cost a donor only $500 under the old law, costs $630 under current law. This aspect of the matter raised some puzzling questions for the Trump Administration. On the one hand, President Trump tried (not very successfully, one must add) to reduce federal appropriations for the arts, relying on the justification that if the government withdrew support, private donors would respond by taking up the slack – an argument clearly implying that when government assistance to the arts grows, it displaces private donations. On the other hand, he also cut marginal tax rates and therefore weakened the incentive to make private donations. (We return to these issues below.)

The table can also be used to illustrate the effect a progressive tax rate structure has on incentives to donate. Assume now that in column B the top row shows taxable income of $50,000 instead of $100,000. Then the table can be interpreted as showing that when an individual's income rises from $50,000 (column B) to $100,000 (column A), he or she rises into a higher marginal tax bracket (50% instead of 37%), and the tax saving achieved by making a charitable donation accordingly rises from 37 cents to 50 cents on the dollar. In other words, under a progressive income tax structure, the higher your income, the stronger your incentive to make charitable donations.

The rate structure of the US federal income tax is progressive, but not as significantly as it was in the past. Before the passage of the 1986 reform, rates ranged from 14% to a maximum of 50%. From 1965 until 1980, the top rate (not including occasional surtaxes) had been 70%. This meant that a charitable gift cost the donor only 30 cents on the dollar, or even less if the donor lived in a state or city that also levied an income tax. Keeping in mind the fact that benefactors of museums, symphony orchestras, hospitals, and universities sometimes have the pleasure of seeing galleries, auditoriums, clinics, or dormitories named after them (and/or their spouses), it is easy to see why a strong tradition of giving away 30 cent dollars developed in the United States. It is also plausible that once the habit of charitable giving was in place, subsequent reductions in the progressivity of the income tax, which raised the donor's cost of giving, did not necessarily or immediately bring a cutback in donations.

13.3   Donating Works of Art

For museums, private support takes the form of donations not only of cash but also of works of art, and these, too, have been heavily influenced by tax considerations. For many years, the donor was allowed to claim as a charitable deduction the market value of the work at the time the donation was made in the United States. That provided a powerful incentive to make donations in kind to museums, especially since the prices of high-quality works of art have risen sharply in recent years (see the discussion in Chapter 10). Consider the alternatives faced by a potential donor. Suppose that she had paid $10,000 for a painting in 1995, and that by 2020, its market value has risen to $200,000. If the owner then sells it and donates the proceeds to the museum, he or she is not only entitled to a charitable deduction of $200,000 but is also liable for tax on the $190,000 capital gain realized at the sale. In 2020, a donor in the top income tax bracket of 37% would have paid capital gains tax at the rate of 20% (since long-term capital gains were taxed at lower rates than ordinary income), amounting to $38,000 on the gain from the painting. On the other hand, if the owner simply gave the painting to the museum, he or she could still have claimed the $200,000 market value as a charitable deduction, while altogether avoiding the payment of income tax on its gain in value. Thus, the incentive to donate works of art that had appreciated in value was even stronger than the incentive to make gifts of cash. By claiming a deduction at market value, a donor could often save in taxes far more than the work of art had actually cost. Not surprisingly, both museum directors and potential donors of valuable art were delighted by these arrangements.

13.4   Individual, Corporate, and Foundation Support

Private donational support for the arts in the United States comes not only from individuals but also from private corporations and foundations. Corporate contributions are encouraged by tax provisions analogous to those for individual taxpayers: In calculating liability for the corporation's income tax, the firm may deduct charitable contributions as an expense up to an amount equal to 10% of taxable income. The net cost of a donation is therefore $(1-t)$ (amount of the gift), where t is the effective tax rate. The top-bracket income tax rate on corporations varied between 40% and 50% during the 1970s and early 1980s before being stepwise reduced, most recently to 21% by the Tax Cuts and Jobs Act of 2017. Thus, ironically, the tax incentive for corporate giving, like that for individual donations, was substantially weakened just at the time that a business-oriented Republican administration was calling for increased private-sector support for social, cultural, and educational endeavors.

How do the sources of private contributions rank in relative size? A perspective on private giving can be obtained by asking what percentage of recipients' income is accounted for by gifts from each category of sources. Table 13.3 displays such percentages for constant samples of theater and opera companies in 2015 and 2019. It also shows the percentage change in the dollar amount of income from each source. Contributions accounted for 50% and 47% of theater company income in each of the two years. The proportion was higher for opera companies: 51% in 2015 and 59% in 2019.

Table 13.3 Income sources, US theater and opera companies

Theatre Communications Group, 84 theaters	2015 (%)	2019 (%)	Change in dollar amount 2015–19 (%)
Total income	100.0	100.0	17.8
Earned income	49.6	53.3	26.6
Contributed income	50.4	46.7	9.2
Private	45.8	41.8	7.6
Individuals	21.0	17.7	−0.7
Corporations	2.9	2.3	−5.3
Foundations	10.2	11.6	33.2
Other	11.7	10.3	3.2
Public	4.6	4.8	25.0
Federal	0.4	0.5	34.2
State	2.2	1.2	−33.3
Local	2.0	3.1	87.1
Opera America, 88 companies	2015 (%)	2019 (%)	2015–2019 (%)
Total income	100.0	100.0	−23.5
Earned income	48.7	41.4	−34.9
Contributed income	51.3	58.6	−12.6
Private	48.6	56.4	−11.2
Individuals	29.0	36.9	−2.4
Corporations	2.9	3.6	−5.3
Foundations	7.9	13.0	25.7
Other	8.9	3.0	−74.4
Public	2.7	2.2	−38.3

Source: Theatre Communications Group, *Theatre Facts 2019* and Opera America, *Annual Field Report 2016* and *2020*.

During the period covered, public support for theater remained about unchanged. Contributions from local governments rose but have been offset by declines at the state level. In contrast, public aid to opera fell from a low 2.7% to 2.2% of income.

This decline, however, was partly offset by an increase in private support from foundations, but not enough to leave the share of total contributions unchanged.

Table 13.3 also tells us that the corporate share in private support was the lowest among private donors. However, in addition to making charitable contributions, corporations also provide support for the arts through expenditures charged to their advertising and promotion budgets. For example, a corporation might sponsor in that way a series of summer "concerts in the park." Like any other increase in costs, such outlays also reduce profits and therefore cut corporate tax liability. Advertising and promotion outlays for the arts are not included in any of the contributions' totals discussed in this section. In fact, the total value of such expenditures is simply unknown.

These comparisons probably understate the corporate share in private giving since the individual and foundation totals include donations to a range of activities that comprise culture

Table 13.4 Corporate donational activity

Year	Donations in 2020 US dollars (millions)	Five-year change (%)	Percentage to culture and the arts	Estimated total to culture and the arts ($ million)
2000	16,060	29.3	–	–
2005	20,147	25.4	–	–
2010	18,711	−7.1	5	936
2015	19,920	6.5	6	1,195
2020	16,880	−15.3	4	675

Notes: Inflation adjustments are made through the CPI Inflation Calculator provided by US Bureau of Labor Statistics.
Source: Giving USA Foundation (2019), *Giving USA: The Annual Report on Philanthropy for the Year 2018 and Giving USA 2021 Infographic.* CECB, *Giving in Numbers 2021*, and earlier editions.

and the humanities as well as the arts, while the figure for corporations includes only the latter. Moreover, some corporate giving occurs through the corporations' own foundations and was therefore counted in the foundation total.

A profile of corporate donation activity from 2000 to 2020 is presented in Table 13.4. The left-hand column shows contributions in constant dollars to all sectors, including health, education, and other areas in addition to the arts. The next column gives the percentage increase in each five-year segment. Clearly, corporate contributions are quite volatile and depend much on the wider economy. In particular, we can observe decreases in 2010, not long after the financial crisis, and at the onset of the COVID-19 pandemic in 2020. (We return shortly to the issue of volatility of corporate contributions.) The third column shows the percentage of corporate donations that went to the arts, as reported in sample studies by the Conference Board. The fourth column is an estimate of their dollar value as the product of column one times column three.

Data on which forms of art and culture corporate donors favor have been tabulated only sporadically. In the 2021–2022 season, Arts Council England estimated corporate giving by artform and found that the three leading categories were combined arts (24%), visual arts (14%), and theater (13%) (Arts Council England, 2022). We have more to say about this below in this chapter, where we will also see that private contributions play a much smaller role in financing the performing arts in Europe.

13.4.1 Motives for Charitable Giving

It seems entirely reasonable that those who are actively interested in the arts and can afford to give a little something to charity should make donations to one or more arts enterprises. And just as churchgoers will probably give to the church they attend and college graduates to their alma mater, so devotees of the arts are most likely to make donations to the museums or performing arts companies they regularly attend. Clearly, such support is not entirely disinterested. Donors hope to contribute, in however small a way, to the maintenance or improvement of enterprises that are a source of personal pleasure. In addition, most nonprofit arts organizations nowadays actively encourage donations by offering potential supporters a range of benefits that increases in scope with the size of the donation. In the case of a ballet company such as the New York City Ballet, a minimum $100 donation may bring in return complimentary tickets to working rehearsals and demonstration programs, and a subscription to the company newsletter. At the other end of the scale, large donors will have priority in reserving choice seats and will be invited to an annual party, with the opportunity of meeting star members of the company. A museum will typically seek support through "memberships" that carry with them, for the lowest ranks, privileges such as free admission to ordinary events, a discount at the museum store, and a subscription to the ubiquitous newsletter. More expensive memberships will entitle donors to free lectures, preopening guided tours of special exhibitions, and so on. The benefits thus conferred on supporters are designed not only to give pleasure (which for the initiate they undoubtedly do), but also (consider the newsletter) to cultivate in donors a sense of "belonging to the family" or of being in the inner circle, which helps to perpetuate the charitable tie.

All of this costs a lot of money to carry out (mailing lists, direct mail solicitations, record keeping, paying for special events), but the motto is, "You have to spend money to make money." In 2019, the Metropolitan Opera is reported to have employed a staff of about thirty-eight and spent $11.1 million on fund-raising. By so doing, they raised about $174.3 million from individuals, corporations, foundations, and government agencies (The Metropolitan Opera Association, 2019). It is now taken for granted in the United States that fundraising from the private sector is an important function within any nonprofit arts institution. Indeed, public agencies would probably be reluctant to make grants to a nonprofit organization that did not appear to be "pulling its weight" in private fund-raising.

It is not surprising that corporate motives for giving are somewhat different from those of individuals. Some corporate managers may, indeed, believe that it is morally important for their firms to *be* good corporate citizens, but one suspects that they believe it is even more important that they be *seen* in that light. Thus, corporations are attracted to forms of giving that are visible or even attention grabbing. That explains, for example, the prominence of corporate support for public television programming. "Special events" to which the company name can be attached, such as a blockbuster art exhibition or a series of summer concerts in the park, also attract generous corporate support. Hence, a large share of corporate donations goes, respectively, to museums and to musical performances.

Some observers worry that corporate support may eventually corrupt culture by bending artistic production too much in the direction of whatever it is that corporations are willing to pay for and away from the more provocative and controversial forms of art that they admittedly try to avoid. It is well to be on guard against that threat, but the danger seems insufficient to justify shunning corporate support. Most arts institutions (and most of their audiences) probably would endorse a policy of "take the money and run."

13.5 Why So Little Private Support for the Arts in Europe?

In Europe private contributions play a much smaller role in financing the arts. Americans may find this puzzling, since European devotion to art in all its forms is well known. Many are of the opinion that the explanation must lie in a difference in tax law. In Europe, charitable contributions were either not deductible or deductible only under severe restrictions. For example, tax-deductible individual donations to arts organizations in Denmark are restricted to $2,100 (kr. 15,000) per year and can be directed only to a few preapproved institutions.

The low level of private support in Europe, be it due to tax law, the tradition of charitable giving, or both, is much explained by history (Schuster, 1985, pp. 48–54). In the distant past, major European cultural institutions such as the Comédie Française or the Vienna State Opera owed their origins and subsequently their support to royal, or at least noble, patronage. In the nineteenth and twentieth centuries, these burdens were assumed by republican governments and municipalities. Private citizens, aware that "the government" was subsidizing arts institutions and that they, as taxpayers, were footing the bill, felt no obligation to make voluntary contributions. That is not to say that wealthy collectors might not sometimes donate valuable works of art to national or municipal museums, but a broad-based tradition of private charitable support for the institutions of art and culture never developed.

In the 1980s, the climate of opinion began to change. After a long period of budgetary expansion, most European governments were trying to restrain public spending. Subsidies for the arts were either reduced or prevented from growing at their accustomed pace. For the first time both governments and the arts institutions themselves became seriously interested in what Schuster calls "the American model with its heavy reliance on and encouragement of private sources of funding" (Schuster, 1985, p. 48). The financial crisis of 2008 has further deteriorated budgets for the arts and culture. In times of economic downturns, the political priorities are reassessed and funding is redirected from aid policies for culture toward covering basic public services and repaying the interest on debt (Almeda et al., 2017). Table 13.5 shows the results for recent years in seven European countries and, for comparison, the United States and Canada. In the United Kingdom, where the Thatcher government had long ago begun a drive toward "privatization," private support by 2019 had reached between 18.5% of total income of selected performing arts companies. That was the highest level among the European countries. By contrast, US opera companies obtained 48% of their income from private contributions, and US theater companies obtained 39%. In Canada, private contributions played a larger role than in Europe but were still far short of the level in the United States.

Table 13.5 highlights other important differences, as well. In the United States, the earned revenue of opera and theater companies (mostly from the box office) accounts for 48% or more of total income. In Europe, it usually brings in 25% or less. Again, the United Kingdom differs, with earned income accounting for 46% of the total. In an arithmetic sense, the lower proportion of the earned income in Europe is a result of the higher proportion of public support, which accounts for 60–80% of total income in Swedish, Finnish, and French theaters. But there is obviously a causal connection, as well: Generous government aid allows arts companies to charge low ticket prices, which pleases audiences and stimulates attendance but holds down earned income. Table 13.5 also shows that within Europe the relative importance of central government versus provincial and local support varies widely from place to place.

European data on private support are sketchy, at best. However, it does appear that most of the private support referred to above comes from corporations rather than individuals. That

Table 13.5 Income structure in the performing arts: International comparisons (% of total income)

	Year	Earned income	Private contributions	Public support, total	Central government	Provincial and local	Other
Canada: all not-for-profit companies[a]	2018	48.1	25.2	26.7	9.6	17.2	
Finland: Association of Finnish Symphony Orchestras[b]	2018	14.5	10.8	72.5	22.4	50.1	2.2
Germany: publicly funded music and spoken theatres[c]	2018	17.2	41.2	38.9	0.6	38.3	2.7
Italy: Turin Opera[d]	2018	25.4	14.0	58.0	37.2	20.7	2.7
Sweden: 74 performing arts instititutions[e]	2019	14.0	4.0	82.0	29.0	53.0	–
United Kingdom: 38 orchestras[f]	2019	45.8	18.5	35.2	31.1	4.1	0.5
United States: 86 opera companies[g]	2019	48.0	48.0	4.0	–	–	–
84 theater companies[h]	2019	53.3	39.1	4.8	0.5	4.4	2.8

Sources:

[a] Statistics Canada, Table 21-10-0185-01 Performing arts, sources of revenue, not-for-profit.
[b] Association of Finnish Symphony Orhcestras (2019), *Facts and figures of member orchestras 2018.*
[c] Deutsches Musikinformations Zentrum, Einnahmen der öffentlich finanzierten Theater (Musik- und Sprechtheater).
[d] Teatro Regio Torino, Revenue and costs comparison on teatroregio.torino.it.
[e] Myndigheten för kulturanalys (2022), *Scenkonst i Sverige 2020.*
[f] Association of British Orchestras (2020), *The State of UK's Orchestras in 2019.*
[g] Opera America (2020), *2019 Annual Field Report.*
[h] Theatre Communications Group (2020), *Theatre Facts 2019.*

is emphatically not the case in the United States, as we saw in Table 13.3. We discuss the particular virtues of individual donations in the Section 13.6, when we take up the advantages and disadvantages of both the US model of support and the European.

13.6   Advantages and Disadvantages of Private and/or Public Support

In debating the merits of the European as compared with the US system of arts support, we are not suggesting that the nations in either camp should entirely abandon their own approach in favor of the other. Each system (and its local variations) is the expression of a long-standing cultural and political tradition that has to be understood in its own terms (see Cummings and Katz, 1987; Toepler and Zimmer, 2002). Nevertheless, it is instructive to examine the claims made for each.

Philosophically, those who favor the European system in which arts institutions are supported primarily by government subsidies start from the premise that art and culture are a national heritage and therefore logically deserve to be supported by the nation acting collectively. From an economic viewpoint, since the arts generates collective benefits, as we discussed in Chapter 12, public support may be required to ensure that the quantity of culture supplied is optimum from the society's perspective. At the practical level, an alleged advantage is that the government can provide whatever funds are needed and in so doing relieve the institutions of unremitting and distracting pressure to raise money from private sources. Government funding, it is also argued, would be relatively stable, providing a more reliable basis for long-run planning than does private support. Perhaps more fundamental support from the public budget is seen as a way of insulating the arts from the potential threat to their artistic freedom associated with dependence on the marketplace.

Those who defend the "US system" do not, of course, disparage government support. Rather, they argue that a combination of public and private funding, with heavy reliance on the latter, has some advantages over an almost exclusive reliance on the public budget. First, it diversifies the sources of income, which could make for greater stability than the European system under which arts budgets can be squeezed very hard during a period of public austerity. Second, diversity in funding sources also reduces the concentration of power over arts policy, which, in the European system, rests with government agencies. A secure base in private support gives institutions a freedom of action they lack when largely dependent on the government. Third, US arts institutions, because of their reliance on the individual donor, cultivate the donor's attention, understanding, and goodwill. In the long run, that probably helps broaden the constituency for the arts, which should, in turn, ultimately provide benefits in the political realm. However, too much reliance on donors can be risky as well, especially if their reputation dissipates. For example, there emerged public fury and protests against a series of museums around the world that bear the name on their walls of the Sackler family, once a major donor, and now criticized for their role in the opioid epidemic in the United States (Harris, 2019).

There is plenty of ammunition with which to criticize the arguments on both sides.

13.6.1 The Question of Stability

The alleged stability of government support must also be questioned in light of recent experience in Europe during the financial crisis of 2008 or the COVID-19 pandemic. As for the stability of private giving, while individual donations appear to be a secure form of support in the United States, it is doubtful whether corporate giving will prove as reliable. It is sensitive to changes in the level of profits, which can be volatile over the course of a typical business cycle, and also depends on the location of corporate activity, since a substantial portion of corporate donations goes to arts organizations in cities or regions where the businesses have either their national or regional headquarters or major plants.

A corporate donor supporting artists and the cultural sector locally can not only easiest oversee the effects of a donation but may also get to enjoy it. As an artist who benefited from local corporate support in San Francisco put it, "It's like watering your own front garden" (*The Economist*, 2022). What happens then to arts donations in the cities that lose a corporate presence? They are very likely to be reduced. However, there may be offsetting gains in other cities where operations of companies increase. In any case, the record up to now is that corporate giving is somewhat more variable year to year than are individual donations.

13.6.2 Interference with Artistic Freedom

Whether government agencies or powerful private donors are more likely to interfere with that artistic independence of arts institutions is an open question. Perhaps the word "interfere" is too dramatic (although we cite such a case). More often the donor's influence on artistic policy makes itself felt without direct interference: The recipient institution bends its policy to conform with the agency's or the donor's known preferences. Such effects are subtle and not easily demonstrated. However, no less an institution than the Metropolitan Opera offers a well-documented example of how it commissioned new operas from two US composers. One of these, *The Ghosts of Versailles*, by John Corigliano and William Hoffman, was produced with considerable popular success in 1991–1992. (It was the first new opera to have its premiere at the Met in twenty-five years.) However, it was reported that the Met had canceled the other commission from Jacob Druckman and also postponed plans to produce *Moses und Aron* by Arnold Schoenberg. In fact, it was not before 1999 when Schoenberg's twentieth-century masterpiece was staged at the Met. The Opera's general manager explained to the *New York Times* that it was impractical to try to fill the 3,800-seat auditorium by putting on contemporary works and that influential members of the board of trustees are also opposed to new operas. As he put it, "The people who make contributions to opera are not too excited about contemporary work" (John Rockwell, 1987). Thus, the tastes of private donors do influence the artistic policies of their beneficiaries.

What about the influence of government donors? In Great Britain, Canada, Australia, New Zealand, and the United States, government grants for the arts are filtered through a semi-independent arts council (the Arts Council of Great Britain, founded in 1945, was the first and became the model) under arrangements that are intended to insulate arts policy from the tastes (or whims) of the politicians who vote the funds. Harry Hillman Chartrand and Claire McCaughey explain the system as follows:

The government determines how much aggregate support to provide but not which organizations or artists should receive support. The council is composed of a board of trustees appointed by the government. Trustees are expected to fulfill their grant-giving duties independent of the day-to-day interests of the party in power. Granting decisions are generally made by the council on the advice of professional artists working through a system of evaluation. The policy dynamic tends to be evolutionary, responding to changing forms and styles of art as expressed by the community (Chartrand and McCaughey, 1989, pp. 49–50).

When it comes to public support of the arts there are recognized two seemingly irreconcilable forces: "One is the right of taxpayers to determine how their money is spent. The other is the absolute necessity to protect freedom of expression, particularly in the arts" (Glueck, 1989). How can this impasse be resolved? Members of the arts community do not deny that taxpayers have their rights. Rather, the art world asks the political world, in the interest of free art, not to insist on those rights. If that sounds like an elitist claim, so be it. In a prescient passage written in 1978, Lincoln Kirstein declared:

It is time for the inventive, lyric, poetic, creative elite to come out of their closets and declare themselves – their worth, their difference in kind, their capacity, their energy, and their strength. Most of all – their necessity. Elitism should be a rallying cry for that band of brothers and sisters who bear the culture of their country, for it is this cultivation of the only memorable residue that marks and outlives their epoch which justifies their permission to perform and produce as free agents, whatever the risk or cost to their countrymen. (Kirstein, 1978, pp. 181–197, cited at 197)

13.7 Summary

Building on the somewhat more theoretical foundation of Chapter 12, this chapter explored the practice of arts support in a number of selected countries. A historical review and international comparisons provided useful perspectives for a description and evaluation of both public and private support.

In this and the previous chapter we have observed how heavy is the reliance of art institutions on financial support, whether private or public. As a result, raising funds features high not only on the agenda of the art institution's management, but it is also increasingly often part of the job description of artists employed by the institution. "Do we raise funds in order to make music, or make music in order to raise funds?," asks the superstar conductor Rodriguez, a fictive character in the comedy drama "Mozart in the Jungle" (2014). But being overburdened with fundraising activities is not the only concern that occupies the thoughts of an artist, as we will see in the next chapter, where we take a closer look at the arts as a profession.

SUGGESTIONS FOR FURTHER READING

For more on the interaction between private and public support in the arts sector, see Borgonovi (2006) and Ferreira (2018).

See Cowen (2006) for a discussion about the arts and its funding in a US context.

PROBLEM SET

13.1 Some countries offer income tax deductions for individuals or corporations that provide charitable donations to not-for-profit arts organizations.
   a. Suppose an individual with the marginal tax rate of 0.45 intends to donate half of her annual income of $160,000 to an arts organization. What are the financial implications to the donor, the government, and the arts organization?
   b. Would your answer differ, if the donor would instead donate a painting of the same value as the monetary donation above? Explain why.
   c. Discuss why a government may prefer to support the arts indirectly by foregoing revenue instead of supporting the arts directly with subsidies.

13.2 "It is a government's responsibility to support the arts."

    a. Evaluate the normative statement above by assessing what are the advantages and disadvantages of public support versus private support.

    b. Form two groups, one arguing in favor of public support for the arts and the other in favor of private support. In each group, draft a list of arguments and prepare for a fierce discussion. Let the debate begin!

    c. Write an essay – no more than three double-spaced pages, total – in which you critically assess whether public support should dominate over private support for the arts.

NOTES

1 The extent and consequence of indirect public support in the form of reduced VAT rates in Europe is studied by Borowiecki and Navarrete (2018). On the basis of data for EU-28 countries in the period from 1993 to 2013, Borowiecki and Navarrete show that the reduced VAT rates for books or admission to cultural services were 7.1% and 6.8%, respectively, which is about only one-third of the average standard VAT rate of 19.8%. This constitutes not only significant public support to the arts, but it is also an additional reason of why international comparisons of private and public funding are very difficult to conduct.

2 For an overview of how European countries have built cultural policy systems, depending on different national political histories and cultural fields, see Dubois (2014).

Part V

Art, Economy, and Society

14 The Arts as a Profession
Education, Training, and Employment

LEARNING OBJECTIVES

By the end of this chapter, the reader should be able to:

- Provide an overview of artists' socioeconomic background
- Apply supply and demand concepts to labor markets in the arts
- Explain the phenomenon of superstars
- Describe what are the benefits and costs of becoming an artist

The "starving artist" is one of the enduring stereotypes of Western culture. Are artists really in such dire straits? If so, why would anyone choose to be an artist? In this chapter, we seek to determine whether and to what extent the stereotype has validity; we try to understand what motivates artists to pursue their chosen professions; and we gain some insights into how the arts labor market works. These are not simple tasks. To offer just one example, it is not always clear exactly who is an artist and who is not. We take up this matter in the next section, where we also examine some of the facts about artists. We then develop some economic concepts to help in understanding these facts. Employing these concepts, we next analyze specific "labor markets" in the arts. Finally, we are able to use this framework and applications to consider merits and shortcomings of possible intervention strategies in arts labor markets. Although we draw many examples and applications from artists and their circumstances in the United States, fundamental concepts can easily be extended to other nations, from which we also draw illustrations and relevant data.

Those professions that the US Bureau of the Census classifies as artists are listed in the upper portion of Table 14.1. It should be noted that these definitions do not distinguish between commercial artists and other artists or between whether artists' employers are profit making or not-for-profit. The dancer category may include both Las Vegas showgirls and members of the Minnesota Dance Theatre in Minneapolis. Furthermore, this classification scheme is broader than that typically used by scholars in the field.[1] Individuals are placed in categories in accordance with their own reports of income sources during the reporting period. Hence, the actor who is supporting herself by working as a bartender between performing engagements will be classified in census and employment statistics as a working bartender rather than an unemployed actor.

The lower part of Table 14.1 presents artist definitions and examples of occupational titles according to census data in Finland, a nation which conducts unusually extensive research on its arts sector. While the definitions are quite similar to those in the United States, some differences

Table 14.1 Definition of artists

Occupational category	Description or examples of occupational titles
US Census Bureau data	
Actors and directors	Includes individuals associated with the production and performance of dramatic works for stage, motion pictures, and the broadcasting media
Architects	Includes those involved with building and landscape architecture
Authors	Self-explanatory
Dancers	Self-explanatory
Designers	Includes decorators and window dressers
Musicians and composers	Includes singers and other musicians
Painters, sculptors, craft- artists, and print makers	Intended to be broadly representative of creative visual artists
Photographers	Including video camera operators
Radio and television announcers	Self-explanatory
Teachers	Those who teach art, drama, and music in higher education
Other artists	
Finnish Census Data	
Architects	Includes urban planners, etc.
Visual artists	Includes caricaturists, cartoonists, graphic artists, painters, sculptors, etc.
Commercial designers	Art director, graphic designer, etc.
Writers and critics	Author, columnist, etc.
Industrial designers and artists	Fashion designer, furniture designer, textile conservator, etc.
Pattern makers, etc.	Ceramist, pottery and porcelain mold maker, etc.
Performing artists in theaters and operas	Arranger, dancer, ballerina, singer, actor, etc.
Other performing artists	Acrobat, popular singer, juggler, magician, etc.
Musicians	Cantor, conductor, music teacher, instrumentalist, composer, etc.
Theater and film directors and managers	Motion picture director and producer, choreographer, theater manager, etc.
Other art and entertainment occupations	Film editor, impresario, prompter, wardrobe master, light technician, etc.
Photographers and camera operators	Self-explanatory

Sources: Karttunen (1998).

are apparent. For example, singers are considered musicians in the United States, but in Finland, they are divided between two categories of performing artists and are excluded from the musician's category. This highlights the challenges of achieving universally accepted definitions, and it increases the difficulty of making international comparisons of the status of artists.

Two of the factors that should influence career choice – earnings and other employment characteristics – are indicated by the US data presented in Tables 14.2 and 14.3. The first of these shows labor market conditions for artists and two comparison groups – the total labor

Table 14.2 US labor force and selected performing artists, selected years (numbers in millions)

	2006	2010	2015	2016	2017
Total workers, sixteen years and older					
Labor force	150,811	152,669	156,251	158,364	159,629
Employed	144,427	139,064	148,834	151,436	153,337
Unemployed	6,384	13,605	7,417	6,928	6,292
Unemployment rate	4.2%	8.9%	4.7%	4.4%	3.9%
Professionals					
Labor force	29,825	32,254	34,754	35,382	36,347
Employed	29,187	30,805	33,852	34,498	35,522
Unemployed	638	1,449	902	884	825
Unemployment rate	2.1%	4.5%	2.6%	2.5%	2.3%
All artists					
Labor force	2,141	2,201	2,349	2,448	2,481
Employed	2,063	1,998	2,247	2,327	2,383
Unemployed	78	203	102	121	98
Unemployment rate	3.6%	9.2%	4.3%	4.9%	4.0%
Actors					
Labor force	49	41	66	64	53
Employed	38	25	49	47	40
Unemployed	11	16	17	17	13
Unemployment rate	22.5%	38.5%	26.1%	26.6%	24.2%
Dancers and choreographers					
Labor force	31	17	21	19	23
Employed	28	15	19	17	21
Unemployed	3	2	2	2	2
Unemployment rate	9.7%	13.9%	10.3%	11.4%	7.5%
Musicians					
Labor force	213	199	212	208	194
Employed	203	182	202	192	188
Unemployed	10	17	10	16	6
Unemployment rate	4.8%	8.5%	4.7%	7.7%	2.9%

Source: National Endowment for the Arts (2019).

force and other professional workers – from 2006 to 2017. In the first two years included, 2006 and 2010, as the United States was entering and leaving the "Great Recession," unemployment rates for artists as a whole moved from slightly less to slightly more than the labor force as a whole, suggesting that artists were somewhat more seriously impacted by that event. Since that time, artist unemployment has been roughly the same as that of the labor force, but over the entire period covered, artists have fared less well than comparable professionals. Especially noteworthy is the exceptionally high unemployment throughout of actors, and we will have more to say about that later in this chapter.

Table 14.3 presents selected job characteristics for the artist categories in 2017. Artists constituted only about 1.5% of the total work force. On the whole, they were about the same age

Table 14.3 Artist characteristics, United States, 2017

Category	Number (000)	Age	College graduates (%)	Unemployment rate (%)	Second job (%)	Median income (2016 $)	Self-employed ($)
All workers	159,629	41	35.5	3.9	–	35,390	9.4
All artists	2,481	41	62.9	4.0	12.3	40,560	34.1
Actors	53	37	58.6	24.2	30.3	21,290	37.8
Architects	256	45	90.2	1.3	2.1	70,530	25.5
Authors and writers	235	44	83.4	3.8	12.7	45,240	42.1
Dancers and choreographers	23	26	27.0	7.5	9.0	20,450	26.0
Designers	938	40	58.0	3.2	5.6	42,240	24
Musicians	194	45	54.3	2.9	34.8	25,950	44.6
Art directors, fine artists, animators	247	44	58.1	4.5	14.4	33,050	53.8
Photographers	225	38	50.5	4.8	16.4	26,360	55.9
Other entertainers	71	34	39.8	5.4	9.5	23,410	46.5

Note: Workers are sixteen years and older. The age is median age.
Source: National Endowment for the Arts (2019).

as the overall total, with the clear exception of dancers and choreographers, and the percent who were college graduates was significantly larger than the total. The unemployment rate among artists was comparable to that of all workers, with the marked exception of actors. A significant proportion of artists held more than one job. The median income for "high culture" artists was markedly lower than that for the labor force as a whole, with an even greater gap when compared with the Professionals category. Artists are also 3.6 times more likely to be self-employed than all workers.

14.1 Information from an Artist Survey

In 2007, the Research Center for Arts and Culture at Columbia University conducted a survey of artists in the New York Metro Area. The focus of the survey was on aging artists, which also corresponds with the increasingly older age of participants across all art forms (see Table 3.5). Table 14.4 presents respondent opinions on who is a professional artist. The criterion used by the US Bureau of the Census – source of earnings – ranks fourth and fifth among the responses listed. The first choice – possessed of an "inner drive" – is, of course, very difficult to ascertain or to measure, although the second and third – considers herself/himself an artist and recognized by peers as artist, respectively – could be determined simply by asking the respondent.

The same survey offers some additional information on artist economic welfare. Almost 70% of respondents earned less than $7,000 from their art in 2007, and only 3.2% earned in excess of $40,000 from this source. The mean income from work as an artist, about $8,300, was

Table 14.4 Most important reasons for considering someone a professional artist

Reason	Percent
Inner drive to make art	20.5
Recognized by peers as artist	15.8
Considers her/himself an artist	13.0
Make living as artist	13.0
Substantial time working on art	9.6
Special talent	8.9
Some income from art	5.5
Intent to make living from art	4.1
Formally educated in arts	3.4

Source: Jeffri et al. (2007).

Table 14.5 Is arts practice income sufficient to live on without other income (%)

Region	Yes, comfortably	Yes, barely	No, but almost	No, definitely not	No, it provides none of my income
East Midlands	2	7	7	64	20
East of England	1	6	10	60	23
London	3	6	5	67	18
North East	6	13	6	58	16
North West	4	9	8	65	15
South East	2	6	11	66	15
South West	5	10	5	64	16
West Midlands	4	7	3	68	18
Yorkshire and Humber	4	5	4	68	19

Source: Arts Council England (2018).

approximately a third of mean total income for each respondent, which strongly suggests that artists support themselves with earnings from a second job or a second household income.

A more recent and broader study into how artists live and work has been conducted by the Arts Council England in 2016. The survey asked whether the arts income is sufficient to live on without other incomes. The results, as summarized in Table 14.5, show that about two-thirds of artists can "definitely not" live on their arts income, and another 15–20% earns no income whatsoever from artistic activities. Across England, it is just around 11% of respondents that can live on their artist's income, albeit most of them just "barely." London, an important arts center, but also an expensive city to live in, is on the low end. For most artists, the main income source is non-arts work, which accounts for 63% of their total income.

Having now reviewed some of the statistical descriptions of artists in a labor market context, we move to the economic explanations of how these outcomes develop.

14.2 Labor Markets in the Arts

In Chapter 4, we introduced the principles of supply and demand, and demonstrated their application in the markets for a variety of goods and services. Precisely the same principles can be applied to a "labor market" where the supply of and demand for the services of human resources interact. In the case of a typical product, supply and demand together determine the product price and the quantity of the product sold during some time period. In a labor market for artists, the price is the wage (plus fringe benefits and other compensation) paid to the artist, and the quantity can be thought of as the number of artists employed. Thus, the labor market determines both the earnings of artists and the number of artists who will find work. In this section, we consider in somewhat greater detail the operation of the demand and supply elements in the labor market for artists. We may speak, for example, of the market for new college graduates, the market for computer programmers, or the market for dancers. These markets serve to determine wage levels and other terms of employment for each category of workers, and they allocate labor among its many competing uses.

Despite what many observers might regard as anomalies, the market for artists bears similarities to other labor markets. Arts labor markets generally are not mentioned in standard texts of labor economics. Perhaps this is because the market is so small – artists constituted less than 1% of all civilian workers in 1989 – or perhaps it is because the operations of this market are so poorly understood or are perceived as so divergent from more typical markets. And certainly there are those who resist analysis of this market in conventional terms. Robert Storr, senior curator at New York's Museum of Modern Art, contends that "[Artists] are not a labor force .... An artist's success is completely unquantifiable" (Robert Storr, quoted in Christina Duff, 1998).

Nonetheless, we begin with the assumption that artists display the same motivations and behaviors as everyone else: They are rational utility maximizers who seek the highest combination of monetary and nonmonetary reward for their efforts.[2]

14.2.1 Labor Market Theory and the Arts

In this section, we develop the theory underlying operation of arts labor markets. As already indicated, the fundamental analytical tool is the interaction of the demand for artists, as expressed by a variety of employers and the supply of the artists themselves. In a competitive market, with no market imperfections, the prices of productive factors and the level of their employment are determined by the forces of supply and demand. The basic principles are no different from those that apply in product markets or in other resource markets: The greater the demand or the less the supply of a service, the higher will be its price. Conversely, the less the demand or the greater the supply, the lower will be the price.

The assumptions that underlie the demand side of a market with "perfect" competition are: (1) employers have complete and accurate knowledge of wages, labor availability, labor productivity, and related matters; (2) employers are rational profit maximizers, which means that they employ workers and other factors of production in a fashion consistent with the highest possible profit; (3) no single employer is sufficiently large to influence wages; (4) employers do not collude to influence the market; (5) artists in a given market are homogenous, that is, they are perfect substitutes for each other.

Corresponding assumptions pertaining to the supply side of the artist labor market are: (1) artists have perfect knowledge of market conditions, including employment opportunities and wages; (2) artists respond rationally to differences in wages and other benefits; (3) artists are perfectly mobile between jobs and among geographic regions; and (4) there are no unions or other artificial restrictions on supply. In Section 14.2.2, we discuss the failure of some of these assumptions to coincide with the reality in some arts labor markets, but at this point they help us to develop an understanding of "ideal" market outcomes.

The supply and demand forces in the artist labor market are illustrated in Figure 14.1. The left-hand panel represents the market for, say, actors. The downward-sloping demand curve suggests that should actors ever become less expensive, theaters and other employers will have an incentive to increase the number employed. Conversely, a higher prevailing wage creates an incentive to economize on the employment of actors.[3]

The supply curve slopes upward to the right, indicating a tendency for additional actors to offer their services in the market as wages rise. The point where the two lines cross is, of course, W, the market clearing wage, such that the number of actors offering their services equals the number desired by employers, and that number is N.

The right-hand panel represents the situation facing the individual employer. In a more competitive situation, such as might exist in the New York City market for actors and in a few other very large markets, a typical employer is likely to be quite small relative to the overall market and hence unable to influence the market wage. We refer to such an employer as a "price taker." In this case, the individual theater must pay the market-determined wage of W and is able to hire n actors at that wage. As drawn, the demand curve for the individual organization is relatively inelastic in the short run.

We can use the diagram in Figure 14.2 to explain more fully the distinction between short- and long-run demand and supply curves. The curves labeled D and D' are short-run demand curves; each is observed at some point in time where the conditions underlying demand are unchanged. In moving from D to D', from one short-run demand curve to a second, we have allowed at least one of the underlying conditions – for example, income or consumer tastes – to change. Similarly, S and S' represent two short-run supply curves, and a movement from one to the other indicates that the conditions underlying the supply of artists have altered. Circumstances entailing such changes are explained and illustrated more fully in the next section.

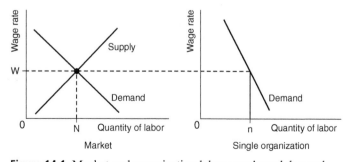

Figure 14.1 Market and organization labor supply and demand.

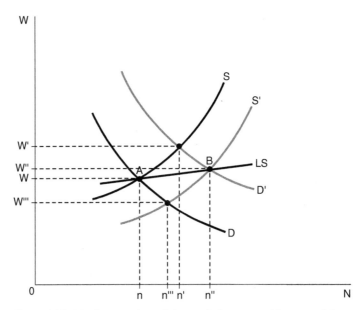

Figure 14.2 Market supply and demand changes and long-run labor supply.

The intersections of *D* and *S* at point *A* and of *D′* and *S′* at point *B* constitute two short-run equilibria, and a line such as *LS* drawn through these points may be said to represent a long-run relationship. The transition from point *A* to point *B* can be an interesting process, as we develop below.

14.2.2 The Demand for Artists

Artists are able to command a salary or wage to the extent that some audience or clientele exists for their work. For example, if no one ever wanted to attend a dance performance and no tickets were sold, there would be no need for dancers and no need to entice anyone to become a dancer. The market demand for dancers would be nonexistent. But if dance is a popular art form, and if people are willing to pay to view a performance, then some dancers will be hired at a salary in return for performing. The demand for dancers is derived from the demand for dance performances. Similarly, if no one ever purchased a painting, there would be no need for painters and no incentive to enter the profession. But if people are both willing and able to acquire paintings, there will be a demand for painters to produce them, and the potential earnings will entice some persons to enter the profession.

The value of the artist to the employer has two components. The first is the artist's marginal productivity, that is, what the artists adds to the "quantity" of the employer's output. The second component is the unit price of that output, since the additional product multiplied by the unit price yields the additional revenue to the employer. If this additional revenue, called the "marginal revenue product" of the artist, exceeds the wage rate, employing the artist adds to the employer's "profit" (or reduces losses).

It follows that the demand for artists depends on those factors that influence demand for their final product. These factors include consumer incomes and consumer tastes and preferences.

For example, if consumer incomes rise, this would be reflected in a shift of the product demand curve, and hence of the artist demand curve, to the right, as depicted in Figure 14.2 by the shift from D to D'. If the conditions underlying supply do not change, so that S remains the supply curve, the result would be a higher wage earned by the individual artist $(W' > W)$ and more artists employed $(n' > n)$.

The same effect might be generated by changes in consumer tastes. For example, many corporations and government units now make a concerted effort to incorporate the visual arts into their working spaces, many going so far as to hire curators to ensure the quality of art acquisitions. This increased desire to acquire works of art is an example of what we mean by a change in consumer taste. In this case, it would cause a rightward shift in the demand curve, just as an increase in consumer income would do. Likewise, arts outreach programs, often supported by public funds, are intended to develop a greater appreciation for the arts – in other words, increasing the taste for art – again shifting the demand curve to the right, for example, from D to D'.[4]

14.2.3 The Supply of Artists

The typical upward-sloping artist supply curve, as portrayed in Figure 14.1, can be interpreted to mean that higher expected earnings can entice additional arts labor into the market. In the short run, higher earnings for, say, dancers, brought about by a change in consumer tastes, may entice those who are sufficiently skilled to abandon their temporary positions as waitpersons and typists and to return to the stage. This is represented by a movement up the short-run curve, S, in Figure 14.2. Due to the higher wage W', $(n' - n)$ additional dancers have entered the market immediately. In addition, more attractive earnings should enhance the long-run appeal of an arts career, so that younger aspirants will enter education and training programs to hone their skills in preparation for eventual employment. With the passage of time, very likely a few years, the supply curve will have shifted to S', meaning that at any given wage level, more artists are offering their services than did previously.

If demand conditions have not altered further, so that D' remains the demand curve, the new equilibrium is point B, and the wage associated with this is W''. It is as if demand shifted along a long-run labor supply curve, LS, with the wage rising from W to W'' while the number of artists employed increases from n to n''. The new, young artists who entered the education and training pipeline in anticipation of the relatively rich reward of W' may be a bit disappointed to discover the somewhat less enticing reward of W''.

Conversely, a reversal of artistic fortunes, such as a decline in public support, may lead to a decline in demand and a decrease in supply. The resulting wage decline and unemployment may send performers scurrying into alternative jobs in the short run. This is illustrated in Figure 14.2 by a movement down of the short-run supply curve S'. As demand falls from D' to D, wages fall to W'''' from W'', and employment levels decline to n''' from n''. In the long run, the dismal pecuniary reward will discourage many aspirants from setting out on the difficult path to artistic employment, so the short-run supply curve shifts from S' back in the direction of S. The final outcome, given full adjustment on the part of those preparing themselves for artistic careers, would be wage and employment levels similar to W and n, respectively.

14.3   Some Realities of the Market for Artists

The arts represent – for us, at least – an unusually interesting application of labor market theory. In the forgoing sections, we relied on some simplifying assumptions to develop a better understanding of how arts labor markets might ideally work. Many of the assumptions of a perfectly competitive market are violated in actual labor markets and especially so among artists. For example, painters and sculptors are not homogenous or perfect substitutes; they differ in talent, style, and media. Neither are dancers, musicians, or actors, whose talent, voice, and practice habits will vary. Members of a corps de ballet may appear virtually identical from the back of the balcony, but they are in fact distinct individuals with different levels of performing ability.

There is little agreement on the value of works of art, that is, the market price, much less perfect knowledge of artist wages.[5] Arts sector employers frequently are incorporated as not-for-profit organizations, which raises the question of whether they can be regarded as profit maximizers in the conventional sense. Like workers in other professions, artists may not be able to move freely from place to place in search of fame and fortune. And many performing artists, especially actors and musicians, are members of unions that effectively support their wages and stipulate work rules.

In addition, the marginal productivity of artists, especially of performing artists, is difficult or impossible to measure. It is not at all clear how much "output" an additional second violin contributes to a symphony orchestra. The conductor, the musicians, and the cognoscenti may recognize a "fuller sound," but those with a less discriminating ear – most of the audience, perhaps – are less likely to notice any change. This makes the worth of an individual performer very difficult to ascertain.

In the sections that follow, we consider a few examples of these complications in some detail. In Section 14.3.1, we explore the impact of unions and make special reference to the performing arts. Then we seek to develop an understanding of the so-called superstar. Finally, we examine the visual artist.

14.3.1   Unions and the Performing Arts

Among the best-known unions in the arts field are Actors' Equity and the American Federation of Musicians, and we confine our inquiry to the markets for the performing artists represented by these unions. In our earlier discussion, we treated the supply of and demand for labor, including artistic labor, as behaving much like supply and demand in any other market. The demand curve has a negative slope and the supply curve a positive one. The intersection of the two is the market wage rate. When we discussed the theory of the arts labor market, we presented a theater's demand curve for actors as a rather typical, downward-sloping relationship between wage and number employed. The short-run demand curve – that exists during a single season, when the theater has committed itself to the fixed costs associated with the season – may in fact be perfectly inelastic, as depicted by line D in Figure 14.3.[6] Given an actor supply curve of S, the theater will hire n actors at a wage of W and a total actor wage expense represented by the area of the rectangle $0\,nAW$. We suppose that this wage is an outcome of

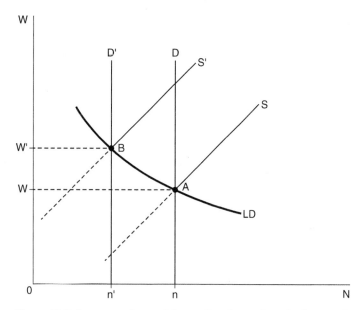

Figure 14.3 Long-run demand for performing artists: single organization.

negotiations between an Actors' Equity local affiliate and the theater management. Since the wage of W is a minimum, the portion of S below W is not attainable and is represented by a dashed line.

If the union successfully negotiates a higher wage such as W' for the ensuing season and if the theater is unable to pass the higher costs on to ticket buyers, then the theater may choose to offer productions with smaller casts. This would be reflected in a shift of the demand curve from D to D' and of actors employed from n to n'. The total actor wage costs would in this instance change to $0n'BW'$.

Consequently, a line drawn through points A and B can be taken to represent a long-run demand curve, where a theater's decision-making is no longer confined to a single season. A shift up in the effective supply curve will, after a period of adjustment, lead to a movement up the long-run demand curve. A clear outcome of actor demands for higher wages is that some actors – equivalent in this case to $n - n'$ – will no longer be employed. And this outcome – a rise in unemployment due to union activity – is widely recognized among economists.

It is not uncommon nowadays for actors to double up, playing multiple roles in a given production, provided their characters are not on stage simultaneously. Many new plays are written, and old plays often are restaged, with fewer parts, so that the expense of actors can be borne more easily. These are consistent with higher rates of unemployment that result from nonmarket wage increases such as those secured by union activity.

A musical organization such as a symphony orchestra in an analogous situation also has an inelastic short-run demand curve for musicians. An employment level such as n in Figure 14.3 may represent both the orchestra's traditional "sound" and a minimum number of musicians as negotiated by the orchestra and the American Federation of Musicians. For example, contracts with the very best US symphony orchestras typically stipulate a minimum number of musicians, often in excess of a hundred. These contracts also include a guaranteed annual salary. For the Chicago Symphony and the Los Angeles Philharmonic, the annual base salary was at $160,000 for a full year (see American Federation of Musicians, 2018). These large and renowned organizations may, through sophisticated fund-raising and marketing activities, be able to cover such higher expenses. Smaller organizations, however, may be discouraged from developing full-sized orchestras, even with much lower salaries. For example, musical talent aside, the Jacksonville Symphony, with fifty-nine musicians, will never achieve the sound of the larger organizations. One might conjecture that more musicians would be employed if the salaries of $52,026 in Jacksonville in 2017 were lower.[7]

These union-negotiated salaries, especially of the major orchestras, seem to be quite attractive – and the figures cited do not include what most might regard as quite generous fringe benefits. According to one source, the estimated 3,000 music performance majors, who graduate from American colleges and conservatories every year, are exposed to fierce competition for 150–269 open positions with full-time orchestras (Gehrke, 2007). Interestingly, some attribute this apparent oversupply not to the attractiveness of union scale but rather to what they regard as the near unscrupulous behavior of music schools, academies, and conservatories, which persist in attracting and graduating students when so few positions are available (Gehrke, 2007). Similarly, in Europe the number of students exceeds the available jobs by far. In the EU-27, arts students comprise 3.9% of all students, whereas artists account for considerably less than 1.6% of the total labor force in 2019. "Considerably less," because the only available estimate includes workers in the arts, entertainment, and recreation (Eurostat, 2020a; 2020b).

Another possible reason for an oversupply of artists is the lure of fame and wealth. Especially since the success stories of some few individuals who "made it" receive the highest visibility, the expectations of artists-to-become may be blurred and they may be overly optimistic in assessing their chances of becoming famous; after all, there can be only very, very few superstars.

14.3.2 The Superstar

Most of the second violins in an orchestra may be regarded as close substitutes for one another.[8] But none of them likely has the drawing power of Midori or Itzhak Perlman. Midori, Perlman, and a number of other especially talented performers are among the "superstars" of the live performing arts. While most of the public might associate stardom with the movies – the box office draws who command salaries well in excess of $1 million per movie – here we focus on the live performing arts.

Performing companies differ in how they utilize the superstar. For example, orchestras rarely have a resident superstar other than, perhaps, the conductor. They rely on itinerant superstars, lining up a number of prominent soloists for each season. Some ballet companies – for example, American Ballet Theater in the not-too-distant past – feature resident superstars as principal dancers, while others – for example, the Joffrey – are less reliant on big names. Broadway productions and major opera companies customarily secure the services of superstars.

We would reasonably expect the more talented performers to command a higher return, but the rewards to superstars seem disproportionately skewed. Sherwin Rosen has attributed this to the interaction of restricted supply of the best talent with expanded demand due to market exposure (Rosen, 1981). According to one observer:

The superstars' fees are high…and they are worth it. The presence on an orchestral program of a great soloist will sell out the concert (and the series of concerts) in many cities. The star system works – audiences will come to see and hear the soloist despite the program or the quality of the orchestra or conductor. (Seltzer, 1989, p. 17)

We can construct an example in the classical music field. Aficionados are likely to acquire a collection of recorded music as one substitute for the more expensive live performance. But since the number of possible soloists available for recording, say, a Beethoven piano concerto, far exceeds the current annual output of new recordings, only a relatively few pianists gain exposure in this fashion. Hence, they become the recognized names – the "riskless commodity" – sought by impresarios and music directors. Although, in point of fact, most listeners would not be able to detect differences in the quality of play among a large number of performers, they seem to prefer the sure thing to the unknown. Robert Frank and Philip Cook characterize this as a "winner-take-all" phenomenon and liken the market to a tournament. The few winners – the superstars – do very well compared with the also-rans (Frank and Cook, 1995).

14.3.3 The Visual Arts

Visual artists – painters, sculptors, and so on – are especially distinct as many are self-employed and, as indicated in Chapter 10, often create speculative works.[9] In this case, the artist engages in "inventory investment," and the inventory is disposed of through some combination of promotional and pricing techniques. The "wage" is the selling price minus the cost of materials, studio expenses, and other related outlays. As an artist becomes more popular, his or her works may command a higher price, which can be interpreted as a greater demand for his or her "labor services" and a higher "wage." An artist will continue to be self-employed, pursuing a livelihood in this manner, so long as the combination of fees for services and expected return on investment (including such nonpecuniary returns as fame) justify the resources expended.

14.4 Becoming an Artist

14.4.1 Investment in Human Capital

The choice of a career is one of the most important, and perhaps most difficult, faced by an individual. Among the factors influencing such a choice are expected earnings, working conditions, training and education requirements, discrimination, and personal preferences. Most people, given a choice between two opportunities that are otherwise similar, will select the one that entails the higher wage or salary. It seems fair and safe to say also that most people will prefer to work fewer hours per day, not to have to undergo lengthy and sometimes expensive training, and select the job that suits them best. Why, then, would anyone select a career that entails notoriously low wages, long and uncertain hours, the possibility of injury, arduous preparation and training, and innate talent, to boot? As we suggest in this chapter, the conventional wisdom holds that careers in the arts have just such characteristics.

As a first step in considering this matter, we must introduce the concept of "human capital." Ordinarily we think of a firm's investment in its physical plant, or productive capability, as the creation of capital. A firm undertakes such an investment, or creates capital, if the expected return justifies the investment. In an analogous situation, an individual will "invest" in education or training, or an employer will invest in an employee, if justified by the expected return. Such investment in a person enhances that person's "human capital." For example, a dancer will incur the costs of classes – investment in his performing ability, or human capital – if he thinks his return (most likely in the form of higher earnings) will be sufficiently enhanced.

To make this concept more precise, we retrieve a concept introduced as Equation (10.5):

$$P_t = \frac{C + P_{t+1} + S}{1+r},\tag{14.1}$$

where P_t is the amount someone would be willing to pay for an asset, the quantity $C + P_{t+1}$ represents the dollar value of the return to acquiring the asset, S is the nonpecuniary return to holding the asset, and r is a market interest rate. With slight modification, and ignoring for the moment the inherent satisfaction variable, S (addressed in Section 14.4.2), we can write

$$F_t = \frac{\Delta W}{1+r},\tag{14.2}$$

where F_t is the fee that the student would be willing to pay for the class if ΔW is the increment in the wage that the dancer will realize as a result of the class. We can make this a bit more concrete with a hypothetical example. Suppose a dancer estimates that a class with a famed teacher will increase her earnings next year by $2,000.[10] The market interest rate is 10%, expressed for our purposes in a decimal form, 0.10. Then the maximum amount the dancer would be willing to pay for the class is

$$F_t = \frac{\$2,000}{1+0.10} = \$1,818.\tag{14.3}$$

If the class is priced at, say, $1,750, which is less than the maximum amount she would be willing to pay, she will invest in herself by taking the class. If, on the other hand, the class is priced at $1,850, she will pass up the opportunity.

More generally, if the perceived return to preparing for and entering an artistic profession is sufficiently high, relative to the cost of investing in human capital, individuals with the appropriate skills will be enticed into that profession. The return, including pecuniary and nonpecuniary components, must compensate the worker for resources expended in training and education and for the risk inherent in artistic endeavors. In addition, the return must at least equal that offered by the best alternative occupation for a given artist. If becoming an artist becomes cheaper, relative to the return, more individuals will become artists at each wage rate, ultimately shifting the supply curve to the right, as we depicted in Figure 14.2. This would occur, for example, if the costs of artistic training were subsidized via public support of a high school of the arts, as is the case in New York City and the state of North Carolina. From the individual artist's perspective, this is an effective reduction of F_t in Equation (14.2), and it makes artistic education seem more worthwhile. The eventual rightward shift of the supply curve results in an increase in employment $(n'' > n')$ but a decrease in the market wage

$(W'' < W')$, an outcome not usually anticipated by those advocating subsidized training. If the performer herself fails to take this into account, she could be sadly disappointed with the level of compensation that does not, in fact, justify her human capital investment.

14.4.2 Thoughts on the Inherent Value of Artistic Work

It is certainly not only the strict financial motive – the amount of income received – that drives people into artistic occupations. One could point at a number of factors associated with high job satisfaction that characterize artistic professions. The work of an artist entails a high variety of tasks and a low level of routine, which makes the work far from boring, and hence less burdensome. Artists have potentially a high degree of personal autonomy in the projects pursued and often a sense of self-fulfillment. They can further enjoy an idiosyncratic way of life, a strong sense of community, and, if they are successful, a high degree of social recognition.

Hans Abbing (2008), writing from the vantage point of being both an artist and an economist, suggests that artists, perhaps more than other professionals, prefer personal satisfaction, recognition, and status to money. Equation (14.1) originally included the variable, S, to represent job satisfaction. We dropped the variable for convenience in subsequent calculations, but now we can explicitly acknowledge its potential importance in explaining artist labor market decisions. According to Abbing, some artists actually lose interest in earning money once they achieve a target income level.

Under the assumption that artistic work is not altogether burdensome, requiring what economists call a "compensating differential," but actually a source of inherent satisfaction, something that makes people better off, David Throsby suggests an important model explaining career choices of a "driven" artist.[11] Throsby's work-preference model explains in particular how much a person is working as an artist and in non-artistic occupations. One of the model's predictions is that an increase in the non-arts wage will induce the artist to spend more time on artistic work and less time on (undesired) nonarts side jobs. The artist is thus largely, but not entirely, oblivious to financial concerns; once the subsistence consumption is reached, she can decrease the volume of nonarts work and dedicate more time to her artistic projects.

14.5 Gender Representation

We have observed in Chapter 3 various characteristics of arts audiences. We have also seen in Table 11.3 that the share of women attending performing arts or visiting an arts museum in 2017 is considerably higher than the share of men. Women appear thus to be relatively keen consumers of the arts, and it is argued sometimes that they socialize through the arts (Ateca-Amestoy, 2008). In contrast to this, in the *production* of arts women are typically underrepresented. Table 14.6 provides a statistical portrait of the artist by gender in the United Kingdom in 2017. Women account for less than half of all workers, and even less – only 46.4% – of all artists. Particularly low is the representation of women among musicians (33.1%) or actors (44.8%), but there are also areas where women dominate: 81.4% of dancers and 58.5% of authors are female.

Table 14.6 Gender inequality in the arts, 2017

Category	Number (000)	Percent female (%)	Women's-to-men's earnings ratio ($)
All workers, sixteen years and older	159,629	47.1	0.79
All artists	2,481	46.4	0.77
Actors	53	44.8	0.89
Architects	256	25.4	0.78
Authors/writers	235	58.5	0.86
Dancers and choreographers	23	81.4	0.63
Designers	938	53.5	0.77
Musicians	194	33.1	0.92
Art directors, fine artists, animators	247	44.6	0.74
Photographers	225	47.1	0.74
Other entertainers	71	45.6	0.74

Source: National Endowment for the Arts (2019).

Table 14.6 shows also that the women's-to-men's earnings ratio is only 0.77 for all artists, which means that female artists earn on average only about three fourths of what male artists earn. The most balanced earnings – at women's-to-men's earnings ratio of 0.92 – are among musicians. The relatively few women who make it into music earn relatively well, albeit still less than men. On the other side, the female dominated category of dance has a women's-to-men's earnings ratio of only 0.63. These patterns seem to suggest that there is a trade-off between entry barriers for women and their earnings. Arts categories that employ relatively many women like dance come with the drawback of significant cuts in their earning relative to men's.

Even more striking is the underrepresentation of women among the "superstars" category, whether nowadays, or in the past. The art historian Linda Nochlin famously asked: "Why have there been no great female artists?" (Nochlin, 1988, p. 145) Throughout history, artworks created by women, when compared to men, have been often overlooked, obscured and undervalued. Lists of the most "famous" artists in history are heavily dominated by men, in the extreme, exclusively so. For example, in one – not so uncritical – ranking of the top 523 Western music composers of all time there is only one female composer (Germaine Tailleferre) (Murray, 2003). However, many female musicians, even though they do not appear on the list of the most prominent, played important roles in music history. For example, the composer Nadia Boulanger has been by far the most important teacher with as many as 413 student composers (followed by Bernard Rogers with only about half as many students) (Borowiecki et al., 2023). The sort of influence exerted by Nadia Boulanger has shaped many generations of composers, including several of those who made it onto the lists of the most famous ones. Furthermore, many of women's works have also been wrongly attributed to male artists (Spence, 2020). As a result, female artists are often rediscovered nowadays and perhaps even sometimes favored by art critics and audiences (Sussman, 2017). However, the male-centered social norms that have been prevalent through most of (art) history and often remain present in societies nowadays have irrevocably diminished the creative potential of our civilization.

14.6   Some Words on the Gig Labor Market

Recent years have seen the rise of the so-called "gig labor market," namely the circumstance whereby workers are essentially self-employed rather than working and developing a career within a single firm or a group of firms in an industry. The standard examples are the chauffer services such as Uber and Lyft, where drivers contract with companies to provide services and are compensated on a "piece-rate" or per unit basis.

Performing artists, especially musicians, understand this type of market very well, since this form has been standard for as long as anyone can remember, especially among musicians. Indeed, the very word "gig" originated among jazz musicians in the 1920s.

In the performing arts, an employer – for example, a theater, an opera company, or a music presenter – would express a "demand" for one or more performers in a pool, or supply, of qualified workers, for a limited-term, one or a few consecutive performances. From an analytical perspective, this means that the relevant labor market is regularly in flux, with frequently shifting supply and demand curves. Musicians who join an orchestra, or dancers who become members of a corps de ballet, may withdraw from the gig labor market for the duration of their employment (although some may continue to have "side-gigs," e.g., an orchestral trombonist who is also in a jazz combo).

14.7   Summary

The factors that influence the supply of and the demand for artists interact to determine artists' incomes, and several economists have sought to identify those that are most relevant. We draw on their work to answer some of the question posed at the outset of this chapter.

Are artists in danger of imminent starvation? It may make a romantic operatic story line, but the data do not support the stereotype. On the other hand, the data make it clear that sole reliance on artistic earnings would be insufficient for a large number of artists. Second jobs are a doubled-edged sword: They enable artists to attain a higher standard of living, but they inhibit investment in artistic human capital by reducing practice, class, studio, and rehearsal time. Artists also earn less than workers with similar educational levels, but we can offer the conjecture that the nonmonetary benefits of an artistic career offer some additional compensation. Although many artists will not be well paid, few are likely to starve, and so long as artistic careers retain some inherent appeal, artists will continue to meet our aesthetic needs.

SUGGESTIONS FOR FURTHER READING

See Wassall and Alper (2006), Abbing (2008), Bille (2020), Schulze (2020), and the collection in Heikkinen and Koskinen (1998) for studies that seek to explain the relationship between artists' income and supply of and demand for artists.

For the role of composer teachers in music history, see Borowiecki (2022) and Borowiecki, Ford and Marchenko (2023).

Refer to Galenson (2023) for an analysis of different approaches to artistic innovation, based on the careers of painters, sculptors, poets, song writers, and others.

PROBLEM SET

14.1 According to the introduction to Chapter 14 of the text, "The 'starving artist' is one of the enduring stereotypes of our culture." This raises the question of whether artists really suffer economic deprivation and, if so, why?

   a. What factors determine the incomes of artists? Are these different from determinants of incomes in other professions? Explain.

   b. What are the implications for the role of schools devoted to preparing young people for artistic careers? (Examples include schools for the arts and music schools.) In developing your answer, distinguish between long- and short-term effects.

14.2 According to the *Billboard* magazine, the Irish rock band U2 has earned $54.4 million in 2018 and has been the highest paid band of that year. The earnings come from streaming revenues ($0.6 million), music publishing royalties ($0.7 million), album sales ($1.1 million), and touring ($52 million). Explain what economic forces enabled this band to earn disproportionately more than other musicians. Discuss what may have been the reasons why the band has predominantly earned from touring.

14.3 Many select a career in the arts, which entails notoriously low wages, long and uncertain hours, the possibility of injury, and arduous preparation and training.

   a. Use the investment in human capital model to explain why many young people make this career choice.

   b. Apply the concept of preferences to explain how some people may be better off as artists with lower wages than in other better paid occupations.

   c. What types of societal problems may this cause and what can be done about it?

NOTES

1 For example, Borowiecki and Dahl (2021) selected only actors and actresses, authors, musicians, and visual artists.

2 This is consistent with the conclusions of Wassall and Alper (2006) who surveyed a number of arts labor market studies.

3 In an imperfectly competitive product market, the demand curve is downward-sloping, and any increase in output fostered by the additional employee will cause a fall in the market price. Accordingly, the value of the employee is determined by multiplying the additional output by the marginal revenue, not the price. For a review of the concept of marginal revenue, see Chapter 5.

4 Consumer taste for the arts can be also influenced by other factors. For example, the revived interest in dance of the early 2010s is alleged by some to have been influenced by the popular television series *Dancing with the Stars*.

5 The reader will remember the importance of trial and error in setting the prices of art works, as discussed in Chapter 10.

6 This is consistent with our treatment in Chapters 6 and 7.

7   The sliding scale represented by the lower salary in Jacksonville, as compared with, say, Chicago, is intended to make allowance for the differing circumstances in smaller cities. Nonetheless, the scale probably exceeds purely market-determined salaries. Data are from American Federation of Musicians (2018).

8   Some contracts specify that the seating of musicians within a section will be rotated from one performance to another, reinforcing a perception of homogeneity or substitutability.

9   Commercial artists, who may work for an employer or who may act as independent contractors, participate in a reasonably well-organized market and very likely have good information about their value in that market.

10 Presumably, such a class would enhance earnings potential over several years, but the treatment of a multiyear period is a bit more complex, although the basic idea is the same. Hence, we stick to just two time periods.

11 Incidentally, the model by explaining labor market decisions of a "driven" artist, defined by Throsby as "a person driven by an irresistible desire to create art," reflects quite precisely the person typically considered an artist, as we have seen in the questionnaire summarized in Table 14.4. According to the NADAC survey, an artist is primary a person who possesses an "inner drive" to make art.

15   The Role of the Arts in a Local Economy

LEARNING OBJECTIVES

By the end of this chapter, the reader should be able to:

- Explain how market size matters for cultural supply
- Explain how economies of agglomeration are relevant for the arts
- Describe trends and the extent of geographic clustering of artists
- Outline why artists cluster

Art and culture of the kind analyzed in this volume – the live performing arts and galleries and museums – are preeminently urban activities. Painters, composers, and playwrights may live anywhere they like, but the economics of live performance as well as gallery and museum display dictate that their output will be seen for the most part in cities. The explanation is quite simple. Like beauty parlors, health clubs, and hospitals, the live performing arts and museums share the characteristic that whatever they offer must be consumed where it is produced. Some restaurants may be willing to deliver a meal to your home, but no theater company, so far as we know, will put on its production in your living room. It is true that an increasing number of cultural institutions employ digital technologies – plays are broadcasted online and museums can be visited virtually – but as we will see in Chapter 16, the potential for substitutability of the "real" experience is limited. Moreover, for most institution, digitization would be a cost rather than an income source. An art exhibition may also travel from the museum that organizes it to other museums and galleries, and some performing arts companies regularly go on tour, but the net income from such endeavors is held down by their high cost in relation to revenue earned.

Thus, even after allowing for possible income from a digital presence, touring companies, and traveling exhibitions, most arts institutions are economically viable only in places where the local arts audience is big enough to support them, basically that means in cities or metropolitan areas that are sufficiently large.[1] How large is large enough depends on two factors: the cost characteristics of the service in question and the density of demand for it. The greater the per capita demand for a service, the smaller the minimum-sized city needed to support it and the larger the number of places that will provide it. On the other hand, the larger the production unit required for efficient operation, the larger a city must be to support that service, and the smaller the number of places that will be served.

The geographic distribution of ordinary retail stores and service activities shows how these principles operate. Small towns provide a market large enough to support a drugstore or barber shop but not a department store or health club. Medium-sized cities can support a department store or health club, but not a stock exchange, investment banking firm, or major league baseball club, for which a very large city is required. For each service, there is a minimum market size, or threshold, below which that activity is not generally viable.

As cities grow larger, they pass successively higher size thresholds and consequently supply not only more of each good but also more kinds of goods. Thus, Chicago not only has more drugstores, supermarkets, and department stores than nearby South Bend, but it also provides types of services that are not found in South Bend at all, for example, investment banking, a commodity exchange, and major league baseball.

15.1 The Concentration of Art and Culture in Urban Centers

Similar considerations govern the location of professional performing arts institutions and art museums. A small city might have only a professional theater. A medium-sized city might have several theaters and, in addition, an art museum, and a symphony orchestra. A large city will probably have additional museums and also an opera company and a ballet. This line of reasoning suggests that arts activity not only increases with city size, but, more interestingly, it increases faster than city size. That being the case, it will also be true that the larger the city, the larger its art and culture industry will be in relation to its economy. Likewise, it would follow that a disproportionately large share of a nation's arts activity would be found in its large cities.

15.1.1 The Role of Economies of Agglomeration

Abetting the concentration of arts activity in large cities is the force of what students of urban development have identified as "economies of agglomeration." These are the savings in unit cost that accrue to certain kinds of firms when a large enough number of them locate in the same city. The savings usually occur because the firms are able to share a common pool of highly specialized inputs, the very existence of which depends on there being a concentration of local buyers. The art and culture industry clearly displays economies of agglomeration. New York City, for example, became a center for producing radio and television programming from the 1920s onward because it already had a vast pool of acting, directing, and writing talent, centered around the Broadway theater, on which radio and later television producers could draw. In the same way, radio and television production was eventually drawn to Hollywood by the pool of talent working in the motion picture industry. And in a reversal of that relationship, a substantial number of motion pictures are now filmed in New York because the city already has the skilled personnel and equipment used to shoot TV programs.

These examples of economies of agglomeration are cases in which one industry is attracted to a given location because it can make use of inputs already drawn to that place by another industry. But economies of agglomeration also operate within single industries. For example, Hollywood became the center for motion picture production because the presence of some firms soon attracted others that could use the same specialized inputs that were unavailable, or at least less abundant, elsewhere. Or look at economies of agglomeration from the perspective of an individual performer: A novice interested in learning modern dance might come to

New York City because that is where the concentration of teachers and job opportunities is greatest. A few years later, that dancer might put together a new company and would base it in New York, because that is where the largest pool of first-rate dance talent can be found. As these cases illustrate, when economies of agglomeration operate, the result can be stated very simply: Activity attracts more activity (Borowiecki and Graddy, 2021; Heilbrun, 1987b).

In Table 15.1, we attempt to substantiate these assertions about the geographic concentration of art and culture. Direct verification is difficult because we lack good data on the extent of arts activity at the local level. The calculations reported in Table 15.1 use the number of artists residing in a given locality as a proxy for arts activity. The data are from the US Population Census tabulation of persons by occupation and place of residence. "Performing artists" include three occupations: musicians and composers, actors and directors, and dancers and choreographers. The single occupation of "painters and sculptors" is taken to represent

Table 15.1 Geographic distribution of performing artists and painters/sculptors

	Performing artists			Painters/sculptors		
	1980	2010	Percent change	1980	2010	Percent change
US total number	270,300	497,100	83.9	183,100	266,700	45.7
	Artist per 10,000 of population					
US total	10.29	13.49	31.1	6.74	7.34	8.9
Metropolitan areas						
Top ten	18.98	23.98	26.3	11.79	11.70	−0.7
New York	41.36	41.79	1.0	18.82	17.91	−4.8
Los Angeles	41.89	66.64	59.1	12.41	20.96	68.9
Next eight	13.32	16.42	23.3	10.83	9.76	−9.8
Second ten	11.05	15.00	35.7	9.32	7.30	−21.6
Third ten	14.04	14.87	5.9	11.46	8.76	−23.6
Fourth ten	11.32	14.00	23.7	7.45	7.28	−2.3
Fifth ten	13.06	15.53	18.9	7.50	5.96	−20.6
Nashville	35.39	45.13	27.5	7.08	5.97	−15.6
Other nine	10.58	11.83	11.8	7.55	5.95	−21.2
Fifty largest	13.69	16.73	22.2	9.50	8.26	−13.0
Remainder of the United States	9.57	12.86	34.4	6.16	7.16	16.3
	Percentage distribution of artists					
Ten largest metro areas	39.9	32.9		32.1	25.5	
Remainder of the United States	60.1	67.1		67.9	74.5	

Notes: US total number of artists is an extrapolation based on the 1% census sample and using person weights. Metropolitan areas are ranked by population size in 1980 and arranged in descending order of size.
Source: US Census and American Community Survey, provided by Integrated Public Use Microdata Series.

the visual arts. The visual arts and performing arts are shown separately because, as it turns out, they exhibit quite different locational characteristics.

15.1.2 Artists per 10,000 of Population

In the middle portion of Table 15.1, we use artists per 10,000 of population to measure the level of artistic activity in the United States as a whole and its pattern of concentration among the fifty largest metropolitan areas, when these are arranged in descending order of size. Since the number of artists rose much faster than total population from 1980 to 2010, artists per 10,000 – which might also be called "artist density" – rose as well. This is consistent with the picture drawn in Chapter 2 of an arts sector growing faster than the general economy.

The second row of Table 15.1 shows that in the United States as a whole, there were 10.29 performing artists per 10,000 in 1980 and 13.49 in 2010. Reading down the columns for performing artists, we see that artist density is higher than the national average in the ten largest metro areas and declines more or less regularly as we move to smaller ones. The notable increase when we reach the fifth group of ten is accounted for by the presence of Nashville, a relatively small metropolitan area that happens to be a national center for the production of popular music and therefore violates the normal locational order. When Nashville is separated out, the other nine areas in the fifth group of ten fall into the normal pattern. The last two rows of the middle portion of the table show that in the fifty metro areas as a whole, the density of performing artists is almost a half greater than in the remainder of the United States, confirming our opening statement that the arts are preeminently an urban activity.

15.1.3 The Special Cases of New York and Los Angeles

Performing arts activity is highly concentrated in New York and Los Angeles, the nation's two leading arts centers. In 2010, the New York metropolitan area had 9.7% and the Los Angeles area had 14.0% of all US performing artists, although their shares of US population were only 3.1% and 3.2%, respectively. That means they each had three or four times their proportionate share of arts activity. This shows up in Table 15.1 as a density of performing artists in New York and Los Angeles that is three or almost five times the national average, respectively (compare Rows 4 and 5 with Row 2). We described above how economies of agglomeration operate in the arts. Undoubtedly, the dominant positions of New York and Los Angeles reflect the fact that, as a result of economies of agglomeration, they became centers not just for the live performing arts but also for mass media productions that require dancers, musicians, composers, actors, and directors.

How much of the concentration of the performing arts in New York and Los Angeles is accounted for by the pull of the mass media and how much by traditional live performance? The labor force data employed in Table 15.1 do not allow us to separate those categories. Some inferences can be drawn, however, from information obtained from the Census of Employment and Wages.[2] In 2010, the United States had 9,783 performing arts companies. Of that total, 14.8% were in the New York metropolitan area, while only 7.7% were in the Los Angeles area. On the other hand, New York is home for 13.5% of the establishments of the motion picture and video production sector, whereas in Los Angeles, this sector's share is 27.2%.

We can conclude that Los Angeles is largely a center for the motion pictures, while New York, though it does some production for the mass media, remains primarily a center for live performance.

15.1.4 Concentration or Deconcentration over Time?

Shifting the perspective slightly, we can ask, is arts activity becoming geographically more concentrated over time? The last two rows of Table 15.1, which show the percentage distribution of artists between the ten largest metro areas and the remainder of the country, help answer that question. Over the last three decades, the answer has been "no." From 1980 to 2010, the proportion of US performing artists residing in the ten largest metro areas dropped from 39.9% to 32.9%. From 1990 onward, however, the distribution remained fairly stable at roughly one third (not shown in the table).[3] The proportion of visual artists found in the ten largest metropolitan areas was lower to begin with than for that of performing artists: It was 32.1% in 1980 and has fallen down to 25.5% in 2010, which reflects the decentralizing forces cited above.

15.1.5 Measuring the Relative Size of the Local Arts Sector

Table 15.1 uses the number of artists per 10,000 of population as a measure of the relative size of the arts sector in a given area. For the nation as a whole, the number of performing artists stood at 13.49 and the number of visual artists at 7.34 per 10,000 of population in 2010. The table also tells us that at the same date, New York and Los Angeles had, respectively, 41.79 and 66.64 performing artists and 17.91 and 20.96 painters and sculptors per 10,000. For the two categories combined, those were by far the highest figures among all US metropolitan areas, confirming what our previous analysis led us to expect, namely, that the largest cities would have the largest arts sectors relative to the size of their economies. Indeed, New York and Los

Table 15.2 Estimated number of cultural establishments

	Performing arts companies			Motion picture and video production			Art dealers		
	1990	2000	2010	1990	2000	2010	1990	2000	2010
US total	10,474	10,795	97,83	10,343	16,278	15,365	6,080	7,130	5,711
Metropolitan areas									
New York	1,638	1,528	1,446	1,740	2,079	2,074	753	737	759
Los Angeles	882	1,227	754	3,228	4,917	4,184	300	348	257
Chicago	270	325	362	328	488	457	152	180	157
Next seven (average)	140	150	124	160	251	183	50	72	87
	Percentage distribution of establishments								
Share of top-10 in US total	35.9	38.3	35.1	62.0	56.8	52.0	25.5	24.9	31.2

Source: Census of Employment and Wages, provided by the US Bureau of Labor Statistics.

Angeles are probably the only US cities in which the business of art and culture is truly important to the local economy.

15.2 Locational Patterns in the Visual Arts

We have already explained why performing arts companies tend to locate in cities, and since the performers themselves must live close to their place of work, they, too, locate in cities. These considerations should apply also to art galleries and dealers, and looking back at Table 15.2, this appears to be the case. In 2010, the ten largest agglomerations had 31.2% of the total number of art dealer establishments, with New York holding by far the highest proportion of 13.3%, followed by Los Angeles with a share of 4.5%. The concentration of art dealers is somewhat higher than that of visual artists, which we observed previously to be around 25.5% in the ten largest agglomerations. It should not surprise us that visual artists are less concentrated in large cities than art dealers, or performing artists, since painters and sculptors need not live or work close to cities. In the language of location theory, they are much more "footloose." For an established visual artist, a few visits per year to a dealer are probably enough to maintain the relationship. For example, Georgia O'Keeffe lived in New Mexico while exhibiting regularly in New York.

As transportation and the technology of communication improved and living costs in urban areas increased, some visual artists who formerly lived in the city have moved to more congenial or less expensive locations. Of course, many continue to live in large cities where, presumably, they find the company of fellow artists stimulating, enjoy the ease of browsing in museums and galleries, or find the social environment, with its tradition of involvement in the arts, to be especially congenial. New York and Los Angeles remain the dominant centers, but Chicago, San Francisco, and Washington, D.C. also have relatively large populations of painters and sculptors.

15.3 Clustering of Famous Artists

The intensity of concentration becomes even more apparent when examining a subsample of famous artists, that is, those who "made it." These artists exhibit a remarkable clustering intensity in relatively few large cities. Hence, the patterns observed in Table 15.1 would most likely be even more remarkable, if density were to be observed in conjunction with the quality of artists.

The observation that the best artists are over-proportionally represented in the largest geographic clusters for the arts offers a very important insight. It suggests that there exists a correlation between locating in a top cluster and becoming famous or being particularly productive. However, the causality – the direction in which this relationship works – is unclear. It could be the case that the best artists migrate to geographic clusters, if creative hubs are simply magnets attracting talented artists. Alternatively, it could be the case that artists located in clusters become more productive, or in other words: Locating in a geographic cluster exerts a positive influence on an artist's production. This discussion may seem abstract, but the knowledge on the causal relationship between creativity and clustering is essential for sound policy making.

It is in general very difficult to establish causal effects between variables, but it may be particularly challenging to estimate whether an artist's decision to locate in a cluster has a causal influence on his or her production. Ideally, we would conduct a randomized experiment in which artists would be by chance assigned – for example, by the means of tossing a dice – into a geographic cluster or some other non-cluster location. The random assignment would ensure that we observe the true effect of locating in a geographic cluster, by comparing the creative production of the two groups after some time.

In reality, however, these types of experiments are not feasible and researchers need to avail of alternative approaches to tackle the issue of causality. One such example is a study by Borowiecki (2013) who estimates the causal impact of geographic clustering – locating in Paris, Vienna or London – on the productivity of music composers born between 1750 and 1899. The historical time period is crucial as it delivers a setting where composers' location choice is as good as randomly assigned (the so-called natural experiment setting). Borowiecki observes how composers' birth places are spread fairly uniformly (in a random-like fashion) across space and documents that depending on the birthplace, the future location choice is affected. This is particularly true during the historical time period in question, when traveling, though possible, was still very difficult and costly. Therefore, geographic distance mattered: Being born closer to a geographic cluster, a composer was more likely to locate there. Exploiting the spread of birth place as a source of random-like assignment into clusters allows Borowiecki to estimate the causal impact of geographic clustering on the productivity of composers. The emerging results support the notion that locating in dense agglomerations may benefit the artist: Composers wrote approximately one additional influential work every three years they spent in a cluster. This implies a productivity increase of close to 50%; quite obviously, a very large boost in one's productivity.

Knowledge about the causal direction allows us to speculate then on how precisely the effect works, and what the mechanisms in play might be. There are several reasons why an artist who decides to locate in a geographic cluster may benefit from that decision. First, artists living and working in proximity to each other, where some kind of face-to-face contact is enabled, may benefit from synergies and spillovers, which influence the individual's ability to innovate. Second, the presence of multiple rivaling artists might be the source of important incentives for outperforming the competitor. Third, in a geographic cluster the presence of a high degree of diversity may be conducive to creative production, as knowledge may spill over between painters and sculptors or between painters and creators from outside the visual arts, for example, music composers or writers. Fourth, location benefits could also be attributed to economies of scale as a result of sharing the same specific cultural infrastructure, access to related supply industries, or distribution channels.

The above presented results and mechanisms on the productivity enhancing role of geographic clustering are conducted at the city level. In reality, there are also significant differences in the density of artistic activity within a single city, where certain districts attract more artists and supply a greater variety of cultural goods and services than other districts. For example, around the turn of the twentieth century many notable artists lived and worked in the Parisian district of Montmartre, probably due to its low rents as well its pervasive bohemian reputation. The list includes several noted composers, such as Erik Satie, but also many visual artists, including Amedeo Modigliani, Claude Monet, Piet Mondrian, Pablo Picasso, Camille Pissarro and Vincent van Gogh.

Moving on to more recent history, the role of cultural districts remains noteworthy. Discussion of creative quarters nowadays may bring to one's mind the neighborhoods of Camden in London, Montmartre in Paris, Kreuzberg in Berlin, or the M50 Art District in Shanghai, but perhaps the most famous example is SoHo in Lower Manhattan, New York City. Recent history has seen the district become an important location for many artistic ateliers, lofts, and galleries, as well as an increasingly popular destination for its range of shops, including both trendy upscale boutiques and large chain store outlets. The case of SoHo is a classic example of inner-city regeneration and gentrification, characterized by socioeconomic, cultural, political, and architectural developments. The downside of these trends is that the artists' neighborhood becomes increasingly fashionable, and hence attracts more businesses and residents, which in turn raises the cost of working and living there. As a result, artists – who are more income constrained, as we saw in the preceding chapter – are forced once again to relocate to other, more affordable neighborhoods. And so, the cycle continues.

15.4 Cultural Tourism

Tourism has experienced continued expansion and diversification since the mid-twentieth century and constitutes one of the largest and fastest growing economic sectors in the world. According to the United Nations World Tourism Barometer, international tourist arrivals have grown from 25 million globally in 1950 to 1.5 billion in 2019; this implies a remarkable annual growth rate of 6.1% (UNWTO, 2020). The COVID-19 pandemic has clearly given a huge blow to the tourism sector and reversed its growth, especially affecting international tourism. However, irrelevant of how many tourism arrivals there are or where they come from, a significant proportion of them constitutes cultural tourists, that is, tourism activity organized primarily or solely for cultural purposes.

For Italy, one of the globally most popular tourist destinations, Figure 15.1 visualizes the relationship between tourist visits by origin and admissions to entertainment activities per province in 2007. The correlation is clearly positive and implies that provinces with a higher admission to entertainment activities experience also higher tourist inflow, be it domestic or foreign visitors. However, it is not clear what type of entertainment activity is related to tourism flow: Are cultural activities attracting tourist visits, or could there also be some other noncultural attractions that are conducive to tourism? For example, one may be concerned that a very similar association would be found with sports activities, which would somehow diminish the value of the arts and culture. Borowiecki and Castiglione explore in more detail the Italian data which allows them to disaggregate entertainment activities participation into various types. Controlling for the wealth and size of each province, and other potentially confounding factors, the authors show that tourism flow is closely related with a wide range of cultural activities, ranging from museum visits to attendance of performing arts (theater, concerts or dance performances), while the role of noncultural activities (such as, for example, sports, amusement parks or open-air shows) in determining tourism flow is largely insignificant.[4] Of

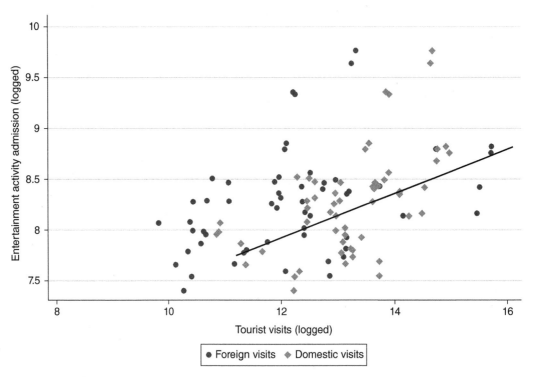

Figure 15.1 Entertainment admissions and tourist visits (Italian provinces in 2007).
Source: Borowiecki and Castiglione (2014).

course, not much can be said on the causal direction of this association, nonetheless, the finding that tourism and cultural participation correlate is quite insightful and potentially of value for cultural and tourism policy making as well.

These results can be further reaffirmed with a Eurobarometer opinion survey of Europeans' preferences toward tourism. According to the extensive questionnaire, which covers twenty-eight member states of the European Union, 25% of tourists mention culture as the main reason for undertaking a travel in 2016 (European Commission, 2016). Even with the survey's rather broad and somewhat vague definition of culture, which includes besides the arts, religion, and gastronomy, it becomes rather obvious that cultural tourism accounts for a nonnegligible part of travel activity in Europe.[5]

Next, we turn to an overview of some popular and yet not uncontroversial approaches to measuring how cultural tourism, and the arts sector in general, interact with and influence economic activity in the city as a whole.

15.5 Economic Impact Studies

In the 1970s, advocates for the arts discovered that assertions about the positive economic impact of the art and culture industry made an effective case for greater state and local government support. The argument worked because it took advantage of two US traditions: first, the long-established interest of state and local governments in promoting economic growth within their borders; second, the hard-headed, show-me-in-dollars-and-cents attitude of locally influential business people whose support was crucial to local arts subsidies. The result was a series of "economic impact studies" that attempted to measure the significance of the local arts industry in actual dollar terms. The word "attempted" is used advisedly because of the conceptual and practical difficulties of carrying out such studies and the questions raised in some quarters about lack of objectivity.

Studies of the economic impact of the arts try to measure the proportion of economic activity in a city that is attributable to its arts industry. The principles involved are perfectly general and could be used to measure the impact of any identifiable local industry. The usual approach is to estimate the size of three flows of spending that originate in the arts sector and that, in combination, measure its impact. The three flows are commonly referred to as direct, indirect, and induced spending and are described in the next sections. Ideally, these flows should be estimated from an input–output model of the local economy. Such a model systematically traces out the dollar value of purchases by each industry from every other industry that are required to produce one year's total output in the economy being studied. Originally developed by Wassily Leontiev in the 1930s and 1940s for the US economy as a whole, input–output models have also been devised for local, state, and regional economies (Reeves, 2002, pp. 54–56). When studies of the economic impact of the arts have been done in metropolitan areas for which such a model does not exist, the researchers have nevertheless usually made use of input–output concepts and borrowed essential parameter values from input–output studies of other localities.

15.5.1 Direct Spending

Direct spending is the easiest category to measure. It consists of the expenditures for goods and services by all institutions defined as being in the local arts sector. The list would presumably include all museums, galleries, and performing arts companies located within the city or metropolitan area. In theory, spending by individual local artists such as painters and sculptors should also be counted, since they are producing art locally, but up to this time lack of data has precluded doing so. The amount of direct spending by the arts sector is usually ascertained by conducting a questionnaire survey of the relevant institutions.

Since the purpose of these studies is to measure the local impact of spending, it is necessary to exclude monies spent to buy goods or services outside the local area. Thus, if a theater has its costumes made in another city, their cost would not be included as part of direct local spending but would be a "leakage" of spending into the outside world. As we see below, the higher the rate of leakage, the smaller the total impact of the arts sector will turn out to be.

15.5.2 Indirect and Induced Spending

The economic impact of the arts sector does not end with its direct spending, for the goods that are directly purchased by arts institutions also have to be produced, and to the extent that they are produced locally that effort gives rise to further rounds of local spending. For example, suppose that a theater company has its programs printed locally. Its payment to the printer is a direct local expenditure, as previously defined. But that is only the first round of local effects. To produce the program the printer buys paper, ink, and electric power, and pays rent in a commercial building. Perhaps the paper and ink are imported from outside the area, so payments for those items are leakages rather than contributions to local activity. But commercial building space and electricity are local products, so the printer's payments for those items constitute a second round of local spending, and to the extent that the commercial landlord and the electric company buy inputs locally, there ensues a third round. Indeed, a series of ever-diminishing rounds continues until the accumulated leakages finally exhaust the initial direct spending impulse. The sum of all rounds of business spending subsequent to the first "direct" round is the "indirect" spending that results from the theater's activity.

In tracing out the secondary effects of direct spending, wages and salaries are treated separately from expenditures on goods and services, but the principle is the same: Wage and salary payments made by the theater to its staff are part of its direct expenditures and give rise to a series of further rounds of activity as the stores in which employees shop purchase local goods to replenish their stocks or the landlords to whom they pay rent spend money on local goods and services to operate and maintain buildings. The sum of these diminishing further rounds is the "induced" local spending attributable to operation of the theater.

15.5.3 Multiplier Effects

The total economic impact of the arts sector on the local economy is the sum of the direct, indirect, and induced spending attributable to it. An input–output model produces these numbers directly. If such a model is not available, the first step is to measure direct local spending of the arts sector by means of a local survey. The amount of total spending attributable to the arts can then be estimated by applying a "multiplier" to the observed level of direct spending, that is, total spending = direct spending × multiplier. The value of the appropriate multiplier can be borrowed from an input–output study carried out for some other city.

It can be shown that the value of the multiplier varies inversely with the rate at which spending "leaks out" of the local economy. One can intuitively see that the smaller the leakage at each round of spending, the higher will be the proportion of each round that is respent locally, and therefore the larger will be the ratio of indirect and induced effects to direct effects. Algebraically, the multiplier is most easily represented as follows: We denote the multiplier as K and the marginal propensity to respend dollar receipts locally as *mprl*.[6] Although a full derivation is not given here, it can be shown that

$$K = 1 / (1 - mprl)$$

In the algebraic statement one can see that the higher the marginal propensity to respend locally, the smaller the value of the denominator and the higher the value of K. To illustrate with plausible values, if, while if $mprl = 0.5, K = 2$. We would expect that the larger the population of the metropolitan area being studied, the larger the value of the multiplier. The analysis of threshold effects at the beginning of this chapter indicated that the larger the metropolitan

Table 15.3 The contribution of the arts to the UK economy in 2011 (million GBP)

	Creative, arts, and entertainment activities	Sound recording and music publishing activities	Book publishing	Total
Direct	2,982	459	1,921	5,362
Indirect	3,062	250	1,647	4,959
Induced	1,433	144	1,105	2,682
Total	7,477	853	4,673	13,003

Note: The table shows the gross value added, which is measured in 2010 GBP.
Source: The contribution of the arts and culture to the national economy, CEBR (2013).

area, the greater the variety of goods and services it would produce. That being so, it follows that the larger the area, the less the need to import, the higher the marginal propensity to respend locally, and therefore the larger the multiplier.

15.5.4 The Arts Industry in the United Kingdom

In 2013 the Arts Council England commissioned a report that measured the size of the arts and culture industry in the UK (Centre for Economics and Business Research, 2013). Table 15.3 summarizes the central findings of the study. The economic activities within the arts and culture industry were divided into three groups: (1) creative, arts, and entertainment activities; (2) sound recording and music publishing activities; and (3) book publishing. For the arts industry as a whole, direct gross value added amounted to £5.36 billion (about $3.3 billion). Total economic impact came to £13 billion, indicating that the multiplier effect, which differed slightly among categories, averaged 2.4.

By themselves, of course, these numbers mean nothing. To put them in perspective, the study offers comparisons with some other UK industries. It is found that in terms of direct revenues, the arts come somewhat ahead of administrative and support services, public administration and defense, health, and wholesale and retail trade. The survey concludes that the arts and culture industry has a high multiplier compared to other sectors. The reason is that for production of an additional unit of output in the arts, the industry requires to consume relatively higher proportions of the outputs of other industries.

15.6 Have Economic Impact Studies Been Misused?

It was pointed out at the beginning of this section that studies of the local economic impact of the arts were developed in the 1970s primarily as an advocacy tool, a way of persuading state and local officials and local business people that art and culture were worthy of generous public and private support. In that role they proved very effective, probably, as it has been suggested, because by relying on dollars-and-cents economic arguments and building on the premise that economic development is a good thing, "they bridge differences or reduce psychological distance between arts advocates and those they must persuade," namely, the business people and public officials who are influential in making funds available for the arts (Radich and Foss, 1987).

However, not all economic impact studies are scrupulous and cautious in the interpretation of the results, and even the best of them may have been misused in subtle ways. There can be no objection to a study that makes an honest and informed effort to measure the sheer size of the arts sector in a local economy. But as Bruce Seaman argues, economic impact studies can be faulted for the fact that those who use them (especially noneconomists) frequently draw incorrect or misleading inferences from them, and the form and content of the studies virtually invite such errors (Seaman, 1987 and Rushton, 2006).

15.6.1 How to Misinterpret an Economic Impact Study

Typical misinterpretations can be illustrated with a single hypothetical example. Suppose that in some medium-sized city, an economic impact study shows the arts industry to account for $40 million of direct and $80 million of indirect spending per year. Advocates using the study emphasize that it proves the arts to be "big business," important to both employment and income in the city. The unstated implication is that if the arts sector were to falter, the city would lose $120 million per year of spending, together with the associated jobs. But this is unlikely to be true because, as Seaman emphasizes, it overlooks the pervasiveness of substitutability among objects of expenditure (Seaman, 1987, pp. 52–55, 57).

Look first at consumer spending. Part of the direct expenditure of arts institutions included in the $40 million total is accounted for in ticket sales by the resident theater company, the local symphony orchestra, and the opera company. But if these institutions did not exist, local citizens would presumably spend their money on something else. Perhaps they would go to the movies more often or spend more on health clubs, restaurant meals, or birthday presents. The pattern of consumer spending would be different, but there is no reason to assume that the total would be smaller, and the same argument extends to the flows of indirect expenditure resulting from the initial spending impulse. However, one possible change in pattern does deserve mention: If the arts were no longer available locally, consumers might travel more frequently to other cities to visit a museum or attend a play, concert, opera, or ballet. That would reduce local spending, just as an increase in imports of other goods and services would. But the effect would probably be very small, since it is likely that only a minor fraction of former arts spending would be diverted to other places.

Substitutability also operates in connection with public support. In most cities a portion of the direct expenditure of nonprofit arts institutions, especially museums, is paid for by local government subsidies. Arts advocates might stress the importance of the jobs and income traceable to that financial support. But again, there is no reason to assume a unique connection. If the city did not subsidize the art museum, it might either spend more on other local services, with a presumably equivalent impact on jobs and income, or else reduce taxes, which would permit an offsetting increase in consumer spending.

One alleged advantage of the arts over some other local service activities is that they can attract visitors from abroad whose spending within the country is a net addition to national income and stimulates economic growth in the same way as an export of goods would do. It is true that not in all countries the export component of arts activity will be significant enough to make or break the case for government or business support. However, in a country like Italy the case for the arts stands much stronger: The direct revenue from tourist demand for all cultural activities is estimated to be about 6% and for the subcategory of museums it is almost 15% (Borowiecki and Castiglione, 2014, table 5, p. 257).

15.7   The Arts and the Local Quality of Life

A final economic argument said to favor promotion of the arts is that their presence can help to attract business firms into a metropolitan area, thus stimulating local economic growth. Circumstantial evidence is shown in Figure 15.2, which shows the existence of a strong and positive relationship between the density of artists and startup activity in US cities in the long run. Even if simple scatter plots are subject to biases due to unobservable factors that potentially matter for the location of arts centers and business clusters, such as educational attainment of local populations, the strength of the disclosed correlation is rather striking.

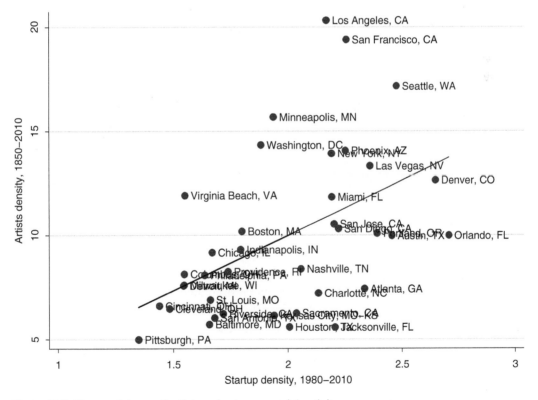

Figure 15.2 The coexistence of artists and entrepreneurial activity.
Notes: Artists include visual artists, musicians, authors, and actors. Densities are measured per thousand people.
Source: Borowiecki and Dahl (2021).

A strong cultural sector helps also to create a favorable image of a city. One study found that officials concerned with local economic development were apt to cite such amenities "as an important indicator of the general level of a community's civility and culture. The presence of these amenities is used to suggest that a community is progressive, resourceful, concerned about itself, and energetic" (Cwi and Lyall, 1977, pp. 21–24). The arts can thus spur civic engagement of the local community, as cultural participation generates networks that span neighborhood boundaries, overcoming so potentially barriers of social class and ethnicity (Stern and Seifert, 2010).

The business community, too, is aware of the importance of art and culture to the local environment. We showed in Chapter 13 that business firms often make substantial contributions to the support of the arts in their home town. While they may be motivated partly by a concern for public relations, it can hardly be doubted that they also believe their contributions are an effective way of making the local community a better place in which to live. Economists, on the whole, would agree with that way of looking at the matter: If the arts deserve local support, it is not because they are instruments of economic development, but because they make an indispensable contribution to the well-being of the women and men who make up the local community.

SUGGESTIONS FOR FURTHER READING

The line of reasoning that larger cities provide a wider array of goods and services is developed in a branch of economic geography known as the "New Economic Geography." The seminal paper on this topic is written by Krugman (1991), but for an introductory overview, see Venables (2016).

Evidence on the clustering of top artists in comparison with average artists in the United States is provided by Borowiecki and Dahl (2021), who also disclose these patterns over the very long term of 150 years.

For a discussion of the uses and abuses of arts impact studies and an extensive bibliography of the subject, see Reeves (2002).

PROBLEM SET

15.1 Choose three cities that differ in size – a small city, a medium-sized city, and a large city – and provide a list of the main cultural amenities offered in each of these places. Discuss how market size determines the cultural supply that you listed. Can you think of other factors that influence the patterns observed?

15.2 It is known that artists have been clustering in specific cities at certain periods. For example, Paris has been the main work location for some of the most famous visual artists or composers of all times.

    a. Discuss whether and how an artist's creative work may benefit from locating in a city like Paris, where many other artists are based as well.

    b. Evaluate what are the negative effects of intensive clustering.

c. Discuss whether and how this may be different for artists nowadays.

15.3 For some state, county, or metropolitan regions that have special interest to you (and for which sufficient data are available) compare employment, total earnings, and average earnings in the "arts" with at least three other sectors, including one or two that you would regard as "superior" and "inferior" to the arts sector. Use the most recent data you can find.

Present your results in an easy-to-read table, and write an essay – no more than three double-spaced pages, total – describing and assessing your findings. What expectations are confirmed? What surprises are uncovered?

NOTES

1 The presence of summer music festivals or summer theater in small rural communities is not an exception to this principle, since the communities are places with a large summer or tourist population, and the performing organizations (other than summer theaters) usually have winter homes in large cities.

2 These data do not come without limitations for the approach pursued here. The Census of Employment and Wages does not include self-employed workers, while multi-job holders will be counted two or more times. Despite these shortcomings, the data presented provide important insights into the question raised previously.

3 This proportion comes, in fact, very close to the proportion of performing arts companies found in the top-10 metropolitan areas as reported in the Census of Employment and Wages, summarized in Table 15.2. The share of performing arts companies has slightly decreased from 35.9% in 1990 to 35.1% in 2010.

4 The results point further to interesting differences across nationalities of tourists. Domestic tourists appear to drive the popularity of theater-type activities, which is possibly related to the ease of access due to a shared language, whereas admissions to museums, concerts, or dance is higher in places with more foreign tourists. For further details, see Borowiecki and Castiglione (2014).

5 The Eurobarometer survey asks also another related question: What would make you go back to the same place for a holiday? Fourteen percent of respondents provide that cultural and historical attractions are the main reason for a return, and this reason is trumped only by the natural features (landscape, weather conditions, etc.). Arguably, weather and views are important determinants for travel, and they are often also so closely related to the appreciation of cultural heritage.

6 In "Keynesian" terms, the marginal propensity to respend locally equals the marginal propensity to consume minus the marginal propensity to import. The multiplier approach is generally traced to the work of John Maynard Keynes (1936, chapter 10).

16 The Mass Media, Digital Access, and the Cultivation of Taste

LEARNING OBJECTIVES

By the end of this chapter, the reader should be able to:

- Discuss how media and digital technologies influence art demand and supply
- Describe trends in consumption of digital arts
- Explain the relationship between digital and traditional cultural consumption

Art is said to be an "acquired" or "cultivated" taste. That is in no way a disparaging statement. It certainly does not imply that a taste for art is somehow unnatural, artificial, or pretentious, as if all those people who claim to enjoy listening to Beethoven's string quartets or Bach's cantatas were just kidding. Rather, it means that one has to be familiar with art to find pleasure in it, and the more familiar with it you become, the more pleasure you find.

As pointed out in Chapter 4, taste is obviously one of the most important variables in determining the level of consumer demand for art (or for any other consumer good). If the public's taste for art increases, the demand curve for art shifts to the right along the supply curve: Unless the supply curve is perfectly vertical, more will be produced and more will be purchased (see Figure 4.7). But if taste itself depends on exposure, we are in danger of being trapped in a suboptimal position, in the following sense. Some expenditure of time and/or money by consumers in making themselves more familiar with art would yield gains in future utility more than sufficient to cover the outlay. The optimal (and rational) decision would be to make the outlay, but since consumers are unaware of the possible future gain, they do not do so. To put it in less formal terms, consumers would greatly enjoy art if they were familiar with it; however, familiarity comes only with exposure, and the public will not expose themselves to it since they have not the taste. This vicious circle can be broken only by policies such as subsidizing the distribution of art (a possibility we discussed in Chapter 12) or providing an effective program of arts education to every student (a proposal we return to in Chapter 17).

16.1 Impact of the Mass Media

From the point of view of high art, the situation is aggravated by the collective impact of broadcast media – traditionally television, radio, motion pictures, and more recently digital media including streaming – and the culture of advertising that uses and is used by them. The taste for popular art is also an acquired one, but in this case the public gets plenty of exposure and is almost guaranteed to acquire the taste because the mass media, by which all our lives are surrounded, or indeed invaded, provide little else. In the competition between popular culture and high art, the commercial broadcast media bias the outcome very sharply in favor of the former. This too can be viewed as a self-reinforcing process or vicious circle. The mass media cater to the taste of the majority, in this case, for popular culture, such as the various forms of rock or country music; exposure through the mass media reinforces that taste; audience surveys then inform commercial producers that popular culture is, indeed, what audiences want and the profit motive ensures that they will continue giving it to them.

There is little doubt that the broadcast media do influence the outcome by catering to the taste of the majority and virtually ignoring everyone else. However, there is a spectrum of tastes in art, recreation, and entertainment reflecting a multitude of influences, among which exposure through the traditional mass media is only one. Another channel that influences taste is the *digital* media that comprises both Internet and mobile mass communication. Digital media by including broadcasting and streaming can come close to broadcast media. The main difference appears though to be that digital media is able to cater better to the individual taste and can provide a more tailored supply – after all, the digital consumer chooses the content she is interested in from the vast array of an online repository.

Table 16.1 shows the share of European's using the Internet daily for private or work-related reasons (Eurostat, 2022). Daily use of the Internet among adult Europeans has grown steadily from 23% in 2004 to 79% in 2019. An equally rapid increase can also be observed for mobile access to the Internet. Forty-three percent have used mobile devices (via mobile or wireless connection) to access the Internet in 2013 and 75% in 2019.

A question more relevant for us is how often the digital means are used to access or consume cultural content? Statistics on the usage of digital technologies is scarce, perhaps even more so than cultural statistics, and available only for selected periods. The Eurobarometer questionnaires, already introduced in Chapter 3 as representative surveys of the population living in one

Table 16.1 Use of the Internet and online services in Europe.

	2004	2007	2010	2013	2016	2019
Daily use of the Internet	23	38	53	62	71	79
Access to Internet at home	–	55	70	79	85	90
Mobile access to the Internet	–	–	–	43	59	75

Notes: Daily use of the Internet measures the use of Europeans 16–74 (in percentage): every day or almost every day on average within the last three months before the survey. Use includes all locations and methods of access and any purpose (private or work/business related). Mobile access to the internet measures the use of mobile devices via mobile or wireless connection: mobile phone (or smart phone), portable computer (e.g., laptop, tablet) or another mobile device (e.g., PDA, e-book reader) away from home or work.
Source: Eurostat (2022).

Table 16.2 Use of the Internet for cultural purposes in Europe in 2007 and 2013.

	Downloading music	Listening to radio or music	Downloading movies or TV programs	Watching TV programs	Visit blogs	Playing computer games
Population as a whole (2007)	27.0	29.0	16.3	11.8	14.1	25.6

	Downloading music	Listening to radio or music	Downloading movies, TV programs or radio programs (podcasts)	Watching TV programs, or streamed or on demand movies	Reading or looking at cultural blogs	Playing computer games	Internet use frequency for cultural purposes	
							Every day	At least once per week
Population as a whole (2013)	31.5	42.6	22.6	27.1	21.5	23.9	10.8	32.1

Note: Based on EU-27, the internet use frequency for cultural purposes includes further culture-related activities, such as searching for cultural information, buying cultural products or reading articles related to culture.
Source: Special Eurobarometer 278 and 399.

of the European Union countries, include helpful questions on the usage of digital technologies for the consumption of culture. And despite the fact that many of the relevant questions differ across the years, insights can be provided into the intensity and perhaps change in the usage of the Internet for a range of specific cultural purposes in or between 2007 and 2013. In Table 16.2, we can observe that the share of population using the Internet to download music increased moderately from 27% in 2007 to 31.5% in 2013. A relatively bigger increase is in the share of those who listen to radio or music on the Internet, which grew from 29% in 2007 to 42.6% by 2013.

All in all, roughly between around 20–40% engage with one of the digital cultural consumptions summarized in 2013, and 42.8% of those engage in more than one of these digital activities (European Commission, 2013). The 2013 wave contains further the explicit question on how often the Internet is used for cultural purposes such as, for instance, searching for cultural information, buying cultural products, or reading articles related to culture. As can be viewed in the last two columns of Table 16.2, 10.8% of the respondents use the Internet for cultural purposes on daily basis, while about one-third use it at least once per week. These results highlight that the use of the Internet for cultural purposes is not only widespread but also frequent across the European society.

The presented numbers illuminate also some interesting changes in the access patterns. Most noticeable is the shift from downloading to streaming of cultural content. With an improving speed and lowering cost of internet connections, increased network coverage, and reliability, including free wi-fi access in many public spaces, it comes perhaps not as a surprise that users consume more content directly from the Internet via streaming technologies, as opposed to downloading, which requires hard-drive storage space. Another observation is that due to the rapid pace at which the technology and usage patterns change, it becomes difficult for statistical offices to keep up with the collection of the right data and posing survey questions that reflect best the current practices.

16.1.1 Some Caveats

Before we go further, two caveats are in order. First, the broadcast and digital media are so complicated that a single chapter cannot possibly do justice to it and is therefore in danger of oversimplifying complex issues. Indeed, it was explained in the Introduction to this volume that broadcasting, writing and publishing, and the motion picture industry would be omitted from the field to be studied because, among other reasons, each would require a book unto itself. The digital media are discussed in this chapter only in respect to their special role in the development of taste and the dissemination of culture. No attempt is made at a full description of the economics of the broadcasting or digital industries.

Second, it must be kept in mind that digital culture is subject to almost continuous transformation (a part of which we discuss below) as wave after wave of technological innovation sweeps through it. There is no reason to believe that the development will be less dynamic in the future. Thus, almost anything written about it today is in danger of sounding outdated tomorrow, especially in a world just after COVID-19, when digital innovations are very volatile and advancements in AI technology are expanding exponentially, and at the time of writing, data are mostly unavailable.

16.1.2 Digital Cultural Consumption

The data introduced in Section 16.1.1 on internet usage for cultural purposes in Europe raise the question on whether the observed digital cultural consumption affects – and if so, how – traditional cultural consumption, such as attendance at live performing arts or visits to museums and art galleries? Accessing music, movies, or TV programs online occurs in the limited leisure time of an individual, and potentially takes away time available for the consumption of experience goods, such as a theater. After all, with the onset of fast and reliable *online* access to culture from the comforts of one's home, leisure activities may increasingly move to the digital space.

Table 16.3 shows how the exposure to traditional culture (attending theater, ballet, dance or opera, concerts, or visiting museums or art galleries) differs for those who engage in one of the five digital activities related to culture. The most closely related online and offline activities are probably the use of the Internet to access music and concert attendance. With this regard, we observe that more than half of those who download music or who listen to music or radio online attend music concerts (55.7% and 53.9%, respectively), which is about two-thirds higher than the average share of concert goers (33.8%).

Interestingly, higher traditional cultural consumption is visible also for activities which do not appear to be in a clear relationship to each other. For example, those who download or stream audiovisual content are more likely to participate in any of the four cultural activities relative to the population as a whole. This suggests that digital cultural consumption appears to be positively associated with consumption via traditional means, which implies a complementary relationship.

16.1.3 The Impact of Live Broadcasting on Live Attendance

We have described in Chapter 8 how digital broadcasting technologies can increase revenues of performing arts institutions. The utilization of these new technologies impacts, however, not only the revenue but also the audiences. For example, the live broadcast of the play "War Horse," produced by the Royal National Theatre in London, has been viewed in UK cinemas by about 120,000 on a single night in 2014, compared with the 1,040 seat capacity of the theater where it was staged (National Theater, 2019).

Table 16.3 Cultural participation and digital media exposure in Europe in 2013 (values in percent).

	Population as a whole	Downloading music	Listening to radio or music	Downloading movies, TV programs, or radio programs (podcasts)	Watching TV programs or streamed or on-demand movies	Reading or looking at cultural blogs
Theater	26.9	38.4	38.5	39.1	43.7	47.5
Ballet, dance, or opera	17.4	25.7	26.9	26.5	32.5	34.5
Concert	33.8	55.7	53.9	53.9	58.3	57.4
Museum or gallery	36.4	52.8	53.5	54.2	60.3	65.5

Note: See Table 16.2.
Source: Special Eurobarometer 399.

The success of broadcasting technologies raises the question: What is the impact on attendance at the live performing arts? Does technology really generate new audiences or is the public only substituting the physical performance with the digital counterpart? On the one hand, broadcasting promotes the show as well as the venue, and this may lead to a higher demand for performances at the theater. People who enjoy the broadcast may be tempted to view the live performance. On the other hand, live transmissions may "cannibalize" attendances at the broadcasting institution, especially if the new format is seen by the public as a substitute for traditional performances.

With this issue in mind, Bakhshi and Throsby (2014) investigated how the demand for live performances at the Royal National Theatre changed after the institution had launched broadcasting to national cinemas. Since a high proportion of the cinemas participating in the broadcast were located in the commuter belt of London, which is in reasonable proximity to the National Theater, the public had a choice to view the production at the theater itself or at the broadcasting venue. By studying box office sales, which allowed Bakhshi and Throsby to identify from which postal district a booking has been made, they show that live broadcasting was associated with an *increase* in bookings for the live performance, not the opposite. In this case, cinema broadcasting has possibly generated some additional bookings for the theater performance, and the authors conclude that the relationship between a live broadcast and attendance of the actual play appears to be complementary in nature.

Comparable results are also found in a study of the English Touring Opera (Wise, 2014). Based on surveys circulated to cinema audiences attending live screenings, it is disclosed that live broadcasting is more likely to stimulate future attendance at another cinema screening, as opposed to deteriorate live theatre attendance. Live screenings are thus expected to neither drag away nor create new audiences for live opera but instead to establish a new audience specifically for screened opera. Interestingly, the "new" digital audience is not completely new to art and culture; according to the questionnaires, they were already moderate or frequent operagoers.

It is perhaps encouraging – or at least a relief – for some live performance arts institutions that broadcasted content is likely viewed independently from the live performance. One concern remains though, and it is related to the effect of the live broadcasting of world-class performances on the attendance at local, lower tier performing arts institutions. It is a nonnegligible consideration that transmissions of high-quality performances from globally leading institutions may have a negative effect on live performance attendance locally. For example, Met Opera transmits among others to the Philharmonic Orchestra in Łódź, a city in central Poland with a population of about 700,000. The third largest city in Poland has its own opera house and company, but it struggles sometimes to fill the venue. This raises the concern of whether Met's broadcasting of outstanding-quality performances offered typically at a lower price than a live performance may negatively affect the attendance of live opera. According to Krzysztof Bogusz from Teatr Wielki in Łódź, a negative impact of broadcasting is not felt, but then systematic data have neither been collected nor analyzed (Bogusz, 2018, e-mail communication).

The Met, being an early adopter of HD broadcasting technology, experiences clearly a first-mover advantage and claims a significant share of the growing market for live broadcasts. However, by having a monopolized position in some countries, the broadcast may disincentivize opera production locally, which could be a concern for local cultural institutions.

16.2 Digital Cultural Heritage

Cultural institutions open to the public, such as museums, have undergone many stages of reinventing their function and role in society over the decades. None of these developments have been, however, as dramatic as those ignited by the onset of digital technologies and the emergence of virtual museums, which host a collection of digitally recorded exhibits that can be accessed through electronic media. Although these changes are not mere transpositions of real museums on the Internet. In the digital age, museums do not just become archives of digitized cultural objects, but instead they have the potential to transform into "complex and interactive systems that allow access to a broader level of knowledge, experience, emotions" (Digital Meets Culture, 2021). Museums by means of digital technologies can therefore reinvent themselves by providing new, richer, and easier accessible content.

Digital technology has made possible the visit to the galleries remotely, for instance through Google Arts and Culture, which allows the visitor to walk through the exhibition rooms of over 2,000 leading museums and art galleries from 80 countries (Carle, 2020). In addition, some images of artworks are available in extra-high-resolution (hence called gigapixel images), enabling the visitor to zoom in on paintings for a view that goes well beyond what can be seen by the naked eye or to view it in augmented reality. These are the examples of how the museum experience can change with the use of digital technology.

Innovations are introduced not only from outside the cultural sector, but also a number of museums have begun to exploit digital technologies themselves. For example, the Tate Gallery has launched in 2012 a temporary online exhibition under the name The Gallery of Lost Art. Over the course of one year, visitors were able to explore artworks that were lost, whether by destruction, theft, or other reasons, and could no longer be seen physically. The virtual gallery enabled access to a wide range of materials, including archival images, films, interviews, and essays, documenting the loss of works by over forty artists across the twentieth century, including by Marcel Duchamp, Pablo Picasso, and Joan Miró. The exhibition has received substantial acclaim from the media and has been visited by around 100,000 visitors from not fewer than 153 countries (Mundy, 2013).

Another example is the live broadcasting of cultural heritage. In 2013, the British Museum was among the first to broadcast blockbuster exhibitions by using similar technologies as the performing arts does, however, applied to physical objects and exhibits. The broadcast can be watched not only live but also in replay mode, thus bringing the exhibition closer to the visitor. There is one additional advantage of the live broadcast in the form of visitor engagement. During the broadcasts, the viewers were able to comment and ask questions, which enabled a unique real-time exchange between the interested public and the museum. This example illustrates how new technologies make it possible for members of the public to take part and to contribute actively to what goes on inside a museum.

An emerging question is how an online presence of a museum relates to the physical visits it receives. Table 16.4 sheds some light on this issue by showing for a global sample of leading museums the number of onsite visits and three measures of online activity in 2019: the number of Facebook likes, Twitter followers, and Instagram followers (*The Art Newspaper*, 2020) and

Table 16.4 Top twenty museums based on onsite visits and online popularity.

Onsite ranking	Institution	City	Country	Onsite visitors (in millions)	Facebook likes (in thousands)	Twitter followers (in thousands)	Instagram followers (in thousands)
1	Musée du Louvre	Paris	France	9.6	2,591	1,526	4,494
2	National Museum of China	Beijing	China	7.4	–	–	–
3	Vatican Museums	Vatican City	Vatican City	6.9	220	–	147
4	Metropolitan Museum	New York	US	6.5	2,013	4,344	3,847
5	British Museum	London	UK	6.2	1,616	2,082	1,996
6	Tate Modern	London	UK	6.1	1,190	4,803	3,905
7	National Gallery	London	UK	6.0	1,017	892	1,815
8	State Hermitage	St. Petersburg	Russia	5.0	74	781	678
9	Reina Sofia	Madrid	Spain	4.4	396	772	397
10	National Gallery of Art	Washington D.C.	US	4.1	863	272	458
11	Victoria and Albert Museum	London	UK	3.9	704	1,383	1,545
12	National Palace Museum	Taipei	Taiwan	3.8	214	–	–
13	Musée d'Orsay	Paris	France	3.7	869	735	1,271
14	Museo Nacional del Prado	Madrid	Spain	3.5	1,086	1,276	810
15	National Museum of Korea	Seoul	South Korea	3.4	87	–	–
16	Centre Pompidou	Paris	France	3.3	710	1,078	1,058
17	Moscow Kremlin Museums	Moscow	Russia	3.1	30	187	169
18	Tokyo Metropolitan Art Museum	Tokyo	Japan	2.9	25	0.8	–
19	Somerset House	London	UK	2.8	122	279	179
20	State Tretyakov Gallery	Moscow	Russia	2.8	2	321	506

Note: Onsite visitors are for 2019 and have been obtained from *The Art Newspaper* (2020). Facebook likes and Twitter/Instagram followers are of the official museum site.
Source: The author.

authors' own data collection). The list opens the Louvre Museum in Paris with 9.6 million onsite visitors, which are about 30% more visitors than the second placed National Museum of China (7.4 million). The Louvre has also the most likes on Facebook (2.6 million) and Instagram followers (4.5 million), and it is placed fourth in terms of followers on Twitter (1.5 million). The highest number of Twitter followers is observed for the Tate Modern in London and the Metropolitan Museum of Art (4.8 million and 4.3 million, respectively). On average, the top-25 museums in terms of onsite visits have obtained more than 600,000 Facebook likes and close to 1 million followers on Twitter and Instagram. These numbers would be higher if we excluded institutions that do not have an official account on either of these social media platforms.

The available information could be used to quantify the correlations between onsite visits and online activity. Using the available observations, one can, in fact, estimate a simple econometric model in which unobserved differences between countries, such as the internet penetration, are accounted for. Estimating this model shows that obtaining one more Facebook like corresponds with 2.7 more onsite visits. More formally, we estimate a country fixed-effects regression. Since this simple estimation delivers only a correlation coefficient, we could interpret it the other way round as well: One additional onsite visit corresponds with 0.28 Facebook likes. The association is also strong and positive for Twitter and Instagram subscriptions: One additional follower on either of the two platforms corresponds with 0.7–1.2 more onsite visits. Despite the limited insights about the causality of this relationship, which likely works in both directions (online and onsite visits reinforce each other mutually), it appears probable that museums with a stronger online presence are also able to attract more onsite visits.

16.3 Video Games and Cultural Consumption

Video games, whether played on a personal computer, dedicated platforms connected to the TV, portable consoles, or smart devices, are increasingly often characterized as the new mass media. This is because of its wide reach and also the high intensity of consumption by larger shares of societies. But it is not the increasing role within the mass media spectrum that warrants this section – some argue that video games have potentially more in common with art and culture than it may appear (Borowiecki and Bakhshi, 2018; Borowiecki and Prieto-Rodriguez, 2017; Cowen, 2008).

Looking closer at video games, one can detect several similarities with the performing arts. For instance, the video gamer views a live (game) performance – perhaps not so dissimilar from what one would view in performing arts. Moreover, the video gamer, by playing the roles of a protagonist, can influence and interact with the performance. This becomes particularly visible in large-scale online games, where millions of characters are entangled in gripping plots, often exposed to intrigue and drama. The gamer, by directing her protagonist, plays out choices, interacts in various ways with other players (co-performers), and together they shape a spectacle. This does not fall far from what a drama performer would do.

Another parallel can be drawn to visual arts, especially considering the games' iconographic landscapes, architectural creations, or cutting-edge couture of the characters. In fact, the cultural significance of the esthetic aspects of video games and their design prompts some of the leading art museums to include video games in their exhibitions. Most notably, Museum of Modern Art in New York has opened in 2012 a permanent exhibition showcasing the best in video game design and esthetics (Eveleth, 2012). The definite answer on whether video games are an art form or not has to be left to curators, critics, art historians, and possibly game designers. Instead, we direct our attention to the issue on how video games playing relates to the consumption of art and culture more in general.

The profiles and behaviors of video gamers can be studied in several ways. One increasingly popular approach is based on questionnaires asked to a representative sample of the population. These surveys contain detailed questions regarding free-time activities, including the incidence and frequency of video games playing.

In a study of video gamers' affinity and preference toward traditional cultural goods and artistic activities, Borowiecki and Prieto-Rodriguez (2015) availed of a comprehensive survey conducted in Spain over the period from 2010 to 2011.[2] The results of the study indicate that those who play more often video games watch also more television and listen more to music, which perhaps may not come as a surprise. However, more interesting, frequent video gamers engage also more in writing and traditional visual arts (such as painting or drawing). Furthermore, those who play are more likely to be involved in photography – as an art form – or video recording activity. The finding that alternative cultural goods or the involvement in artistic activities exhibit a positive association with video games consumption is quite insightful, as it seems to support the notion that video games tend to be complementary to cultural consumption and practices.

16.4 Music Consumption

The music industry is also rapidly changing and evolving due to new technology. The high accessibility and exposure to music via various digital platforms affect the consumption of culture via traditional means. For example, attendance at popular music concerts became particularly complementary to album sales and was reflected in rising ticket prices (Krueger, 2005). Music listeners engage also often in preordering of albums, which enable access to exclusive content, be it merchandise or nonphysical, such as access to the musician's Twitter account that provides updates from places like the music production set. Whereas the sales of fan boxes, which contain not only the music album but also various fan paraphernalia, account for a significant share of total music sales and do not seem to be doomed to disappear in the new world of streaming (Turner-Williams, 2022).

16.5 Summary

Digital progress, now much accelerated by the COVID-19 pandemic, brought the production process of culture closer to the consumer, both in terms of geographic distance and socioeconomic distance, since now the online content caters not only to the average consumer but also to the niche user. Consumers can participate in and share culture, which transforms cultural markets, and leads often to the widening of cultural supply, especially when the consumer becomes a cocreator of new content.

Digital technologies and digital applications open new ways of communication, investigation, and consumption of products and services in the cultural sector. These insights complement what we have observed in Chapter 10, namely how digital technologies and NFTs have affected art markets and investments into artworks. The application of the digital factor to the different forms of production, distribution, and consumption of culture demonstrates several benefits in terms of effectiveness; cost reduction; visibility; and social, cultural, and educational inclusion. However, as with the introduction of any new technology, very real challenges may arise, and these need to be recognized, understood, and managed by all involved in culture-related work.

SUGGESTIONS FOR FURTHER READING

For an overview on how digital technologies affect the production processes, for example, by changing business models within creative industries, see Towse and Handke (2013), or how culture and cultural heritage decenters away from institutional structures toward the individual in the age of digitization, see Borowiecki et al. (2016).

Digitization of heritage collections as an indicator of innovation is studied by Borowiecki and Navarrete (2016, 2017).

One of the early volumes on digital transformation of creative industries in a developing country is provided for China by Chrétien-Ichikawa and Pawlik (2022).

PROBLEM SET

16.1 Some kindergartens and schools run programs that expose their pupils to art.
   a. Discuss how such a practice may influence a person's long-term interest in art.
   b. Design your own policy that would change the attitudes toward the arts of a group of people. (You can be creative in your choice!) Be specific about how you would implement the policy and outline a strategy to evaluate its success.

16.2 In Chapter 2, we have concluded that live performing arts is a commodity that "has to be consumed at the point of production." Explain how live broadcasting technologies lessen this assumption.

16.3 Taste is one of the most important variables determining the level of consumer demand, including demand for art.
   a. Discuss how mass media shapes consumer's taste in art.
   b. What is the difference between traditional mass media and digital media in terms of reflecting and influencing the taste of consumers? And how do you think will digital media matter for the future cultivation of taste?

16.4 CNN Style wrote: "Social media and smartphones are the most significant technological developments to impact the art world since the invention of the camera."
   a. Evaluate the statement by referring to the rising importance of digital technologies.

b. Form two groups, one arguing in favor of digital technologies for the art world and the other against it. In each group, draft a list of advantages or drawbacks of digital technologies and prepare your arguments. Let the discussion begin!

c. Write an essay – no more than three double-spaced pages, total – in which you assess whether the "significant technological developments," referred to in the quote above, are a good thing or not.

NOTE

1 Borowiecki and Prieto-Rodriguez (2015) construct econometric models in which they can control for observable socioeconomic characteristics of the video gamer, such as age, gender, and educational attainment. Without the inclusion of socioeconomic controls, the estimated correlation between traditional cultural consumption and video games playing could be biased. For example, the younger respondents are typically playing video games and engage less in other cultural consumptions, however, the latter possibly because of their age and not necessarily due to playing video games.

17 Innovation, Diversity, and the Future of Art and Culture

LEARNING OBJECTIVES

By the end of this chapter, the reader should be able to:

- Understand how the high arts compete with popular culture
- Evaluate the degree of diversity in the arts
- Describe how arts education can stimulate the demand for art
- Analyze the past and future trends of the high arts

It has been a theme of this book that the arts with which it deals – and especially the live performing arts – must compete for the consumer's attention with a popular culture that is powerfully propagated by the mass media of radio, television, the movies, and – more recently – digital broadcasting and streaming, and the culture of advertising and promotion in which they are enmeshed. In the face of that competition, the arts have not fared badly.

We demonstrated in Chapter 2 that there was a measurable arts boom in the 1970s and that growth continued into the early 2000s but with increasing signs of weakness in some sectors. We also showed that the COVID-19 pandemic brought sharp reductions in spending on the arts. These setbacks, coupled with the various pandemic-related restrictions, put many arts institutions in financial jeopardy. Were these merely troubles of the moment, or was the long-run trend now running against the arts? Understandably, there was a great deal of anxiety in the art world about the answer to that question.

It is always risky to simply extrapolate into the future from recent experience. It may be worthwhile, nevertheless, to consider the situation of the arts sector by sector in order to reason out what we think the future may bring.

17.1 Competition, Sector by Sector

Competition between popular culture and the high arts can be analyzed at two different levels of aggregation. At the macro level, involvement with popular culture, especially through the medium of television, claims so much of most Americans' or Europeans' leisure time that many have not developed the familiarity with the high arts that might lead them to become participants.

When asked in 2016 to indicate barriers to increased attendance at the arts, only 38% of interested nonattendees checked "costs too much," but 56% selected "lack of time," making it by far the leading answer (National Endowment for the Arts, 2020, table 9). The weak position of the high arts in competition with popular culture is the result of very powerful cultural trends that will be difficult to alter, but a major effort to promote arts education might modify them. We examine that possibility at the end of this chapter.

At the micro level, the ability of the individual live performing arts to compete with popular culture varies across art forms. We propose to look at two factors that help to explain that variation. The first is *technological* innovation. Here the question is, how powerful is the competition of non-live modes of production with the particular live art form? The second factor is *artistic* innovation. In this case the question becomes, how effectively do artistic innovations in the particular art form build and hold an audience?

17.1.1 Symphony Concerts

Among the four live performing arts we have considered – theater, symphony concerts, opera, and dance – symphony concerts have clearly suffered the most from the competition of non-live performance. (See the decline in attendance shown in Table 2.2.) In Chapter 3, we pointed out that, in theory, the availability of art through the mass media could either stimulate demand and thereby increase the rate of live participation or satisfy demand and therefore reduce the rate of live attendance. In the case of music, recordings and sound systems have been developed through wave after wave of technological innovation to the point that they compete very strongly, indeed, with live sound. Moreover, the availability of digital streaming technologies, accelerated during the COVID-19 pandemic, enables an unprecedented selection of music and also ease of access. It is difficult not to believe that these remarkable technologies have, in fact, reduced the demand for attendance at symphony concerts. You can hear a concert of your own choice in any location that has internet access, and at much less expense of time and money than would be required to hear it live. No doubt, live performance is better (unless the recorded artists are notably superior to those in the concert hall), but is it enough better to justify the expense and bother? Evidently, a great many music lovers think not.

At the same time, artistic innovation in the composition of "serious" music has not in recent decades been sufficiently attractive and exciting to build and hold audiences. In the eighteenth and nineteenth centuries, audiences listened to the music of their own time and were, for the most part, charmed by the innovations of contemporary composers. Writing about those centuries, William and Hilda Baumol (1994) describe both the rapid growth of demand for contemporary compositions and the lack of interest in what was called "ancient music" – Handel and Bach – who were barely thirty years gone. But in the early twenty-first century, at least in the realm of concert music, contemporary work has largely failed to capture the public's allegiance. If we assign Mahler, Sibelius, and Strauss to the nineteenth century, as might be justified on artistic grounds, Stravinsky is probably the only twentieth-century composer whom the public would rank as high as the major figures of earlier times. A few other twentieth-century composers, including Bartók, Ravel, Shostakovitch, Bernstein, and Copland, have entered the standard repertory. Nevertheless, symphony orchestra programs are largely made up of compositions from the distant past. Indeed, our concert halls have often been called musical museums. Data on orchestra repertoire presented by the League of American Orchestras showed that twenty-two out of the twenty-five most frequently performed composers in 2012 in the United States were born in the seventeenth to nineteenth centuries.[1] The contrast with the eighteenth and nineteenth centuries could not be starker: In those days audiences listened mainly to operas written in their own time. Unfortunately, the musical museum has apparently lost its charm, especially for those who have yet to attain middle age.

17.1.2 Dance

For dance as a live art – including both ballet and modern dance – the situation is exactly opposite to that of symphony concerts. The competition from recorded performance is negligible, not because one cannot film dance performances to distribute via television or digital broadcasting, but because dance is a three-dimensional art, and serious dance fans do not find the two-dimensional versions more than minimally satisfying. Without a technological breakthrough into three-dimensional reproduction, recorded dance cannot compete with the live thing. Furthermore, dance benefits from artistic innovation to a far greater extent than does concert music. The field of modern dance is made up of a multitude of mostly rather small companies, each under the guidance of its own chief artist-choreographer. Innovation keeps the level of audience excitement high. Dance fans *expect* to see something new each year, perhaps even at each performance, and return again and again *because* of innovation, not in spite of it.

The situation is not very different for ballet. Although old chestnuts (or, depending on one's point of view, classics) from the nineteenth century, such as *The Nutcracker*, *Sleeping Beauty*, and *Giselle*, are still with us, up-and-coming twenty-first-century choreography can be viewed as well. Despite practical difficulties in trying to combine the old and the new, a tradition of presenting both is well established in almost every company and helps to bring the audience back. Moreover, old works may actually be new for a given audience: Because recorded dance is relatively unsatisfactory, few recordings exist, and for that reason works that actually are not brand new, when mounted for the first time in a given city, can create the same excitement as a newly made work would do. With that built-in advantage, it will be a long time before the ballet world runs out of innovation.

17.1.3 Theater

The competitive situation of the theater is only slightly different from that of dance. It is perfectly possible to record a theatrical production on tape to be shown on television or via streaming. (Indeed, how can we distinguish between a "play" shown on television and a "drama" written specifically for that medium?) In fact, however, very few plays made for the stage are transferred to television or streaming, and only a few are made into movies. If you want to see non-live drama, you can go to the movies or turn to streaming platforms, but what you see will not be the same sort of thing that is put on in live theater. Although the growth of movie audiences after the invention of talking pictures came partly at the expense of live theater, the theater survived and ultimately expanded through the system of permanent regional theaters. (See the discussion in Chapter 2.) It seems clear that the competition of non-live performance is not as strong for the theater as it is in the case of music.

Artistic innovation, which is taken for granted in the theater, helps to maintain audience interest. On Broadway, most of each season's output consists of new plays or new musicals. It is the excitement of seeing new works that brings the habitual theatergoer back, again and again. (Indeed, before the development of Off-Broadway, when the Broadway theater was the only game in town, some theater lovers complained that the classics were not staged often enough.) The nonprofit, regional theater cannot subsist entirely on brand new plays. Most regional theaters try to present a mixture of the classics and the contemporary, but relatively new works do make up a large proportion of their yearly programs.[2] And as in the case of dance, a work written thirty – or 130 – years ago may still be new to the audience in a given town. So, the theater certainly has the advantage of artistic novelty to build and hold its audience.

17.1.4 Opera

It is plausible to argue that the ability of opera to withstand the competition of non-live performance falls somewhere between that of the theater and that of symphonic music. Operatic music can be recorded and played back at the listener's convenience just as successfully as symphonic music can. However, the "production values" that apparently make up a significant part of opera's appeal for many of its devotees are entirely lost on recordings and not very successfully captured on film, television, or streaming. So, the live performance of an opera is a good deal more exciting than the non-live. Moreover, the introduction of "supertitles" is a technological innovation that further enhances the attraction of live performance for many attendees.

What about artistic innovation? The answer is best divided into two parts. On the one hand, opera programming (probably because of the high cost per production) is almost as conservative as the programming of symphony concerts: A recent study of opera repertory found that in the United States during the 2019–2020 season, opera created after 1970 made up just below two-fifths of the aggregate repertory (see Opera America, 2022).

But because opera involves dramatic as well as musical elements (the production values just mentioned), other kinds of innovations are possible: One can mount a new production, set the action in a different period, or alter the dramatic interpretation. Old wine in new bottles, perhaps, yet the combination may be quite attractive. Still, the long-run prospects for opera will much depend on whether new works can be developed that will excite new audiences.

17.1.5 Art Museums

Interestingly, the ability of art museums to attract and hold audiences can be examined under the same headings that we have applied to the live performing arts. There is the same problem of competition between the object itself (the original work of art) and a reproduction of it, in high resolution and, if applicable, increasingly often three dimensional, made possible by modern technology. Or to speak more realistically, the actual object on display in a given museum competes for the art lover's attention not so much with its own reproduction, as with the thousands of reproductions of great art from all over the world that the interested viewer can find in handsomely printed books or online, one mouse-click away. If the museum is small, or its collection not very distinguished, that competition may be very strong, indeed. Until recently, a reproduction was never the same as the real thing: It was usually much smaller and bound to lack the texture or three dimensionality of the original, to say no more. However nowadays, many museums offer online access not only to high-resolution images of artworks and cultural artifacts, but even to something more by showing parts of the painting that a naked eye cannot see. For example, hidden layers of an artwork can be revealed with infrared imaging technologies and X-radiation, which provide details of the artists' working methods and clues to original and changing artistic intentions. Edward C. Banfield, the political scientist and art collector whose definition of art was quoted in Chapter 10, has argued that high-quality reproductions deserve to be given a serious role in the art life of the nation. He specifically points out the advantages they offer to the millions of people who do not live close to a major museum (Banfield, 1984, chapter 6).

As for artistic innovation, whatever one may think of them, one cannot accuse contemporary painters and sculptors of failing to provide that. And innovation does appear to fire up the interest of collectors in buying contemporary work. So far as museums are concerned, however, innovation has a different meaning. With the exception of a few that specialize in contemporary art, most museums are devoted to assembling and preserving the great works of the past. New acquisitions in any one year, unless from a major bequest, are rarely sufficiently exciting to affect attendance. How then can museums overcome the public's feeling of being already thoroughly familiar with its collection? The answer is through special exhibitions and the occasional blockbuster. These are the "innovations" that stir up public attention and increase attendance. Moreover, they can be defended as artistically worthy events rather than mere promotional stunts when, as is often the case, they have genuine aesthetic power. (See the discussion in Chapter 11).

Our discussion of artistic and technological innovation has focused on the latter as a source of non-live art that eventually offers serious competition to the live forms. There is another side to the story, however. Technological innovation can also stimulate, or become the means to, artistic innovation within the traditional fields. For example, electronic synthesizers are now employed by some composers, dance can be extended into what are called "multimedia" performances, and visual artists blend computer code into their interactive artworks. Without question, theatrical writing and production have been influenced by motion picture and television technique. A notable instance of technology stimulating design was cited in Chapter 8: The modern movement in architecture had its origin in the desire of architects to adapt their art to the industrial age by using machine-made materials and new methods of construction in place of designs based on the ancient handicrafts. It is not for the authors of this volume to judge the success or failure of these technologically inspired innovations. We must recognize, however, that technological change is often the root of artistic innovation. Thus, it provides an aesthetic opportunity, as well as a source of competition for traditional forms.

17.2 The Question of Audience Age

There may well be a connection between artistic innovation, audience age, and potential audience development. Anyone who has attended the live arts may have noticed that dance and theater audiences are younger, on average, than the audiences at symphony concerts or the opera. Based on surveys of public participation in the arts, we summarized the average age of participants across art forms in Chapter 3 (see Table 3.5). In 2012, the average age of participants for ballet and modern dance was found to be forty-seven and forty-six, respectively, and for theater, it was forty-nine, as compared with fifty-two and fifty-one for symphony and opera audiences, respectively. The average age for art museums was forty-seven. However, it is probably the greater ease (because hours are flexible and no reservation is required) and the much lower cost of visiting an art museum than attending the live performing arts, rather than anything attributable to innovation, that attracts a relatively younger audience to museums.

It was suggested in the previous section that theater and dance companies present the public with new and innovative works far more frequently than do symphony orchestras and opera companies. The age data just cited are consistent with that argument. The young are more open than their elders to exploring and appreciating new works of art. Hence, the more innovative art forms attract younger audiences. But whether having a younger audience is, in itself, favorable for future audience development is unclear. It is favorable if the institution can hold onto its young members as they grow older, while continuing to attract young entrants to the audience, as well. But if people grow more resistant to innovation as they age, then the more innovative art forms will lose older audience members for the same reason they are gaining younger ones. Perhaps, there is a lifetime taste cycle typified by the playgoer who was attracted by the innovative works of Tennessee Williams in the 1950s but did not go to the theater in the 1990s because "they don't make plays like that anymore." In that case, having a younger audience today need not augur well for the future.

It should be recalled, however, that artistic innovation may be favorable to audience growth in the live performing arts not only through its efficacy in attracting the young, but also because it can keep live performance one step ahead of the non-live versions that compete with it for attention. But to speak at a deeper level, innovation is part of the creative process in art. We demean art itself if we imply that artistic innovation is no more than a promotional strategy.

17.3 Diversity and the High Arts

Very little has been said in this book on the subject of multiculturalism, a topic that might be thought to lie beyond the economics with which we have been dealing. Yet in speculating about the future of art and culture, one cannot ignore it. Take the United States as an example. Non-European ethnic minorities – African, Hispanic, and Asian Americans – now make up a substantial proportion of the US population and, sometime in the next century, may well constitute a majority. However, the modes of art discussed in this book developed largely out of European cultures. The prospects for continued growth of "high art" in the United States may depend in part on how well they can adapt in an increasingly multicultural society.

In the fields of theater and dance, this may appear to be less of a challenge. Black playwrights, actors, and actresses are increasingly represented in theatre (and in motion pictures), and well-established dance companies such as the Dance Theater of Harlem have paved the way for academies and companies committed to diversity in professional ballet. However, despite signs of increasing diversity, producers and consumers of the performing arts continue to be predominantly white.

The Survey of Public Participation in the Arts provides data on who attends performing arts and visits art museums (see Table 11.3): Four-fifths of performing arts audiences are white and so are three in four art museum visitors. As shown by Borowiecki and Dahl (2021), who study artists backgrounds by art domain in the United States from 1850 to 2010, the share of non-whites has been slowly increasing throughout the decades and has accelerated since the 1970s, but non-whites remain underrepresented among artists relative to their share of the overall population.

Music in general is the most racially mixed domain, according to data presented by Borowiecki and Dahl. However, the results vary by musical genre. For symphony and opera, 86% of musicians were white in 2014 (Aaron Flagg, 2020).[3] The future growth of these genres may be limited if they do not appeal to non-European segments of the population. Managers and boards of directors of opera companies and symphony orchestras have embarked upon a number of initiatives aimed at increasing the non-white share of their audiences. This is particularly vital since these institutions are primarily based in large cities, where ethnic minorities are most highly concentrated. At this point, however, it is unclear if these efforts have met with much success.

17.3.1 Access to the Arts

The arts and cultural industries have seen a long history of discrimination. We have just approached the topic of racial inequality, and in Chapter 14 discussed gender (under)representation in arts professions. It may be true that women are well represented among the consumers of arts, as we have seen in Chapter 3 (e.g., Table 3.3), but significant barriers continue to impede the entry of women into artistic professions. The MeToo movement has exposed the widespread sexual abuse, harassment, and gender-based discrimination faced by women within the film industry.

The injustices of centuries of discrimination are hard to comprehend, and beyond the scope of this book. The important point here is that by arbitrarily excluding from artistic activity large parts of the society, we harm the arts and diminish the value of our cultural heritage. If we want to enhance creativity in the arts of the future, the artistic domains need to welcome and support people of different races, nationalities, genders, and ages. Few have described the value of diversity so eloquently, as did the late Elijah Cummings:

Diversity is not our problem, it's our promise. It's our promise because it leads to unparalleled heights of creativity, expression, and excellence. It's our promise because it leads to higher performing and more sustainable institutions. And it's our promise because it allows us to live by our democratic ideals of fairness and equality. (Elijah Cummings, speaking at the League of American Orchestras 2016 National Conference, quoted in League of American Orchestras, 2021)

There are also other, more objective barriers that prevent larger parts of the society from entering the arts, namely the lack of access to financial resources. We have seen in Chapter 14 that artists' earnings are, on average, quite low, and it is obviously difficult for an artist to thrive if she has to worry about sustaining her living. There is also a matter of time: artists who need to engage in secondary jobs in order to get by have less time for their creative endeavors. Other things equal, this advantages those who have access to private (family) financial resources.

It is perhaps not surprising that art history furnishes many anecdotes of important artists with bourgeois or upper-class backgrounds. The father of Leonardo da Vinci's was an affluent notary; Michelangelo descended from a family of bankers (though not as prosperous as the banker father of Paul Cézanne); and the parents of Édouard Manet were a judge and the god-daughter of a Swedish prince. Borowiecki and Dahl (2021) more systematically analyze the role of family wealth in influencing the likelihood that an individual undertakes an artistic profession. The authors confirm that artists have been earning below average, in line with our earlier discussion. However, they also find that the probability someone becomes an artist increases if she comes from a wealthier household. While a part of this finding could be driven by the fact that individuals from wealthier backgrounds may benefit from a better network or access to better education or training, it is likely that having a safety net in the form of family wealth helps one endure the hardship of an artist's career over a longer period.

On a more positive note, this sort of inequality is increasingly recognized by cultural policy makers. For example, Creative Europe, an arts and culture funding initiative, with a budget of €2.4 billion over the period from 2021 to 2027 intends to reinforce cultural diversity, help millions of Europeans train professionally, and reach new audiences. This is a welcome initiative, but probably more are needed, especially in the less developed parts of the world. Additionally, further research is required to help us determine the most effective ways to support artists.[4]

17.4 Arts Education

While pondering the future of art and culture, one will want to ask what role can or should arts education play in shaping that future? After all, education and innovation are closely related concepts. Moreover, those who speak for the arts have long argued that elementary and secondary schools often neglect arts education. Critics have therefore advocated a radical expansion and, in some cases, an equally radical restructuring of in-school arts education. Calls have also been made for the expansion of adult education in the arts.

Advocates for arts education undoubtedly share a deep conviction that understanding art is as necessary to our well-being as is the command of those other great objects of our schooling: languages, mathematics, science, history, and social studies. But for those involved with the arts, there is also a more practical motive for advocacy: the hope that more and better arts education will help to protect and enlarge the domain of art.

17.4.1 Unresolved Issues

It must also be said that the cause of arts education has probably been held back by the persistence of important unresolved questions within the field itself. Among the "perennial" issues listed by Fowler (who must be ranked as a very friendly critic), one finds the following (Fowler, 1988, chapter 3). First, there is no agreement as to which arts should be taught. Visual art and music are the two that have been traditionally included in the curriculum. What ought to be added? The possibilities include dance, drama, design, film, creative writing, poetry, and assorted crafts. Can or should these be offered, as well?

Second, there is the question of who ought to do the teaching. Should the arts be taught by the classroom teacher or by a specialist? If a specialist, what expertise is wanted – training in the art form, in pedagogy, or both?

Third, whose culture is to be taught? Ethnic minorities in the United States increasingly insist that their own cultural traditions not be neglected when art and culture are made part of the public school curriculum. Multiculturalism is now accepted by politicians, government agencies, and educators as a desirable policy, but it is not easily translated into curriculum and course content in a way that will satisfy all parties. How, for example, does one achieve a balance between teaching the dominant culture and giving weight to the cultures of ethnic minorities?

Fourth, should arts courses emphasize creating art or appreciating it? Historically in the United States, most precollege courses have tried to teach creativity. Students were given a hands-on opportunity to paint, to model in clay, or to perform music. Some critics argue that the relatively low status of the arts in the educational hierarchy is a direct result. The whole enterprise could be dismissed by an unsympathetic observer as just fooling around in the studio. An alternative curriculum, now endorsed by the Getty Center for Education in the Arts, has been called "discipline-based arts education" and would try to give students an understanding not only of art production, but also of the more "academic" approaches to art through art history, criticism, and aesthetics. Its supporters argue that, among other things, the discipline-based approach would be more rigorous, and would therefore attract support for arts programs from those who are sympathetic with the demands of the excellence-in-education movement, now so influential in the United States.

Finally, there is the question of evaluation. Very little is known about the effectiveness of alternative approaches to arts education. Should students who have taken such courses be regularly tested to see what they learned? Supporters of discipline-based arts education obviously think that they should, and that such tests would enhance the "academic respectability" of the field. Adherents of the older "creativity" approach argue that one cannot readily test for its results and that courses devised to have testable outcomes are likely to be incompatible with that approach. Predictably, recognition of these questions gives rise within the field to a demand for more research.

17.4.2 Can Arts Education Stimulate the Demand for Art?

As we explained in Chapter 4, economists think of taste, or consumer preferences, as one of the principal determinants of demand. We also argued that the taste for art can be described as a "cultivated" taste, meaning that one has to be familiar with a given form of art to develop a taste for it, and the more familiar one becomes, the stronger the taste grows. The economist Tibor Scitovsky was a notable advocate of investing in "consumption skills," so that we will better know how to enjoy the use of our increasing wealth and leisure. He pointed to a liberal arts education as one source of training in those skills (see Scitovsky, 1972; reprinted in Tibor Scitovsky, 1986, pp. 37–45, esp. pp. 39–42). Advocates for the arts might well hope that arts education, by helping to cultivate the appropriate tastes, will directly stimulate the public's demand for the "higher" forms of art and protect them against the powerful competition of "popular" culture.

We do not know much about the effectiveness of arts education. In the nature of the case, it is difficult to evaluate a student's understanding of art, but in any event, few evaluative studies of arts education have been carried out. Some insights have been gained, however, from research into factors associated with adult participation in the arts. Several such studies have found that early childhood socialization in the arts is positively correlated with adult attendance. Socialization comprises such experiences as childhood lessons, youthful participation or attendance, or growing up with parents who were interested in the arts.

Questions on this topic are included in the Taking Part Surveys carried out for the UK Department for Culture, Media, and Sport. Analyzing the responses for the years 2006 to 2010, Babatunde Buraimo and coauthors found that going to museums or art galleries, or attending theater, dance, or classical music performances when growing up were all associated with higher adult participation rates. Such socialization experiences persist even if controls for educational attainment or the occupation background is accounted for (see table 3 in Buriamo et al., 2011). A paper by Charles M. Gray confirms that years of education is an important factor, that arts education is positively associated with participation in the performing arts even when other relevant factors are controlled, and that out-of school training is more effective than in-school classes (Gray, 1996).

Thus, after all the caveats have been entered, we are entitled to believe that arts education *does* stimulate demand for the arts. To put it another way, if we choose to do so, we *can* push that demand curve to the right!

17.5 The Future of the High Arts

17.5.1 The Arts and Innovations

What will the future bring? Providing an answer to this question will be difficult for anybody who does not own a crystal ball. However, it is rather certain that there will be changes and many of them will be driven by technological innovations. Take as an example the overview of technologies used to consume culture presented throughout the different editions of the underlying textbook. The first edition in 1993 discussed the consumption of culture via videocassettes, the second in 2001 focused on CDs, and this presents streaming of cultural content. One can only speculate what technologies would be covered in the fourth edition, but in what follows, we will consider a couple of emerging trends, which will likely play an ever-increasing role in the arts and culture.

With further development of virtual reality technologies, the term "virtual museum" will likely receive a very new meaning. One could wonder, for example, how will the demand for physical attendance to the Louvre change, if people are able to visit the museum via virtual reality headsets, or to admire via augmented reality a Mona Lisa painting hanging in their dining room?

In the performing arts, an audience equipped with smart glasses may perhaps be able to experience special effects or fantastic stage sets, generated and projected via a computer code, and probably at a fraction of the cost. This would not only be an example of technology-driven artistic innovation, but by potentially saving production costs, it may also decrease the "symptoms" of Baumol's cost disease, which we presented in Chapter 8. Moreover, augmented reality could perhaps also be used to project supertitles in the desired language, which may diminish some of the language barriers to the theater, as we discussed in Chapter 15.

Digital technologies can also create completely new arts markets, like the marketplace for digital assets that represent real-world art or music objects, also known as NFTs. These assets are bought and sold online, often with cryptocurrency, and they are generally encoded to ensure the uniqueness of each artwork. This may sound ludicrous to some or a niche to others, but the NFT market achieved $17.6 billion in sales in 2021, compared to $65.1 billion of global sales in the overall art and antiques market worldwide in the same year (L'Atelier, 2021; Statista, 2022).

The stark difference of smart technologies, compared to the inventions of the past, is that using them more makes them even smarter and hence better. Some computer programs are already so "intelligent" that they can create art on their own. While some debate whether it is really true art, the first paintings created by a computer algorithm – or artificial intelligence – have been auctioned for rather significant amounts. For example, a portrait printed on canvas and hung in a gilded wood frame was sold for more than $430,000 in 2019 (Christie, 2018). The piece looks like the work by an eighteenth-century painter and only upon closer inspection, the artist's signature – the mathematical formula $\left(\min G \max D \times \left[\log\left(D(x) \right) \right] + z \left[\log\left(1 - D\left(G(z) \right) \right) \right] \right)$ – reveals that the artist was not human.

Artificial intelligence can also enhance creativity in music. Though some musicians may protest, AI innovations offer new and potentially valuable experiences to audiences, like, for example, a play by Shakespeare rapped in a computer-generated voice of a famous rap artist (Hochberg, 2020). It remains to be seen whether computer programs of the future will also be able to give us more compositions by Wolfgang Amadeus Mozart or perhaps complete some of the unfinished classical works by past masters, and whether any of this would change the repertoires or audience profiles of orchestras and opera.

Some of the new technologies could be good for the artist's earnings too, especially innovations that enable new income sources. We have already covered the streaming of classical music concerts in Chapter 8, but increasingly many streaming services also enable individual musicians to disseminate their music, and the personalization of content, which characterizes streaming platforms, is found to be particularly beneficial to the lesser known artists (Datta et al., 2018). Emerging artists may also benefit from new forms of finance and funding, among others enabled by crowd-funding platforms, which can be used to secure the necessary finances in order to prepare and execute artistic projects (Loots et al., 2022). There are also more curious inventions, which, for example, enable more established artists (and other celebrities) to sell personalized content like video messages with occasional wishes. Some inventions are path-breaking, others are incremental, but many of them have in common that they affect the consumption of arts and change the opportunities for artists.

17.5.2 The COVID-19 Pandemic and Its Aftermath

In considering the future of the arts, one should also contemplate what changes have been brought by the COVID-19 pandemic. The global health crisis has clearly changed our lives, including the ways in which we spend our leisure time and consumer culture. It has also set in motion or accelerated trends that have relevance for the arts of tomorrow. In our considerations here, we will refrain from assessing how the coronavirus crisis has affected the arts in general, which has been diligently covered in an edited volume by Salvador et al. (2021), but instead, we will take the pandemic as a departure point, in order to consider what the post-COVID future might look like.

Some of the technological advancements presented above, or in Chapter 16, have been enhanced by the COVID-19 pandemic. For example, the accessibility to online museums or streaming of cultural content has grown significantly during the pandemic, and will likely remain with us (UNESCO, 2021). In other cases, the pandemic stimulated artistic innovation, when artists have been inspired to rethink and adapt to the new circumstances. For instance, several philharmonics ventured into performing from their homes, such as the thirty-eight players of the English National Ballet Philharmonic who played the Swan Lake Overture via a video communications software from the comforts of their living rooms, bedrooms, kitchens, or the shed (the timpanist). And while performing remotely comes with many difficulties, innovations in virtual collaboration tools may enable musicians to continue with virtual rehearsals and perhaps even performances (see also O'Hagan and Borowiecki, 2021).

One of the areas most affected by the COVID-19 pandemic has been the tourism sector. The pandemic hit international tourism in particular, which includes cultural tourism (covered more deeply in Chapter 15), and hence it is very relevant for the arts. It has also redirected some of the tourism flows to more local areas, including to the periphery, which has cultural heritage that may be lesser known, but often is invaluable. This trend has been appreciated by those, who were increasingly concerned by excessive numbers of tourists in a few highly popular destinations. Overcrowding from an excess of tourists is not only unsustainable for the environment and results in conflicts with locals, but it is also a threat to cultural heritage, when it is overused (UN World Tourism Organization, 2018). It remains to be seen whether cultural and tourism policy makers will succeed in retaining some of the tourism flows to the periphery, but the tourism trends set into motion by the pandemic provide a promising starting point.[5]

17.5.3 The Value of Theory and Economics

In light of the discussed potential or ongoing innovations and trends, one could worry that the content of this book will be outdated by the time it is read. However, this is unlikely going to be the case. While the examples and context presented in this book will certainly change with time, the theory introduced, which remained unchanged throughout the past editions of the book, will remain applicable to contexts that will emerge in the future. This is the true value of a textbook that is theory based. Even though the surroundings change, sometimes rapidly and dramatically, economic theories do not, and they remain robust and applicable throughout time. Take for example the theory of demand for arts, which powerfully, persistently, and reliably explains the consumption levels of cultural products and services (independent of the consumption medium).

Research methods are also evolving with time, and so scholarship in economics has become increasingly reliant on advanced econometric analyses. The advantages of sophisticated quantitative methods are many, and include the increased reliability of the results of a given study, or the possibility to pin down causal relationships, as opposed to just correlations. The latter advantage is particularly important if one wants to understand in what way different factors depend on one another, and how cultural policy should be designed to become effective and efficient. These developments coincide with improving access to data that become increasingly real time, detailed and "big," and thus provide opportunities to reassess and expand our knowledge on a variety of different topics related to the arts. However, econometric progress comes also with the drawback that few nonexperts (typically noneconomists) are able to understand and appreciate the technicalities of new research. Therefore, it is very important that economists remain in close dialogue with cultural policy makers and managers. Platforms like *Economists Talk Art*, which explain economic research and provide research-based policy analysis and commentary for cultural policy makers, managers and the wider public, are increasingly appreciated (and also a great way to get an exposure to recent scholarship in the area).

17.6 Summary

In this chapter we contemplated the future of the arts and the future of cultural economics. In doing this, we presented many trends and innovations that matter for the arts and involved stakeholders. However, no matter how useful or path-breaking the inventions of the future will become, it remains important not to lose touch with the past, especially considering that very much can be learned from history. The long-term trends, the effects of various innovations throughout history, or the consequences of the discrimination of the past can be all assessed and learned from in the present.

Throughout the book, we have often referred to historical anecdotes or research based on historical data and context; not only because the authors of this book find pleasure in writing about history, or because our cultural heritage and its value are defined by past context, but also since very much can be learned from it. In fact, insights from the past can be as valuable as those from the present, especially in cases when it is difficult to answer a question using conventional contemporaneous approaches. Some examples presented in the book illustrate how economic history of the arts has enabled us to answer important questions that are of relevance for policy makers or societies nowadays (see Chapter 15 for examples).[6] From history we can also learn what mistakes have been made, such as the discrimination against people of a particular skin color or gender. None of this can be reversed, but by understanding and acknowledging it, we can perhaps lessen the mistakes of today or tomorrow. In doing this, and equipped with a better understanding of economics and the discipline's theories and tools, we may be able to contribute toward a stronger and better arts and culture of the future.

Lincoln Kirstein, that venerable and eloquent prophet, described art and culture as "the only memorable residue that marks and outlives one's epoch." In the same essay, he said of the arts that "our prime complaint is not what we do, or how it is done, but how little we have for what we might do" (Kirstein, 1978, pp. 197, 194).

SUGGESTIONS FOR FURTHER READING

For an overview of research in the economic history of the arts, see Borowiecki and Greenwald (2024).

A study of students' achievement in arts-related courses in 2016 is provided by National Assessment of Educational Progress (2017).

For a guide on how to make orchestras more impartial, diverse, and inclusive, refer to League of American Orchestras (2021).

Insights into what factors determine the conservative repertoires at opera houses are provided by Cancellieri and Turrini (2016).

See how COVID-19 spurred the digitization in cultural and creative industries in Naylor et al. (2021) and Australia Council for the Arts (2022).

PROBLEM SET

17.1 Choose an invention presented in the chapter and evaluate whether it may affect the production and/or consumption of culture in the future, and if yes, then how? In particular, are you concerned that the technological innovation will become another source of competition for the high arts, or do you assess that it will instead enhance cultural consumption?

17.2 In Chapter 16, we have presented a list of top museums based on onsite visits in 2019. In Table 17.1, we provide similar data for the top fifteen museums in 2013.

    a. Now it is time for you to apply your analytical skills to real data. Compare and assess what has changed in between 2013 and 2019. Be observant and creative in your analysis of the data.

    b. Try to forecast what will be the number of onsite visits at top museums in the year 2030. In which parts of the world do you expect top museums of the future to be located?

    c. Conduct a survey in your class and find out which of the top museums have been visited by your classmates. Evaluate whether the distribution of museum visitors in your class is consistent with the global distribution of visitors to top museums. Comment what could be the reasons for any deviations toward a museum, city, or country.

17.3 Identify and collect your own data on visitors for a sample of museums over time (or at least at two points of time). Use the data to repeat the analysis from above. In particular, assess what are the changes in onsite visits following major events, such as the COVID-19 pandemic, the 2022 Russian invasion of Ukraine, or other global or more regional events.

    Present your results in an easy-to-read table and write an essay – no more than three double-spaced pages, total – describing and assessing your findings. What expectations are confirmed? What surprises are uncovered?

Table 17.1 Top fifteen museums in 2013 based on onsite visits popularity

Onsite ranking	Institution	City	Country	Onsite visitors (in millions)
1	Louvre Museum	Paris	France	9.3
2	British Museum	London	United Kingdom	6.7
3	The Metropolitan Museum of Art	New York City	United States	6.2
4	National Gallery	London	United Kingdom	6.0
5	Vatican Museums	Vatican City	Vatican City	6.0
6	Tate Modern	London	United Kingdom	4.9
7	National Palace Museum	Taipei	Taiwan	4.5
8	National Gallery of Art	Washington, D.C.,	United States	4.1
9	National Museum of Modern Art	Paris	France	3.7
10	Musée d'Orsay	Paris	France	3.5
11	Victoria and Albert Museum	London	United Kingdom	3.3
12	Museo Reina Sofía	Madrid	Spain	3.2
13	Museum of Modern Art	New York City	United States	3.1
14	National Museum of Korea	Seoul	South Korea	3.1
15	The State Hermitage Museum	St. Petersburg	Russia	2.9

Note: Onsite visitors are for 2013 and have been obtained from the European Museums Network (2022).

NOTES

1 Calculated from data presented in League of American Orchestras (2013, table "Most frequently performed composers").

2 The British Theatre Consortium and UK Theatre/Society of London Theatre, based on data from 274 venues in Britain, calculated that 51% of the productions in 2014 are of new plays, whereas only 33% are revivals (the remaining 16% are collaborative devised shows); see British Theatre Consortium (2016).

3 Over the period from 2002 to 2014, there has been almost no change in the share of African American or Hispanic musicians, but the share of Asian musicians increased from 5.3% to 9.1%.

4 Anecdotally, the field of cultural economics may be particularly well suited to studying and supporting diversity and equality in the arts, as it is one of the most gender-balanced fields in economics and, perhaps, even in social sciences. For a report on gender equality in cultural economics, see Borowiecki and Mauri (2019).

5 Worth to notice are also various projects that study and support tourism activity in the periphery, such as the EU-funded INCULTUM project (https://incultum.eu/).

6 The value of historical approaches is further elevated by the fact that what happened in the past has often consequences for nowadays, and the historical persistency has also implications for the arts (Borowiecki, 2015b).

Bibliography

1991. *The Broadcasting Yearbook.*
New Providence, NJ: R. R. Bowker.

1997. "Artists' Royalties." *The Economist,*
June 21, 1997: 18–19.

Abbing, Hans. 2008. *Why Are Artists Poor? The Exceptional Economy of the Arts.* Amsterdam, Netherlands: Amsterdam University Press.

Abrams, Dore, Farra Bracht, and Martha Prinz. 1996. "Determinants of State Government Funding of the Arts in the United States." Paper presented at the *9th International Conference on Cultural Economics*, Boston, MA, May 8–11.

Adams, Henry. 2018. "What Happened to the Blockbuster Art Exhibition?" *The Conversation*, January 2. Available at http://theconversation.com/what-happened-to-the-blockbuster-art-exhibition-34644

Addleson, Mark. 2001. "Stories about Firms: Boundaries, Structures, Strategies, and Processes." *Managerial and Decision Economics,* 22(4–5): 169–170.

Agard, M. B. and June Spencer. 1987. *50 Cities, Local Government and the Arts.* Madison, WI: Opinion Research Associates.

Agnello, R. J. and R. K. Pierce. 1996. "Financial Returns, Price Determinants, and Genre Effects in American Art Investment." *Journal of Cultural Economics,* 20(4): 359–383.

Alford, J. 1998. "A Public Management Road Less Traveled: Clients as Co-producers of Public Services." *Australian Journal of Public Administration,* 57(4): 128–137.

Alford, J. 2007. *Engaging Public Sector Clients: From Service Delivery to Co-production.* Houndmills, Basingstoke: Palgrave Macmillan.

Allen, Greg. 2005. "The X Factor: Is the Art Market Rational or Biased?" *New York Times*, May 1. Available at www.nytimes.com/2005/05/01/arts/design/the-x-factor-is-the-art-market-rational-or-biased.html?searchResultPosition=1

Almeda, Pere, Albert Sagarra, and Marc Tataret. 2017. *Public Spending on Culture in Europe 2007–2015.* Barcelona: Fundacio Catalunya Europa.

Alper, N. O. and G. H. Wassall. 2000. *More than Once in a Blue Moon: Multiple Job Holdings by American Artists.* National Endowment for the Arts, Research Division Report #40. Santa Ana, CA: Seven Locks Press.

American Alliance of Museums. 1989. *Data Report of the 1989 National Museum Survey.* Washington, DC: American Alliance of Museums.

American Federation of Musicians. 1997–98 season. "Wage Scales and Conditions in the Symphony Orchestra 1997–98 Season."

American Federation of Musicians. 2018. "Wage Scales and Conditions in the Symphony Orchestra 2017–18 Season."

Americans for the Arts. (undated). "Local Arts Agency Facts 1998." *Monographs,* 2(3): 1–36.

Americans for the Arts. 1997. "Theatre Facts 1996." *American Theatre,* 14(10): 26–30.

Americans for the Arts. 1999. *United Arts Fundraising 1998: A Report about the Nation's United Arts Fund Campaigns in 1997.* Washington, DC: Americans for the Arts.

Americans for the Arts. 1999. *United States Urban Art Federation 1999.* Washington, DC: Americans for the Arts.

Americans for the Arts. 2010. *National Arts Index: 2010 Annual Report.* Washington, DC: Americans for the Arts.

Americans for the Arts. 2016. *National Arts Index: 2016 Annual Report*. Washington, DC: Americans for the Arts.

Americans for the Arts. 2021. *Nonprofit Charitable Giving Policy: Encouraging Charitable Giving and Supporting Public Access to the Arts*. Washington, DC: Americans for the Arts.

Anderson, Robert. 1974. "Paintings as an Investment." *Economic Inquiry*, 12(3): 13–26

Andersson, Å. E. and D. E. Andersson. 2006. *The Economics of Experiences, the Arts and Entertainment*. Cheltenham, UK: Edward Elgar.

Applebome, Peter. 1998. "Endowment Nominee's Broad View of the Arts; Moving Beyond Country Music to a Political Stage." *New York Times*, March 23.

Arndt, O., R. Bartuli, B. Creutz, and B. Wankmüller. 2022. *COVID-19 Impact on the Cultural and Creative Industries in Germany. Economic Effects in a Scenario Analysis for 2020, 2021 & 2022*. Berlin, Germany: The Federal Government's Centre of Excellence for the Cultural and Creative Industries.

Arts Council England. 2018. Livelihoods of Visual Artists Report: 2016 Data Report. Available at www.artscouncil.org.uk/publication/livelihoods-visual-artists-report

Arts Council England. 2022. Private Investment in Culture Survey Report 2022. Available at www.artscouncil.org.uk/publication/private-investment-culture-survey-report-2022

Ashenfelter, Orley and Kathryn Graddy. 2003. "Auctions and the Price of Art." *Journal of Economic Literature*, 41(3): 763–787.

Ashenfelter, Orley and Kathryn Graddy. 2011. "Sale Rates and Price Movements in Art Auctions." *American Economic Review, Papers and Proceedings*, 101(3): 212–216.

Association of Art Museum Directors. 2018. Art Museums by the Numbers. Available at https://aamd.org/our-members/from-the-field/art-museums-by-the-numbers-2018

Ateca-Amestoy, V. 2008. "Determining Heterogeneous Behavior for Theater Attendance." *Journal of Cultural Economics*, 32(2): 127–151.

Auden, W. H. 1956. *Introduction to Selected Writings of Sydney Smith*. New York: Farrar, Straus & Cudahy, xiv.

Auletta, Ken. 1998. "Dept. of Airwaves." *The New Yorker*, November 9: 34–35.

Australian Bureau of Statistics. 1998. "Attendances at Cultural Venues: Why Are They Declining?" Discussion paper, October 1998, mimeo.

Australian Council for the Arts. 2020. "Creating Our Future: Results of the National Arts Participation Survey." August 2020.

Australia Council for the Arts. 2022. Impacts of COVID-19 on the Cultural and Creative Industries. Arts and Cultural Audiences, Organisations, Artists and Creative Workers.

Bakhshi, Hasan and David Throsby. 2014. "Digital Complements or Substitutes? A Quasi-field Experiment from the Royal National Theatre." *Journal of Cultural Economics*, 38(1): 1–8.

Balfe, J. H. and J. C. Heine. 1988. *Arts Education beyond the Classroom*. New York: American Council for the Arts.

Balfe, J. H. and M. J. Wyszomirski. 1985. *Art, Ideology, and Politics*. New York: Praeger.

Banfield, E. C. 1984. *The Democratic Muse: Visual Arts and the Public Interest*. New York: Basic.

Banternghansa, C. and Graddy, K. 2011. "The Impact of the Droit de Suite in the UK: An Empirical Analysis." *Journal of Cultural Economics*, 35: 81–100.

Barnes, Brooks. 2003. "Back to the Boom?" *Wall Street Journal*, November 7: W1ff.

Baumol, W. J. 1987. "Unnatural Value or Art Investment as Floating Crap Game," in D. V. Shaw et al., eds., *Artists and Cultural Consumers*. Akron, OH: Association for Cultural Economics and University of Akron, 1–14.

Baumol, W. J. 1996. "Children of Performing Arts, the Economic Dilemma: The Climbing Costs of Health Care and Education." *Journal of Cultural Economics*, 20(3): 200–203.

Baumol, W. J. 2012. *The Cost Disease: Why Computers Get Cheaper and Healthcare Doesn't*. London, UK: Yale University Press.

Baumol Hilda and W. J. Baumol. 1984. "The Mass Media and the Cost Disease," in W. S. Hendon et al., eds., *The Economics of Cultural Industries*. Akron, OH: Association for Cultural Economics, 109–123.

Baumol, Hilda and W. J. Baumol. 1985. "The Future of the Theater and the Cost Disease of the Arts," in Mary Ann Hendon et al., eds., *Bach and the Box: The Impact of Television on the Performing Arts*. Akron, OH: Association for Cultural Economics, 7–31.

Baumol, W. J. and Hilda Baumol. 1994. "On the Economics of Music in Mozart's Vienna." *Journal of Cultural Economics*, 18(3): 171–198.

Baumol, W. J. and W. G. Bowen. 1966. *Performing Arts: The Economic Dilemma*. New York: Twentieth Century Fund.

Beck, Kirsten. 1983. *Cultivating the Wasteland*. New York: American Council for the Arts.

Beggs, Alan and Kathryn Graddy. 2009. "Anchoring Effects: Evidence from Art Auctions." *American Economic Review*, 99(3): 1027–1039.

Benedict, Stephen, ed. 1991. *Public Money and the Muse*. New York: Norton, for the American Assembly of Columbia University.

Benhamou, Francoise. 1996. *L'Economie de la culture*. Paris: Editions La Decouverte, 11.

Benhamou, Francoise. 1998. *Mini Chiffres Clés 1998*. Paris: Ministère de la Culture et de la Communication.

Besanko, David et al. 2017. *Economics of Strategy*. 7th ed. New York: John Wiley & Sons.

Bille, Trine. 2008. "Cohort Effects, Age Effects, and Period Effects in the Participation in the Arts and Culture in Denmark: 1964–2004." *International Journal of Cultural Policy*, 14(1): 113–137.

Bille, Trine. 2020. "Artists' Labour Markets," in *Handbook of Cultural Economics*, 3rd ed. Cheltenham, UK: Edward Elgar Publishing.

Blaug, Mark, ed. 1976. *The Economics of the Arts*. London: Martin Robertson.

Blaug, Mark. 2001. "Where Are We Now on Cultural Economics?" *Journal of Economic Surveys*, 15(2): 123–143.

Blumenthal, Ralph. 1995. "Museums Share More Art to Survive Leaner Times." *New York Times*, December 7.

Borgonovi, F. 2006. "Do Public Grants to American Theatres Crowd-Out Private Donations?" *Public Choice*, 126(3): 429–451.

Borowiecki, Karol J. 2012. "Are Composers Different? Historical Evidence on Conflict-induced Migration (1816–1997)." *European Review of Economic History*, 16(3): 270–291.

Borowiecki, Karol J. 2013. "Conflict-induced Migration of Composers: An Individual-level Study." *Cliometrica*, 7(3): 237–266.

Borowiecki, Karol J. 2013. "Geographic Clustering and Productivity: An Instrumental Variable Approach for Classical Composers." *Journal of Urban Economics*, 73(1): 94–110.

Borowiecki, Karol J. 2014. "Artistic Creativity and Extreme Events: The Heterogeneous Impact of War on Composers' Production." *Poetics*, 47: 83–105.

Borowiecki, Karol J. 2015a. "Agglomeration Economies in Classical Music." *Papers in Regional Science*, 94(3): 443–468.

Borowiecki, Karol J. 2015b. "Historical Origins of Cultural Supply in Italy." *Oxford Economic Papers*, 67(3): 781–805.

Borowiecki, Karol J. 2017. "How Are You, My Dearest Mozart? Well-being and Creativity of Three Famous Composers Based on their Letters." *Review of Economics and Statistics*, 99(4): 591–605.

Borowiecki, Karol J. 2022. "Good Reverberations? Teacher Influence in Music Composition since 1450." *Journal of Political Economy*, 130(4): 991–1090.

Borowiecki, Karol J. 2020. Chapter 15: Creativity, in R. Towse and T. N. Hernández eds., *Handbook of Cultural Economics*, Third Edition. Cheltenham, UK: Edward Elgar Publishing.

Borowiecki, Karol J. and Catarina Marvão. 2017. "May I Have This Dance? Dance Participation and Attendance in Denmark." *Cultural Trends*, 26(2): 155–167.

Borowiecki, Karol J. and Caterina Mauri. 2019. "Economics and the Arts: A Virtuous Example of Gender Equality." Unpublished.

Borowiecki, Karol J. and Christian M. Dahl. 2021. "What Makes an Artist? The Evolution and Clustering of Creative Activity in the US since 1850." *Regional Science and Urban Economics*, 86, 103614.

Borowiecki, Karol J. and Concetta Castiglione. 2014. "Cultural Participation and Tourism Flows: An Empirical Investigation of Italian Provinces." *Tourism Economics*, 20(2): 241–262.

Borowiecki, Karol J. and Diana Greenwald. 2024. "Arts and Culture," in Claude Diebolt and Mike Haupert, eds., *Handbook of Cliometrics*, Second Edition. Heidelberg: Springer.

Borowiecki, Karol J. and Georgios Kavetsos. 2015. "In Fatal Pursuit of Immortal Fame: Peer Competition and Early Mortality of Music Composers." *Social Science & Medicine*, 134: 30–42.

Borowiecki, Karol J. and Hasan Bakhshi. 2018. "Did You Really Take a Hit? Understanding How Video Games Playing Affects Individuals." *Research in Economics*, 72(2): 313–326.

Borowiecki, Karol J. and John O'Hagan. 2012. "Historical Patterns Based on Automatically Extracted Data: The Case of Classical Composers." *Historical Social Research (Section 'Cliometrics')*, 37(2): 298–314.

Borowiecki, Karol J. and John O'Hagan. 2013. "Impact of War on Individual Life-cycle Creativity: Tentative Evidence in Relation to Composers." *Journal of Cultural Economics*, 37(3): 347–358.

Borowiecki, Karol J. and Juan Prieto-Rodriguez. 2015. "Video Games Playing: A Substitute for Cultural Consumption?" *Journal of Cultural Economics*, 39(3): 239–258.

Borowiecki, Karol J. and Juan Prieto-Rodriguez. 2017. "The Cultural Value and Variety of Playing Video Games," in J. Prieto-Rodriguez, V. M. Ateca-Amestoy, V. Ginsburgh, I. Mazza, and J. O'Hagan, eds., *Enhancing Cultural Participation in the EU: Challenges and Methods*. Heidelberg: Springer, 323–336.

Borowiecki, Karol J. and Kathryn Graddy. 2021. "Immigrant Artists: Enrichment or Replacement?" *Journal of Economic Behavior and Organization*, 191: 785–797.

Borowiecki, Karol J. and Trilce Navarrete. 2016. "Changes in Cultural Consumption: Ethnographic Collections in Wikipedia." *Cultural Trends*, 25(4): 233–248.

Borowiecki, Karol J. and Trilce Navarrete. 2017. "Digitization of Heritage Collections as Indicator of Innovation." *Economics of Innovation and New Technology*, 26(3): 227–246.

Borowiecki, Karol J. and Trilce Navarrete. 2018. "Fiscal and Economic Aspects of Book Consumption in the European Union." *Journal of Cultural Economics* 42, 309–339.

Borowiecki, Karol J., Neil Forbes, and Antonella Fresa. 2016. *Cultural Heritage in a Changing World*. Switzerland: Springer.

Borowiecki, Karol J., Nicholas Ford, and Maria Marchenko. 2023. "Harmonious Relations: Quality Transmission among Composers in the Very Long Run." *European Review of Economic History*, https://doi.org/10.1093/ereh/head005

Borrup, Tom. 2018. "Creative Disruption in the Arts: Special Issue Introduction." *Journal of Arts Management, Law, and Society*, 48(4): 223–226.

Brickley, James, C. W. Smith, and Jerold Zimmerman. 2021. *Managerial Economics and Organizational Architecture*. 7th ed. New York, NY: McGraw-Hill.

Brida, J. G., M. Disegna, and R. Scuderi. 2014. "The Behaviour of Repeat Visitors to Museums: Review and Empirical Findings." *Quality & Quantity*, 48(5): 2817–2840.

British Theatre Consortium. 2016. "The British Theatre Repertoire 2014."

Brooks, A. C. 2000a. "Is There a Dark Side to Government Support for Nonprofits?" *Public Administration Review*, 60(3): 211–218.

Brooks, A. C. 2000b. "Public Subsidies and Charitable Giving: Crowding Out, Crowding in, or Both?" *Journal of Policy Analysis and Management*, 19(3): 451–464.

Brooks, A. C. and J. I. Ondrich. 2007. "Quality, Service Level, or Empire: Which Is the Objective of the Nonprofit Arts Firm?" *Journal of Cultural Economics*, 31(2): 129–142.

Brudney, J. L. and R. E. England. 1983. "Toward a Definition of the Coproduction Concept." *Public Administration Review*, 43(1): 59–65.

Bryan, Michael F. 1985. "Beauty and the Bulls: The Investment Characteristics of Paintings." *Economic Review, Federal Reserve Bank of Cleveland* (First Quarter): 2–10.

Buckley, Cara. 2021. "Mystery Donor, Serious Money, Joyous Artists." *New York Times*, May 30, p. 16.

Bulletin of the Whitney Museum of American Art. 1989–90. p. 104.

Buriamo, B., Jones, H., and Millward, P. 2011. *Participation and Engagement in Cultural Activities: Analysis of the Taking Part Survey*. London, UK: Department for Culture, Media and Sport.

Byrnes, W. J. 2008. *Management and the Arts*. 4th ed. Waltham, MA: Focal Press.

Cahalan, Margaret. 1989. *A Sourcebook of Arts Statistics: 1989*. Washington, DC: National Endowment for the Arts, April 1990.

Cameron, L. and Williams, J. 2001. "Cannabis, Alcohol and Cigarettes: Substitutes or Complements?" *Economic Record*, 77(236), 19–34.

Cancellieri, G. and Turrini, A. 2016. "The Phantom of Modern Opera: How Economics and Politics Affect the Programming Strategies of Opera Houses." *International Journal of Arts Management*, 18(3): 25–36.

Carle, E. 2020. "Now That we're at Home, Bring the Great Artists to You" [Blog post]. The Keyword | Google. Arts and Culture. Available at https://blog.google/outreach-initiatives/arts-culture/at-home-bring-the-great-artists-to-you/.

Carnegie Commission. 1979. *A Public Trust: The Report of the Carnegie Commission on the Future of Public Broadcasting*. New York: Bantam.

Carnegie Commission on Educational Television. 1967. *Public Television: A Program for Action*. New York: Harper & Row.

Castañer, Xavier and Lorenzo Campos. 2002. "The Determinants of Artistic Innovation: Bringing in the Role of Organizations." *Journal of Cultural Economics*, 26(1): 29–52.

Caust, Jo. 2003. "Putting the 'Art' Back into Arts Policy Making: How Arts Policy Has Been 'Captured' by the Economists and the Marketers." *International Journal of Cultural Policy*, 9(1): 51–63.

Caves, R. E. 2000. *Creative Industries: Contracts between Art and Commerce*. Cambridge, MA: Harvard University Press.

Caves, R. E. 2002. "Contracts between Art and Commerce." *Journal of Economic Perspectives*, 17(2): 73–84.

Centre for Economics and Business Research. 2013. "The Contribution of the Arts and Culture to the National Economy." Report for Arts Council England and the National Museums Director's Council. CEBR.

Chambers, David, Elroy Dimson, and Justin Foo. 2015. "Keynes the Stock Market Investor: A Quantitative Analysis." *The Journal of Financial and Quantitative Analysis*, 50(4): 843–868.

Chambers, David, Elroy Dimson, and Christophe Spaenjers. 2020. "Art as an Asset: Evidence from Keynes the Collector." *The Review of Asset Pricing Studies*, 10(3): 490–520.

Champernaud, Luc, Victor Ginsburgh, and Philippe Michel. 2008. "Can Public Arts Education Replace Arts Subsidization?" *Journal of Cultural Economics*, 32(2): 109–126.

Chang, Sharon and Renuka Mahadevan. 2014. "Fad, Fetish or Fixture: Contingent Valuation of Performing and Visual Arts Festivals in Singapore." *International Journal of Cultural Policy*, 20(3): 318–340.

Chapman, L. H. 1982. *Instant Art, Instant Culture*. New York: Teachers College Press.

Chartrand, H. H. 2000. "Toward an American Arts Industry," in J. M. Cherbo and M. J. Wyszomirski, eds., *The Public Life of the Arts in America*, chapter 2. New Brunswick: Rutgers University Press.

Chartrand, H. H. and Claire McCaughey. 1989. "The Arm's Length Principle and the Arts:

An International Perspective: Past, Present and Future," in Milton C. Cummings, Jr., and J. Mark Davidson Schuster, eds., *Who's to Pay for the Arts? The International Search for Models of Arts Support*. New York: American Council for the Arts, 43–80.

Cherbo, J. M. and M. J. Wyszomirski, eds. 2000. *The Public Life of the Arts in America*. New Brunswick: Rutgers University Press.

Chrétien-Ichikawa, S. and K. Pawlik. 2022. *Creative Industries and Digital Transformation in China*. Singapore: Palgrave Macmillan.

Christie's. 2018. "Is Artificial Intelligence Set to Become Art's Next Medium?"

Christina Duff. 1998. "In Payscales, Life Sometimes Imitates Art." *Wall Street Journal*, May 22, 81.

Coase, R. H. 1937. "The Nature of the Firm." *Economica*, 4(16): 386–405.

Coase, R. H. 1960. "The Problem of Social Cost." *Journal of Law and Economics*, 3: 1–44.

Colonna, Carl, and Carol Colonna. 1982. "An Economic and Legal Assessment of Recent Visual Artists' Reversion Rights Agreements in the United States." *Journal of Cultural Economics*, 6(2): 77–85.

Commission for Cultural Affairs. 1983. "Funding for Culture: The Cultural Policy of the City of New York." A report to the mayor by the Mayor's Advisory Commission for Cultural Affairs, June.

Cowell, Ben. 2007. "Measuring the Impact of Free Admission." *Cultural Trends*, 16(3): 203–224.

Cowen, Tyler. 1997. "Why I Do Not Believe in the Cost-Disease." *Journal of Cultural Economics*, 20(3): 207–214.

Cowen, Tyler. 1998. *In Praise of Commercial Culture*. Cambridge, MA: Harvard University Press.

Cowen, Tyler. 2006. *Good and Plenty: The Creative Successes of American Arts Funding*. Princeton: Princeton University Press.

Cowen, Tyler. 2008. "Why Everything Has Changed: The Recent Revolution in Cultural Economics." *Journal of Cultural Economics*, 32(4): 261–273.

Cowen, Tyler and Alexander Tabarrok. 2000. "An Economic Theory of Avant-Garde and Popular Art, or High and Low Culture." *Southern Economic Journal*, 67(2): 232–253.

Cox, Meg. 1986. "Boom in Art Market Lifts Prices Sharply, Stirs Fears of a Bust." *Wall Street Journal*, November 24.

Cox, Meg. 1988. "What Effrontery! Art Dealers Are Told to Price Their Stuff." *Wall Street Journal*, March 17.

Cummings, Jr., M. C. 1982. "To Change a Nation's Cultural Policy: The Kennedy Administration and the Arts in the United States, 1961–1963," in K. V. Mulcahy and C. R. Swaim, eds., *Public Policy and the Arts*. Boulder, CO: Westview, 141–168.

Cummings, Jr., M. C. 1991. "Government and the Arts: An Overview," in Benedict, ed., *Public Money and the Muse: Essays on Government Funding for the Arts*, 31–79.

Cummings, Jr., M. C. and R. S. Katz, eds. 1987. *The Patron State: Government and the Arts in Europe, North America, and Japan*. New York: Oxford University Press.

Cwi, David, and Katherine Lyall. 1977. "Economic Impacts of Arts and Cultural Institutions: A Model for Assessment and a Case Study in Baltimore." National Endowment for the Arts, Research Division, *Report no. 6*, November 21–24.

Dance/NYC. 2016. State of NYC Dance & Workforce Demographics 2016.

Datta, H., G. Knox, and B. J. Bronnenberg. 2018. "Changing their Tune: How Consumers' Adoption of Online Streaming Affects Music Consumption and Discovery." *Marketing Science,* 37(1): 5–21.

Davenport, Ken. 2011. "The Incredible Shrinking Cast Size." Available at kendavenport.com/the-incredible-shrinking-cast-size/.

Dees, J. G. 2012. "A Tale of Two Cultures: Charity, Problem Solving, and the Future of Social Entrepreneurship." *Journal of Business Ethics*, 111: 321–334.

Dekker, Erwin. 2015. "Two Approaches to Study the Value of Art and Culture and the Emergence of a Third." *Journal of Cultural Economics*, 39(4): 309–326.

Department for Digital, Culture, Media and Sport. 2021. *Museums Partnership Report: Sharing Collections 2019/20*.

Department for Digital, Culture, Media and Sport. 2022. *Charities Act 2022*. Available at www.gov.uk/guidance/charities-act-2022-implementation-plan#provisions-of-the-act-expected-to-come-into-force-autumn-2022. Accessed 21 October 2022.

Department of Cultural Affairs. 1999. Letter to the authors from Kathleen Hughes, Assistant Commissioner. City of New York, January 8.

Dickieson, J. D. W. 2018. "The Deaccession Dilemma: Themes in the American Debate about Art Museum Deaccessions." *The Museum Scholar: Theory and Practice*, 1.

Digital Meets Culture. 2021. *Virtual Museums and Photographic Heritage 2016*. Available at www.digitalmeetsculture.net/article/virtual-museums-and-photographic-heritage-seminar-in-pisa/. Accessed 4 May 2021.

DiMaggio, P. J. 1984. "The Nonprofit Instrument and the Influence of the Marketplace on Policies in the Arts," in W. McNeil Lowry, ed., *The Arts and Public Policy in the United States*. Englewood Cliffs, NJ: Prentice-Hall, for the American Assembly of Columbia University, 57–99.

DiMaggio, P. J. 1991. "Decentralization of Arts Funding from the Federal Government to the States," in Benedict, ed., *Public Money and the Muse: Essays on Government Funding for the Arts*, 216–252.

DiMaggio, P. J. and Kristen Stenberg. 1985a. "Why Do Some Theatres Innovate More Than Others? An Empirical Analysis." *Poetics*, 14(1–2): 107–122.

DiMaggio, P. J. and Kristen Stenberg. 1985b. "Conformity and Diversity in American Resident Theaters," in Balfe and Wyszomirski, eds., *Art, Ideology and Politics*, 116–139.&&

DiMaggio, P. J., Michael Useem, and Paula Brown. 1978. "Audience Studies of the Performing Arts and Museums: A Critical Review." National Endowment for the Arts, Research Division, *Report no.* 9.

Dobrzynski, J. H. 1996. "Have Show, Will Travel (within Limits)." *New York Times*, February 25, 1996.

Dokko, Jane. 2008. "Does the NEA Crowd Out Private Charitable Contributions to the Arts?" Board of Governors of the Federal Reserve System, Finance and Economics Discussion Series 2008–10.

Dubois, V. 2014. "Cultural Policy Regimes in Western Europe," in *International Encyclopedia of the Social and Behavioral Sciences*. 2nd ed.

The Duluth Manifesto on Cultural Entrepreneurship. Available at www.linkedin.com/pulse/duluth-manifesto-cultural-entrepreneurship-olaf-kuhlke/

Dunning, Jennifer. 1985. *But First a School: The First Fifty Years of the School of American Ballet*. New York: Viking.

Eckert, R. D. and R. H. Leftwich. 1988. *The Price System and Resource Allocation*. 10th ed. New York: Dryden Press.

Economist. 2022. Silicon Valley's Plutocrats Are Shaking up Culture in the Region. Available at www.economist.com/culture/2022/10/19/silicon-valleys-plutocrats-are-shaking-up-culture-in-the-region.

Eduniversal. 2021. 2021 Best Masters and MBA Survey. Available at www.eduniversal-survey-mastersranking.com/

EGMUS. 2022. Data Table. European Group on Museum Statistics. Available at www.egmus.eu/nc/es/statistics/complete_data/z/0/

Ekelund, R. and S. Ritenour. 1999. "An Exploration of the Beckerian Theory of Time Costs: Symphony Concert Demand." *American Journal of Economics and Sociology*, 58(4): 887–899.

Ellmeier, Andrea. 2003. "Cultural Entrepreneurialism: On the Changing Relationship between the Arts, Culture and Employment." *International Journal of Cultural Policy*, 9(1): 3–16.

Etro, Federico, and Pagani, Laura. 2012. "The Market for Paintings in Italy During the Seventeenth Century." *The Journal of Economic History, Cambridge University Press*, 72(2): 423–447.

European Commission. 2013. "Special Eurobarometer 399. Cultural Access and Participation." TNS Opinion and Social. Brussels.

European Commission. 2016. "Flash Eurobarometer 432. Preferences of Europeans towards Tourism." TNS Opinion & Social. Brussels.

European Museums Network. 2022. The Most Visited Museums in the World. Available at http://museums.eu/highlight/details/105664/the-most-visited-museums-in-the-world.

Eurostat. 2020a. Employment by Sex, Age and Detailed Economic Activity (from 2008 and onwards, NACE Rev. 2 two digit level) – 1 000 (LFSA_EGAN22D). Available at https://ec.europa.eu/eurostat/databrowser/bookmark/847c2ba0-4498-4a12-9c1d-000d37450190?lang=en

Eurostat. 2020b. Students Enrolled in Tertiary Education by Education Level, Programme Orientation, Sex, Type of Institution and Intensity of Participation. (EDUC_UOE_ENRT01). Available at https://ec.europa.eu/eurostat/databrowser/bookmark/a1a4456e-85a9-4b5a-bd18-8e4b9fb40d07?lang=en.

Eurostat. 2022. Households – level of internet access (ISOC_CI_IN_H). Available at https://ec.europa.eu/eurostat/databrowser/bookmark/c188b60d-8496-4bf8-b48d-877a71d34ab2?lang=en

Evans, Graeme, Phyllida Shaw, and Judy White. 1998. *Artstats, Digest of Arts Statistics and Trends in the UK 1986–87 to 1995–96*. London: Arts Council of England.

Eveleth, Rose. 2012. "Video Games Are Officially Art, according to the MoMA." *Smithsonian Magazine*. December 3, 2012.

Falk, Martin, and Tally Katz-Gerro. 2016. "Cultural Participation in Europe: Can We Identify Common Determinants?" *Journal of Cultural Economics*, 40(2): 127–162.

Fama, Eugene and Michael Jensen. 1983. "Separation of Ownership and Control." *Journal of Law and Economics*, 26(2): 301–326.

Federico, John. 1992. "Theatre Communications Group, Memo to the Authors." *Finances of the Performing Arts*, vol. 1, February 14.

Opera America, *Annual Field Report 1996*.

Feist, Andy, Rod Fisher, Christopher Gordon, and Charles Morgan with Jane O'Brien. 1998. *International Data on Public Spending on the Arts in Eleven Countries*. London: The Arts Council of England, Research Report No. 13.

Feldstein, Martin, ed. 1991. *Economics of Art Museums*. Chicago and London: University of Chicago Press.

Felton, M. V. 1994. "Evidence of the Existence of the Cost Disease in the Performing Arts." *Journal of Cultural Economics*, 18(4): 301–312.

Fernández-Blanco, V., Rodriguez-Álvarez, A., and Wiśniewska, A. 2019. "Measuring Technical Efficiency and Marginal Costs in the Performing Arts: The Case of the Municipal Theatres of Warsaw." *Journal of Cultural Economics*, 43(1): 97–119.

Ferreira Neto, A. B. 2018. "Charity and Public Libraries: Does Government Funding Crowd out Donations?" *Journal of Cultural Economics.* 42(4): 525–542.

Filer, Randall. 1984. "A Theoretical Analysis of the Economic Impact of Artists' Resale Royalties Legislation." *Journal of Cultural Economics*, 8(1): 1–28.

Filer, Randall. 1986. "The 'Starving Artist' – Myth or Reality? Earnings of Artists in the United States." *Journal of Political Economy*, 94(1): 56–75.

Finlay, Leslie. 2022. "A Simple 4-Step Guide to Great Theatre Marketing."

Flagg, Aaron. 2020. *Anti-Black Discrimination in American Orchestras*. League of American Orchestras. Available at https://americanorchestras.org/wp-content/uploads/2020/08/Anti-Black-Discrimination-in-American-Orchestras.pdf

Flanagan, R. J. 2012. *The Perilous Life of Symphony Orchestras: Artistic Triumphs and Economic Challenges*. New York: Yale University Press.

Florida, Richard. 2002. *Rise of the Creative Class*. New York: Basic Books.

Ford Foundation. 1974a. *The Finances of the Performing Arts*. Vol. 1. New York: Ford Foundation.

Ford Foundation. 1974b. *The Finances of the Performing Arts*. Vol. 2. New York: Ford Foundation.

Foster, A. W. and J. R. Blau, eds. 1989. *Art and Society: Readings in the Sociology of the Arts*. Albany: State University of New York Press.

Fourmouzi V., M. Genius, and P. Midmore. 2012. "Demand for Organic and Conventional Produce in London, UK: A System Approach." *Journal of Agricultural Economics*, 63(3): 677–693.

Fowler, Charles. 1988. *Can We Rescue the Arts for America's Children?* New York: American Council for the Arts, 13–19.

Francis Haskell. 1990. "Titian and the Perils of International Exhibition." *New York Review*, August 16: 9.

Frank, Robert, and Phillip Cook. 1995. *The Winner-Take-All Society*. New York: Free Press.

Frateschi, C., E. Lazzaro, and L. Palma Martos. 2009. "A Comparative Econometric Analysis of Museum Attendance by Locals and Foreigners: The Case of Padua and Seville." *Estudios de Economía Aplicada*, 27(1): 175–196.

Frey, B. S. 1994a. "The Economics of Music Festivals." *Journal of Cultural Economics*, 18(1): 29–39.

Frey, B. S. 1994b. "Art: The Economic Point of View," in Peacock and Rizzo, eds., *Cultural Economics and Cultural Policies*, chapter 1: 3–16.

Frey, B. S. 1998. "Superstar Museums: An Economic Analysis." *Journal of Cultural Economics*, 22(3): 113–125.

Frey, B. S. and Reiner Eichenberger. 1995. "On the Rate of Return in the Art Market: Survey and Evaluation." *European Economic Review*, 39: 528–537.

Frey, B. S. and S. Meier. 2006. *The Economics of Museums. Handbook of the Economics of Art and Culture: Vol. 1*. Amsterdam: Elsevier.

Frey, B. S. and W. W. Pommerehne. 1988. "Is Art Such a Good Investment?" *Public Interest*, 91: 79–86.

Frey, B. S. and W. W. Pommerehne. 1989. *Muses and Markets: Explorations in the Economics of the Arts*. Oxford: Basil Blackwell.

Galbraith, J. K. 1958. *The Affluent Society*. Boston: Houghton Mifflin.

Galenson, D. 2023. *Innovators*. Oxford: Oxford University Press.

Gapinski, James H. 1986. "The Lively Arts as Substitutes for the Lively Arts." *American Economic Review*, 76(2): 20-25.

Gaquin, Deirdre. 2008. *Artists in the Workforce: 1990 to 2005*. Washington, DC: National Endowment for the Arts. *Research report*, 48.

Gast, D. V. 1988. "Pricing New York Galleries." *Art in America*, 76(7): 86–87.

Gehrke, Karl. 2007. "Odds Are against Graduating Orchestra Hopefuls." *MPR News*.

Getty Center for Education in the Arts. 1985. *Beyond Creating: The Place for Art in America's Schools*. Los Angeles: Getty Center for Education in the Arts, 3–7, 12–21.

Ginsburgh, Victor. 2017. "Contingent Valuation, Willingness to Pay, and Willingness to Accept," in B. S. Frey and D. Iselin, eds., *Economic Ideas You Should Forget*. Cham: Springer, 65–66.

Ginsburgh, Victor, and David Throsby, eds. 2003. *Handbook of the Economics of Art and Culture*. Amsterdam: Elsevier.

Ginsburgh, Victor, and P. M. Menger, eds. 1996. *Economics of the Arts: Selected Essays*. Amsterdam: Elsevier.

Giving USA. 1997. *Giving USA, 1997*. New York: AAFRC Trust for Philanthropy. 199.

Globerman, Steven and S. H. Book. 1974. "Statistical Cost Functions for Performing Arts Organizations." *Southern Economic Journal*, 40(4): 668–671.

Glueck, Grace. 1989. The Arts, for What They're Worth. *New York Times*, November 19.

Goetzmann, W. N. 1996. "How Costly Is the Fall from Fashion?" in Ginsburgh and Menger, eds. 71–84.

Goff, Sharon. 1989. *Legislative Appropriations for State Arts Agencies: A Twenty-Year Perspective*. Washington, DC: National Assembly of State Arts Agencies.

Gordon, R. J. 2016. *The Rise and Fall of American Growth*. Princeton, NJ: Princeton University Press.

Goudriaan, Rene and G. J. van't. Eind. 1985. "To Fee or Not to Fee: Some Effects of Introducing Admission Fees in Four Museums in Rotterdam," in V. L. Owen and W. S. Hendon, eds., *Managerial Economics for the Arts*. Akron, OH: Association for Cultural Economics, 103–109.

Grammp, William. 1989. *Pricing the Priceless: Art, Artists, and Economics*. New York: Basic.

Gray, C. M. 1984. "The Smell of the Greasepaint, the Roar of the Crowd: What Are They Worth?" Presented at the Annual Meeting of the Midwest Economics Association, Chicago, April.

Gray, C. M. 1992. "Arts Costs and Subsidies: The Case of Norwegian Performing Arts," Chapter 25 in Towse and Khakee, eds., *Cultural Economics*. Berlin: Springer-Verlag, 267–273.

Gray, C. M. 1995. *Turning On and Tuning In: Media Participation in the Arts*. Santa Ana, CA: Seven Locks Press.

Gray, C. M. 1996. "The Cultivation of Taste? Early Exposure to the Arts and Adult Participation." Presented at the 9th International Conference on Cultural Economics, Boston, May 8–11, 1996.

Gray, C. M. 1998. "Hope for the Future? Early Exposure to the Arts and Adult Visits to Art Museums." *Journal of Cultural Economics*, 22(2–3): 87–98.

Gray, C. M. 2007. "Gifts in Kind and Other Illiquid Assets," Chapter 10 in D. R. Young, ed., *Financing Nonprofits: Putting Theory into Practice*. Lanham, MD: AltaMira Press.

Gray, C. M. 2016. "Strategic Pricing in the Nonprofit Arts: A Case Study of Orchestra Behavior." Unpublished working paper.

Gray, C. M. 2017. "Baumol's Cost Disease," in Palgrave Macmillan, eds., *The New Palgrave Dictionary of Economics*. London: Palgrave Macmillan.

Gray, C. M. 2020. "Consumption Skills and Coproduction in the Arts: Theory and Application." Presentation prepared for Annual Meetings of Association for Cultural Economics, International, and Social Theory, Politics, and the Arts. Both canceled due to COVID.

Gray, C. M. and James Heilbrun. 2000. "Economics of the Nonprofit Arts: Structure, Scope, and Trends," in Cherbo and Wyszomirski, eds., *The Public Life of the Arts in America*, chapter 8, 202–225.

Haag, E. v. d. 1979. "Should the Government Subsidize the Arts?" *Policy Review*, 10 (Fall): 63–73.

Hall, E. C. 1997. "Survey and Analysis of the Repertory of Twenty-Six American Symphony Orchestras: 1982–1983 through 1993–1994." *Ph.D. dissertation*, Johns Hopkins University.

Hancock, D. 2015. *Event Cinema: A Sector in Full Swing*. IHS Technology Cinema Intelligence Service.

Handke, Christian and Ruth Towse. 2013. *The Handbook on the Digital Creative Economy*. Cheltenham, UK: Edward Elgar.

Hansmann, Henry. 1986. "Nonprofit Enterprise in the Performing Arts," in Paul J. DiMaggio, ed., *Nonprofit Enterprise in the Arts*. New York: Oxford University Press, 17–40.

Harris, Elizabeth A. 2019. "The Met Will Turn Down Sackler Money amid Fury over the Opiod Crisis." *New York Times*, May 15.

Hart, Philip. 1973. *Orpheus in the New World: The Symphony Orchestra as an American Cultural Institution*. New York: W. W. Norton & Company.

Harvey, J. Levin. 1980. *Fact and Fantasy in Television Regulation*. New York: Russell Sage Foundation.

Heikkinen, Merja, and Sari Karttunen. 1995. "Defining Art and Artists as a Methodological Problem and a Political Issue." Working paper, Research and Information Unit, Arts Council of Finland, Helsinki.

Heikkinen, Merja, and Tuulikki Koskinen, eds. 1998. *Economics of Artists and Arts Policy*. Helsinki: Arts Council of Finland.

Heilbrun, James. 1984. "Once More with Feeling: The Arts Boom Revisited," in W. S. Hendon et al., eds., *The Economics of Cultural Industries*. Akron, OH: Association for Cultural Economics, 34–46.

Heilbrun, James. 1987a. "Growth and Geographic Distribution of the Arts in the US," in Douglas Shaw, William Hendon, and C. Richard Waits, eds., *Artists and Cultural Consumers*. Akron, OH: Association for Cultural Economics, 24–35.

Heilbrun, James. 1987b. *Urban Economics and Public Policy*. 3rd ed. New York: St. Martin's Press.

Heilbrun, James. 1988. "Nonprofit versus Profit-Making Firms: A Comment." *Journal of Cultural Economics*, 12(2): 87–92.

Heilbrun, James. 1996. "Growth, Accessibility and the Distribution of Arts Activity in the United States: 1980 to 1990." *Journal of Cultural Economics*, 20(4): 283–296.

Heilbrun, James. 2001. "Empirical Evidence of a Decline in Repertory Diversity among American Opera Companies 1991/92 to 1997/98." *Journal of Cultural Economics*, 25(1): 63–72.

Heimenz, J. 1980. Sharps and Flats: A Report on Ford Foundation Assistance to American Music. Ford Foundation, July 1980.

Helm, Scott and Frederik O. Andersson. 2011. "Beyond Taxonomy: An Empirical Validation of Social Entrepreneurship in the Nonprofit Sector." *Nonprofit Management and Leadership*, 20(3): 259–276.

Hendon, W. S. 1979. *Analyzing an Art Museum*. New York: Praeger.

Hendon, W. S. 1987. "Evaluating Cultural Policy Through Benefit/Cost Analysis," in Radich and Schwoch, eds., *Economic Impact of the Arts: A Sourcebook*, 159–183.

Hendon, W. S. et al., eds. 1984. *The Economics of Cultural Industries*. Akron, OH: Association for Cultural Economics.

Hewitt, Chris. 2017. "Ticket Prices Have Become a Moving Target at Some Twin Cities Theaters." *Star Tribune*, November 19. Available at www.startribune.com/ticket-prices-have-become-a-moving-target-at-some-twin-cities-theaters/458509153/

Hewitt, Chris. 2018. "The Secret Price of Seats." *Star Tribune*, November 11. Retrieved at www.startribune.com/what-you-don-t-know-about-seating-at-guthrie-ordway-and-other-top-twin-cities-theaters/500085181/

Hewitt, Chris. 2020. "Keeping the Lights On." *Star Tribune*, November 8: E3.

Hill, Kelly, and Kathleen Capriotti. 2009. *A Statistical Profile of Artists in Canada: Based on the 2006 Census*. Ottawa: Canada Council for the Arts.

Hirschey, Mark. 2009. *Fundamentals of Managerial Economies*. 9th ed. Mason, OH: Cengage Learning.

Hochberg, Bill. 2020. "YouTube Won't Take Down a Deepfake of Jay-Z Reading Hamlet – To Sue, Or Not To Sue." Forbes.

Horowitz, Harold, et al. 1989. "Public Support for Art: Viewpoints Presented at the Ottawa Meetings." *Journal of Cultural Economics*, 13(2): 1–19.

Hutter, Michael, and David Throsby, eds. 2008. *Beyond Price: Value in Culture, Economics, and the Arts*. Cambridge: Cambridge University Press.

Institute of Museum Services. 1977–1987. *The Collaborative Spirit: Partners in America, Tenth Anniversary*. Washington, DC: n.p., n.d., 5.

Institute of Museum and Library Services. 2018. *Museum Data Files*. Accessed at www.imls.gov/research-evaluation/data-collection/museum-data-files#museumdatafile

Institute of Museum and Library Services. 2022. *Mission*. Retrieved at www.imls.gov/about/mission

Irwin, Neil. 2017. "Why Surge Prices Make Us So Mad: What Springsteen, Home Depot and a Nobel Winner Know." *New York Times*, October 14. Retrieved at www.nytimes.com/2017/10/14/upshot/why-surge-prices-make-us-so-mad-what-springsteen-home-depot-and-a-nobel-winner-know.html?_r=0

Isard, Walter. 1960. *Methods of Regional Analysis: An Introduction to Regional Science*. New York: Wiley; Cambridge, MA: MIT Press.

Jackson, Ray. 1988. "A Museum Cost Function." *Journal of Cultural Economics*, 12(1): 41–50.

Janowitz, Barbara. 1990. "Theatre Facts '89." *American Theatre* 7(1): 32–43.

Jeffri, Joan, and Robert Greenblatt. n.d. *Information on Artists-2*, Abstract. Research Center for Arts and Culture, Columbia University.

Jeffri, Joan, Spiller Michael W., Heckathorn Douglas D., and Jenifer Simon. 2007. *Above Ground. Information on Artists III: Special Focus New York City Aging Artists*. New York, NY: Research Center for Arts and Culture, Columbia University.

Jenkins, Simon. 1984. "Paying for the Arts." *Economist*, 293(7368) (November 17): 1–4, 13–16.

Jensen, M. C. 1972. "Capital Markets: Theory and Evidence." *Bell Journal of Economics and Management Science*, 3(4): 357–398.

Jensen, M. C. and W. H. Meckling. 1976. "Theory of the Firm: Managerial Behavior, Agency Costs and Ownership Structure." *Journal of Financial Economics*, 3(4): 305–360.

Johnson, Ken. 2007. "The Hidden Cost of Sky-High Art Prices: Museums Are Less Likely to Acquire Major Works." Retrieved at http://archive.boston.com/ae/theater_arts/articles/2007/06/03/the_hidden_cost_of_sky_high_art_prices/

Kahneman, Daniel, J. L. Knetsch, and Richard Thaler. 1986. "Fairness as a Constraint on Profit Seeking: Entitlements in the Market." *American Economic Review*, 76(4): 728–741.

Karttunen, Sari. 1998. "Profile of the Artistic Labour Force in Finland Based on the Population Censuses 1970–1995." Paper presented at the *Tenth International Conference on Cultural Economics*, Barcelona, June 14–17. Unit for Media and Culture, Statistics Finland.

Keaney, Emily. 2008. "Understanding Arts Audiences: Existing Data and What It Tells Us." *Cultural Trends*, 17(2): 97–113.

Keynes, J. M. 1936. *The General Theory of Employment, Interest, and Money*. New York: Harcourt, Brace.

Kim, Mirae, Sheely Pandey, and S. K. Pandey. 2018. "Why Do Nonprofit Performing Arts Organizations Offer Free Public Access?" *Public Administration Review*, 78(1): 139–150.

Kimmelman, Michael. 1990. "What on Earth Is the Guggenheim Up To?" *New York Times*, October 14.

Kimmelman, Michael. 1992. "At the Guggenheim, Bigger May Be Better." *New York Times*, June 21.

Kirchberg, Volker. 1998a. "The Changing Face of Arts Audiences." The Kenneth Myer Lecture, Deakin University, Geelong, Victoria, Australia, October 1998.

Kirchberg, Volker. 1998b. "Entrance Fees as a Subjective Barrier to Visiting Museums." *Journal of Cultural Economics*, 22(1): 1–13.

Kirstein, Lincoln. 1978. "The Performing Arts and Our Egregious Elite," in W. M. Lowry, ed., *The Performing Arts and American Society*. Englewood Cliffs, NJ: Prentice-Hall, 181–197.

Knowles, Jemilla. 2012. "Google's Art Project Grows Larger with 151 Museums Online across 140 Countries." TNW Google Blog. The Next Web.

Kräussl, Roman. 2010. "Art Price Indices." Chapter 3 in McAndrew, ed.: 63–86.

Krueger, A. B. 2005. "The Economics of Real Superstars: The Market for Rock Concerts in the Material World." *Journal of Labor Economics*, 23(1): 1–30.

Krugman, P. 1991. "Increasing Returns and Economic Geography." *Journal of Political Economy*, 99(3): 483–499.

Kushner, R. J. 2011. "Scale, Scope, and Structure in the Community Chorus Industry." *Journal of Arts Law, Management, and Society*, 41: 38–54.

Kushner, R. J. and Randy Cohen. 2011. "Measuring National-Level Cultural Capacity with the National Arts Index." *International Journal of Arts Management*, 13(3): 20–40.

Kushner, R. J. and Randy Cohen. 2017. "Creating a Policy Index for the Arts." *Stanford Social Innovation Review*, 15(4): 48–53.

L'Atelier. 2021. "The 2021 NFT Market Report: Presented by NonFungible and L'Atelier BNP Paribas."

Landis, John, C. A. Kroll, and B. J. Johnson. 1990. *Responses to High Housing Prices: Economies, Firms and Households*. Vol. 1.

Berkeley: Center for Real Estate and Urban Economics of the University of California, August 1990.

Lange, Mark, James Bullard, William Luksetich, and Philip Jacobs. 1985. "Cost Functions for Symphony Orchestras." *Journal of Cultural Economics*, 9(2): 71–85.

Last, A.-K. and Heike Wetzel. 2010. "The Efficiency of German Public Theaters: A Stochastic Frontier Analysis Approach." *Journal of Cultural Economics*, 34: 89–110.

Last, A.-K. and Heike Wetzel. 2011. "Baumol's Cost Disease, Efficiency, and Productivity in the Performing Arts: An Analysis of German Public Theaters." *Journal of Cultural Economics*, 35(3), 185–201.

League of American Orchestras. 2013. *Orchestra Repertoire Report 2012–2013*. New York City: League of American Orchestras.

League of American Orchestras. 2020. *Orchestras at a Glance 2020*. New York City: League of American Orchestras.

League of American Orchestras. 2021. *Making the Case for Equity, Diversity, and Inclusion in Orchestras: A Guide from the League of American Orchestras*. New York City: League of American Orchestras.

Lee, Susan. 1988. "Greed Is Not Just for Profit." *Forbes*, April 18: 65–70.

Levine, L. W. 1988. *Highbrow/Lowbrow*. Cambridge, MA: Harvard University Press.

Light, P. C. 2008. *The Search for Social Entrepreneurship*. Washington, DC: Brookings Institution Press.

Little, S. W. 1972. *Off-Broadway: The Prophetic Theater*. New York: Coward, McCann, and Geoghegan.

Loos, Ted. 2020. "Museums Are Back, and Changing." *New York Times*, October 25: 2.

Loots, Ellen, Diana Betzler, Trine Bille, Karol J. Borowiecki, and Boram Lee. 2022. "New Forms of Finance and Funding in the Cultural and Creative Industries. Introduction to the Special Issue." *Journal of Cultural Economics*, 46: 205–230.

Luksetich, William, Mark Lange, and Philip Jacobs. 1987. "The Effectiveness of Museum Fund-Raising Efforts," in Harry Hillman-Chartrand et al., eds., *Paying for the Arts*. Akron, OH: Association for Cultural Economics, 187–197.

Luksetich, William, and Mark Lange. 1995. "A Simultaneous Model of Nonprofit Symphony Orchestra Behavior." *Journal of Cultural Economics*, 19: 49–68.

Madden, Christopher. 2005a. "Indicators for Arts and Cultural Policy: A Global Perspective." *Cultural Trends*, 14(3): 217–247.

Madden, Christopher. 2005b. "Cross-Country Comparisons of Cultural Statistics: Issues and Good Practice." *Cultural Trends*, 14(4): 299–316.

Maloney, Jennifer. 2014. "New York's Metropolitan Opera Opens Its Budget Curtain." *The Wall Street Journal*. May 30.

Mandel, B. R. 2009. "Art as an Investment and Conspicuous Consumption Good." *American Economic Review*, 99(4): 1653–1663.

Martorella, Rosanne. 1989. "The Relationship between Box Office and Repertoire," in A. W. Foster and J. R. Blau, eds., *Art and Society: Readings in the Sociology of the Arts*. Albany: State University of New York Press, 307–324.

Max, Frankel. 1999. "Word & Image." *New York Times*, February 21: 28–30.

McAfee, R. P. and John McMillan. 1987. "Auctions and Bidding." *Journal of Economic Literature*, 25(2): 699–738.

McAndrew, Clare, ed. 2010. *Fine Art and High Finance: Expert Advice on the Economics of Ownership*. New York: Bloomberg.

McAndrew, Clare. 2022. *The Art Market 2022*. Basel, Switzerland. Art Basel & UBS.

McAndrew, Clare and Lorna Dallas-Conte. n.d. *Implementing Droit de Suite (artists' resale right) in England*. London, UK. Arts Council of England.

McCain, Roger. 1989. "Artists' Resale Dividends: Some Economic-Theoretic Considerations." *Journal of Cultural Economics*, 13(1) (June): 35–51.

McCarthy, K. F., Arthur Brooks, Julia Lowell, and Laura Zakaras. 2001. *The Performing Arts in a New Era*. Santa Monica, CA: Rand.

McCarthy, K. F. and Kimberly Jinnett. n.d. *A New Framework for Building Participation in the Arts*. Santa Monica, CA: Rand.

McGrath, Tara, Renaud Legoux, and Sylvain Senecal. 2016. "Balancing the Score: The Financial Impact of Resource Dependence on Symphony Orchestras." *Journal of Cultural Economics*. DOI 10.1007/s10824-016-9271-z.

McKenzie, Jordi. 2009. "How Do Theatrical Box Office Revenues Affect DVD Retail Sales? Australian Empirical Evidence." *Journal of Cultural Economics*, 34(3): 159–179.

Mei, J. and Michael Moses. 2005. "Vested Interest and Biased Price Estimates: Evidence from an Auction Market." *The Journal of Finance*, 60(5): 2409–2435.

Meiksins, Rob. 2018. "Nonprofits On and Off Broadway: The Search for Enterprise Models." *Nonprofit Quarterly*, February 26. Retrieved at https://nonprofitquarterly.org/2018/02/26/nonprofits-off-broadway-search-enterprise-models/

Menzmer, Melissa. 2015. *The Arts in Early Childhood: Social and Emotional Benefits of Arts Participation*. Washington, DC: National Endowment for the Arts.

Miernyk, W. H. 1965. *Elements of Input-Output Analysis*. New York: Random House.

Milgrom, Paul and John Roberts. 1992. *Economics, Organization, and Management*. Englewood Cliffs, NJ: Prentice-Hall.

Miller, Derek. 2016. "Average Broadway." *Theatre Journal*, 68: 529–553.

Miller, Judith. 1996. "As Patrons Age, Future of Arts Is Uncertain." *New York Times*, February 12. Retrieved at www.nytimes.com/1996/02/12/us/as-patrons-age-future-of-arts-is-uncertain.html

Mitchell, R. C. and R. T. Carson. 1989. *Using Surveys to Value Public Goods: The Contingent Valuation Method*. Washington, DC: Resources for the Future.

MNEWS. 1991. A Press Release from the Museum of Fine Arts. Boston, October 24.

Molotsky, Irvin. 1993. Tax Break to Aid Museums. *New York Times*, August 19.

Montgomery, Sarah. 1992. Private communication to the authors, January 22.

Montias, J. M. 1973. "Are Museums Betraying the Public Trust?" *Museum News*, 51(9): 25–31,

Moore, T. G. 1968. *The Economics of the American Theater*. Durham, NC: Duke University Press.

Morrison, W. G. and E. G. West. 1986. "Subsidies for the Performing Arts: Evidence on Voter Preference." *Journal of Behavioral Economics*, 15: 57–72.

Mozart in the Jungle (TV Series 2014–2018). Retrieved at www.imdb.com/title/tt3502172/.

Mundy, Jeniffer. 2013. *Lost Art: Missing Artworks of the Twentieth Century*. London: Tate Publishing.

Murray, Clare. 2003. *Human Accomplishment: The Pursuit of Excellence in the Arts and Sciences, 800 B.C. to 1950*. New York: Harper Collins.

Murray, Clare. 2020. Functions of Art Museums: What Visitors and Museum Staff Believe. *The Museum Review*, 5(1).

Musgrave, R. A. 1959. *The Theory of Public Finance*. New York: McGraw-Hill.

Musgrave, R. A. and P. B. Musgrave. 1984. *Public Finance in Theory and Practice*. 4th ed. New York: McGraw-Hill.

Nansen. 2022. *NSN-NFT500 Index*. Retrieved at https://pro.nansen.ai/nft-indexes/nft-500?platform=All

National Assembly of State Arts Agencies. 1989a. *State Arts Agencies Legislative Appropriations Annual Survey, Fiscal Years 1989 and 1990*. Washington, DC: National Assembly of State Arts Agencies.

National Assembly of State Arts Agencies. 1989b. *The State of the State Arts Agencies, 1989*. Washington, DC: National Assembly of State Arts Agencies.

National Assessment of Educational Progress. 2017. *The Nation's Report Card: 2016 Arts Assessment*. National Assessment of Educational Progress.

National Commission on Excellence in Education. 1983. *A Nation at Risk*.

Washington, D.C.: US Department of Education.

National Endowment for the Arts. (undated). *A New Look, Guide to the National Endowment for the Arts.* Washington, DC: National Endowment for the Arts.

National Endowment for the Arts. 1981a. "Economic Impact of Arts and Cultural Institutions." Research Division Report no. 15. Washington, DC.

National Endowment for the Arts. 1981b. Research Division Report no. 11. Washington, DC.

National Endowment for the Arts. 1988a. "Toward Civilization: A Report on Arts Education." Washington, DC.

National Endowment for the Arts. 1988b. "The Arts in America: A Report to the President and to the Congress." Washington, DC.

National Endowment for the Arts. 1988c. The Arts in America: A Report to the President and to the Congress. Washington, DC.

National Endowment for the Arts. 1988d. "The Arts in America: A Report to the President and to the Congress." Washington, DC.

National Endowment for the Arts. 2015. "A Decade of Arts Engagement: Findings from the Survey of Public Participation in the Arts, 2002–2012." Washington, DC.

National Endowment for the Arts. 2019. "Data Tables." *Artists and Other Cultural Workers: A Statistical Portrait (2012–2016).* Washington, DC.

National Endowment for the Arts. 2019. "U.S. Patterns of Arts Participation: A Full Report from the 2017 Survey of Public Participation in the Arts." Washington, DC.

National Endowment for the Arts. 2020. *Why We Engage: Attending, Creating, and Performing Art.* Washington, DC: Office of Research and Analysis.

National Endowment for the Arts. 2022. "New Data Show Economic Impact of COVID-19 on Arts & Culture Sector." Retrieved at www.arts.gov/news/press-releases/2022/new-data-show-economic-impact-covid-19-arts-culture-sector.

National Endowment for the Humanities. 1998. *1998 Annual Report.*

National Gallery of Art. 2021. *Financial Statement FY2021.* KPMG LLP. VA.

National Theater at Home. 2019. www.warhorseonstage.com/. Accessed 24 June 2019.

Naylor, R., Todd, J., Moretto, M., and Traverso, R. 2021. *Cultural and Creative Industries in the Face of COVID-19: An Economic Impact Outlook.* Paris, France: UNESCO.

Neligan, Adriana. 2006. "Public Funding and Repertoire Conventionality in the German public Theatre Sector: An Econometric Analysis." *Applied Economics*, 38(10): 1111–1121.

Nelson, Philip. 1970. "Information and Consumer Behavior." *Journal of Political Economy*, 78: 311–312.

Netzer, Dick. 1978a. *The Subsidized Muse, a Twentieth Century Fund Study.* Cambridge, UK: Cambridge University Press.

Netzer, Dick. 1978b. "How Big Is the Arts Industry?" *New York Affairs*, 4(4): 4–6.

Netzer, Dick. 1978c. "The Arts: New York's Best Export Industry." *New York Affairs*, 5(2): 50–61.

Netzer, Dick. 1986a. "Changing Economic Fortunes of the Dance in the U.S." Urban Research Center of New York University, May.

Netzer, Dick. 1986b. "Dance in New York: Market and Subsidy Changes." *American Economic Review*, 76(2) (May): 15–19.

Netzer, Dick. 1992a. "Cultural Policy in an Era of Budgetary Stringency and Fiscal Decentralization: The US Experience," in Ruth Towse and Abdul Khakee, eds., *Cultural Economics.* Berlin: Springer-Verlag, 237–245.

Netzer, Dick. 1992b. "Arts and Culture," In Charles Clotfelter, ed., *Who Benefits from the Nonprofit Sector?.* Chicago: University of Chicago Press, 174–206.

New York City Ballet, Inc. 2020. Financial Statements June 30, 2019 and 2018.

Noam, E.M, eds. 1985. *Video Media Competition.* New York: Columbia University Press.

Noble, J. V. 1970. "Museum Manifesto." *Museum News*, 48(8): 17–20.

Nochlin, Linda. 1988. *Women, Art and Power & Other Essays.* New York: HarperCollins.

Noll, R. G. et al. 1973. *Economic Aspects of Television Regulation.* Washington, DC: Brookings Institution: 50–51.

Noonan, Douglas S. 2003. "Contingent Valuation and Cultural Resources: A Meta-Analytic Review of the Literature." *Journal of Cultural Economics*, 27(3/4): 159–176.

O'Hagan, John. 2016. "European Statistics on Cultural Participation and Their International Comparability." *International Journal of Cultural Policy*, 22(2): 291–303.

O'Hagan, John, and Adriana Neligan. 2005. "State Subsidies and Repertoire Conventionality in the Non-Profit English Theatre Sector: An Econometric Analysis." *Journal of Cultural Economics*, 29(1): 35–57.

O'Hagan, John, and Karol J. Borowiecki. 2010. "Birth Location, Migration and Clustering of Important Composers: Historical Patterns." *Historical Methods: A Journal of Quantitative and Interdisciplinary History*, 43(2): 81–91.

O'Hagan, John, and Karol J. Borowiecki. 2021. "Orchestrating Change: The Future of Orchestras post Covid-19," in Elisa Salvador, Trilce Navarrete, and Andrej Srakar, eds., *Creative Industries and the COVID-19 Pandemic: A European Focus.* London: Routledge.

Olson, Mancur. 1969. "The Principle of 'Fiscal Equivalence': The Division of Responsibilities among Different Levels of Government." *American Economic Review*, 59(2): 479–487.

O'Neal, K. M. 2008. "Bringing Art to Market: The Diversity of Pricing Styles in a Local Art Market." *Poetics*, 36: 94–113.

Opera America. 1996. "*Finances of the Performing Arts.*" Vol. 1. Annual Field Report.

Opera America. 2018. "Annual Field Report 2017."

Opera America. 2022. "Annual Field Report 2021."

Orend, R. J. 1987. "Socialization in the Arts." A report to the NEA under contract no. NEA-C86–179, dated April 22, 1987 (ERIC no. ED 283 768).

Ostrom, Elinor. 1997. "Crossing the Great Divide: Coproduction, Synergy, and Development." GAIA Research Series, accessed at http://escholarship/org/uc/item/38h154v3.

Pankratz, D. B. 1989. "Arts Education Research: Issues, Constraints and Opportunities," in Pankratz and Mulcahy, eds., *The Challenge to Reform Arts Education*, 1–4.

Pankratz, D. B. and Kevin V. Mulcahy, eds. 1989. *The Challenge to Reform Arts Education: What Role Can Research Play?* New York: American Council for the Arts.

Pankratz, D. B. and V. B. Morris, eds. 1990. *The Future of the Arts: Public Policy and Arts Research.* New York: Praeger.

Panzar, John C. and Robert D. Willig. 1977. "Economies of Scale in Multi-Output Production." *The Quarterly Journal of Economics*, 91(3): 481–493.

Panzar, John C. and Robert D. Willig. 1981. "Economies of Scope." *The American Economic Review*, 71(2): 268–272.

Paquette, Jonathan. 2019. "Organizational Theories in Arts Management Research." *Journal of Arts Management, Law, and Society*, 49(4): 221–223.

Parks, R. B. et al. 1981. "Consumers as Coproducers of Public Services: Some Economic and Institutional Considerations." *Policy Studies Journal*, 9 (Summer), 1001–11.

Passell, Peter. 1990. "Vincent Van Gogh, Meet Adam Smith." *New York Times*, February 4.

Peacock, Alan. 1969. "Welfare Economics and Public Subsidies to the Arts." *Manchester School*, 37(4): 323–335.

Peacock, Alan, and Ilde Rizzo, eds. 1994. *Cultural Economics and Cultural Policies.* Boston: Kluwer.

Pear, Robert. 1983. "Reagan's Arts Chairman Brings Subtle Changes to the Endowment." *New York Times*, April 10.

Pechman, J. A. 1987. *Federal Tax Policy.* 5th ed., table A.1. Washington, DC: Brookings Institution, 313–314.

Peers, Alexandra. 1989. "Art Index of Sotheby's Is Really More Art Than Index, Some Say." *Wall Street Journal*, March 23.

Perloff, J. M. 2018. *Microeconomics*. 8th edition. Global Edition. London, UK: Pearson Education.

Pesando, J. G. and P. M. Shum. 1996. "Price Anomalies at Auction: Evidence from the Market for Modern Prints," in Ginsburgh and Menger, eds., 113–134.

Peterson, R. A. 1990. "Audience and Industry Origins of the Crisis in Classical Music Programming: Toward World Music," in Pankratz and Morris, eds., *The Future of the Arts: Public Policy and Arts Research*. New York: Praeger, 207–227.

Peterson, R. A., D. E. Sherkat, J. H. Balfe, and Rolf Meyersohn. 1996. "Age and Arts Participation with a Focus on the Baby Boom Cohort." National Endowment for the Arts, Research Division Report 34.

Pfitzinger, Scott. 2017. *Composer Genealogies: A Compendium of Composers, Their Teachers, and Their Students*. Lanham, MD: Rowman & Littlefield Publishers.

Pignataro, Giacomo. 1994. "Imperfect Information and Cultural Goods: Producers' and Consumers' Inertia," in Peacock and Rizzo, eds., *Cultural Economics and Cultural Policies*, Chapter 5, 55–68.

Plaza, Beatriz. 2010. "Valuing Museums as Economic Engines: Willingness to Pay or Discounting of Cash-flows?." *Journal of Cultural Heritage*, 11: 155–162.

Pogrebin, Robin. 2019. "Clean House to Survive? Museums Confront Their Crowded Basements." *New York Times*, March 10. Retrieved at www.nytimes.com/interactive/2019/03/10/arts/museum-art-quiz.html?action=click&module=Top%20Stories&pgtype=Homepage

Pompe, J., L. Tamburri, and J. Munn. 2011. "Factors Influencing Programming Decisions of US Symphony Orchestras." *Journal of Cultural Economics*, 35: 167–184.

Porter, Michael. 1985. *Competitive Advantage*. New York City, NY: Free Press.

Preece, Stephen. 2005. "The Performing Arts Value Chain." *International Journal of Arts Management*, 8: 21–32.

PUCK. 2012. "European Culture and Development." November 2012. Oviedo.

Rabkin, Nick, and E. C. Hedberg. 2011. "Arts Education in America: What the Declines Mean for Arts Participation." Washington, DC: National Endowment for the Arts. Research Report 52.

Radich, A. J. and S. K. Foss. 1987. "Economic Impact Studies of the Arts as Effective Advocacy," in Radich and Schwoch, eds., *Economic Impact of the Arts: A Sourcebook*. National Conference of State.

Radich, A. J. and Sharon Schwoch, eds. 1987. *Economic Impact of the Arts: A Sourcebook*. Denver, CO: National Conference of State Legislatures.

Ravanas, Philippe. 2008. "Hitting a High Note: The Chicago Symphony Orchestra Reverses a Decade of Decline with New Programs, New Services, and New Prices." *International Journal of Arts Management*, 10(2): 68–78.

Reeves, Michelle. 2002. *Measuring the Economic and Social Impact of the Arts*. London: The Arts Council of England.

Reif, Rita. 1989a. *New York Times*, June 1, 1989.

Reif, Rita. 1989b. "Getty Museum Buys a Manet for a Record Price." *New York Times*, November 15: C3. Retrieved at www.nytimes.com/1989/11/15/arts/getty-museum-buys-a-manet-for-a-record-price.html?searchResultPosition=4

Reitlinger, Gerald. 1961. *The Economics of Taste: The Rise and Fall of the Picture Market, 1760–1960*. New York: Holt, Rinehart & Winston.

Renneboog, L. and C. Spaenjers. 2013. "Buying Beauty: On Prices and Returns in the Art Market." *Management Science*, 59(1): 36–53.

Resch, Magnus. 2016. *Global Art Gallery Report 2016*. Berlin: Phaidon Verlag GmbH.

Reyburn, Scott. 2014. "Can an Economist's Theory Apply to Art?." *New York Times*, April 20. Available at www.nytimes

.com/2014/04/21/arts/international/Can-an-Economists-Theory-Apply-to-Art.html?searchResultPosition=1

Robbins, Lionel. 1932. *An Essay on the Nature and Significance of Economic Science*. London: Macmillan.

Rockwell, John. 1987. Met Opera Narrows Repertory Plans. *New York Times*, May 27.

Rose, B. G. 1986. *Television and the Performing Arts: A Handbook and Reference Guide to Cultural Programming*. Westport, CT: Greenwood.

Rosen, Sherwin. 1981. "The Economics of Superstars." *American Economic Review*, 71(5): 845–858.

Rosenbaum, Lee. 2007. "The Walton Effect: Art World Is Roiled by Wal-Mart Heiress." *Wall Street Journal*, October 10: D11.

Rosenquist, James. 1982. "Artists and Planning," in L. E. Caplin, ed., *The Business of Art, 1982*. Englewood Cliffs, NJ: Prentice-Hall, 21–28.

Ross, Jenna. 2016. "Rescuing the Season Ticket." *Star Tribune*, October 16: E5.

Roth, Evan. 1990. "Deaccession Debate." *Museum News*, 69(2): 42–46.

Ruijgrok, E. C. M. 2006. "The Three Economic Values of Cultural Heritage: A Case Study in the Netherlands." *Journal of Cultural Heritage*, 7: 206–213.

Rushton, Michael. 2006. "The Changing Role of Economic Analysis in Arts Advocacy." Paper prepared for ARNOVA Conference, Chicago, November 2006.

Salmon, Felix. 2018. "Blockbuster Shows Are Ruining Art Museums." *Slate*. Available at https://slate.com/business/2018/05/blockbuster-shows-like-kusama-and-bowie-ruining-art-museums.html

Salvador, Elisa, Trilce Navarrete and Andrej Srakar eds., *Creative Industries and the COVID-19 Pandemic: A European Focus*. London: Routledge.

Salvatore, Dominick. 1986. *Microeconomics: Theory and Applications*. New York. Macmillan.

Samuelson, P. A. 1954. "The Pure Theory of Public Expenditure." *Review of Economics and Statistics*, 36(4): 386–389.

Samuelson, P. A. 1955. "Diagrammatic Exposition of a Theory of Public Expenditure." *Review of Economics and Statistics*, 37(4): 350–356.

Santagata, Walter and Giovanni Signorello. 2000. "Contingent Valuation of a Cultural Public Good and Policy Design: The Case of 'Napoli Musei Aperti'." *Journal of Cultural Economics*, 24: 181–204.

Sattout, E. J., S. N. Talhouk, and P. D. S. Caligari. 2007. "Economic Value of Cedar Relics in Lebanon: An Application of Contingent Valuation Method for Conservation." *Ecological Economics*, 61: 315–322.

Scherer, F. M. 2001. "An Early Application of the Average Total Cost Concept." *Journal of Economic Literature*, 39(3): 897–901.

Schneider, Freiderich and Werner Pommerehne. 1983. "Analyzing the Market of Works of Contemporary Fine Arts: An Exploratory Study." *Journal of Cultural Economics*, 7(2): 41–67.

Schulze, Günther G. 2020. "International Trade," in *Handbook of Cultural Economics*. 3rd ed. Cheltenham, UK: Edward Elgar Publishing.

Schuster, J. M. D. 1985. *Supporting the Arts: An International Comparative Study*. Washington, DC: US Government Printing Office.

Schuster, J. M. D. 1987. "Perspectives on the American Audience for Art Museums." Unpublished research monograph based on the 1985 Survey of Public Participation in the Arts, MIT, Cambridge, MA.

Schuster, J. M. D. 1989a. "Determinants and Correlates of Arts Support by States," in Douglas V. Shaw et al., eds., *Cultural Economics, '88: An American Perspective*. Akron, OH: Association for Cultural Economics, 211–224.

Schuster, J. M. D. 1989b. "Government Leverage of Private Support: Matching Grants and the Problem with 'New Money.'" in M. J. Wyszomirski and Pat Clubb, eds., *The Cost of Culture*. New York: American Council for the Arts, 63–97.

Schwarz, Samuel, and M. G. Peters. 1983. "*Growth of Arts and Cultural Organizations in the Decade of the 1970s.*" National Endowment for the Arts. Study prepared for the Research Division Rockville, MD: Informatics General Corporation.

Scitovsky, Tibor. 1972. "What's Wrong with the Arts Is What's Wrong with Society." *American Economic Review*, 62(2): 62–69.

Scitovsky, Tibor. 1976. *The Joyless Economy*. Oxford, UK: Oxford University Press.

Scitovsky, Tibor. 1986. *Human Desire and Economic Satisfaction*. New York City, NY: New York University Press.

Seaman, B. A. 1987. "Economic impact studies: A fashionable excess," in Radich and Schwoch, eds., *Economic Impact of the Arts: A Sourcebook,*. Washington, DC: National Conference of State Legislatures, 43–75.

Seaman, B. A. 2006. "Empirical Studies of Demand for the Performing Arts," in V. Ginsburgh and D. Throsby, eds., *Handbook of the Economics of Art and Culture, I.* Amsterdam: Elsevier, 416–472.

Seltzer, George. 1989. *Music Matters*. Metuchen, NJ: Scarecrow Press.

Sesser, Stan. 2011. "The Art Assembly Line." *Wall Street Journal*, June 3: D1.

Shanahan, J. L. 1980. "The Arts and Urban Development," in W. S. Hendon, J. L. Shanahan, and A. J. MacDonald, eds., *Economic Policy for the Arts*. Cambridge, MA: Abt Books, 295–305.

Shaw, D. V. et al., eds. 1987. *Artists and Cultural Consumers*. Akron, OH: Association for Cultural Economics.

Sheets, Hilarie M. "Two Museums Tried to Sell Art. Only One Caught Grief about It." *New York Times*, October 30, 2020.

Singer, Leslie. 1978. "Microeconomics of the Art Market." *Journal of Cultural Economics*, 2: 21–39.

Sisario, Ben. 2021. "Musicians Speak Up for Creative Equity." *New York Times*, May 9: 7.

Smith, Thomas M. 2003. Raising the Barre: The Geographic, Financial, and Economic Trends of Nonprofit Dance Companies: A Study (Vol. 44). National Endowment for the Arts.

Smithsonian Institution. 2021. *Annual Report FY 2021*. Office of International Relations.

SMUDataArts. 2019. Return on Fundraising Index: "What Is the Return on Fundraising?"

Spence, Rachel. 2020. "Women Step into the Light." FTWeekend – Arts: 11.

Spulber, D. F. 2003. "The Intermediation Theory of the Firm: Integrating Economic and Management Approaches to Strategy." *Managerial and Decision Economics*, 24: 253–266.

Statista. 2022. Sales Value of the Art Market Worldwide from 2007 to 2021 (in Billion US Dollars).

Stein, J. P. 1977. "The Monetary Appreciation of Paintings." *Journal of Political Economy*, 8(5): 1021–1035.

Steiner, Faye. 1997. "Optimal Pricing of Museum Admission." *Journal of Cultural Economics*, 21(4): 307–333.

Steiner, Lassse. 2016. "Arts and Happiness," in Tachibanaki, T., ed., *Advances in Happiness Research: Creative Economy*. Tokyo: Springer.

Sterling, C. A. and J. M. Kittross. 1990. *Stay Tuned: A Concise History of American Broadcasting*. 2nd ed. Belmont, CA: Wadsworth.

Stern, Mark J. and Susan C. Seifert. 2010. "Cultural Clusters: The Implications of Cultural Assets Agglomeration for Neighborhood Revitalization." *Journal of Planning Education and Research* 29(3): 262–279.

Stockhausen, Karlheinz. 1996. "*Helikopter-Streichquartett.*" Grand Street 14, no. 4 (Spring, "Grand Street 56: Dreams"): 213–25. ISBN 1-885490-07-0.

Storch, P. S. 1990. "How to Equip Your Conservation Laboratory for Success." *Museum News*, 69(3): 92–94.

Studenmund, A. H. and H. J. Cassidy. 1987. *Using Econometrics: A Practical Guide*. Boston: Little, Brown and Company.

Sullivan, K. M. 1991. "Artistic Freedom, Public Funding, and the Constitution," in Benedict, ed., *Public Money and the Muse: Essays on Government Funding for the Arts*. New York City, NY: W.W. Norton & Company.

Sussmann, Anna Louie. 2017. "Why Old Women Have Replaced Young Men as the Art World's Darlings." Art Market. Artsy. net.

Sussmann, Leila. 1984. "Anatomy of the Dance Company Boom, 1958–1980." *Dance Research Journal*, 16(2): 23–28.

Svenson, Arthur. 1982. "State and Local Arts Agencies," in Mulcahy and Swaim, eds., *Public Policy*, 195–211.

Taleb, N. N. 2007. *The Black Swan: The Impact of the Highly Improbable*. New York City, NY: Random House.

Theatre Communications Group. 2018. *Theatre Facts 2017*.

Theatre Communications Group. 2020. *Theatre Facts 2019*.

Theatre Communications Group. 2022. *TCG Member Theatres*. Retrieved at www.tcg.org/ Default.aspx?TabID=1665. Accessed 7 April 2022.

The Art Newspaper. 2020. "Art's Most Popular: Here Are 2019's Most Visited Shows and Museums."

The Art Newspaper. 2022. "Art Is Now Accepted as a Financial Asset, But It Is Still a Questionable Investment."

The Broadway League. 2022. Broadway Season Statistics. Retrieved at www .broadwayleague.com/research/statistics- broadway-nyc/.

The Independent Commission. 1990. *A Report to Congress on the National Endowment for the Arts*. Washington, DC: The Independent Commission.

The Metropolitan Opera. 2020. *Annual Report 2018–19*. Retrieved at www.metopera.org/ about/annual-reports/

The Metropolitan Opera. 2021. *Annual Report 2019–20*. Retrieved at www.metopera.org/ about/annual-reports/

The Metropolitan Opera Association. 2019. Return of Organization Exempt from Income Tax [Form 990].

The Port Authority of New York and New Jersey. 1993. "The Arts as an Industry: Their Economic Importance to the New York-New Jersey Metropolitan Region."

The Rockefeller Panel Report. 1965. *The Performing Arts: Problems and Prospects*. New York: McGraw-Hill.

Thompson, E., M. Berger, G. Blomquist, and S. Allen. 2000. "Valuing the Arts: A Contingent Valuation Approach." Unpublished report to the Kentucky Arts Council. Center for Business and Economic Research, University of Kentucky, Lexington.

Throsby, C. D. 1977. "Production and Cost Relationships in the Supply of Performing Arts Services," in K. A. Tucker, ed., *Economics of the Australian Service Sector*. London: Croom Helm, 414–432.

Throsby, C. D. 1990. "Perception of Quality in the Demand for Theatre." *Journal of Cultural Economics*, 14(1): 65–82.

Throsby, C. D. 1994. "The Production and Consumption of Arts: A View of Cultural Economics." *Journal of Economic Literature*, 32: 1–29.

Throsby, C. D. 1999. "Cultural Capital." *Journal of Cultural Economics*, 23, 1–2: 3–12.

Throsby, C. D. 2003. "Determining the Value of Cultural Goods: How Much (or How Little) Does Contingent Valuation Tell Us?" *Journal of Cultural Economics*, 27: 275–285.

Throsby, C. D. 2008a. "Modeling the Cultural Industries." *International Journal of Cultural Policy*, 14(3): 217–232.

Throsby, C. D. 2008b. *Economics of Cultural Policy*. Cambridge: Cambridge University Press.

Throsby, C. D. 2011. "Looking Ahead: Challenges to the Arts, Culture, Management and Policy in the Next 20 Years." Keynote presentation, 11th AIMAC Conference, Antwerp, July.

Throsby, C. D. and G. A. Withers. 1979. *The Economics of the Performing Arts*. New York: St. Martin's Press.

Throsby, C. D. and G. A. Withers. 1983. "Measuring the Demand for the Arts as a Public Good: Theory and Empirical Results," in J. L. Shanahan et al., eds., *Economic Support for the Arts*. Akron, OH: Association for Cultural Economics, 37–52.

Toepler, Stefan. 2001. "Culture, Commerce, and Civil Society: Rethinking Support for the Arts." *Administration & Society*, 33(5): 508–522.

Toepler, S. and A. Zimmer. 2002. "Subsidizing the Arts Government and the Arts in Western Europe and in the United States." in D. Crane, N. Kawashima and K. Kawasaki, eds., *Global Culture*. Milton Park, UK: Routledge, 39–58.

Tommasini, Anthony. 2020. "Graying Audiences Are a Lifeline, Not a Risk." *New York Times*, August 9: AR9.

Tomassini, Anthony. 2021. "Reinventing the American Orchestra." *New York Times*, February 14: AR4.

Törmä, Taneli. n.d. *Front Page*. Retrieved at www.tanelitorma.com. Accessed 7 February 2016.

Towse, Ruth. 1997a. Introduction, in Ruth Towse, ed., *Cultural Economics: The Arts, the Heritage and the Media Industries*, vol. 1. Cheltenham, UK: Edward Elgar.

Towse, Ruth, ed. 1997b. *Baumol's Cost Disease, the Arts and Other Victims*. Cheltenham, UK: Edward Elgar.

Towse, Ruth. 1993. *Singers in the Marketplace*. Oxford: Clarendon Press.

Towse, Ruth, ed. 2011. *A Handbook of Cultural Economics*. 2nd ed. Northampton, MA: Edward Elgar.

Towse, Ruth and Abdul Khakee, ed. 1992. *Cultural Economics*. Berlin: Springer-Verlag.

Turner-Williams, Jaelani. 2022. "Five Reasons Why Beyonce's Return to a Traditional Rollout Makes Sense for 'Renaissance'." Billboard. June 21, 2022.

UN World Tourism Organization. 2018. "'Overtourism'? Understanding and Managin Urban Tourism Growth beyond Perceptions."

UNESCO. 2021. *Museums around the World in the Face of COVID-19*. Paris, France: UNESCO.

UNWTO. 2020. *International Tourism Growth Continues to Outpace the Global Economy*. Retrieved at www.unwto.org/international-tourism-growth-continues-to-outpace-the-economy.

Useem, Michael. 1987. "Trends and Preferences in Corporate Support for the Arts," in Robert A. Porter, ed., *Corporate Giving in the Arts*, 4th ed. New York: American Council for the Arts.

US Bureau of Economic Analysis. 2022. *Arts and Culture Production Satellite Account, US and States, 2020*. Retrieved at www.bea.gov/data/special-topics/arts-and-culture.

US Bureau of Labor Statistics, Nonfarm Business Sector: Labor Productivity (Output per Hour) for all Employed Persons [PRS85006092], (Retrieved at Federal Reserve Bank of St. Louis, April 8, 2022).

US Department of Commerce, Bureau of the Census. 1991a. Statistical Abstract of the United States, 1991.

US Department of Commerce, Bureau of Economic Analysis. 1991b. *National Income and Product Accounts of the US* Table 2.4, as revised 1991.

Van Lent, Daan. 2014. "Toppositie Concertgebouworkest in gevaar om geldgebrek." NRC Handelsblad. 2 September.

de la Vega, P., Suarez-Fernandez, S., Boto-García, D., and Prieto-Rodríguez, J. 2020. "Playing a Play: Online and Live Performing Arts Consumers Profiles and the Role of Supply Constraints." *Journal of Cultural Economics*, 44(3): 425–450.

Venables, A. J. 2016. "New Economic Geography," in *The New Palgrave Dictionary of Economics*. London: Palgrave Macmillan.

Verschuere, B., T. Brandsen, and V. Pestoff. 2012. "Co-production: The State of the Art in Research and the Future Agenda." *Voluntas*. DOI 10.1007/s11266-012-9307-8.

Voss, Z. G. et al. 2016. *Orchestra Facts: 2006–2014. A Study of Orchestra Finances and Operations, Commissioned by the League of American Orchestras*. League of American Orchestras. Available online at www.americanorchestras.org/knowledge-research-innovation/orchestra-facts-2006-2014.html.

Walmsley, B., A. Gilmore, D. O'Brien, and A. Torreggiani. 2022. *Culture in Crisis: Impacts of Covid-19 on the UK Cultural Sector and Where We Go from Here*. Leeds, UK: Centre for Cultural Value

Wassall, Gregory, and Neil Alper. 1984. "Determinants of Artists' Earnings," in Hendon et al., eds., *The Economics of Cultural Industries*. Akron, OH: Association for Cultural Economics, 213–230.

Wassall, Gregory, and Neil Alper. 1985. "Occupation Characteristics of Artists: A Statistical Analysis." *Journal of Cultural Economics*, 9: 13–34.

Wassall, Gregory, and Neil Alper. 1992. "Toward a Unified Theory of the Determinants of the Earnings of Artists," in Ruth Towse and Abdul Khakee, eds., *Cultural Economics*. Berlin: Springer-Verlag, 187–200.

Wassall, Gregory, and Neil Alper. 2006. "Artist's careers and their Labor Markets," in *Handbook of the Economics of Art and Culture*, edition 1, volume 1, chapter 23. Amsterdam, Netherlands: Elsevier, 813–865.

Wassall, Gregory, Neil Alper, and Rebecca Davison. 1983. *Art Work: Artists in the New England Labor Market*. Cambridge, MA: New England Foundation for the Arts.

Waterman, David. 1987. "Arts and Cultural Programming on Cable Television: Economic Analysis of the US Experience," in *Economic Efficiency and the Arts*. Akron, OH: Association for Cultural Economics, 240–249.

Wechsler, Dana. 1989. "A Treacherous Market." Forbes, November 27: 292–294.

Weil, S. E. 1983. "Custody without Title." In a collection of his papers entitled Beauty and the Beasts: On Museums, Art, the Law, and the Market. Washington, DC: Smithsonian Institution Press.

Weil, S. E. 1990. *Rethinking the Museum*. Washington, DC: Smithsonian Institution Press.

West, E. G. 1987. "Nonprofit versus Profit Firms in the Performing Arts." *Journal of Cultural Economics*, 11(2) (December): 37–47.

Wheatley, Daniel and Craig Bickerton. 2016. "Subjective Well-Being and Engagement in Arts, Culture, and Sport." *Journal of Cultural Economics*, 41(1): 23–45.

Whitaker, G. P. 1980. "Coproduction: Citizen Participation in Service Delivery." *Public Administration Review* (May–June): 240–246.

White, J. L. 1996. "When It's OK to Sell the Monet: A Trustee-Fiduciary-Duty Framework for Analyzing the Deaccessioning of Art to Meet Museum Operating Expenses." *Michigan Law Review*, 94: 1041–1066, cited at 1065.

Williamson, Oliver. 1983. "Organizational Form, Residual Claimants, and Corporate Control." *Journal of Law and Economics*, 26(2): 351–366.

Williamson, Oliver. 2010. "Transaction Cost Economics: The Natural Progression." *American Economic Review*, 100: 673–690.

Wise, Karen. 2014. "English Touring Opera – Opera in Cinemas Report." Creative Works. London. Available at www.creativeworkslondon.org.uk/wp-content/uploads/2014/05/ETO-Working-paper-May-2014.pdf

Withers, G. A. 1983. "The Cultural Influence of Public Television," in J. L. Shanahan et al., eds., *Markets for the Arts*. Akron, OH: Association for Cultural Economics, 31–43.

Wittlin, A. S. 1970. *Museums: In Search of a Usable Future*. Cambridge, MA: MIT Press.

Wolf, Thomas. 1992. Speech to the 1992 Conference of the American Symphony Orchestra League in *The Financial Condition of Symphony Orchestras*. Washington, DC: American Symphony Orchestra League, June 1992, pt. 1, appendix A.

Wooldridge, J. M. 2010. *Econometric Analysis of Cross Section and Panel Data*. 2nd ed. Cambridge, MA: MIT Press.

Working Group for Public Broadcasting. 1988. *Public Broadcasting: A National Asset to Be Preserved, Promoted and Protected*. Columbus: Ohio State University School of Journalism, December.

World Travel & Tourism Council. 2022. Travel & Tourism Economic Impact Global Trends 2022. London.

Woronkowicz, Joanna. 2016. "Do Artists Have a Competitive Edge in the Gig Economy?" Available at www.arts.gov/national-initiatives/

creativity-connects/report/do-artists-have-a-competitive-edge-in-the-gig-economy

Wyszomirski, M. J. 1982. "Controversies in Arts Policymaking," in Kevin V. Mulcahy and C. Richard Swaim, eds., *Public Policy and the Arts.* Boulder, CO: Westview Press, 12–15.

Wyszomirski, M. J. and J. H. Balfe. 1985. "Coalition Theory and American Ballet," in Balfe and Wyszomirski, eds., *Art, Ideology and Politics.* New York: Praeger, 210–241.

Yermack, David. 2017. "Donor Governance and Financial Management in Prominent US Art Museums." *Journal of Cultural Economics*, 41: 215–235.

Zhang, Wenyi. 2022. Number of museums in China from 2011 to 2021. Statista. Retrieved at www.statista.com/statistics/226450/number-of-museums-in-china/. Accessed June 2023.

Zeigler, Joseph. 1973. *Regional Theatre.* Minneapolis: University of Minnesota Press.

Zieba, Marta. 2009. "Full-Income and Price Elasticities of Demand for German Public Theatre." *Journal of Cultural Economics*, 33: 85–108.

Zorloni, Alessia. 2005. "Structure of the Contemporary Art Market and the Profile of Italian Artists." *Industrial Organization*, 8(1): 61–71.

Index